ADVANCES IN
EXPERIMENTAL SOCIAL PSYCHOLOGY

VOLUME 16

Theorizing in Social Psychology:
Theoretical Perspectives

CONTRIBUTORS TO VOLUME 16

Carl W. Backman

Janet Landman

Melvin Manis

William J. McGuire

Arthur W. Staats

Sheldon Stryker

ADVANCES IN

Experimental

Social Psychology

EDITED BY

Leonard Berkowitz
DEPARTMENT OF PSYCHOLOGY
UNIVERSITY OF WISCONSIN—MADISON
MADISON, WISCONSIN

VOLUME 16
Theorizing in Social Psychology:
Theoretical Perspectives

 1983

ACADEMIC PRESS, INC.
Harcourt Brace Jovanovich, Publishers
Orlando   San Diego   San Francisco   New York   London
Toronto   Montreal   Sydney   Tokyo   São Paulo

ACADEMIC PRESS, INC.
Orlando, Florida 32887

United Kingdom Edition published by
ACADEMIC PRESS, INC. (LONDON) LTD.
24/28 Oval Road, London NW1   7DX

LIBRARY OF CONGRESS CATALOG CARD NUMBER: 64-23452
ISBN 0-12-015216-9

PRINTED IN THE UNITED STATES OF AMERICA

83 84 85 86   9 8 7 6 5 4 3 2 1

CONTENTS

A Contextualist Theory of Knowledge: Its Implications for Innovation and Reform in Psychological Research

William J. McGuire

Social Cognition: Some Historical and Theoretical Perspectives

Janet Landman and Melvin Manis

Paradigmatic Behaviorism: Unified Theory for Social-Personality Psychology

Arthur W. Staats

v

Social Psychology from the Standpoint of a Structural Symbolic Interactionism: Toward an Interdisciplinary Social Psychology

Sheldon Stryker

Toward an Interdisciplinary Social Psychology

Carl W. Backman

CONTRIBUTORS

Numbers in parentheses indicate the pages on which the authors' contributions begin.

Carl W. Backman (219), *Department of Sociology, University of Nevada, Reno, Reno, Nevada 89507*

Janet Landman (49), *Department of Psychology, University of Michigan, and V. A. Medical Center, Ann Arbor, Michigan 48109*

Melvin Manis (49), *Department of Psychology, University of Michigan, and V. A. Medical Center, Ann Arbor, Michigan 48109*

William J. McGuire (1), *Department of Psychology, Yale University, New Haven, Connecticut 06520*

Arthur W. Staats[1] (125), *Social Science Research Institute, University of Hawaii, Honolulu, Hawaii 96822*

Sheldon Stryker (181), *Department of Sociology, Indiana University, Bloomington, Indiana 47405*

[1]Present address: Department of Psychology, University of Hawaii, Honolulu, Hawaii 96822.

PREFACE

In the preface to the first volume in this series, I quoted a comment made by W. I. B. Beveridge in his book *The Art of Scientific Investigation*. This quotation and my subsequent remarks are worth repeating here.

> Facts obtained by observation or experiment usually only gain significance when we use reason to build them into the general body of knowledge. Darwin said: "Science consists in grouping facts so that general laws or conclusions may be drawn from them." In research it is not sufficient to collect facts; by interpreting them, by seeing their significance and consequences, we can often go much further. (Beveridge, 1957, p. 123)

As I commented in the first volume, the papers in this series, then, will do more than report research findings. Interpretations and generalizations will also be offered so that we can see the "significance and consequences" of the data and (hopefully) can go much further.

> The last phrase deserves some additional comment [I went on to say]. There is no claim . . . that the theoretical statements presented in these volumes are the last word and will remain unaltered as additional information is obtained. We can be assured that most of the hypotheses listed in these pages will be found wanting in one way or another as the years go by. By presenting their hypotheses, the writers have contributed to the data collection and theory development that will question their own formulations. Their theoretical statements will help social psychology go further.

This volume is offered in the same spirit that guided those remarks almost 20 years ago. These *Advances* have continually sought to publish papers that provide a theoretically oriented integration of the data collected in particular research areas in the belief that theories largely determine the significance of observations. Furthermore, as I noted a generation ago, theories change, especially in social psychology. These alterations stem partly from the accumulation of evidence highlighting the deficiencies in existing formulations (a point I made in 1964) but also from changes in theoretical fashions. Just consider what has taken place in only the past 20 years. The relatively concentrated but active interest in social learning theory based on associationist learning concepts has dwindled further and many of the theory's leading advocates have taken up other concerns, such as self-conceptions and the operations of schemas in person perception. Research on balance theory is almost nonexistent, and there is even comparatively little attention being given to dissonance theory. The study of casual attributions spurted ahead for a number of years and now seems to be dying down somewhat as more and more attribution theory investigators have turned their interests to judgments and information processing and memory. After a generation of such changes in social psychology's leading formulations, it may be time for us to step back and take a look at our theories and analyses as a whole.

This volume and the next one to come aim to provide this broader perspective so that social psychologists can better judge where they are in their theory development and where they might go from here. This volume, 16, offers a wide-ranging scan of the theoretical horizons, a metatheoretical examination of the more specific approaches that social psychologists have employed in collecting and integrating their data. In one way or another the authors all urge social psychologists to extend their theoretical outlook. McGuire argues that all our theories have something to contribute to our understanding of human behavior. Staats calls for an integration of social behaviorist–associationist conceptions with other, more cognitive formulations. And Stryker and Backman summarize the theoretical ideas guiding much of the work in contemporary sociological social psychology. All essentially say that no particular conception in the field today is the only road to the truth. The chapter by Landman and Manis is somewhat more narrowly focused. It concentrates on cognitive theorizing in present-day social psychology, but even in this narrower domain, their treatment is fairly eclectic. Here, too, the emphasis is on what can be learned from each of the analyses in the area.

The next volume, 17, is more specialized still, and covers research and theorizing in particular areas of social psychology.

But whatever the specific coverage of the views favored by the writers represented in these volumes, these books can help social psychologists take stock. I do not believe that our discipline is in a serious crisis, but I do think that we can all profit from a reexamination of the analyses we have developed and the problems we have investigated. I anticipate that Volumes 16 and 17 will contribute to this reexamination.

ADVANCES IN

EXPERIMENTAL
SOCIAL PSYCHOLOGY

VOLUME 16

Theorizing in Social Psychology:
Theoretical Perspectives

A CONTEXTUALIST THEORY OF KNOWLEDGE: ITS IMPLICATIONS FOR INNOVATION AND REFORM IN PSYCHOLOGICAL RESEARCH*

William J. McGuire

DEPARTMENT OF PSYCHOLOGY
YALE UNIVERSITY
NEW HAVEN, CONNECTICUT

A "contextualist" epistemology is proposed in this chapter as an appropriate metatheory for psychology, after the meanings of theory and of the more generic term "knowledge" are first clarified. Contextualism's implications for reforming both the process and product of psychology are then discussed. Two phases of needed process reforms are described, that of creatively generating hypotheses and that of developing them by means of empirical confrontation. Finally, the psychological product is discussed by reviewing the various theoretical depictions of the person that have guided and grown out of the research process.

*The writing of this chapter was substantially aided by a grant to the author, Grant Number 5 RO1 MH 32588 from the National Institutes of Mental Health, Interpersonal Processes and Problems Section (BR-S).

1

I. The Nature and Tragedy of Knowledge

Because theory is an abstract type of knowledge, its meaning can be better understood if the more generic concept of "knowledge" is first clarified. One knows an object by representing it to oneself, perhaps by constructing in one's cognitive arena an analog that is in one-to-one correspondence to the known aspect of the object; this representation reduces and distorts the object as required to represent it within the knower's cognitive capacities. The average person may have less of a frenzied need to know than is assumed by dwellers in the house of intellect who regard the unexamined life as not worth living; but many people do have at least a modest need to know because the environment's complexity or strangeness often exceeds one's capacity to deal directly with its fullness, so that one can cope with it only by representing it to oneself in a reduced and conventionalized form. Typically, the environment presents the person with more information than the human cognitive system can meaningfully process (McGuire, 1983b), requiring one to cope by reducing the thing-in-itself to a knowledge representation that assimilates a manageable portion of its information to one's available cognitive categories while ignoring its other aspects.

"Knowing" involves the inherent tragedy that these necessary representations of the known are necessarily misrepresentations: One cannot survive without doing it but one cannot do it well. All the operations into which the knowing process can be analyzed, such as those shown in Table I, produce falsifications both in the form of oversimplifications (ignoring most aspects of the known, overlooking unique features of entities grouped together, reducing a complex entity to its aspects on a few dimensions, etc.) and in the form of distortions (capriciously slicing up the seamless web of reality, locating axes of meaning arbitrarily in reality-space, distorting unique experiences so that they fit preexisting categories, assuming that everything else is equal, etc.). Knowledge representations are adaptive insofar as the inevitable oversimplifications are brilliantly apt and the distortions largely irrelevant for the task at hand. One can reasonably hope that phylogenetically acquired genetic endowment and ontogenetically acquired experiential structures will have shaped the human cognitive system so that our concrete knowledge of recurrent, important situations will typically involve such adequate representations.

There is less reason for such optimism when we turn to theory, which is knowledge writ large in the form of generalized abstractions applicable to a wide range of experiences but representing each only vaguely, making it likely that dangerous oversimplifications and distortions will arise when a theory is applied to a specific case. Brilliant theorists may aptly apply a theory to specific situations within their range of expertise, but often theories will be overgeneralized to additional situations where their misrepresentations become more devastating

TABLE I

THE REPRESENTATIONAL ACT OF KNOWING: MISREPRESENTATIONS AT EACH STEP OF THE PROCESS AS IT EVOLVES TOWARD THEORY

Process	Set operation	Products yielded	Misrepresentations involved
1. Focusing, noticing, awareness	Set assembly	Observations	Elected ignorance of most of the field; arbitrarily slicing the seamless web of reality
2. Analyzing, fractionating	Set partition	Discriminations	Ignoring similarities
3. Categorizing, entitizing, constancies	Partial definition by enumeration	Objects of thought, entities	Ignoring differences; ignoring nonfitting peculiarities
4. Abstracting	Properties	Dimensions of judgment (variables)	Arbitrary placement of axes of meaning
5. Predicating	Partial definition by properties	Propositions, judgments, assignments of objects to dimensions	Ignoring other aspects of the object
6. Relating	Logical set operations	Hypotheses, inferring object's location on one dimension from its location on another	"Everything else equal" fallacy
7. Generalizing	Going from sets to supersets	Principles (hypotheses with broad variables)	Extrapolations distorted by values, wishes, inadequate information
8. Systematizing	Axiom systems	Theory (set of principles relating a domain of variable)	Incompleteness, Gödelian arbitrariness
9. Utilizing	Models	Applications	Oversimplification; distortion

unless the ubiquitous oversimplifications and distortions intrinsic to theories have been kept explicit. An appropriately poignant image of the knower (and especially of the theorist) is that of a rope walker who, on arriving at a precipice of ignorance, ties one end of a chain of inferences to a stake on its brink, and, flinging the free end as far as possible out over the abyss, runs quickly along the thrown chain to get the maximum distance before plunging to disaster. These theoretical chains of inference do not permit great leaps forward but simply allow a little advance beyond the previous Furthest North. Limited knowledge representations being all we have, the only thing worse than generating and using them is not doing so (Edge, 1983).

Knowing is a human adaptation that evolved as a means rather than as an end. The consummate intellectual may come to feel that it is an end in itself, but knowing makes survival sense only as an intermediate stage of some larger process. Thomas à Kempis used the words of Ecclesiastes in asserting that the eye is not fulfilled by seeing and analogously the evolution of knowing is explicable only within the context of the further operations that it evokes or channels. In everyday life, the knower's (mis)representation of the environment may serve to guide behavior, generate affective reaction to the situation, terminate concern about it, etc. In the more sophisticated realms of art or science, knowing may lead to more elaborate responses: a writer or sculptor who imagines an inspiring representation may express it in a novel or statue; a scientist who formulates a theoretical representation may develop it by putting it in jeopardy by empirical confrontation. In recent years I have been developing a contextualist philosophy of science (McGuire, 1973, 1983c) that recognizes and exploits the loss and distortion of information necessarily involved in knowledge and especially in abstract theoretical knowledge. In the next section I describe this contextualist position by tracing its evolution through two millennia of epistemological development. Later sections discuss its implications for the reform of social psychological research.

II.   Toward Contextualism: Two Millennia of Theory-Testing Criteria

Intellectuals have always recognized the possibility that theories (particularly other people's theories) may be in error and so have proposed evaluating their appropriateness by a variety of internal and external criteria. The internal criterion most often used to judge a theory's adequacy is its internal consistency in not yielding mutually contradictory derivations. On the other hand, a researcher does not have to be a Marxist to judge a theory by the rather opposite criterion of how well it plays a more active dialectical role in knowledge generation by provoking new insights; judged by this standard, an internal contradiction between a thesis and antithesis could be a most useful way of evoking a new synthesis. Other internal criteria sometimes used to judge a theory's attractiveness are that it be parsimonious or broadly relevant or seem certain or be elegantly beautiful. Alternatively, it may be judged by its novelty in being more than just a minor variation on a familiar theme; on the other hand, some judge a theory by its plausibility in fitting within the prevailing metatheory without introducing any eccentric new factor such as extrasensory perception. That these various internal criteria for judging the relative adequacy of competing theories are not only independent of one another but sometimes even mutually contradictory illustrates a basic descriptive (and prescriptive) tenet of contextualism that will be developed in the following.

The relative adequacy of theories can be judged also by various external criteria. The status of a theory's author or advocate is one such criterion, not only in dogmatic religious and political circles, but even in some sycophantic scientific circles (which is the reason for periodical calls for "blind" reviews of research proposals and journal manuscripts). A more rationalistic external criterion is whether a formulation is derivable from or at least compatible with some accepted set of principles such as the Euclidean axioms or the Hullian behaviorist postulates. Pragmatists judge theories by their usefulness for human survival or some other highly valued end. The external criterion most revered currently by the orthodox scientist is ecological validity such that the theory, on being empirically tested, conforms to some interpersonally observable reality that it is supposed to describe. The Establishment consensus for the preferred external criterion of a theory's truth has evolved during the past two millennia of European thought through at least four stages that are worth singling out here for brief discussion—dogmatism, rationalism, positivism, logical empiricism—before describing our new contextualist position.

A.   PRE-CONTEXTUALIST POSITIONS ON THE DEDUCTIVE-INDUCTIVE ANTITHESIS

1.   Dogmatism

Within this orientation, the preferred criterion of truth is the hypothesis's conformity to a set of propositions whose legitimacy is recognizable by such signs as the superior credibility of their author, their having stood the test of time, or the compellingness of their content. This was the Establishment meta-theory during the late Roman Empire and early medieval periods when the criterion dogma was the Judeo-Christian Scriptures as interpreted by the teaching office of the Church or the exegeses of the Talmudic rabbis for theorists such as Athanasius, Augustine of Hippo, Gregory, Rashi, etc. While dogmatism ceased to be the dominant epistemology a thousand years ago, it is still the working criterion of current Islamic, Hebrew, and Christian fundamentalists, Freudians and Marxist-Leninists of the strict observance, and other ideologues of one book.

2.   Rationalism

The rationalistic criterion of a theory's truth is that it be internally consistent and deducible from a set of reasonable postulates such as self-evident axioms (e.g., the principle of sufficient reason) and inductions based on widespread observations (such as that all life comes from life). This rationalistic metatheory began to gain acceptance when the disruptive Viking and Magyar predations subsided in the tenth century. This allowed exploitation, in a pattern of production suitable to northern European conditions, of the previous centuries' technological innovations such as the heavy wheeled plow, the scythe, the shoulder harness' replacement of the yoke (which permitted efficient use of the horse as a draft animal), the three-field crop rotation system, and the integration of animal husbandry with agriculture. The resulting surplus provided a basis for the tenth-century Carolingian revival, which included the professionalization of speculation and a clerical ascendancy, producing epistemological consequences that ended the dogmatic hegemony that had characterized the first millennium of the Common Era. Intimations of a developing rationalistic ascendancy are discernable as early as Anselm's *Monologian* in 1077 of the Common Era in response to his monks' request for a derivation of the Christian corpus of belief on the basis of reason without making use of Scripture. A generation later Abelard in his *Sic et non* went beyond showing that the dogmatic approach is unnecessary by showing that it is inadequate as well, since Scripture and patristic writing include contradictory statements even on basic issues. By the thirteenth century, theorists such as Thomas Aquinas, Averröes, Maimonides, Duns Scotus, along with their precursors such as Peter Lombard and successors such as Nicholas of Cusa and William of Occam, used this rationalistic metatheory to build knowledge edifices as impressive as the contemporaneous cathedrals of stone and stained glass.

3. Positivism

The hegemony shifted from rationalistic to positivistic epistemologies by the seventeenth century. While the term *positivism* was popularized only by the nineteenth-century writings of Comte, this epistemology was formalized as early as Francis Bacon's *Novum Organum* in 1620 and was adumbrated in the hypothetico-deductive method of Robert Grosseteste and the empiricism of his pupil Roger Bacon. Its elevation by the seventeenth century to the Establishment epistemology is exhibited in the contribution of Locke, Voltaire, Hume, Diderot, etc. Positivism stands the deductivism of the rationalists on its head by using an extreme inductivist criterion of truth, identifying direct sensory experience as the source of all knowledge and as the criterion against which any theory must be tested.

4. Logical Empiricism

Early in our own century, the Vienna Circle took a great roll forward by reconciling the deductive and inductive extremes of the two previous Establishment epistemologies. While its positivistic predecessor was basically an opposite reaction to the prior rationalist ascendancy, the logical empiricist movement achieved a more creative synthesis of its two predecessors, the deductive thesis and the inductive antithesis. What Schlick, Carnap, Hempel, Feigel, Bergmann, and others within the Wienerkreis did was give the first word to deduction and the last to induction by prescribing that the researcher start out with a hypothesis validly deducible from an a priori theory and then test its and the theory's truth by subjecting it to the jeopardy of disconfirmation via an empirical test. Within this elegant epistemology, a hypothesis has scientific meaning and validity to the extent that it is embedded in both a more abstract theory and a more concrete empirical manifestation.

B. THE CONTEXTUALIST POSITION

The contextualist position here proposed as a new descriptive and prescriptive epistemology for social psychology (and, indeed, for other scientific disciplines) incorporates two of logical empiricism's innovative premises while departing from it radically in two other regards. Contextualism and logical empiricism agree on one basic assumption about hypothesis generating and one about hypothesis testing: namely, that derivations of a hypothesis from broader theories should precede and guide a scientist's empirical observations and that empirical confrontation is essential for developing the hypothesis's scientific meaning and validity. The disagreements between logical empiricism and contextualism likewise involve one hypothesis-generating and one hypothesis-testing assumption. Departing radically from logical empiricism's tenet that some theories are right and others wrong, contextualism maintains that all theories (including even mutually contradictory ones) are right. Departing from the logical empiricist position that the empirical confrontation is a test of whether a given theory is correct (or better, in the method of strong inference, which of several opposed theories is correct and which wrong), contextualism asserts rather that empirical confrontation is a discovery process to make clear the meaning of the hypothesis, disclosing its hidden assumptions and thus clarifying circumstances under which the hypothesis is true and those under which it is false.

As regards the first of these innovative positions, that all hypotheses are true, contextualism maintains that a theory (like knowledge on any other level) is an oversimplified and distorted representation of any situation. It can be a brilliant cost-effective representation in certain contexts and dangerously misleading for others. Because all hypotheses are true, all are false. A hypothesis or its contradictory is each adequately true in a few appropriate contexts and each is dangerously false in many others. Contextualism's second disagreement with logical empiricism is its regarding empirical confrontation, not as a test to determine whether the hypothesis is true or not, but rather as a continuing discovery process to disclose the hypothesis's full meaning by revealing its hidden assumptions and so specifying in which contexts its misrepresentations are tolerable and in which seriously misleading. By an adequately designed empirical program, the social psychologist can ascertain the theory's pattern of adequacy over a range of contexts, elaborating its subtleties to provide insight into the conditions that determine when a theory provides powerful guidance and when it misleads.

That the contextualist metatheory includes a coherent bundle of interrelated insights increases the richness of its implications but raises problems of nomenclature. We have successively called the position *interactionism, transactionism, constructionism, constructivism,* and now *contextualism.* Each term has focused on a different emphasis of the approach. For example, the meaning of a theory develops in "interaction" with empirical observation, one "constructs" rather than tests theories through empirical confrontation, and any theory is true in some "contexts" but not in others. The name changes have been carried out, not so much because the earlier terms are inappropriate or because we wished to present a moving target to our enemies, but rather to avoid confusion with partially related positions as when we switch here to *contextualism* from our previous term *constructivism* (McGuire, 1980) to avoid confusion with Vladimir Tatlin's *constructivism* movement (Milner, 1980) in abstract art or, closer to social psychology, to Holzkamp's (1970, 1972) *Konstruktivismus* or Swanson's (1981) *constructivist* formulation. The fullness of the contextualist approach which makes any simple label too narrow also gives the position a rich set of implications for the process and product of social psychological research. In the remainder of this chapter, these implications are described, first for the process of developing psychological theory and then as regards the product, the theories that emerge from the process.

III.   Psychology as Process: The Developing of Theoretical Knowledge

Psychology has dual aspects of becoming and being, process and product, the process of developing knowledge and the knowledge product that results. The research psychologist is more preoccupied with the process while such interest as the lay person develops for the field is focused mainly on the product. This divergence of interests results in misunderstandings illustrated by the classroom conflict with the psychologist-teacher on one side spending a great deal of time discussing the methods from which findings emerge and arguing that the meaning of findings cannot be grasped without an appreciation of the investigative processes that yielded them. On the other hand the lay person-student wants to hear more about whatever body of knowledge psychology has produced and complains that the psychologist is more preoccupied with proving that the field uses scientific methods than with demonstrating that it has found something interesting. In discussing contextualism's implications, I shall be more even-handed by first discussing psychology as process, reviewing methodological procedures by which its theory is produced, and then discussing psychology as product, surveying the theoretical representations of the person that have developed out of and guide this process. However, since the writer is a professional, process will be given more space than product. I discuss the process of psychology first as regards a priori procedures for generating hypotheses and then a posteriori procedures for refining hypotheses through empirical confrontation, stressing four classes of reforms in current psychological research called for by contextualism.

A.   THE PROCESS OF GENERATING PSYCHOLOGICAL
     THEORIES AND HYPOTHESES

1.   The Strange Neglect of the Hypothesis-Generating Phase of Research

Most scientists would grant that the research process includes generating hypotheses as well as empirically testing them and might even agree that the former is the more important since a hypothesis must be formulated before it can be tested. Why then do discussions of scientific method focus almost exclusively on hypothesis-testing topics such as manipulational versus correlational tests, experimental design, measurement, descriptive and inferential statistics? The strange neglect of the important hypothesis-generating phase of the research process probably reflects, not failure to appreciate its importance, but rather the opinion that discussing it is futile because it is largely dependent on the inborn creativity of the researcher and because creative processes can hardly be described, much less taught. At most, a mentor may simply encourage the student to read publications of creative researchers or work in an apprentice relationship with them, on the chance that the creative knack for generating interesting hypotheses may be acquired by some kind of intellectual osmosis.

The contextualist view of knowledge as (mis)representations of the known whose validities vary vastly with circumstances implies that theorizing is commonplace since even everyday acts of knowing involve considerable and perhaps excessive creativity. Hence, the contextualist is more optimistic about the possibility of actively promoting creative theorizing and hypothesis generation by both strategic and tactical means. First, institutional arrangements can promote creativity by establishing research settings that encourage scientists to produce creative theoretical representations (Pelz & Andrews, 1976; Andrews, 1979;

Latour & Woolgar, 1979; Goodfield, 1981), and second, one can train individual researchers in the use of heuristics that facilitate creative hypothesis generating (Stein, 1974; Amabile, 1983). To correct any feeling that the creative process cannot be described, much less taught, I have been assembling lists such as the one shown in Table II that includes 44 creative heuristics that have been used in psychological theory generation and in whose use researchers can be trained. Space limitations allow our describing here only one illustrative heuristic from each of the five categories shown in Table II but others are described elsewhere (McGuire, 1973, 1980, 1982).

TABLE II

EXAMPLES OF CREATIVE TECHNIQUES USED TO GENERATE PSYCHOLOGICAL HYPOTHESES

A. Heuristics involving analyses of naturally occurring events
    1. Intensive case studies
    2. Account for paradoxical incidents
    3. Explain practitioners' rules of thumb
    4. Extrapolate from similar problems already solved
    5. Find solution in the existence of an opposite problem
    6. Introspect on own experience in comparable situation
    7. Role play (self or another) in the situation
    8. Participant observation

B. Heuristics involving simple, direct conceptual analyses
    9. Push a reasonable hypothesis until its implications become implausible
  10. Mentally reduce a factor to zero in a given situation
  11. Thought experiment to explore the limits
  12. Reverse the direction of a commonsense hypothesis
  13. Functional (adaptivity) analysis
  14. Linguistic analysis
  15. Partition partial definitions of a variable into distinctive subsets
  16. Reverse the focus between dependent and independent variables
  17. Utilize imagery (e.g., physiognomic or right-hemisphere thinking)
  18. Disrupt ordinary state of consciousness
  19. Focus on essentials and diverge; refocus
  20. Analyze into (sequential) subcomponents

C. Heuristics involving complex, mediated inferential analyses
  21. Posit multiple mediators of a known relationship
  22. Induce a broader generalization and deduce other implications
  23. Identify trade-off factors
  24. Hypothetico-deductive method
  25. (Computer) simulation
  26. Generate or find a checklist and apply it to the problem
  27. Construct a heuristically provocative generating structure
  28. Analogy; transfer a conceptual scheme from one area to another
  29. Reverse the known and unknown, the independent and dependent variables

TABLE II (*Continued*)

D. Heuristics involving analyses of previous research
    30. Reconcile conflicting outcomes or failures to replicate
    31. Deviant case analysis
    32. Interpret a serendipitous interaction effect
    33. Analyze a nonmonotonic relationship into rectilinear underlying functions
    34. Posit factors that account for irregularities in an obtained relationship
    35. Write a review article to organize current knowledge on the topic
    36. Bring together two striking past experiments

E. Heuristics involving collection of new or re-analyses of old data
    37. Pit two factors against one another
    38. Directly measure and subtract out a given mediating process
    39. Mathematical modeling
    40. Multivariate fishing expedition
    41. Add exploratory independent variables for serendipitous interactions
    42. Allow open-ended responses and do content analysis
    43. Active participation in research routine (data collection, etc.)
    44. Explore a new technique

2. Some Heuristics for Generating Hypotheses

The eight heuristics shown in the first category of Table II all involve taking notice of striking, naturally occurring events or anecdotal observations sufficiently to provoke explanations. For example, heuristic 5 involves juxtaposing two opposite problems so that each suggests the other's solution. Several years ago I attended back-to-back National Institutes of Health conferences, one a Heart, Lung and Blood Institute meeting to investigate why so few hypertensive patients took the drugs that had been prescribed for them and the other, an alcohol and drug abuse conference on why Americans are such pill-poppers. Since the two institutes perceived opposite problems of under- and over-use of drugs, the contrasting factors involved could be used to suggest reciprocal solutions to the problems. This heuristic 5 of putting opposite problems into confrontation nicely exploits contextualism's basic premise that all relationships (including mutually contradictory ones) have some ecological validity, given the wide range of possible contexts.

A second category of heuristics, including numbers 9 through 20 in Table II, goes beyond mere observation by requiring at least a simple conceptual manipulation. Number 12, conceptually reversing the direction of a common-sense hypothesis, is a heuristic particularly in tune with the contextualist approach to theorizing. It involves taking an obvious relationship and standing it on its head by hypothesizing a contrary relationship and then thinking of special contexts in which this reversed relationship might obtain. For example, the "forewarning of persuasive intent" research was at first based on the obvious assumption that people will be less influenced by a message if it comes from a source whom they suspect is out to persuade them. However, one can assert the contrary hypothesis, that forewarned people will be *more* persuaded, at least in contexts such as when a receiver wants to ingratiate a romantically attractive or powerful source by agreement (Mills & Aronson, 1965) or uses anticipatory attitude change to avoid seeming persuadable later (McGuire & Millman, 1965) or for other reasons reviewed by McGuire (1969c).

The third group of heuristics (numbers 21 through 29 in Table II) involves using more complexly mediated inference, illustrated by heuristic 20, which posits multiple mediators for an obtained relationship. Researchers trying to account for a relationship almost always stop after generating one or two hypothetical explanations, but the contextualist approach reminds us that any domain to be explained can be sliced up in innumerable knowledge planes so that it is worth inferring a variety of mediating processes in accounting for an obtained relationship, each of which would yield different mediator and interaction predictions and suggest new meanings of the variables. When Hovland, Lumsdaine, and Sheffield (1949) found that the World War II army indoctrination films sometimes produced delayed action effects, they conjectured that this might be due to the "discounting cue" process (on which much of the subsequent sleeper effect research has focused) but then—atypically but commendably—they continued to think creatively about the process and hypothesized a half-dozen additional mediating processes, each of which invites further research (McGuire, 1983a). Likewise, Adorno *et al.* (1950), while especially interested in the authoritarian-personality mediation of anti-Semitism, also described other syndromes leading to this bias.

Heuristics 30 through 36 in Table II represent a fourth category that requires not only conceptual analyses but also utilization of provocative outcomes of previous research. Again, a number of heuristics in this fourth category are particularly suggested by the contextualist approach, such as reconciling conflicting outcomes of previous work, deviant case analysis, and interpreting serendipitous interaction effects. An example of the latter heuristic is our introducing potentially provocative interaction variables into studies of the spontaneous self-concept (McGuire, McGuire, & Winton, 1979). This led to the finding that ethnicity and gender are more salient in the negation self-concept (given in response to a "Tell us what you are not" probe) than in the affirmation self-concept (in response to "Tell us about yourself"), especially in females, provoking conjectures as to why and with what effects children and especially girls think of themselves in terms of not being the other gender more than in being the gender that they are.

A final category, including the last 8 of the 44 Table II heuristics, requires collecting new or reanalyzing old data. Heuristic 37, pitting two factors against one another, can be illustrated by the research on whether peer or expert sources have more persuasive impact. Conceptual analysis suggests that peer sources gain in attractiveness by being similar to the receiver, whereas experts gain in perceived credibility by superior knowledgeability (Brock, 1965). Pitting these two factors against each other has yielded some interesting if elusive findings such as the pratfall effect (Helmreich, Aronson, & LeFan, 1970; Deaux, 1972) and the nonmonotonic relationship between source's age and his or her influentiality (Stukát, 1958).

Illustrations of the other heuristics are available elsewhere (McGuire, 1980, 1982). The purpose here is not to demonstrate intensively or exhaustively the efficacy of one or all heuristics but to illustrate the point that the teaching of research methodology, now focused almost exclusively on hypothesis-testing procedures, can productively deal also with the hypothesis-generating processes. Obviously one must find one's hypothesis before one can test it and so more thought should be given to establishing research settings that are provocative or at least supportive of new insights and to training students in techniques (such as the use of heuristics illustrated in the preceding) that actualize their hypothesis-generating potential. Contextualism, by stressing the multifaceted nature of explanation, counsels prodigality in hypothesis production.

B. EMPIRICAL CONFRONTATION AS DISCOVERY RATHER THAN TEST

The previous section dealt with contextualism's implication that the a priori hypothesis-generating phase of the research process should be given greater emphasis in methodology discussions as a corrective to the current tendency to discuss only the second, a posteriori, hypothesis-testing phase. In turning here to this latter phase of bringing the generated hypotheses into empirical confrontation, I stress three additional implications of contextualism for basic reforms in the current teaching and practice of psychological research, namely, exploiting the empirical confrontation as a discovery process rather than a mere testing of what is already known, developing an integrated research style, and explicitly planning research on the strategic as well as the tactical level.

1. Experimentation as Continued Discovery

Contextualism stresses the continuity rather than contrast between the two phases of research. Current conventions emphasize the contrast between the two, depicting the first phase as a creative divergent process of a priori hypothesis generating and the second as a critical convergent process of a posteriori hypothesis testing. Contextualism points out that research is a more continuously creative process in that the first phase of a priori hypothesis generation is followed by a second empirical-confrontation phase that continues rather than reverses the discovery process. In the contextualist vision of science, empirical confrontation is not so much a testing of the hypothesis as it is a continuing revelation of its full meaning made apparent by its pattern of confirmations and disconfirmations in a strategically programmed set of observable situations. Contextualism reminds us that each of a wide range of hypotheses, including even contradictory ones deriving from contrasting theories about human nature or social situations, can be valid under the peculiar circumstances assumed (often only implicitly) by each theory. Hence, the scientist should subject his or her a priori theoretical speculations to empirical confrontations, not to test if they are true, but to discover the pattern of contexts in which each adequately represents the observation, thus bringing out more fully the meaning of each theory by making explicit its limiting assumptions and yielding a more sophisticated appreciation of the complex factors operative across the spectrum of situations.

Most theorists grant that restrictive assumptions surround any hypothesis, and they might even assert that these assumptions are so obvious that they can go without saying. However, engaging in research tends to generate a polemic force that encourages imperialistic thinking, driving the researcher to suppress restrictive assumptions and to apply the hypothesis in a wider range of contexts than originally envisioned until an initially "among other things" conjecture becomes treated as a "nothing but" universal. Such imperialism can be creatively provocative in the a priori hypothesis-generating phase (indeed, heuristic 9 in Table II calls for pushing a reasonable hypothesis until its implications become implausible and suggest a limiting force) but it becomes counterproductive when excessive preoccupation with and loyalty to the original insight blinds the thinker to other explanations. Dissonance theorists began by ingeniously conjecturing that under certain conditions reducing the person's reward for counter-attitudinal advocacy would enhance internalized attitude change (Festinger, 1957) but tended in the heat of controversy to overgeneralize this hypothesized negative relationship between incentive size and internalization so that a tedious program of research became necessary to rediscover the restrictive context (Collins & Hoyt, 1972).

2. Corrupting Effects of the "Hypothesis-Testing" Conceptualization

The Establishment fiction that empirical confrontation serves the narrow function of testing hypotheses and the theories from which they are derived, that it simply tells one whether or not one's a priori formulation had been right in the first place, has numerous unfortunate effects on the way research is taught in the classroom, done in the laboratory or field, reported in the journals, and applied in society. What tends to be published is a sanitized version of research, the well-done demonstration of the confirmed hypothesis, which makes visible only the superficial portion of a great iceberg of research, leaving hidden the greater and more informative part of the process. In actuality, the enthusiastic researcher who has devised an interesting hypothesis will typically set up a laboratory situation that promises to confirm the inferred relationship but will usually have to go through considerable mental gymnastics because of disenchanting failure experiences in which the results do not come out "right." The well-trained researcher does not thereupon reject the hypothesis but rejects the experiment. She or he reanalyzes the theory and the experimental conditions in order to detect what went "wrong" and beefs up the situation to enhance the likelihood that the predicted outcome will be found. These responses to the initial disconfirmations include such "improvements" as using more appropriate tasks and participants, more reliable and valid measuring instruments, stronger and more theory-relevant independent variable manipulations, better control of extraneous variables, and more sensitive statistical analyses. A researcher ingenious enough and persistent enough will at last design an experiment that comes out "right" and it is only this sanitized experiment, the final outcome that rests on a series of turkeys—or turtles—all the way down that becomes the sole portion of the research program revealed in the manuscript submitted to the dissertation committee or the journal.

Far from being condemned as deceptive, this procedure is currently applauded as eminently proper, and full disclosure is condemned. Were a doctoral candidate to submit a dissertation giving proportionate space to all the prestudies, the bulky manuscript might patronizingly be accepted as an indulgence tolerable in a student, but only after the candidate is sternly admonished to correct such prolixity before submitting the study for publication. The student is reminded that one inevitably has to do a series of prestudies in order to get meaningful control over the variables in the theory but that a reader should not have to wade through a description of all this preliminary work before hearing about the "real" experiment. A journal editor who receives a manuscript describing the prestudies in which the hypothesis was not confirmed as well as the final confirming study might reply bitingly that the researcher's intellectual odyssey in the course of meandering toward the actual experiment may be very interesting to her or his mother but the space crunch in the journal hardly makes it appropriate for publication.

The contextualist is disturbed because this current sanitized style of reporting omits the richest information obtainable from the empirical confrontation. The final study confirming the hypothesis is not particularly informative: It can be taken for granted that some set of circumstances can be found to confirm any expressible relationship, provided that the researcher has sufficient stubbornness, stage management skills, resources, and stamina sooner or later to find or construct a situational context in which the predicted relationship reliably emerges. The more valuable information obtainable through empirical confrontation emerges from the pattern of contexts in which the predicted relationship obtains as contrasted with those in which the contrary relationship or none at all obtains, information revealed more by the series of prestudies than by the final confirmation or failure to confirm. Publication conventions imposed by the current fiction that the empirical confrontation is a "test" of the original hypothesis leads to publishing only the final sanitized outcome, thus losing most of the information in the suppressed "exploratory" phase of the empirical confrontation.

The misleading publication style is the end product of the current erroneous mode of research training that emphasizes hit-and-run, one-experiment-at-a-time research planning derived from the misconception that empirical confrontation should serve as a test of the hypothesis. Students are taught to muddle through this exploratory stage with tunnel vision directed at modifying the conditions so that the hypothesis will be confirmed, rather than systematizing the prestudy phase into a program of studies as required by contextualism. Currently, even the most respected graduate programs strive to turn out good "stage managers" with a knack for setting up hypothesis-testing experiments that come out "right" (McGuire, 1973). The well-regarded departments turn out such students by attracting and retaining adept stage managers and keeping out of their way as they pass through or perhaps even by enhancing their impressario skills by apprenticing them to past masters or mistresses of the theatrical arts and crafts.

At an earlier period I conjectured (McGuire, 1967, 1969a) that this skilled-artificer concept of the researcher as forging confirmations of his or her theory in the smithy of the laboratory could be corrected by moving research to field settings in the natural world, since confirming the hypothesis in a natural field setting assures one that there is at least one realistic context in which the hypothesis works adequately. However, I soon realized (McGuire, 1973) that the flight to the field would simply encourage the bright young researcher to change from being a laboratory stage manager to becoming a natural world "finder" (to use a term from real estate and commerce). The field-oriented departments would end up trying to turn out researchers with a knack for finding special natural world settings in which a given hypothesis will come out right. For example, a field-oriented researcher who hypothesizes that heterogeneous groups will be more (less) productive than homogeneous ones might first attempt to test it in terms of the points per game or variety of plays used by high school basketball teams of varying demographic heterogeneity. Should (as is terribly likely) the results come out wrong in this first experiment, the researcher would probably not reject the hypothesis but rather, to the extent that resources, stamina, and ingenuity allowed, would try to find different group contexts in which the hypothesis works better, perhaps studying the gunnery scores of tank crews or number of options considered in deliberations of the League of Women Voters, etc., until finally a real-world group context is found in which the prediction is confirmed. The published manuscript describing this research would focus on the final success story in which an appropriate group setting was at last found in which the hypothesized relationship was demonstrated. The unsuccessful "prestudies" that came out in wrong directions typically go unreported or are mentioned only in an embarrassed paragraph in the discussion section or as a footnote in the methods section, more in the spirit of a guilty admission of the writer's initial obtuseness than as an effort to exploit the information in this pattern of confirmations and disconfirmations. The contextualist approach implies rather that researchers should be trained in research strategy (as discussed in Section D) to conduct these prestudies explicitly organized in a program of research that has been deliberately designed to reveal how the pattern of relationships between the variables of interest changes from context to context as suggested by alternative theories.

3. Ubiquity of the Hypothesis-Testing Fallacy

The contextualist proposition that empirical confrontation involves hypothesis discovery and clarification rather than hypothesis testing is not a prescription needed only by the social and behavioral sciences because of their purportedly more complicated or value-laden subject matter, or their less manipulable or more hidden variables, or their peculiarly unpredictable or reactive units of observation, or whatever. Rather, for the physical scientist as well as the social scientist, empirical confrontation is and ought to be a discovery procedure to make explicit hidden assumptions more than as a testing procedure to determine if the original hypothesis is or is not true. Imagine a contemporary Galileo/Stevin who, to test the hypothesis that bodies fall with an acceleration independent of their mass, trudges wearily to the top of the Leaning Tower of Pisa and drops simultaneously a ping-pong ball and a bowling ball, predicting that their moment of impact will be observed as simultaneous by a collaborator on the ground below. But this collaborator will obviously observe that, contrary to the prediction, the heavier bowling ball arrives long before the ping-pong ball floats to the ground. If the researcher then rushes to the publishing house crying, "Stop the presses, Galileo is wrong," he or she would be laughed to scorn with the explanation that everyone knows that the prediction was made only within the context of objects falling in a friction-free vacuum. Should the researcher protest that the "law" is frequently asserted misleadingly without these qualifying phrases, he or she would be told it goes without saying that no physicist for centuries has even thought of bodies falling in anything but a vacuum. The empirical confrontation at the Leaning Tower of Pisa would have served, not to test the theory of mass-free acceleration of falling bodies, but to make its meaning clearer to the researcher, revealing its hidden assumptions about the contexts within which Galileo's prediction may obtain versus the more common contexts in which quite different theories better predict the behavior of falling bodies.

Thus for the physical as well as the social scientist, empirical confrontation is best considered, not as a critical hypothesis-testing corrective of an earlier a priori phase of creative hypothesis generating, but rather as an a posteriori continuation of the discovery process. This fallibilism may be applied even beyond the empirical sciences to the analytical propositions of mathematics (Davis & Hersh, 1981): One's faith in the postulate that $2 + 2 = 4$ is hardly weakened by the empirical discovery that two cups of sugar plus two cups of warm water yield far less than four cups of warm sugar water. Such a kitchen confrontation would lead, not to one's rejecting the proposition that $2 + 2 = 4$, but rather to a better understanding of the restrictive contexts in which it applies to models in the natural world.

C.   STYLES OF PSYCHOLOGICAL RESEARCH

The contextualist theory of knowledge that there are innumerable theoretical representations for any situation, one or another being the less inadequate depending on the context, suggests a third reform of current psychological practices, that we give more attention to the integrated stylistic aspects of research and particularly that we develop a new systems style in place of the current unilinear styles of doing research. "Style" here refers to the pattern of options selected at the two dozen or so successive choice points met in doing an empirical study. In taking each of these steps the researcher must choose among numerous available options. Tbe complete set of choices characteristically made by a researcher, constituting a preferred path in going through the multistep research process, is what I call a research "style."

Since numerous options are available for taking each of the several dozen steps, there are a vast number of potential paths through the complete research process but in any given era of a scientific discipline only a very few of the many possible styles are popular among researchers, perhaps one preferred Establishment style (for example, the laboratory manipulational experiment) and one or two alternative dissident styles (for example, the field experiment and the multivariate correlational study), each with minor variants. The convergence on just a few styles is partly historical accident, but there is some intrinsic determination in that one's selection of a given methodological option at one choice point tends to narrow one's options at later choice points. During the past quarter century, psychologists' metatheory has concentrated most research within one or the other of two unilinear styles that we call "convergent" and "divergent," the former somewhat more popular at mid-century but losing ascendancy to the divergent by the 1970s. The contextualist theory of knowledge calls for an alternative "systems" style of research to supplement these two unilinear styles. These three styles—the convergent, divergent, and systems—will be described successively.

1. The Convergent Unilinear Style

This style, especially popular in mid-century social psychology, is typified by Hovland *et al.'s* (1949, 1953) attitude change research. Convergent researchers begin by noticing an interesting relationship that calls for an explanation (rather than, as with the divergent style, beginning with a fascinating theory to be applied). For example, a convergent stylist might become interested in an observed relationship (such as delayed action effect in persuasion, the risky shift, the enhancing of liking by mere exposure, or the elicitation of aggression by witnessing violence), and then try to account for the maximum amount of variance in this relationship by drawing eclectically on a wide range of explanatory theories. I call this style "convergent" as regards theory use because the researcher brings a broad range of explanatory theories convergently to bear on the relationship of interest, each theory accounting for only a small amount of the relationship.

This convergent purpose typically leads to employing complex experimental designs that include multiple independent variables whose main and interaction effects on the dependent variable are predicted by one or another of the theories. Usually these independent variables are orthogonally manipulated by fairly weak operational procedures. For example, the participants might be given booklets each of whose pages contains a paragraph whose wording varies from booklet to booklet to place the recipients on different levels of one of the independent variables. In contrast to this rather casual manipulation of the independent variable, convergent theorists tend to measure dependent variables quite carefully, using multiple items each with a finely graded response scale to allow the kinds of statistical analyses that are sensitive enough to pick up small main and interaction effects.

These experimental design choices largely determine the convergent stylist's typical modes of data collection and analysis. Settling for superficial but simple manipulations of the independent variables by written paragraphs varying subtly from booklet to booklet allows the convergent stylist to use a large number of cases because participants can be run economically in large groups. It also allows each person to serve on different issues, permitting sensitive within-person comparisons and replicating the results across multiple issues (or other types of materials). The convergent stylist's careful multi-levelled measure of the dependent variable allows the use of sensitive differences-among-means descriptive statistics and powerful analysis of variance inferential statistics that estimate the magnitude (or at least significance) of interaction as well as main effects.

2. The Divergent Unilinear Style

In contrast to the convergent stylist's starting with a fascinating relationship to be explained and converging on it from a variety of eclectically chosen theoretical viewpoints, the divergent theorist begins with a single fascinating theory, applying it "divergently" to a wide variety of relationships in order to explain a little of the variance in each relationship. This reversal of initial purposes channels the divergent stylist into choosing options opposite to those usually chosen by the convergent stylist at a number of subsequent decision points in the research process. For example, whereas the convergent stylist is dependent-variable focused, using elegant and sensitive measures of the effects while only superficially manipulating the independent variables, the divergent stylist oppositely stresses independent over dependent variables, attempting precise and sizable manipulation of the one theory-crucial independent variable while being rather casual about measuring the dependent-variable effect. Typically the divergent theorist runs participants individually through elaborate inductions designed to put them exactly on the intended level of the independent variable and to hold constant other variables and to prevent the operation of mediating processes other than the theoretically relevant one. Usually the manipulation is carefully checked out and participants eliminated if not found to be on the level intended. In contrast to their careful independent variable manipulations, divergent stylists tend to be quite casual about dependent variable measurement, often settling for a gross measure by a single dichotomous response scale such as whether or not participants sign a petition, or which of the two booklets they select, or whether they choose to wait alone or in a room with other persons.

The divergent stylist's need to manipulate the independent variable sizably and precisely and to eliminate extraneous variables typically requires that each person participate individually in laborious manipulational procedures that might involve several experimenters and/or confederates. This individualized treatment typically restricts divergent-style studies to a relatively few participants and a single issue or other material, limiting generalizability. The small number of cases and gross scaling of the dependent variable typically limit the divergent stylist to insensitive descriptive statistics such as contingency coefficients and to relatively low parametric inferential statistics such as sign tests, chi squares, or at best, t tests.

3. The Systems Style of Research

Both convergent and divergent styles are "unilinear" in depicting some variables as independent and others as dependent with the main causal flow from the independent to the dependent. The contextualist theory of knowledge on the other hand calls for a contrasting systems style that allows knowledge representations more adequately to reflect the complexities of the real-world situations being represented which have reciprocal links and remote feedback loops that allow multiple and bidirectional causal paths. Hence, a systems stylist includes a complex set of variables within the research design. While initially some may be conceptualized as independent, others as mediating, and still others as dependent variables, all are allowed to covary naturally. This is necessary to detect complex relationships, including multiple causal pathways whose relative contribution to the covariance can be shown to fluctuate from one to another of the differing contexts established by the other variables in the design.

Besides starting with a multiplicity of interrelated independent, mediating, and dependent variables, the systems stylist typically presents a low profile to the participants, for example, observing persons in a natural situation or presenting open-ended probes that allow a wide range of participant-chosen responses instead of limiting the participant to multiple-choice response options on a researcher-chosen dimension. This permissiveness as regards responding yields data that are onerous to analyze (often requiring content analysis, a dummy variable approach to nonordered response categories, etc.) but in compensation yields more information than the unilinear reactive approaches. The systems style also encourages employment of time-series designs in which participants are measured on the variables at several different times in order to trace complex, bidirectional causal pathways among the variables.

Such complicated designs lead the systems stylist to select elaborate data analysis options such as multivariate analyses to reduce the number of variables, exploratory computer simulations to limit the number of paths that need to be searched, or estimate the criticality of values assigned to parameters and structural equation models to ascertain the strength and directions of various causal paths (Coleman, 1981). The contextualist system style calls also for a corrective reemphasis on descriptive statistics over inferential statistics. Both the convergent and divergent unilinear styles are rather simplistic in their descriptive statistics (except among the multivariate analysts who are premature contextualists), often testing only the null hypothesis of no relationship without regard for the shape of the relationship or even the effect size. In contrast, a contextualist system style would use exploratory data analyses (Tukey, 1977; Leinhardt & Wasserman, 1978; Hoaglin, Mosteller, & Tukey, 1983) that exploit descriptive statistics as discovery procedures rather than simply inferring whether a rectilinear horizontal null hypothesis can be rejected at some conventionally accepted level of significance. Even when practical difficulties confine measures to dichotomous frequency counts, the systems stylist can use log-linear models to exploit the information in multidimensional contingency tables (Haberman, 1978, 1979; Coleman, 1981). There is a worrisome danger of post-factum capitalization on chance in the systems style but steps can be taken to contain this danger. Contextualism makes the systems style especially inviting; more generally, it stresses the importance of recognizing the concept of research style and of training the researcher to develop whatever organically integrated style he or she finds most provocative.

1. The Nature of Research Strategy

Contextualism's fourth general implication for the reform of the psychological research process is that more attention be given to developing research strategy as a corrective to the current overemphasis on research tactics. Tactics deal with specific methodological issues that arise within the conduct of a single study, whereas strategy involves the broader issues that arise in designing a multistudy program of research, including choice of topic, planning an integrated series of studies, and deciding where to start. Social psychological research, especially that using the divergent style, has been criticized since the 1960s for its hit-and-run quality (Ring, 1967; McGuire, 1967) in which the investigator plans and conducts an isolated study and when an outcome can be reported in accord with her or his preferred theory (and probably with a half-dozen other theories as well), the researcher, instead of pursuing the topic through a program of studies, drops it and designs a study to confirm some new derivation from the theory. The contextualist view of knowledge stresses that an adequate understanding of either a phenomenon or a theory requires that it be investigated through a program of research planned to reveal the wide range of circumstances that affect the phenomenon and the rich set of implicit assumptions that limit the theory, thus making explicit the contexts in which one or another relationship obtains.

By the 1980s the hit-and-run aspect of social psychological research has abated at least to the point that a researcher's pursuing the investigation of a relationship through a program of multiple experiments is no longer perceived as a sign of creative deficit. Pedagogy here again lags behind practice because methodology courses continue to deal exclusively with research tactics for conducting the individual experiment. While teaching students the options available and the criteria for choosing among them at various choice points within the single study, these courses continue to ignore the broader issues of research strategy that arise in planning a program of experiments that will cumulatively explicate a theory or phenomenon. Rarely is there discussion of how to select problems on where to begin a program of research or of how to establish priorities for deciding among the directions in which to pursue an issue programmatically. A rare exception to past pedagogic neglect of the strategic level of research has been these Berkowitz (1964–1983) *Advances* volumes in which authors are encouraged to describe the programmatic nature of their cumulative work rather than the usual presentation of individual studies in isolation. I shall describe the pedagogic possibilities for training students in the strategic level of research, first in terms of general principles and then in the form of a concrete example.

2. Principles of Research Strategy

The researcher should consider the broad programmatic aspects even when undertaking a narrow study. When investigating the concrete prediction of a specific relationship, it might seem unnecessary to fit this study explicitly within a broad programmatic strategy, but paradoxically such an effort is especially necessary with such ad hoc inspirations. When the prediction has been derived from an explicit theoretical formulation, the theory would have provided some strategic guidance from the start. With both phenomenon and theory instigated hypotheses, strategic planning on three different levels of abstraction is called for. First, on the hypothesis's own level of abstraction, conceptual clarification of its variables and their relationship should be carried out. Second, on a more abstract level, alternative theoretical structures that predict either the hypothesis or its contrary should be made explicit. Third, on a more concrete level, a program of empirical studies should be planned to clarify the pertinence of the alternative theoretical formulations to the empirical domain of interest. I shall briefly sketch strategic procedures that can be used on each of these three levels of abstraction.

a. Strategies for Clarifying a Hypothesis on Its Own Level of Generality. Strategic research planning can begin on the hypothesis's own level of abstraction by clarifying the predicted relationship and the meanings of the variables themselves. To begin by clarifying the relationship, it should be recognized that researchers differ among themselves as to which way of expressing a hypothesis best enhances its meaningfulness and provocativeness. Hence, research training should demonstrate that the hypothesis can easily be transformed among verbal, graphical, tabular, etc., modes of expression without changing its meaning. Verbal statements of the hypothesized relationship can be in the form of an ordinary declarative sentence (i.e., "People's liking for a stranger increases with the extent that the stranger's eyes have large pupillary openings"), to a conditional statement ("If a stranger's pupils are more dilated, then he or she will be better liked"), or a statement of covariation ("The greater the stranger's pupil dilation, the more liking he/she will evoke"), to more austerely symbolic formalizations ("As regards evoked liking, large pupil dilation > small"; or "liking $= f^+$ (pupil dilation)").

Researchers who are more visually oriented may find a graphical mode of representing the relationship more comprehensible or provocative. For example, the hypothesis may be represented on a graph whose abscissa is scaled for the independent variable (size of pupil dilation) and the ordinate for the dependent variable (being liked), with each stranger being entered as a point within the enclosed space located by his or her scores on these two variables. An alternative graphical representation sometimes preferred by beginning researchers is to let each successive abscissa point represent a different stranger, with his or her pupil dilation and likability scores being entered in that column in accordance with ordinate scales of the independent and dependent variables so that the covariation of the two curves can be observed.

Researchers more comfortable with numbers may prefer tabular modes of representing the hypothesis, perhaps depicting it as a table whose three columns partition the strangers into three groups on the independent variable (as being below, at, or above average in pupil dilation), and entering the stranger's dependent variable score (amount that the stranger is liked) in the appropriate column and predicting the ordering of the magnitudes of the columns' mean (being-liked scores would increase as pupil dilation increases from low, to medium, to high).

Giving a student a lesson in translating her or his hypotheses among such alternative modes of representation demystifies the logic of empirical predictions, makes arcane expressions of hypotheses conceptually accessible, enhances ability to transform expressions from one mode to another when the type of hypothesis or the stage of research makes switching convenient, eases the translation from talking about the relationship to designing the experiment and setting up the data analysis and facilitates the expression of more complex interaction hypotheses.

A second hypothesis-clarifying step is exploring the meaning of one's variables whose full significance is often grasped only precariously. One initially perceives covariation between two or more dimensions on which one's units of observation differ and then forms an image or verbal label of each dimension that subsequently guides its conceptual use and measurement. If the initial label is unwisely chosen, the researcher's later conceptualizing and operationalizing may be drawn away from his or her initial inspiration and the fit to the empirical domain may be diminished. Besides preventing the initial intuition from slipping away, explicit clarification of the variables discloses the heuristically rich ambiguities and complexities in the variables. Conceptual clarification might start with an informal discursive description of the variable in the form of a short written paragraph, which can be studied to yield a more formal definition in the form of genus plus specific difference. The connotative meaning can then be sketched by listing essential properties, typical concomitants, negative descriptors, etc., which can then be organized into a logical structure. Generating an antonym domain clarifies each property in accord with the contrast principles of Saussurian structuralism and can be used to produce an alternative structure for cross checking. One can check out competing interpretations in terms of their fit to one's initial extended description. Alternatively, rival interpretations can be evaluated by going to the variable's denotative meaning: One can list people whose ordering on the variable seems clear and can ascertain which of the competing descriptions better conserves this denotative ordering. When the uncertainty cannot be resolved, the researcher may include subscales that provide separate scores for each of the conflicting meanings. Explicitly carrying out a definitional analysis of this sort allows the researcher to exploit the full richness of the original insight and to appreciate the hypothesis's true complexity.

b. Strategies for Embedding the Hypotheses in Abstract Theories. After clarifying and enriching the hypothesis on its own level of abstraction by developing the meanings of its variables and by multiple representations of the predicted relationship between them, strategic analysis can proceed to a more abstract level by mapping alternative theoretical structures in which the prediction is embedded. The first step, making explicit at least one broader theory from which the hypothesis can be derived, is one on which the divergent stylist has an advantage since it will have been a theoretical insight that initially attracted her or him to the hypothesis; however, the convergent stylist, while more preoccupied with the predicted relationship itself, should also start by making explicit a broader theoretical conceptualization that houses the prediction. By a broader theoretical explanation I mean a set of propositions on a higher level of abstraction than the hypothesis from which it can be derived. Typically, it would involve a series of general propositions, each stating how one broad variable will be related to another, plus definitional propositions that tie in each of the hypothesis's more specific variables with a broader variable contained in one of the general propositions. For example, a hypothesis that people enjoy associating with others to the extent that others are similar to themselves might be explained by (derived from) a social reinforcement theory that contains a series of general propositions about association responses being enhanced by past rewards plus definitional propositions that relate interpersonal similarity to rewardingness.

Once an initial salient explanatory theory has been generated, the researcher should take a second step of generating additional theories that also imply the hypothesis. Researchers are so likely to neglect this step that in Table II we have suggested as creativity heuristic 21 that the researcher not stop with a single explanation of a phenomenon but continue to generate up to a half-dozen alternative explanations that could also account for it. Contextualist epistemology with its stress on the multiplicity of possible knowledge representations for any situation, each adequate in some but not in other contexts, makes especially obvious this need for sketching out a variety of alternative theories from which the predicted relationship can be derived, each theory suggesting additional variables that need to be worked into one's program of empirical confrontation.

The third step in this abstract level of research strategy is to stand the hypothesis on its head and generate several theories that predict this contrary relationship between the variables. For example, if one initially hypothesized that people's liking for others increased with the others' past helpfulness, and then generated three or four different theories that would account for this plausible prediction, here in the third step one has the more formidable task of generating theories that identify contexts in which the contrary relationship obtains, such that people find others to be less attractive to the extent that the others have been helpful in the past. While the original hypothesis was trivially obvious, this third step of generating theories yielding the opposite prediction becomes more difficult but also more rewarding. Indeed, Table II includes as heuristic 12 for enhancing research creativity this procedure of mentally reversing the direction of a commonsense prediction and thinking of special circumstances in which the reversal would obtain. The importance of this third hypothesis-inverting step in strategic theorizing is especially apparent within the contextualist working assumption that all theories and even their contraries are likely to be true, given one or another special context. By this strategy of generating multiple theories that account for the initial hypothesis and several more that yield the contrary prediction, the researcher makes explicit suppressed assumptions of each theory and calls attention to limiting situational contexts in which any given formulation will be valid.

When one starts with an obvious hypothesis (for example, that people like others to the extent they perceive the others as liking them, or that people's own levels of aggression increase with the amounts of violence to which they are exposed), the strategy of generating multiple theoretical explanations, rather than stopping with a first momentarily salient one, enriches one's empirical research strategy, as will be described in the next section. However, with such obvious hypotheses it might seem perverse to bother with step 3 of dredging up exceptional circumstances in which the typical commonsense prediction would be reversed. However, it is just such oddities that allow scientific psychology to provide new insights rather than confirm old commonsense prescientific understandings: the commonsense bubbapsychological relationship may have far wider ecological validity but discovering how in exceptional circumstances a tritely familiar relationship may be reversed is often more enlightening (as when a physical scientist or engineer speculates about peculiar reversals of commonly experienced "laws" of motion that would occur in a vacuum, rare as a vacuum may be).

c. Research Strategies on a Third, More Concrete Level. Strategic thinking on the hypothesis's own level by clarifying its variables and on more abstract levels by generating theories from which it and its contrary can be derived escalates the complexity of the conceptualization. To exploit these complications for insight enhancement rather than to be confused by them calls for a third, more concrete level of strategic planning in which a program of empirical research is developed to reveal the pattern of empirical contexts in which the alternative conceptualizations manifest themselves. Training in this third level of strategic planning gives the researcher tools for untangling the theoretical complexities and thus enhances his or her courage to face and exploit these complexities. A half-dozen of these untangling tools will be described here.

A first conceptual procedure for untangling theoretical complexities is to analyze each of the explanations as regards which intervening variable it assumes is mediating the predicted relationship, and then add to the design a direct measure of each of the implied mediators. Partial correlation or analysis of covariance can then be used to determine the extent to which each mediator accounts for a significant portion of the relationship between independent and dependent variables (indicating that the theory implying this mediator may indeed be an explanation of the relationship) but also to determine if a significant relationship between independent and dependent variables remains even when the effect of each mediator is partialled out (indicating that other mediators and other theories are also involved).

A second untangling technique is to add to the design additional independent variables, each of which is predicted uniquely by one of the theories to interact with the original independent variable to affect its relationship to the dependent variable so that an obtained interaction effect would indicate the given theory's appropriateness. Adding multiple independent variables, each uniquely predicted by a different theory to produce an interaction effect, helps the researcher to appreciate that explanation is not a zero-sum game: however firmly one believes in Boyle's law, one need not reject Charles's law. A diverse set of theorized processes may be operative with wide variation from situation to situation in the proportion of the common variance contributed by each of the mediators. For example, positive covariation between exposure to violence depictions and viewers' subsequent aggressiveness can be accounted for by a variety of explanations involving disinhibition, activation, response availability, etc., each of which yields a rich set of interaction predictions. A research design that includes interaction variables each suggested by a different theory is an example of the heuristic value of the contextualist approach.

Four other untangling techniques will be given only cursory description here. Redundant and conflicting theories can be empirically disentangled by analyzing the dependent variable into several subdimensions, each most relevant to one of the theories, as when questions about the relative importance of ideological versus demographic similarity in determining interpersonal liking led to theoretical and empirical analyses to identify the different domains of liking in which each type of similarity is especially operative. Another untangling technique is to manipulate the independent variable in different theory-distinctive ways, as when researchers used different types of forewarnings of persuasive attacks to determine the extent to which anticipatory attitude change is due to informational or self-esteem mechanisms. A fifth approach is to combine several theorized processes to make a composite prediction of a bottom line (often nonmonotonic) net relationship, as when activation versus avoidance explanations of stress effects (e.g., coping with the threat versus with the fear) are combined to predict an overall inverted-U nonmonotonic relationship between stress level and response to social influence. A sixth approach is to collect data in an inclusive multivariable naturalistic design and then use structural equation models or other causal analyses to tease out alternative paths and directions of causality among a set of the variables as is currently being done in exploring the pertinence of alternative explanations of the interrelations among cognitions, affects, and actions toward attitudinal objects.

Acquainting the researcher with techniques such as the half-dozen just described here for strategically planning the conflicting empirical level of research facilitates exploiting the heuristic provocation offered by the concrete implications of the redundant and contrary theoretical explanations generated on the abstract strategic level. Acquaintance with the availability of such solutions also gives the researcher courage and skill to undertake strategic research planning on all three levels of abstraction. Contextualism makes the need for strategic planning particularly salient but one need not be a card-carrying contextualist to agree that current narrow preoccupation in methodology courses with within-study tactical issues should be corrected by paying more attention to the broader strategic issues that arise when one is deciding where to begin and how to pursue a multistudy program of research.

3. An Illustration of Research Strategy

While some issues involved in the strategic level of research (such as those previously described) can be usefully discussed in terms of general procedures, the strategic levels of methodology have received so little attention that many of the issues can best be indicated in terms of a concrete example. My own current research on widely shared preferences in seemingly arbitrary word orderings serves as a basis for description of these issues. This research is not concerned with intrinsically-demanded word orderings where sequence affects meaning (as when "John loves Mary" has a significance sufficiently different from "Mary loves John" so that the nonequivalence is the stuff of great stories and great sorrows). The research centers rather on the innumerable cases in which almost everyone uses one seemingly arbitrary word order that neither rhyme nor reason demands. Of interest, for example, is the general consensus on using such word orderings as "large white house" or "I put on my shoes and socks" when there would be no grammatical error or change in meaning were one to say "white large house" or "I put on my socks and shoes" (and in fact the latter would more accurately describe the sequence in which the dressing usually occurs). The prevalence of such asymmetrical preferences in word orderings for which there is no compelling reason but for which a variety of possible explanations suggest themselves promises that its study may reveal unsuspected principles of cognitive and social functioning.

Strategic decisions about where to begin and how to pursue such a broad program of research are needed once one recognizes the numerous options offered by the multiplicity of (1) the phenomenon's manifestations, of (2) the methods that can be used, and of (3) the types of explanations that can be theorized. With respect to word-order's manifestations, shared preferences occur in diverse families of noun pairs (niece and nephew, knife and fork, bacon and eggs, etc.), adjective series (high and mighty, flimsy wooden fence, etc.), verbs (to cut and run, to trick or treat, etc.), and other parts of speech (and/or, in and out, etc.). Should one concentrate in depth on one manifestation of the phenomenon or make a full-court press? Among the diverse methods by which the phenomenon can be investigated, one could use rating tasks (asking people if they would usually say "We visited our aunt and uncle" or "We visited our uncle and aunt") or could content analyze spontaneous orderings of "aunt and uncle" versus "uncle and aunt" in natural discourse, perhaps elicited by open-ended probes such as "Tell me about your family," or perhaps as analyzed in concordances to the writings of famous authors. With respect to the diverse explanations that a contextualist could offer to account for discretionary word-order regularities, possible bases for priority include phoneme recognizibility, ease of utterance, cognitive availability, psychodynamic involvement, sociocultural evaluation, etc.

The total investigatory space created by these three dimensions—domains of manifestation, method of study, and theoretical explanations—is illustrated in Fig. 1. Strategic choices must be made regarding where in this space to begin the research and in which direction to pursue it. The very act of asking such a question is a noteworthy initial strategic decision, since all too often the researcher neglects the a priori sketching out of the total research domain as shown in Fig. 1 and so stumbles into a decision on where to begin without adequate deliberation.

In deciding where to start in the word-order case, we ruled out a full-court press strategy in the form of one grand data-collection design that would include all domains of word-order manifestations (nouns, adjectives, verbs, etc.), all methods (rating tasks, natural utterances, etc.), and all classes of theories (phonological, cognitive, etc.). Such a strategy of collecting all possible data before doing any of the analyses should seldom be the approach of choice because it requires making a vast investment before obtaining any information that might show that some variables make so little difference that they could have been eliminated early in the research program with a vast saving of effort and little loss

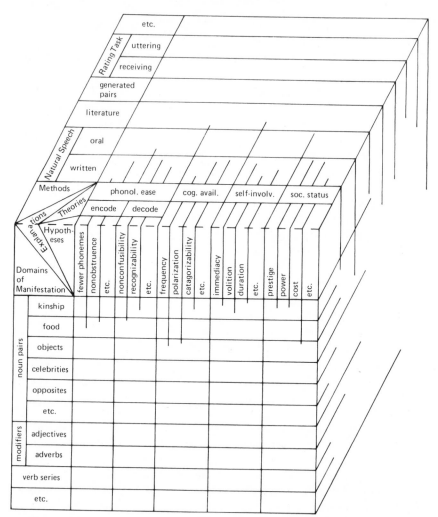

Fig. 1. Domains of research on word order regularities within which strategy decisions have to be made.

of information. For example, if one limited one's initial data collecting to a relatively simple semantic domain such as kinship noun pairs (fathers and sons, niece and nephew) and investigated it by a wide range of methods, these relatively simple initial studies might show that similar results are obtained whether one uses the simpler rating task or the more onerous natural discourse method. If so, one would be encouraged to economize from then on by dispensing with the onerous natural discourse method and instead studying the other domains of word-order manifestations by the simpler rating method. The full-court press method would have required one to drag the costly natural discourse method through all the domains of material perhaps only to learn at the end that its information yield may be largely redundant with what could have been found by using just the undemanding rating method. The strategic methodological principle illustrated is that one should begin by bringing multiple methods to bear on a narrow manifestation of the phenomenon of interest in order to identify the simplest set of methods that yield the full information, thus discovering which of the more onerous methods one can dispense with in the subsequent steps of one's research program.

Having decided to make our basic exclusionary cut by focusing within one narrow semantic domain at a time, we had to select the word-order manifestation with which to begin. We decided to start with the domain of kinship noun pairs (brother and sister, mom and pop, etc.) and then turn to the slightly more complicated but comparably vital domain of food pairs (soup and sandwich, lettuce and tomatoes, scotch and soda). Only later, after some theoretical mastery of word-order phenomenon has been gained, will we tackle semantic domains that armchair analysis indicates to be more difficult to explain, such as the orderings within adjective series (large brick house, dirty old man, etc.). Important strategic criteria for choosing to start with kinship pairs is that they include a manageable universe of terms (only 13 basic English words plus compounds). Also, kin and food are significant and familiar domains of human experience, making it likely that they will reflect basic human processes and will occur with sufficient frequency in natural discourse to allow data to be accumulated economically. The familiarity of the kin and food domains also makes them accessible to and suggestive of interpretive insights. For example, in interpreting ordering preferences within kinship pairs one can confidently make use of such contextual information as each kin's relative social status, emotional valence, frequency of contacting, etc. Within food pairs one can use contextual information about which tends to be the better liked, more nutritious, more generously represented in the usual portions, etc. Another criterion for our choosing kin and food pairs is that, while they have been important meaning domains at all times and places, there have been some recognizable cross-cultural and cross-era variations that promise to allow comparative data to untangle cognitive from linguistic and sociocultural theoretical explanations. Also, both kin and food terms have fairly clear objective referents, making for easy cross-language translation.

An important reason for our strategic decision to study one semantic domain at a time is that it facilitates the development of separate explanatory theories for each domain since we can exploit our grasp of the minutia of each limited familiar domain to provoke a particularly apt theoretical interpretation of word-order preferences within it while allowing the emergence of overlapping but somewhat divergent theories for each separate domain. For example, if one of the theoretical propositions that accounts for kin-pair orderings is that the higher status member of the pair tends to be named first, and if a rule of food-pair primacy turns out to be that the more expensive item tends to be named first, then the two principles, status and cost, can easily be combined into a more general proposition. In other domains a more radically different set of theoretical principles may emerge to explain word order but, far from being an embarrassment, such divergence of explanatory principles is one of the attractions of this strategy since the divergencies can be creative springboards for the higher-order theoretical synthesis of a broader abstract theory. The broad theory would fit a wide range of semantic contexts (each vague and with frequent errors in detail), while each lower-order theoretical subset would fit its own specific domain more provocatively and precisely, with its ad hoc dimensions being given deeper meaning and heuristic power by the higher-order theory. Theoretical representations of word-order regularities are interesting, not so much because they tell us more about consensus in discretionary word-order preferences than most people really want to know, but because of what they disclose about the structure and functioning of human cognitive systems and social structure.

Current methodology discussions and training do not pay sufficient attention to the kind of strategic issues discussed in this section D, with a resulting neglect of the thoughtful overall analysis and sequencing of research on the across-study programmatic level. The unorthodox contextualist position that the empirical confrontation phase of research is a continuing discovery process (rather than a test of whether or not one's a priori theory and hypothesis are true) calls attention to the importance of expanding current methodological thinking beyond mere within-study tactics to deal also with the among-study strategic aspects of programmatic research design.

IV. Psychology as Product: The Theoretical Yield from Analytical and Empirical Research

Here we turn from process to product, from the process of creating psychological knowledge to the knowledge produced as we discuss the substance of the psychological theories that both underlie and grow out of the research process. We shall first distinguish four types of psychological theories (categorical, process, systems, and guiding-idea theories) before concentrating in a little more detail on sixteen of the latter, guiding-idea theories that have dominated psychological research for the past half century.

A.   FOUR TYPES OF THEORIES GUIDING AND EMERGING
     FROM THE RESEARCH PROCESS

1. Categorical Theories

The simplest theoretical representations of the complex human environment involve chunking the innumerable independent variables into a manageable set of categories, perhaps five to ten, each of which can be further partitioned into several levels of more specific subcategories. An example of this type of knowledge representation is the partition of persuasive communication variables into five classes, including source, message, channel, receiver, and target (that is, into variables concerning who says what via which medium to whom regarding what issue), each of which classes of variables may then be further subdivided on additional levels (McGuire, 1978, 1983a) as when message variables are subdivided into message styles, arguments, motivational appeals, inclusions, orderings, etc., and message style in turn is further subdivided into such variables as clarity, vividness, speed, literalness, and humorousness. Other examples of categorical theories are Adorno *et al.'s* (1950) distinguishing among numerous subtypes of persons high and low in anti-Semitism and S. Cook's (1975) identifying types of conditions under which interracial contacts are most likely to result in intergroup harmony.

These categorical (or "descriptive") theories are relatively primitive types of knowledge representation that handle information overload by several cognitive conveniences: Complex realities are reduced to their characteristic on one dimension of variability, this dimension is partitioned with a few broad intervals, and all entities falling into the same interval are treated as equal and as different from entities falling into other intervals on that dimension, thus allowing the researcher to concentrate on and work creatively with a few essential features while ignoring others. Categorical theories also allow the researcher the option of taking a broad perspective by staying at the level of general categories or of taking a narrower and deeper look, zooming in on microprocesses by concentrating on the subcategories of just one domain. Categorical theories are particularly useful to the phenomenon-oriented convergent stylist who can use the categories and subcategories as a checklist of independent variables that may need investigating to account for the total variance in a phenomenon. Though they lack charisma, these categorical chunking theories have often served useful purposes.

2. Process Theories

While categorical theories organize the independent variables into arbitrarily ordered sets of inputs, the somewhat more sophisticated process theories typically analyze dependent variables into sequentially ordered proximal and distal output steps, perhaps depicting the output behavior of interest and its mediators as a flow chart like those often used to facilitate writing a computer program. For example, McGuire (1983a) analyzes the persuasion process into a dozen of successive output steps such as getting exposed to the social pressure, attending to it, involvement in it, comprehension, skill acquisition, agreement, action, etc. Another example is Janis and Mann's (1977) analysis of the decision process into various successive steps, including both a main line of progression and secondary feedback loops. The process theorist, unwilling to settle for an end-product prediction, aims to develop a process simulation with a one-to-one correspondence between the steps in the theoretical representation and the micro-processes through which the behavior is actually channeled.

A combination of categorical and process theories can provide a particularly useful representation of a complex psychological domain if a categorical analysis of the independent variables and a process analysis of the dependent variables can be joined to form an input-output matrix. An example is McGuire's (1969b, 1983a) communication–persuasion matrix whose column headings are the various categories of the communication input variables (e.g., aspects of source, message, etc.) and whose row headings are the successive output steps that constitute the process of being persuaded (exposure, attention, comprehension, agreement, action, etc.), with each cell entry specifying the relationship between its column independent variable and its row dependent variable. Such input–output matrices are efficient representational structures for making complex domains of reality intellectually accessible, facilitating the digesting of new information, the recognition of gaps in existing knowledge, the manipulation of the processes involved, and the evaluation of applied programs. They are susceptible of such further elaboration as erecting theoretical superstructures on the column or row categories, subdividing the categories, adding further dimensions to the two-dimensional matrix, etc.

3. Axiomatic Theories

"Systems" or "axiomatic" knowledge representations are particularly elegant and productive theories that start with a set of conceptually independent postulates, usually fewer than a dozen in number, each sufficiently self-evident or empirically well established as to seem trite but in combination yielding some surprising theorems. The avatar of axiomatic theories is Euclidean geometry whose relatively banal initial postulates combine to allow deduction of a startling variety of theorems and corollaries. Spinoza's *Ethics* is another classic example. Within psychology, Clark Hull developed such "hypothetico-deductive" theories to describe memorization (Hull *et al.*, 1940) and choice behavior (Hull, 1952). Freud's theory of human personality is at least implicitly an axiomatic theory though its formal structure is more apparent in systematizations by his interpreters (Schafer, 1976) than in Freud's own writings. Examples in social psychology are McGuire's (1968) persuasibility theory whose six axioms and two corollaries yield a wide variety of theorems about individual differences in susceptibility to social influence, the probabilogical theory of cognitive structure and attitude change (McGuire, 1981a), and Anderson's (1981) information integration–functional measurement theory.

4. Guiding-Idea Theories

Theories in this fourth category are partial views of the system (e.g., the person), each of which exploits the provocative implications of a selective depiction of the process (e.g., human nature). Guiding idea theories in psychology may depict the person as an information processor, or as a power seeker, or an ego-defender, etc. Typically the partial depiction is first formulated not as an aggressively "nothing but" formulation but simply to make use of the notion that "among other things" people behave as if they were information-processing machines or whatever; however, in the polemical atmosphere that often arises in research, each of these mutually supplementary theories may be pushed imperialistically to the point of being perceived as antagonistic to the others. Because such guiding-idea formulations continue to be the most popular kind of knowledge representations used in social psychology, we shall devote the next section to describing 16 of these partial views of human nature that together give direction to most social psychological research.

B. SIXTEEN GUIDING-IDEA THEORIES OF HUMAN NATURE

Any student of social psychology should be able with little effort to discern a half-dozen or more guiding-idea theories that have inspired research in the field, for example, social learning theory depicting the person as a reward-maximizer, consistency theories that represent the person as striving to maximize internal congruence, hermeneutic–attribution theories depicting the person as striving to interpret and give meaning to experiences, etc. To retrieve the full variety of these various guiding-idea theories and describe them systematically and inclusively, I have isolated four dimensions and have dichotomized them in Saussurian contrasts to identify the range of such polarized partial views of human nature (McGuire, 1974, 1980, 1981b). I first describe the four dichotomized dimensions themselves and then the 16 guiding-idea theories that they define.

Two of the distinguishing dimensions have to do with forces that instigate human action and two with forces that terminate it. The first, "stability versus growth" or "being versus coming" dimension contrasts theories that depict the person as instigated to action by the need to maintain the current equilibrium (stability, homeostasis) from those stressing the need to grow, actualize, or achieve a higher level of complexity. A second "active versus reactive" instigating dimension distinguishes theories that depict behavior as actively evoked by forces within the person versus theories representing behavior as a reaction to outside forces. The other two dimensions concern the forces postulated to terminate action. The third, "cognitive versus affective" dimension, distinguishes theories that represent human action as terminating with the attainment of some kind of cognitive meaning (ideational) state versus theories depicting action as terminating when a certain affective (feeling, emotional) state is attained. A final "internal versus external" dimension distinguishes theories that depict action as terminating with the attainment of some specified arrangement among the internal aspects of the person from those describing action as terminating when some specified relationship is established between the self and the external environment.

Guiding-idea theories take a stand, implicitly at least, at one or the other opposing pole on each of these four dimensions, yielding the 2^4 structure of possible theories shown in Table III, whose column headings are furnished by the two instigating dimensions and whose row headings are supplied by the two terminating dimensions. In each of the 16 cells of the Table III matrix is named a family of guiding-idea theories whose depiction of human nature is specified by

TABLE III

Sixteen Partial Views of Human Nature that Have Served as Guiding-Idea Theories for Psychological Research

Action termination	Action initiation			
	Need for stability		Need for growth	
	Active instigation	Reactive instigation	Active instigation	Reactive instigation
Cognitive state				
External relationship	1. Consistency	2. Categorization	5. Stimulation	6. Problem solver
Internal relationship	4. Hermeneutic	3. Inductional	8. Autonomy	7. Teleological
Affective state				
External relationship	13. Tension reduction	14. Ego defensive	9. Attraction	10. Identification
Internal relationship	16. Expressive	15. Repetition	12. Assertion	11. Contagion

the four descriptors supplied by its column and row headings. For example, cell 1 in the upper left-hand corner of the matrix includes the various consistency theories (balance, dissonance, congruity, etc.) that characterize the person as acting to maintain the current equilibrium rather than for growth and as acting to reduce a disequilibrium within the person (for example, between attitudes and actions) rather than as reacting to some press from the environment; as regards termination of action, these cell 1 consistency theories depict the behavioral sequence as ceasing with the attainment of a cognitive rather than feeling state (adjusting the components into cognitive congruity) and with the attainment of an internal coherence among components of the self rather than establishing some relationships between the self and the outside environment. The sections that follow describe briefly each of the 16 partial views of human nature named in the Table III cells, taking them up in quadrants by starting with the four in the upper left-hand corner of the matrix and proceeding clockwise through the other three quadrants.

1. The Cognitive Stability Theories

Theories in the four cells that make up the upper left-hand quadrant of Table III all depict the person as acting to maintain or reestablish an equilibrium and as terminating action with the attainment of a cognitive goal state, but they differ among themselves on the other two dimensions, active versus reactive instigation and internal versus external terminal states. Of the four families of theories in this quadrant, I start with the consistency theories in the upper left-hand cell and then proceed clockwise around the other three cells of the quadrant, describing each family of theories as regards the partial aspect of human nature that it stresses and mentioning some of its major users.

"Consistency" theories, which dominated social psychology in the 1960s, represent the person as balancer, maximizing connectedness and coherence among cognitions, affects, and behavior, much as an honest broker trying to keep any one aspect from getting noticeably out of line with the others, perhaps tending toward a least-squared-deviations solution. Many variants of consistency theories emerged—balance, congruity, psychologics, probabilogics, dissonance, symmetry, social exchange, equity, etc.—differing among themselves on such issues as what components the person tries to keep coherent, what modes of inconsistency reduction are preferred, etc. Theorists associated with this partial representation include Heider, Osgood & Tannenbaum, Abelson & Rosenberg, Newcomb, Festinger, Brehm, Aronson, McGuire, Homans, Adams, etc. A succinct review can be found in McGuire (1966) and detailed ones in Abelson *et al.* (1968) and Wicklund and Brehm (1976).

Cell 2 "categorization" theories (sometimes called "perceptual") depict the person as a filing clerk handling an excess of incoming information by sorting it into an available set of cognitive cubbyholes whose affective and behavioral tags channel the person's responses. This representation of human nature suggests that changing the person's behavior is not so much a matter of attaching a new response to the old stimulus, but of presenting the old stimulus in a way that will cause the person to categorize it differently. This viewpoint is represented in psychological theories involving such concepts as schema, frames of reference, stereotypes, adaptation level, assimilation–contrast, framing, etc., and on the fringes of psychology by symbolic interactionism and the various structuralist schools. Theorists utilizing this filing clerk view of the person include Luchins, Sherif, Asch, Helson, Upshaw, Tversky, Blumer, Moscovici, Piaget, Lévi-Strauss, etc.

The family of theories in cell 3, cryptically termed "inductional" theories here, depict the person as a lazy conceptualizer trying to make sense of experience but only in response to some externally imposed need to know. Examples of inductional theories are Bem's (1972) radical behaviorism which depicts the person as formulating attitudes when external demands require it, various self-labeling theories such as the foot-in-the-door formulations, and revisions of consistency theory which hold that incongruities lead to behavioral and attitude change only when they involve the frustration of some other need such as self-esteem (Wicklund & Frey, 1981).

Cell 4 "hermeneutic" formulations depict the person as much more actively cognizing, as an implicit theorist habitually generating explanations of self and environment in a search for meaning. These theories trace back to Helmholtz's doctrine of unconscious inference (Hochberg, 1981) and is represented by Michotte's early work on the person as an implicit physicist, Festinger's social comparison theory, Lerner's just world notion, Jones's ingratiation research, Kelley's attribution theory, etc. These hermeneutic theories stressing the person's need to attribute meaning to his or her world dominated social psychology during the 1970s, replacing the consistency theories' hegemony in the 1960s. Recent work using this meaning-seeker view of the person is reviewed briefly by Kelley and Michela (1980) and at more length by Harvey and Weary (1981).

2.   The Cognitive Growth Theories

The four families of theories shown in the upper right-hand quadrant of Table 3 agree with the four just considered in depicting the person as striving after a cognitive state, but this new tetrad depicts the person as striving after cognitive growth rather than cognitive stability. These four differ among themselves on the other two dimensions.

The first family of cognitive growth theories, the cell 5 "stimulation" partial views, stress the person's stimulus hunger, curiously seeking after novelty, playful capriciousness, proneness to fads, and avidity to avoid boredom. This aspect of the person was slighted during the midcentury behavioristic ascendancy and came into its own only when the animal learning theorists themselves (for example, Berlyne, Harlow, Kendler, Dember, etc.) began to stress this notion in studies of rats' and monkeys' alternation behavior, need exploration, curiosity drive, etc. This need for complexity or curiosity drive view has been best developed by Berlyne (1960) and has received focused study as a human need by Bieri *et al.* (1966) and by Zuckerman (1979).

The cell 6 "problem solver" theories stress the utilitarian aspect of the person, avid to maximize gain and taking pleasure in meeting and coping with challenges and enhancing his or her skills. This representation of the person received early emphasis in Tolman's purposive theory, Lewin's goal-oriented field theory, Katz's functional theory, and in the numerous variations of the attribution $\times$ evaluation conceptualization, especially in its instrumentality $\times$ evaluation versions but also in its attribution $\times$ property versions. Hence it underlies the research of many in the Michigan–Illinois "school" such as Peak, M. Rosenberg, Dulaney, Raven, Fishbein, Triandis, etc. Fishbein's (1980) theory of reasoned action is an especially influential version. The achievement motivation branch of this work, stemming from McClelland, is reviewed by Weiner (1974) and Fyans (1980).

The "teleological" (or "purposive" or "template") theories shown in cell 7 are currently more inspired by analog computer and guided missile imagery than by the theological preconceptions formerly implied by the term "teleological." They depict humans as pattern matchers with end state cognitions in accord with which they attempt to bring their perception of the world, the match being achieved either by locomoting through the environment until it presents a suitable sensory match to the image or by working on the environment to transform it so that it accords with the picture in the head. This partial view of the person enters psychology from Dilthey via Weber and lies behind such midcentury notions as Tolman's cognitive map, Hebb's concept of cell assembly, Miller, Pribram and Galanter's plan concept, etc. It came into its own with the proliferation of computer-generated imagery underlying cybernetics, operations research, systems theory, etc. Currently it underlies Powers' (1978) notion of behavior as the control of perception and reviews can be found under terms such as scheme (Eckblad, 1981), script (Abelson, 1981), and rule (Harré, 1981) theory.

The partial views of human nature shown in cell 8 are called "autonomy" theory because they stress the human need for freedom and control (or at least the illusion of control) over one's own life and environment. Preoccupation with the person as striving for autonomy seems to fluctuate in a 20-year cycle, having been popular in the 1930s work of Gordon Allport and Henry Murray, and again in 1950s theorizing of Erik Erikson and Abraham Maslow, and showing a resurgence in the 1970s research on locus of control (Lefcourt, 1981), reactance theory (Brehm, 1966; Wicklund, 1974), illusion of control (Steiner, 1980), and self-determination (Deci, 1980). Especially good use has been made of this notion by health psychologists such as H. Leventhal, Lazarus, and Rodin. Perlmuter and Monty (1979) provide a review of this family of theories.

3. The Affective Growth Theories

In contrast to the previous eight theories' stress on the person as striving for various cognitive (thought, ideological) goal states, the next eight guiding-idea theories of human nature stress the person as striving for various affective (emotional, feeling) states. The four families of theories in the lower right quadrant of Table III, like the four just considered, depict the person as striving to grow rather than to maintain current stability but stress needs for affective growth rather than for cognitive growth.

Cell 9 "attraction" theories in their most basic form depict the person as driven by a gregarious need, as in Giddings or McDougal's early formulations or more recently in Harlow's or Ainsworth et al.'s (1978) work on attachment patterns in infants. Many theorists in this group postulate that beyond a congregating behavioral manifestation, this attraction tendency shows itself also in a need to love and be loved, a research topic particularly popular in the 1970s' social psychological research as reviewed by Berscheid and Walster (1978). Still other affiliation theorists go further by postulating an altruistic aspect such that the person seeks after and gets gratification from helping others, as illustrated by Sorokin's and psychobiological altruism theorizing, and by Berkowitz's empirical social responsibility research, as reviewed by Staub (1979) and Rushton (1980).

Cell 10 "identification" theories depict the person with a need for self-creation, as gaining gratification from ego-expansions that embellish the self-concept through identification with others and acquisition of new roles. This partial view of the person is stressed by humanistic formulations such as Maslow's self-actualizing theory and E. Erikson's adolescent identity theorizing and by the role, reference-group and self-presentation notions associated with Linton, Newcomb, Sarbin, Allen, Sherif, Hyman, Goffman, etc. A review of role theory conceptualizations can be found in Biddle (1979).

The "contagion" (or "imitation") theories shown in cell 11 represent the person as shaped by modeling, social facilitation, imitation, social learning, etc. Variant forms of this position stress the person as copying the behavior of others, as empathizing with others' feelings, or as introjecting others' stereotypes. Some of these theorists attribute the imitation tendency to inbred genetic patterns focused by phylogenetic selection and others to ontogenetically acquired habits shaped by social reinforcements of imitating during early years of life. This partial view of the person in society has been the central inspiration of fin-de-siècle French theorists such as LeBon, Tarde, Binet, and Charcot, and of current social facilitation, modeling, and social learning theorists such as Miller and Dollard, Bandura (1977), Zajonc, Cottrell, etc.

Fairly popular prescriptively as well as descriptively during the past decade have been the cell 12 "assertion" theories that stress the status- and power-oriented aspects of human personality. Some of these formulations depict the person as striving for goals whose attainment enhances self-respect while others add an interpersonal aspect such that the person seeks successes that win the admiration of others or, to look at the opposite pole, as striving to avoid guilt and shame. The interpersonal aspect may even be represented as competitive, with the person depicted as striving to win over others or even attaining dominance in a Hobbsean notion of society as a war of each against all. In recent decades these notions of the person as selfish and predatory have been promoted both within and outside the social and behavioral sciences by failed playwrights and ento-mologists-manqués. Theorists associated with these various depictions of the person as assertive and power-oriented range from Alfred Adler, McClelland, Winter, etc., to Lorenz, Morris, Tiger & Fox, Dawkins, and the sociobiologists. Empirical reviews of this assertion–power notion are provided by Baron (1977), Ng (1980), and Henderson (1981), while its philosophical basis is discussed by Dubarle (1978).

4. The Affective Stability Theories

The final tetrad of theories, shown in the lower left-hand quadrant of Table III, agrees with the quartet just considered in stressing the person's striving for affective states; however, these last four focus on the person's need to maintain affective stability rather than their striving after affective growth as stressed by the previous four theories.

The "tension reduction" theories shown in cell 13 represent the person as an energy discharge system, experiencing pleasure in the release of accumulated tension. Diverse theories sharing this partial view of the person range from religious, individuality-annihilating views such as the Hindu mokshya and Buddhist nirvana concepts to Freud's thanatotic notion which derives from the materialistic imagery of the second law of thermodynamics. Other examples are the drive-reduction position popular with behaviorists since Miller and Dollard and the catharsis theories that have been popular with students of human fantasy from Aristotle to a few current television-effects theorists. Some revisionists such as Berlyne and Solomon have posited that an intermediate level of tension is optimal, the person acting to restore this intermediate level if felt stress falls above or below it.

Cell 14 "ego-defensive" theories emphasize the person as striving to maintain a favorable self-image by avoiding, distorting, or repressing unacceptable interpretations or impulses from within or from outside agents. Psychoanalytical theories such as Freud, Adorno, etc., describe the variety of adjustment mechanisms by which the person keeps suppressed the ego-threatening material while allowing its vicarious expression as in the "authoritarian personality" syndrome. Functional theorists such as D. Katz and motivational researchers such as Dichter describe manifestations of this ego-defensive need in the form of distorted perception, selective recall, etc.

The theories shown in cell 15 are called somewhat inadequately "repetition" theories to reflect their stressing a reverberation tendency in the person such that his or her having acted in a certain way in a situation increases the likelihood of acting in that same way when later placed in the same situation. This notion, deriving from earlier philosophical associationism, dominated mid-century psychology in the form of S-R reinforcement theories of Hull and Skinner. Reinforcement theories added the assumption that for facilitation to occur, performance of the act must be followed by reward, since they postulated that stimulus-response contiguity without reward, and especially if followed by punishment, would have an opposite extinguishing effect. On the other hand, the "mere" contiguity position has always had its supporters from 18th Century British–Scottish–French associationists to current contiguity and statistical learning theorists such as Guthrie and Estes and Zajonc's "mere exposure" demonstrations. Social learning theorists (Dollard and Miller, Bandura, R. F. Weiss, etc.) have particularly utilized this partial view of human nature to depict the behavior of the person in society, as reviewed by Staats (1975).

The cell 16 "expressive" theories stress the acting out, play aspects of the person, the individual as attaining gratification through self-expression, taking joy in experiencing emotion and intense external stimulation (Cherfas & Lewin, 1980). This partial view of human nature has been used to explain phenomena as diverse as nightmares, the literary attraction of horror stories and tear jerkers, the popularity of loud music and psychedelic lights and colors, and the appeals of rallies, regalia, and enthusiasms associated with mass movements focused on political demagogues, pop stars, and charismatic religious figures. Theorists stressing this partial view of the person include Huizinga, Leont'ev, Bühler, Peckham, and Stevenson.

Each of the 16 guiding-idea theories of human nature just described is a partial view of the person, valid in the sense that the tendency stressed does represent the person in one of her or his numerous aspects and thus is of value in depicting human behavior in certain contexts in which this aspect becomes a relatively commanding determinant of action. However, any one guiding-idea theory will contribute only trivially to behavioral variance in a wide range of contexts in which other unrelated or even contradictory aspects of the person are in the ascendance. As emphasized in the contextualist position, any of these guiding-idea theories can be useful in provoking hypotheses about human experience and behavior that may prove accurate in a limited domain of contexts but each guiding-idea theory will lead the researcher astray in many other contexts. The wise researcher uses these partial-view theories as supplementary rather than antagonistic to one another and must be constantly on guard lest the psychodynamics of controversy drive these "among other things" theories toward becoming "nothing but" theories. Contextualism suggests that the researcher exploit each of these guiding-idea theories for its heuristic potential while remaining sensitive to its numerous inadequacies in most situations and to the availability of the alternative partial views.

This tour of the horizon from the contextualist vantage point has suggested a number of fundamental reforms in social psychology as both process and product. As regards process, it calls for the corrective emphasizing of the hypothesis-generating aspect of research method relative to its hypothesis-testing aspect. It reveals the advantage of treating the empirical confrontation phase of scientific method as a continuing discovery process in which the a priori theory is not so much tested as developed through empirical confrontations that bring out its hidden assumptions and define the pattern of contexts in which it is and is not valid. Contextualism also calls for our being more aware of the rather restricted "styles" of research within which research tends to be confined at any given period and of the advantages currently in switching from the convergent and divergent unilinear styles to a systems style. It also directs attention to the need for and ways of grappling more explicitly with the strategic, programmatic aspects of method that guide our going from study to study rather than as at present restricting discussions of methods to the tactical level of procedural options within an individual study.

As regards the product or content aspect of social psychology, contextualism reveals the need for a more ecumenical stance toward theory, for recognizing the existence and utility of a wide variety of formulations to generate useful insights into the contents and determinants of experience and behavior, while also appreciating the limited usefulness and distorting nature of any one formulation. It calls for a delicate balance in using any theory to shed light on some aspects of the phenomenon without allowing it to blind us to other aspects. Many other current epistemologies and philosophies of science downplay the limitations of knowledge in representing the richness of the known, but contextualism strengthens the researcher's courage to appreciate and utilize these limitations.

REFERENCES

Abelson, R. P. The psychological status of the script concept. *American Psychologist*, 1981, **36**, 715–729.

Abelson, R. P., Aronson, E., McGuire, W. J., Newcomb, T. M., Rosenberg, M. J. & Tannenbaum, P. H. (Eds.). *Theories of cognitive consistency:* A sourcebook. Chicago, Illinois: Rand McNally, 1968.

Adorno, T. W., Frankel-Brunswick, E., Levinson, D. J., & Sanford, R. N. *The authoritarian personality.* New York: Harper, 1950.

Ainsworth, M. D. S., Blehar, M. C., Walters, E., & Wall, S. *Patterns of attachment.* New York: Wiley, 1978.

Amabile, T. M. *The social psychology of creativity.* Secaucus, New Jersey: Springer-Verlag, 1983.

Anderson, N. H. *Foundations of information integration theory.* (Vol. 1). New York: Academic Press, 1981.

Andrews, F. M. (Ed). *Scientific productivity: The effectiveness of research groups in six countries.* New York: Cambridge University Press, 1979.

Bandura, A. *Social learning theory.* Englewood Cliffs, New Jersey: Prentice-Hall, 1977.

Baron, R. A. *Human aggression.* New York: Plenum, 1977.

Bem, D. Self perception theory. In L. Berkowitz (Ed.), *Advances in experimental social psychology* (Vol. 6). New York: Academic Press, 1972, 2–63.

Berkowitz, L. (Ed.). *Advances in experimental social psychology* (Vols. 1–15). New York: Academic Press, 1964–1983.

Berlyne, D. E. *Conflict, arousal, and curiosity.* New York: McGraw-Hill, 1960.

Berscheid, E., & Walster, E. H. *Interpersonal attraction* (2nd ed.). Reading, Massachusetts: Addison-Wesley, 1978.

Biddle, B. J. *Role theory: Expectations, identities, and behaviors.* New York: Academic Press, 1979.

Bieri, J., Atkins, A. L., Briar, S., Leaman, R. L., Miller, H., & Tripodi, T. *Clinical and social judgment: The discrimination of behavioral information.* New York: Wiley, 1966.

Brehm, J. W. *A theory of psychological reactance.* New York: Academic Press, 1966.

Brock, T. C. Communicator-recipient similarity and decision change. *Journal of Personality and Social Psychology,* 1965, **1,** 650–654.

Cherfas, J. & Lewin, R. *Not work alone: A cross-cultural view of activities superfluous to survival.* Beverly Hills, California: Sage, 1980.

Coleman, J. S. *Longitudinal data analysis.* New York: Basic Books, 1981.

Collins, B. E., & Hoyt, M. F. Personal responsibility-for-consequences: An integration and extension of the "forced compliance" literature. *Journal of Experimental Social Psychology,* 1972, **8,** 558–593.

Cook, S. W. The impact of cooperative learning experiences on cross-ethnic relations and attitudes. *Journal of Social Issues,* 1975, **31,** 219–244.

Davis, P. J., & Hersh, R. *The mathematical experience.* Boston, Massachusetts: Birkhauser, 1981.

Deaux, K. To err is humanizing: But sex makes a difference. *Representative Research in Social Psychology,* 1972, **3,** 20–28.

Deci, E. L. *The psychology of self-determination.* Lexington, Massachusetts: Heath, 1980.

Dubarle, D. (Ed.). *Le pouvoir.* Paris: Editions Beauchesne, 1978.

Eckblad, G. *Scheme theory: A conceptual framework of cognitive-motivational processes.* New York: Academic Press, 1981.

Edge, D. Essay review: Is there too much sociology of science? *Isis,* 1983, **74,** 250–256.

Festinger, L. *A theory of cognitive dissonance.* Stanford, California: Stanford University Press, 1957.

Fishbein, M. A theory of reasoned action: Some applications and implications. In H. Howe & M. Page (Eds.), *Nebraska Symposium on Motivation, 1979,* **27,** Lincoln, Nebraska: University of Nebraska Press, 1980, 65–116.

Fyans, L. J., Jr. (Ed.). *Achievement motivation: Recent trends in theory and research.* New York: Plenum, 1980.

Goodfield, J. *An imagined world: A story of scientific discovery.* New York: Harper & Row, 1981.

Haberman, S. J. *Analysis of qualitative data* (Vols. 1 and 2). New York: Academic Press, 1978 and 1979.

Harré, R. Rituals, rhetoric, and social cognition. In J. P Forgas (Ed.), *Social Cognition*. London: Academic Press, 1981, 211–224.

Harvey, J. H., & Weary, G. *Perspectives on attributional processes*. Dubuque, Iowa: Brown, 1981.

Helmreich, R., Aronson, E., & LeFan, J. To err is humanizing—sometimes: Effects of self-esteem, competence, and a pratfall on interpersonal attraction. *Journal of Personality and Social Psychology*, 1970, **16**, 259–264.

Henderson, A. *Social power: Social-psychological models and theories*. New York: Praeger, 1981.

Hoaglin, D. C., Mosteller, F., & Tukey, J. S. (Eds.). *Understanding robust and exploratory data analysis*. New York: Wiley, 1983.

Hochberg, J. On cognition in perception: Perceptual coupling and unconscious inference. *Cognition*, 1981, **10**, 127–134.

Holzkamp, K. Wissenschraftstheoretische voraussetzungen kritisch-emanzipatorischer Psychologie. *Zeitschrift für Sozialpsychologie*, 1970, **1**, 5–21; 109–141.

Holzkamp, K. *Kritische Psychologie. Vorbereitende Arbeiten*. Frankfurt am Main: Fischer Taschenbuch, 1972.

Hovland, C. I., Lumsdaine, A. A., & Sheffield, F. D. *Studies in social psychology in World War II*. Vol 3: *Experiments on mass communication*. Princeton, New Jersey: Princeton University press, 1949.

Hovland, C. I., Janis, I. L., & Kelley, H. H. *Communication and persuasion*. New Haven, Connecticut: Yale University Press, 1953.

Hull, C. L. *A behavior system*. New Haven, Connecticut: Yale University Press, 1952.

Hull, C. L., Hovland, C. I., Ross, R. T., Hall, M., Perkins, D. T., & Fitch, F. B. *Mathematico-deductive theory of rote learning*. New Haven, Connecticut: Yale University Press, 1940.

Janis, I. L., & Mann, L. *Decision making*. New York: Free Press, 1977.

Kelley, H. H., & Michela, J. L. Attribution theory and research. *Annual Review of Psychology*, 1980, **31**, 457–501.

Latour, B., & Woolgar, S. *Laboratory life: The social construction of scientific facts*. Beverly Hills, California: Sage, 1979.

Lefcourt, H. M. (Ed.). *Research with the locus of control construct*. Vol. 1: *Assessment methods*. New York: Academic Press, 1981.

Leinhardt, S., & Wasserman, S. S. Exploratory data analysis: An introduction to selected methods. In K. F. Schuessler (Ed.), *Sociological Methodology 1979*. San Francisco, California: Jossey Bass, 1978, 311–365.

McGuire, W. J. The current status of cognitive consistency theories. In S. Feldman (Ed.), *Cognitive consistency*. New York: Academic Press, 1966, 1–46.

McGuire, W. J. Some impending reorientations in social psychology. *Journal of Experimental Social Psychology*, 1967, **3**, 124–139.

McGuire, W. J. Personality and susceptibility to social influence. In E. F. Borgatta & W. W. Lambert (Eds.), *Handbook of personality theory and research*. Chicago, Illinois: Rand-McNally, 1968, 1130–1187.

McGuire, W. J. Theory oriented research in natural settings: The best of both worlds for social psychology. In M. Sherif & C. Sherif (Eds.), *Interdisciplinary relations in the social sciences*. Chicago, Illinois, Aldine, 1969, 21–51.(a)

McGuire, W. J. The nature of attitudes and attitude change. In G. Lindzey & E. Aronson (Eds.), *Handbook of social psychology* (Vol. 3, 2nd ed.) Reading, Massachusetts: Addison-Wesley, 1969, 136–314.(b)

McGuire, W. J. Suspiciousness of experimenter's intent as an artifact in social research. In R.

Rosenthal and R. Rosnow (Eds.), *Artifacts in behavioral research*. New York: Academic Press, 1969, 13–57.(c).

McGuire, W. J. The yin and yang of progress in social psychology: Seven koan. *Journal of Personality and Social Psychology*, 1973, **26**, 446–456.

McGuire, W. J. Psychological motives and communication gratification. In J. G. Blumler & E. Katz (Eds.), *The uses of mass communications: Current perspectives on gratifications research*. Beverly Hills, California: Sage Publications, 1974, 167–196.

McGuire, W. J. The communication/persuasion matrix. In B. Lipstein & W. J. McGuire (Eds.), *Evaluating advertising: A bibliography of the communication process*. New York: Advertising Research Foundation, 1978, xxvii–xxxv.

McGuire, W. J. The development of theory in social psychology. In R. Gilmour & S. Duck (Eds.), *The development of social psychology*. London: Academic Press, 1980, 53–80.

McGuire, W. J. The probabilogical model of cognitive structure and attitude change. In R. E. Petty, T. M. Ostrom, & T. C. Brock (Eds.), *Cognitive responses in persuasion*. Hillsdale, New Jersey: Erlbaum, 1981, 291–307. (a).

McGuire, W. J. Theoretical foundations of public communication campaigns. In R. Rice & W. Paisley (Eds.), *Public communication campaigns*. Beverly Hills, California: Sage, 1981, 41–70.(b).

McGuire, W. J. Putting attitude research to work in marketing practice. *Marketing News*, 14 May 1982, **15**, No. 23, 2–18.

McGuire, W. J. Attitudes and attitude change. In G. Lindzey & E. Aronson (Eds.), *Handbook of social psychology* (3rd ed.). Reading, Massachusetts: Addison-Wesley, 1983, in press.(a).

McGuire, W. J. Search for the self: Going beyond self-esteem and the reactive self. In R. A. Zucker, J. Arnoff, and A. I. Rabin (Eds.), *Personality and the prediction of behavior*. New York: Academic Press, 1983, in press.(b).

McGuire, W. J. Toward social psychology's second century. In S. Koch & D. E. Leary (Eds.), *A century of psychology as science*. New York: McGraw-Hill, 1983, in press.(c).

McGuire, W. J., McGuire, C. V., & Winton, W. Effects of household sex composition on the salience of one's gender in the spontaneous self-concept. *Journal of Experimental Social Psychology*, 1979, **15**, 77–90.

McGuire, W. J., & Millman, S. Anticipatory belief lowering following forewarning of a persuasive attack. *Journal of Personality and Social Psychology*, 1965, **2**, 471–479.

Mills, J., & Aronson, E. Opinion change as a function of communicator's attractiveness and desire to influence. *Journal of Personality and Social Psychology*, 1965, **1**, 173–177.

Milner, J. *Russion revolutionary art*. New York: Hippocrene Books, 1980.

Ng, S. H. *The social psychology of power*. London: Academic Press, 1980.

Pelz, D. C., & Andrews, F. M. *Scientists in organizations: Productive climates for research and development* (Rev. ed.). New York: Wiley, 1976.

Perlmuter, L. C., & Monty, R. A. (Eds.). *Choice and perceived control*. Hillsdale, New Jersey: Erlbaum, 1979.

Powers, W. T. Quantitative analysis of purposive systems: Some spadework at the foundation of scientific psychology. *Psychological Review*, 1978, **85**, 417–435.

Ring, K. Experimental social psychology: Some sober questions about some frivolous values. *Journal of Experimental Social Psychology*, 1967, **3**, 113–123.

Rushton, J. P. *Altruism, socialization and society*. Englewood Cliffs, New Jersey: Prentice-Hall, 1980.

Schafer, R. *A new language for psychoanalysis*. New Haven, Connecticut: Yale University Press, 1976.

Staats, A. W. *Social behaviorism*. Homewood, Illinois: Dorsey, 1975.

Staub, E. *Positive social behavior and morality*. (Vol. 2). New York: Academic Press, 1979.

Stein, Morris I. *Stimulating creativity.* Vol. 1: *Individual procedures.* New York: Academic Press, 1974.

Steiner, I. D. Attribution of choice. In M. Fishbein (Ed.), *Progress in social psychology* (Vol. 1). Hillsdale, New Jersey: Erlbaum, 1980, 1–47.

Stukát, K. G. *Suggestibility: A factorial and experimental analysis:* Uppsala: Appelbergs Boktryckeri Ab, 1958.

Swanson, D. L. A constructivist approach. In D. D. Nimmo and K. R. Sanders (Eds.), *Handbook of political communication.* Beverly Hills, California: Sage, 1981, 169–191.

Tukey, J. W. *Exploratory data analysis.* Reading, Massachusetts: Addison-Wesley, 1977.

Weiner, B. *Achievement motivation and attribution theory.* Morristown, New Jersey: General Learning Press, 1974.

Wicklund, R. A. *Freedom and reactance.* Hillsdale, New Jersey: Erlbaum, 1974.

Wicklund, R. A., & Brehm, J. W. *Perspectives on cognitive dissonance.* Hillsdale, New Jersey: Erlbaum, 1976.

Wicklund, R. A., & Frey, D. Cognitive consistency: Motivational and nonmotivational perspectives. In J. P. Forgas (Ed.), *Social cognition.* London: Academic Press, 1981, 141–163.

Zuckerman, M. *Sensation seeking: Beyond the optimal level of arousal.* Hillsdale, New Jersey: Erlbaum, 1979.

SOCIAL COGNITION: SOME HISTORICAL AND THEORETICAL PERSPECTIVES

Janet Landman and Melvin Manis

DEPARTMENT OF PSYCHOLOGY
UNIVERSITY OF MICHIGAN
AND
V. A. MEDICAL CENTER
ANN ARBOR, MICHIGAN

I. Introduction

The topic of thinking has always fascinated and always daunted psychology. As Mandler and Mandler (1964) note, psychology has:

worried it as a dog worries a precious bone. It was always there, sometimes buried, sometimes dug up again and brought to a high sheen, never quite cracked or digested, and never

49

forgotten. Even the Wundts and the Hulls promised themselves to get back to the problem sooner or later. (p. 1)

But as a concept in its own right, social cognition is relatively new. According to Taylor (1981), social cognition was only about 5 years old in 1981. In 1982 the journal *Social Cognition* was established to serve as a new forum for the ever-increasing numbers of investigations in this emerging field. Given the signs of vigorous activity all around, this seems to be a propitious time in which to examine social cognition rather closely, to see where it has come from and whether it has reached the "age of reason"—whether social cognition has acquired some sense of its own task which is founded in reasoned theory.

Let us begin by defining terms. What is cognition and what is social cognition? The Latin derivation of the word *cognition* is *cognoscere*—to become acquainted with, to know. Narrowly defined, cognition refers to thinking or knowing and is distinguished from affection and conation. According to Neisser (1976), "Cognition is the activity of knowing: the acquisition, organization, and use of knowledge" (p. 1).

The central concerns of cognitive psychology are representation and processing (e.g., Klatzky, 1975; Mandler, 1981). These issues require the building and testing of theoretical constructs and models, since no one has yet directly observed the formation or processing of representations and since introspection regarding cognitive processes remains problematic (Nisbett & Wilson, 1977; Skinner, 1953; but see Ericsson & Simon, 1980; Kraut & Lewis, 1982). But what is representation?

In general, a representation is something that stands for something else. In the realm of cognitive psychology, what is of direct interest is not a physical entity ("hardware") but a cognitive or mental one ("software") (Hofstadter, 1979; Neisser, 1976). Models of representation have proliferated in cognitive psychology. They include at least these seven types: template, neural network, digital matrix, multicomponent vector, feature set, list of propositions, and relational network (Palmer, 1978). Since social cognition has made most use of the first and last models in this list—template and network models—it is these two that will command most of our attention in this chapter.

Whereas representation is the structural or "building-blocks" aspect of cognitive psychology, *processing* is the functional or "building" aspect. There are at least two levels of processing of interest to psychology: the purely cognitive level (e.g., how perception, memory, inference work) and the level at which thought motivates action. (A third possible level at which cognition can be studied is the physiological or neurophysiological level, but this is not the domain of direct interest to cognitive psychology or to cognitive social psychology.) Cognitive theories in social psychology are virtually unanimous in asserting that overt behavior is vitally influenced by the actor's cognitions. The prevailing view thus emphasizes that, in contrast to so-called black box or stimulus-response models, social behavior can most effectively be explained by means of a stimulus–cognition–behavior paradigm.

Theories of this general type have a good deal of face validity, for we all can remember many occasions in which we consciously sought to understand some situation in which we found ourselves, with the goal of mapping out an appropriate plan of action. Similarly, when we review our past actions (or are asked by some roving attributionist to explain our behavior), we have little difficulty in sketching a coherent account of the sort of thinking that (may have) guided us. With respect to processing then, the study of social cognition has been directed toward the first two levels of analysis noted—the rather self-contained level of the mind itself, and the less circumscribed level at which thought is presumed to urge action.

What is *social cognition?* In everyday life, some type of social cognition is undoubtedly going on nearly every waking moment—from remembering whose name goes with whose face at a party, to appreciating a particular individual's sense of humor, to knowing how to behave at a concert. Taylor's (1981) definition of social cognition is simply "any work that emphasizes how an individual cognizes his or her social world" (p. 195). Within social psychology some authors distinguish social cognition from cognitive social psychology, with social cognition emphasizing the role of *cognition* in social phenomena and with cognitive social psychology emphasizing the role of cognition in *social* phenomena (Isen & Hastorf, 1982).

In another definition of social cognition (Hamilton, 1981), what is emphasized are the content areas and methods peculiar to social cognition: "the direct investigation of the cognitive structures and processes underlying person perception, often using experimental techniques borrowed from cognitive psychology" (p. 136). A generic experimental paradigm used in social cognition research involves the practice of exposing subjects to certain stimuli under controlled conditions and measuring various aspects of subjects' cognition—for example, what they perceive, what they remember, what they can identify as having seen before, the inferences they draw and the judgments they make on the basis of the stimuli presented. In experimental and cognitive psychology, the stimuli have often been impersonal—for example, nonsense syllables, geometric figures, or lists of fruits, furniture, or animals. In social cognition research, however, the stimuli usually have something to do with the self, another person or groups of persons—for example, lists of personality traits or behaviors, and segments of film portraying an interpersonal or group interaction.

The fact that both Hamilton's and Taylor's definitions of social cognition include reference to "the how," or to process, also distinguishes social cognition to some extent from its ancestors in social psychology. Social psychology has in the past more often addressed issues of cognitive content than process. In contrast, cognitive psychology has from the beginning concentrated on cognitive processes (Manis, 1977). Social cognition tries to do both.

Perhaps perversely, it seems somehow natural to define cognition, social or nonsocial, in contrast to what it is *not*. Cognition is usually distinguished both from raw sensation and behavior, on the one hand, and from emotion or motivation, on the other—at least from within the information processing framework which is the dominant cognitive approach. When cognitive psychology was born, it promised to usher in a new zeitgeist and a new paradigm—a zeitgeist and a paradigm that departed from that of behaviorism (Mandler, 1981; Solso, 1975). Mandler and Mandler (1964) describe it this way: "the psychology of thinking has frequently had the character of a resistance movement against the mainstreams of hard-headed experimental psychology" (p. 2). In contradistinction to its behavioristic progenitor, cognitive psychology concerns itself with unobservable mental constructs. In order to investigate such constructs, cognitive psychology evolved in the form of a "theory-rich psychology" (Mandler, 1981, p. 14). In these respects cognitive psychology in general and social cognition in particular represent a radical departure from behaviorism, as well as from what Mandler calls the "physiological imperialism" (1981, p. 4) characteristic of much of psychology prior to the so-called cognitive revolution.

Besides representing a self-consciously theory-rich reaction against behaviorism, the research enterprise called social cognition to some extent also reflects a reaction against the perceived deficiencies of the psychodynamic approach—for example, a tendency toward reification and overgeneralization (Mischel, 1979). Many social psychologists embraced a cognitive approach out of a rejection of psychodynamic explanations and a preference for what they felt were more parsimonious cognitive accounts (Nisbett & Ross, 1980).[1]

In this chapter we examine current theories of social cognition and the intellectual history out of which social cognition has arisen. This examination reveals, we believe, the pervasive and continuing influence of two generic traditions within psychology: associationism and constructionism. We feel that it is salutary at this point in the development of social cognition to explore its intellectual history, its associationist and its constructionist traditions, so as to be in a position to address the question of whether or not social cognition represents an important theoretical advance. Thus, we explore the roots of associationism as well as its present application in social cognition research, the roots of constructionism and its present application in social cognition research, and the rather surprising wedding of these perspectives in recent investigations of social cognition. For the sake of explication we present issues of structure and process

---

[1]Social psychology is not unique in this pattern of development. Anthropology, for example, has experienced a similar evolution, with a cognitive approach appearing recently in reaction on the one hand against a type of anthropology that tends to hypostatize culture, and on the other hand, against a form of anthropology that reduces culture to behavior (Geertz, 1973).

separately, although to divide the two is to cleave artificially what are undoubtedly overlapping and interdependent aspects. Finally, let us point out that this review is not an exhaustive one (the attribution literature and its relation to social cognition remains unexamined, to mention only one lacuna), but it focuses on those investigations of social cognition that fairly explicitly apply associationist or constructionist theory.

II.   Historical Roots of Social Cognition

Social cognition's associationsit roots lead it to pose this question: How do elements of the social world get combined by the perceiver? From within the constructionist perspective the corresponding question is: How does the perceiver construct ideas about the social world? The use of passive versus active voice in these two formulations is indicative of the differential processing assumptions of the associationist and the constructionist approaches, respectively. Another major difference is the associationist emphasis on bottom-up linkage of elements versus the constructionist stress on the top-down influence of higher-order cognitive processes.

Ever since psychology established itself as a separate discipline, associationism has been the reigning theory of learning, memory and representation, either explicitly or implicitly (Jenkins, 1974; Solso, 1979). In J. J. Jenkins's words, associationism is for psychology "the oldest theory of them all" (1974, p. 795). Indeed, it is probably fair to say that "many of us confuse the dicta of associationism with the grounds of empirical science itself" (Jenkins, 1974, p. 796). Associationism assumes basic units. Larger units are built up from smaller units by associative linkage. In classical associationism these more complex cognitive units are assumed to be qualitatively the same as the smaller units of which they are composed.

A.   CLASSICAL ASSOCIATIONISM AND ITS INADEQUACIES

In the third century B.C., Aristotle had already articulated the elementary principles of associationism. For Aristotle memory was active, a "mental movement" (1952, p. 694), a process by which a person "move[s], solely by his own effort, to the term next after the starting point" (p. 693). (This is in contrast to Plato's doctrine of innate ideas and his concomitant emphasis on static structure.) In order to explain what factors facilitate recollection, Aristotle introduced the principles of *similarity* (and *contrast*), *contiguity, frequency,* and *good form.* By the principle of similarity is meant the idea that elements that are alike in some way tend to be recalled together. Contiguity of elements, or closeness in space or time, also facilitates their linking in memory. And the frequency principle asserts that the more often elements are experienced, the more likely they are to be remembered. Aristotle's comments on the facilitating effects of organization or good form are particularly relevant to modern formulations, such as schema theory: "things arranged in a fixed order, like the successive demonstrations in geometry, are easy to remember [or recollect], while badly arranged subjects are remembered with difficulty" (1952, p. 693).

The British associationists (Hobbes, Locke, Berkeley, etc.) accepted Aristotle's principles of association but downplayed the Aristotelian view of the mind and its functions as being active. Thus, late in the seventeenth century John Locke asserted that complex knowledge is built up in accordance with associative principles from simple ideas, sensations, or muscular movements, which force themselves onto a passive mind. Locke's choice of simile for the mind as being like a "white paper" exemplifies what has been more recently called a "bottom-up" orientation, that is, the assumption that the content of the mind is created through the summing of sensations or perceptions to form ideas.[2]

Ebbinghaus (1885) brought to early psychology a brand of associationism that owed more to the British associationists than to Aristotle's more dynamic model. In Ebbinghaus's experimental paradigm the nonsense syllable functioned as the unit of memory; Ebbinghaus observed that memory for a particular nonsense syllable depended on the number of repetitions of the syllable. When Ebbinghaus studied nonsense syllables within lists, he noted that recall also depended on contiguity.

Along with experimental procedures designed to study memory, Ebbinghaus also bequeathed to psychology a version of associationism that assumed a minimal concept of mental structure. In the "oldest theory of them all," cognitive structure was reduced to pairs or chains of associations. Even complex associative units were conceived as relatively unstructured and decomposable.

With respect to processing, Ebbinghaus enumerated the following associative principles: repetition, contiguity, intensity of interest in the content, nature of the content, and individual differences. He chose to focus on the first two of these factors in his own work, because they were "capable of numerical determination" (1885, p. 9). Ebbinghaus utilized nonsense syllables as stimuli in order to control for the last three factors (interest, content, and personal preferences and capacities) while manipulating the factors of contiguity and repetition.

Although he was careful not to claim the status of law for these "formulae of so vague a character" (p. 90), Ebbinghaus was also careful to distinguish his approach from one that would postulate memory as the "unitary act of a unitary

---

[2]In fact, Locke posited a second method by which ideas are formed, that is, reflection. However, psychology has tended to ignore this more rationalist (more "top-down") aspect of Locke's thought in favor of his more empiricist (more "bottom-up") notion.

soul'' (p. 109), thereby putting himself—and early experimental psychology—in the "bottom-up" and not the "top-down" camp.

Behaviorism uncritically took up associative concepts, attempting to explain thought and memory in terms of stimulus–response (S–R) bonds. Absent from early behaviorism was the Lockeian admission of ideas or other sorts of unobservable cognitive structures as elements to be connected. Although later behaviorists, such as Osgood (1953), emphasized the importance of mediating responses as a physicalistic equivalent of the "idea" concept, the principles of association came to be equated with classical conditioning principles. Since there is nothing active, selective, or voluntary about a reflex, behavioristic associationism postulated passive, automatic processes.

The principles of instrumental learning, although goal-oriented, were similarly lacking in mental constructs. According to J. B. Watson (e.g., 1914) and E. L. Thorndike (1932), learning was a matter of strengthening bonds between a stimulus and a response rather than a matter of forming new associations. In early behaviorism, learning was a mechanical process of gradually hitting upon a successful response and strengthening it by repetition or reward. Thus in the behavioristic incarnation of associationism, the role of the mind (if its existence was not denied) was construed as a passive one of receiving environmental stimuli and automatically associating them with certain responses, under favorable external conditions.

The limits of early associationism within psychology became more apparent as the twentieth century advanced. The behavioristic version of associationism came under attack for its refusal to consider mental concepts such as ideas. Some theorists (e.g., N. E. Miller, 1959; Russell, 1927) pointed out that unobservable intervening variables are not only necessary to explain human language and thought, but also are more theoretically economical than S–R chains, particularly when there is more than one possible stimulus and/or more than one possible response.

Criticism was also directed at associationism's neglect of levels of organization beyond the paired associate or the simple S–R chain. Deese (1965, 1968) succinctly asserts that "what is important about associations is not what follows what, but how sets of associations define *structured patterns* of relations among ideas" (1965, p. vii, emphasis added). Theorists such as Piaget and Chomsky, with their focus on higher-order cognitive structures, also challenged the atomistic proclivities of associationism.

In addition to its neglect of complex mental units, early associationism failed to explain *how* its elements were linked (Anderson & Bower, 1973; Bartlett, 1932; Lewin, 1938; Mandler, 1968). Fifty years ago Bartlett (1932) criticized early associationism as lacking explanatory value. He argued that associationist principles like contiguity and similarity are valuable as long as they are kept on the "plane of descriptive analysis" (p. 305). It is when these principles are erroneously given causal or functional status that they prove problematic, for example, when it is asserted that certain "details are together *because* they are similar" (Bartlett, 1932, p. 305).

Along with the conceptual critiques, data-based criticisms of early associationism began to mount. The simple principles of associationism (such as pairwise association based on frequency, recency, or similarity) were inadequate to explain complex cognitive phenomena like hypothesis-formation, hypothesis-testing, tip-of-the-tongue phenomena, and certain types of errors of memory.

Problems such as these caused some researchers (e.g., Lewin, Bartlett, Jenkins, Deese) to abandon associationism. Others remained within the associationist tradition, but sought to develop more complex models to supplant the simple models limited to paired associates or to chains of associates linked by dint of frequency, recency, contiguity, similarity, or reinforcement alone.

B.   NEO-ASSOCIATIONIST MODELS

A number of neo-associationist theories arose independently out of cognitive psychology and attempted to address one or more of the deficiencies of traditional associationism. In general, these theories, having evolved out of the verbal learning tradition, emphasize memory more than perception or higher-order cognitive activity. Certain of these theories have found application in the study of social cognition and thus they bear examination.

Neo-associationist theories of cognition were developed by Anderson (1976), Anderson and Bower (1973), Collins and Loftus (1975), Collins and Quillian (1969), Glass and Holyoak (1975), Hayes-Roth (1977), Kintsch (1974), Norman and Rumelhart (1975), and Quillian (1969). Although they differ to some degree, these theorists propose associative network models that have common structural and process aspects. A typical network model posits hypothetical *cognitive structures,* or nodes, that are connected by associative pathways, resulting in an orderly arrangement of knowledge. These nodes represent cognitive elements ranging in generality from *smaller* units such as cogits (Hayes-Roth, 1977), concepts, properties, and features (e.g., Collins & Loftus, 1975) through structures of *intermediate* size like propositions (Anderson & Bower, 1973; Anderson, 1980) and cogit assemblies (Hayes-Roth, 1977) to the *larger* and more inclusive schemas (Anderson, 1980).

In most neo-associative models, the cognitive units represent data, information, concepts, and similar substantive elements of thought. However, in some models (e.g., Norman & Rumelhart, 1975; Winograd, 1972), processes, principles, or procedural rules are also capable of representation via cognitive structures or nodes.

In addition to hypothetical cognitive elements, all associative network models postulate associative *pathways* that serve to connect the various nodes. These pathways also go by names like pointers, links, or relations. Pathways are required by the assumption that bits and pieces of information do not ordinarily lie about in isolation from other units of knowledge, but are interrelated or associated with one another.

The earliest principles of association, particularly the rules of contiguity, similarity, frequency and recency, are also found in more recent formulations of associative network models. In neo-associative models, associative strength remains a chief principle of *process,* and strength is typically conceived as a function of frequency and recency of exposure to stimuli. Another determinant of associative strength in these theories is similarity or semantic relatedness; the stronger the similarity between nodes, the greater their strength of association, and the more likely it is that activation of one node will spread to the related node. Thus neo-associationism recapitulates the importance of the Aristotelian associationist principles of relatedness, contiguity, frequency and recency and, to some extent, good form. The dominant process assumption in neo-associationist formulations is that memory is a matter of searching and matching. The search is often construed as more or less passive or automatic, being driven by features of the stimulus or by other characteristics of the environment.

What makes a theory *neo*-associationist? By Anderson and Bower's definition, a neo-associationist theory possesses two methodological features: rationalism (reason-based theory building) and empiricism (data-based theory building). Methodological empiricism, of course, is not new but is a characteristic shared by traditional associationism within psychology. Methodological rationalism is an innovation with respect to Ebbinghaus's form of associationism as well as with respect to behaviorism, both of which tended to avoid theoretical or hypothetical constructions in favor of observables. In neo-associationist theories, unobservable or symbolic constructs (e.g., concept nodes, propositions, cogits) take over the role played by neurophysiological entities and observable events such as stimuli and responses in earlier forms of associationism.

Many of the neo-associationist theories had their origin in computer simulation work. The computer offers a number of advantages for theory building and theory testing (also perhaps certain disadvantages—cf. Moscovici, 1981; Searle, 1982) unavailable to earlier associationists, specifically the facilitation of precise, clear, and full specification of a comprehensive system of hypothetical cognitive constructs and processes, and the ability to check whether the specified processes work together as predicted (Anderson & Bower, 1973). Given such a mighty tool, it is not surprising that associationist models of the computer age are broader in theoretical scope and power than earlier formulations.

The three associative network theories of memory that have most directly influenced research and theory on social cognition to date are Anderson and Bower's (1973) associative network theory, Collins and Loftus's (1975) spreading activation theory, and Hayes-Roth's (1977) knowledge assembly theory.

1. Human Associative Memory (HAM)

Human Associative Memory (HAM) is the name of the computer program developed by J. R. Anderson and G. Bower to simulate memory activities. Although HAM has been superseded by newer, revised versions (e.g., ACT; see Anderson, 1976, 1980), it remains of interest for its comprehensiveness and clarity and because of its continuing influence on the study of social cognition. In Anderson and Bower's model the fundamental informational units are simple propositions. Propositions interrelate one or more associations and are assumed to be the "smallest units of meaning that assert things about the world that might be reasonably judged true or false" (Anderson, 1980, p. 4). The proposition is an informationally larger structure than the concepts and properties of other theories (e.g., Collins & Loftus, 1975). Like other theorists (e.g., Collins & Loftus, 1975), Anderson and Bower posit various kinds of associations: context–fact associations, location–time, subject–predicate, and relation–object. An example of a proposition or "proposition tree" that includes all but the last of these four types of associations is, "The pope was shot at the Vatican in May 1981."

If an individual were to read this proposition concerning the pope and later try to answer questions about it (e.g., When was the pope shot?), the person would engage in a process, according to Anderson and Bower, that includes the component phases of (1) parsing the input, or encoding the input into a proposition tree, and (2) matching proposition trees retrieved from long-term memory with this new tree, looking for trees that connect the same nodes in the same way. In a short story pertinently entitled "A Worn Path," Eudora Welty tells a quietly powerful tale of an elderly Negro woman who regularly makes her way from her rural home to a Natches doctor's office to obtain medicine for her ill grandson. At the old woman's arrival, Miss Welty evokes in nontechnical language the search-and-match recognition process simulated by cognitive researchers such as Anderson and Bower: "There she saw the document that had been stamped with the gold seal and framed in the gold frame, which matched the dream that was hung up in her head."

Whereas perception and inference in this model are assumed to be active or "top-down" in nature, the memory component of HAM is assumed to work passively and serially. Anderson and Bower predict that recall operates in an all-or-none manner at the level of the independent proposition. This is in contrast, as we will later discuss, with Gestalt and constructionist approaches, which predict interdependence among elements such that the newly formed complex whole (e.g., a schema, script, stereotype, prototype) becomes the unit of memory.

In HAM it is not the precise words of a proposition that are to be understood or matched. When matching occurs, it is normally at a semantic or abstract level rather than at a lexical level. Recall or recognition results when an input or a probe has been matched with a representation from long-term memory.

2. Spreading Activation Theory

A second neo-associationist theory which has influenced the study of social cognition is the spreading activation theory of Collins and E. Loftus (1975). In order to account for a variety of experimental findings on semantic memory, Collins and Loftus elaborated the associative network theory originally developed by Quillian (1969) and by Collins and Quillian (e.g., 1969). Collins and Loftus, like Quillian, conceive of memory as a process of activation spreading in parallel from the node(s) representing the stimulated concept(s) to connected nodes via pathways. Rate of activation is an inverse function of the number of connections to be traversed. Whether concepts related to an initially stimulated concept node are activated depends on whether strength of activation exceeds threshold. One of this theory's most influential contributions has been the activation metaphor, in general, and the idea of spreading activation, in particular.

A major prediction of both theories just discussed (Anderson & Bower, 1973; Collins & Loftus, 1975) is what is alternatively known as the "fan effect," the "memory set–size effect" (Sternberg, 1966), the "category–size effect" (Klatzky, 1975), or the "interference effect" (Anderson, 1980; Hayes-Roth, 1977). The fan effect prediction goes like this: The greater the number of facts that "fan out" from an input concept, the greater the response time required to recognize, identify, or verify a particular fact. For example, it takes longer to ascertain the correctness of the statement "A canary is an animal" than the statement "A canary is a bird," because of the greater number of links associated with the concept "animal" compared with the concept "bird" (Klatzky, 1975, p. 146).

Collins and Loftus propose a parallel rather than serial search process (as in HAM), so that activation spreads out from an input concept to all its links simultaneously; however, the rate of search depends on the number of paths that are searched, which accounts for the relatively slow verification time when a complex concept is involved. Despite these differences in processing assumptions, both theories predict the same outcome—the fan effect.[3] Later we will discuss the implications of the fan effect for associationist and constructionist

---

[3]Collins and Loftus qualify their formulation by predicting the fan effect only when concepts are conceptually unrelated or when discrimination is difficult.

theories, as well as the way in which social cognition has adopted this associative derivation.

3. Knowledge Assembly Theory

A third neo-associationist theory that is receiving attention from social cognition investigators is the knowledge assembly theory of B. Hayes-Roth. The theory is named with Hebb's (1949) cell assembly theory in mind, since Hayes-Roth considers her theory an extension of Hebb's. In the cell assembly theory, Hebb postulated that repeated activation of particular neurons as a group (e.g., repeated fixation on the three corners of a triangle) eventually culminates in the synthesis of an integrated *new* cell assembly (e.g., corresponding to recognition of a triangle). Similarly, Hayes-Roth (1977) proposed that "learning proceeds as the recursive strengthening and assemblage of cogit representations and assemblies into unitized (higher-order) assemblies—that is, into higher order representations" (p. 262). According to Hayes-Roth, a *cogit* is the functional unit of cognition, the "smallest structure perceptually or cognitively delineated" (p. 261). A cogit is activated in an all-or-none manner.

An interesting feature of cogits is their mutability. Cogits are not thought of as brick-like structures lying about in the mind, but are more like the living cell assemblies of Hebb's formulation. According to knowledge assembly theory, lower-level cogits can be assembled through associations. The strength of the associations is increased with frequency and recency of activation. A cogit's associations may differ in strength of activation, and activation spreads from a cogit representation among its associates in direct proportion to their strength. Eventually, a higher-order or unitized assembly may be synthesized, subsuming the lower-order elements. This unitized assembly then has all the features and capabilities of a lower-order cogit, except that the unitized assembly takes over as the functional unit of cognition. Now the higher-order assembly may itself become associated with other cogit representations and so on.

Hayes-Roth points to a variety of evidence that supports the postulates of knowledge assembly theory. For example, with respect to the hypothesis of gradual construction of unitary higher-order units out of discrete lower-order elements, Hayes-Roth (1977) refers to the results of Chase and Simon (1973), who found that chess masters "chunk" a greater number of pieces than nonmasters when they reconstruct chess positions from memory.

Hayes-Roth's theory predicts that once information has been unitized, information about the structure as a whole will be more accessible than information about any part, because the integrated structure must first undergo decomposition before the parts can be accessed. In support of this prediction, Hayes-Roth (1977) cites a number of studies, for example, N. F. Johnson's (1975) finding that people can more quickly identify visually presented words than their constituent letters.

In his book *Gödel, Escher, and Bach,* Hofstadter (1979) compares the idea of non-decomposable mental units to the quark concept in quantum mechanics, in which protons and neutrons are hypothesized to be composed of trios of quarks bound together so tightly that they cannot be separated. In both cases, the constructs in question are not directly observable but seem to be theoretically powerful nevertheless.

Since publication of Hayes-Roth's theory in 1977, other researchers have produced results that are congruent with certain aspects of this model. The *decomposition* hypothesis (the relative inaccessibility of the parts of an integrated whole) has received considerable support. McGee (1980) for example, presented subjects in two experiments with a large number of words to learn one at a time and instructed them either to form a separate image for each word or to try to interrelate successive pairs (or triads) of words through a relational image. Recognition of each word was then tested by having subjects cross out on a list each word that had not been shown. Subjects who had formed relational images showed poorer recognition of single words than subjects who had formed separate images. McGee concludes that organization impedes the recognition of words that are presented individually on a test list. In the framework of knowledge assembly theory, this result can be explained as the embedding of more than one word into a *unitary* image at encoding, which causes subsequent difficulty in decomposing the newly integrated structure into its original constituent parts (words) when these parts are presented in the recognition test.

Hayes-Roth's theory leads to an interesting set of predictions concerning the fan effect. Recall that the fan effect is the phenomenon in which it takes longer to recognize, identify, or verify a concept the greater the number of associations that are linked to it. Hayes-Roth refines this hypothesis, predicting that the fan effect occurs only with poorly learned material, but not with well-learned or overlearned material. The rationale for these differential predictions is as follows: In the case of poorly learned sets, excitation is spread more thinly the larger the set, causing access interference (a relatively slow reaction time in recognizing a specified element from a large set of possibilities). In the case of well-learned sets, however, the elements are presumed to have been integrated into a unitary assembly so that excitation is not spread out and recognition no longer depends on set size.

In some respects Hayes-Roth's knowledge assembly theory stands midway between associative theories and constructionist theories. The postulates of knowledge assembly theory include both the principles of frequency and recency of association in the earlier stages of learning, as well as higher-order cognitive structures that are processed as units after sufficient experience. Like other neo-associationist theories (see above), Hayes-Roth's theory is essentially passive in its processing assumptions. Also like Anderson and Bower and Collins and Loftus, Hayes-Roth assumes a greater degree of structuredness in the representation of knowledge than was characteristic of traditional associationism.

In contrast to the associationist theorists before her, Hayes-Roth explicitly rejects the (usually implicit) assumption of static structures, assuming instead that networks of associations are capable of significant change both in form and in functioning over time and with experience. Moreover, the integrated structures in Hayes-Roth's model are both quantitatively and *qualitatively* different from the original structures or elements. For example, the fan effect is assumed to characterize the functioning of nonintegrated structures but not unitized structures.

C.   CONSTRUCTIONIST APPROACHES

From its conception, associationism was not without its critics. F. C. Bartlett and members of the Gestalt school emphasized what is now called "top-down" processing, or the active construction of knowledge by the knower, as opposed to a passive copying of stimuli onto the white paper of the mind. As Bartlett (1932) asserted, "remembering appears to be far more decisively an affair of *construction* rather than one of mere reproduction" (p. 205, emphasis added). Whereas in associative perspectives structure is elementaristic, relatively unorganized, and qualitatively immutable, constructionist structure is more holistic, more organized, and qualitatively mutable. Whereas in associative theories processing is passive, context-general, and univocal, constructionist processes are more active, context-dependent, and interdependent. For the sake of simplicity we will refer to the following approaches (Gestalt psychology, Bartlett's schema theory, and Smith's organizational model) as *constructionist* in order to differentiate them from associationism, though this term overstates the similarities within the group and reflects only part of the group's difference from associationism. Each of the following perspectives serves as a critique of some aspect of associationism.

1.   Gestalt Psychology's Configurationism

The Gestalt school challenged the reigning assumptions of associationism, particularly criticizing its atomism and its neglect of organization or form. Indeed, the word *gestalt* means a shape, form, or even a "whole having a form" (Köhler, 1930a, p. 164). The subject matter of Gestalt psychology was the dynamics of perceptual and cognitive organization. This is in contrast with the subject of associationism, which was how perception and cognition were built up through the linking of accumulated pieces of information. Köhler railed against the reductionism and atomism of associationism, charging that "for too long the perceptual field has been treated analytically, in an artificial and unrealistic manner . . . so that an incoherent mosaic of qualities would have to result" (1930b, p. 175).

Köhler saw that early associationism was not only atomistic but also uneconomical, since it required too many pieces and too many links, most of which would be irrelevant in any given cognitive situation. Koffka (1924/1966) criticized Watson and Thorndike for their postulate that learning occurred when certain associations were blindly and gradually strengthened. Instead, Koffka asserted that some learning is a "true development [i.e., a qualitative change], and not a mechanical addition of performances" (p. 225). The Gestaltists contended that people and animals often reorganize a situation not by chance and not by trial-and-error but by reason or insight (sudden learning via cognitive reorganization).

For the Gestaltists, organized wholes, not independent cognitive elements, were the central theoretical constructs. Where the associationism of the day focused on small and separable units of thought (e.g., pairs or chains of nonsense syllables), the members of the Gestalt school demonstrated the functioning of organized cognitive wholes (e.g., melodies) that could not be decomposed without qualitatively changing the phenomenon.

Gestalt psychology's theoretical assumptions were directly counter to the associationists' belief that structure is atomistic, decomposable, relatively unorganized, and static. This familiar Gestalt structural axiom was stated by Köhler in 1930: "In psychology, then, we have wholes which, instead of being the sum of parts existing independently, give their parts specific functions or properties that can only be defined in relation to the whole" (1930a, p. 145). Even more explicitly, Köhler distinguished between Gestalt wholes and associationist wholes, asserting that organized wholes are not just bigger units but are different kinds of units: "a specific sensory whole is *qualitatively* different from the complex that one might predict by considering only its parts in isolation" (1930a, p. 161, emphasis in original).

With respect to the *processes* involved in perceiving, knowing, and remembering, the Gestalt school was also at odds with early associationism. Where associationism assumed univocal, independent, and quantitative principles of cognitive processing, the Gestalt school postulated multiple but interdependent and qualitative principles. The Gestalt school postulated that the process of structuring, organizing, or giving a unitary form to elements took place not in isolation from other cognitive activities but in interdependence; problem-solving depended on comprehension, which depended on recall, with recall in turn depending on organized comprehension: "recall certainly has a significant function in intelligent behavior, but . . . it depends on the organizational process

itself whether or not recall occurs'' (Köhler, 1930b, p. 183). (Both associationists and Gestaltists agreed that the process was a passive—i.e., physiologically determined—one.)

Like other critics of associationism (e.g., Bartlett), these theorists also
argued that associationist accounts were not truly explanatory. In an essay called
"The Nature of Intelligence," Köhler (1930b) attacked early associationism as
lacking explanatory power, warning: "If this is supposed to be a clarification . . . , we must be on guard against it" (p. 173).

Although the Gestalt school of thought had limited impact on the experimental psychology of its day, related principles found their way into social
psychological research undertaken by Lewin, Heider, and Asch. Its emphasis on
organized cognitive wholes can also be traced to modern forms of psychological
theory, both experimental cognitive and social.

2. Bartlett's Schema Concept

F. C. Bartlett was one of the first in a long line of lapsed associationists.
Although Bartlett did not deny the validity of the simple associationist principles
(contiguity, similarity, frequency, recency), he did challenge their sufficiency.
Whereas Ebbinghaus had chosen to focus on the stimulus factors of repetition
and contiguity in his studies of memory, Bartlett preferred to concentrate on
three other factors that Ebbinghaus had identified as influencing what is remembered: the nature of the content, the intensity of interest in the content, and
individual or cultural differences in interest. Of course, interest is not independent of content, and it was this factor of interest in (attitude toward, expectation
of) a given type of material that fascinated Bartlett.[4]

As a social psychologist, Bartlett stressed that one's social group or culture
affects one's memory "by providing a persistent framework of institutions and
customs which acts as a schematic basis for constructive memory" (1932, p.
255). For Bartlett, *schemas* were active, changing, "organized modules" (p.
200). Though he used Sir Henry Head's (1920) term "schema," Bartlett
"strongly disliked" it, judging the schema concept to be "at once too definite
and too sketchy" (p. 201). In this respect, Bartlett tried to forestall both reification and imprecise usage of the schema concept, a concern that bears repeating
even today.

Bartlett cast doubt on the assumption that memory was primarily atomistic
in nature, rejecting the idea that new information functions as "a number of
individual events somehow strung together and stored within the organism" (p.
201). Instead, Bartlett highlighted nonatomistic types of structure and process:
"the past operates as an organized mass rather than as a group of elements each

---

[4]Some argue that interest is also not independent of repetition, recency, and similarity—for
example, the mere exposure effect (see Moreland & Zajonc, 1977).

of which retains its specific character'' (p. 197), thereby anticipating Hayes-Roth's (1977) and Anderson's (1980) unitized knowledge structures which are less atomistic and less decomposable than nonunitized knowledge structures.

Bartlett maintained that Ebbinghaus's reliance on nonsense syllables ''weights the evidence in favor of mere rote recapitulation'' (p. 204) as well as in favor of the copy theory of memory favored by early associationists. When Bartlett had people read and recall stories from unfamiliar cultures (as well as other types of materials that were more complex and more meaningful than nonsense syllables), he found that recall tended to be distorted to fit cultural expectations and personal experiences. This sort of evidence supported Bartlett's claim that memory was an active, constructive, ''top-down'' phenomenon rather than the ''passive patchwork'' (Bartlett, 1932, p. 201) of Ebbinghaus's associationism. In the last paragraph of *Remembering,* Bartlett asserts, ''I have never regarded memory as a faculty, as a reaction narrowed and ringed round, containing all its peculiarities and all their explanations within itself'' (1932, p. 314). For Bartlett, memory was actively constructed in interdependence with other cognitive activities, such as perception, imagination, and inference.

If memory is a matter of active construction of meaningful higher-order units, and not passive reproduction, then its operating principles must include active, person-based processes in addition to the traditional associative ones. To the classic principles of association Bartlett added qualitative principles such as ''conventionalization'' (p. 268). Conventionalization is a general process (akin to Piaget's concept of assimilation) by which new material is actively changed by people in acordance with their own sets of cultural conventions, assumptions, mores, norms, and experiences. In fact, one of the principal kinds of conventionalization, according to Bartlett, is assimilation, the changing of new or foreign elements in memory to fit existing expectations. Other forms of conventionalization are simplification and elaboration, the retention of schema-relevant information, and social constructiveness (creating something new by welding together diverse elements in line with the developmental direction of a group).

Like Bartlett before them, some modern cognitivists have begun to assert the importance of nonquantitative principles of cognition. Minsky (1975), for example, argues that purely quantitative principles such as response probability, subjective probability, and reinforcement ''are not likely to be able to account for sophisticated cognitive activities'' (p. 275). Minsky's frame theory, like Bartlett's, emphasizes the dependence of thought on language and culture rather than on mathematical principles.

Though Bartlett self-consciously formulated his schema theory in contrast to traditional associationism, he did not intend to set one against the other as dichotomies or to supplant associationism with a schema model. He accepted both associationist and constructionist principles, but preferred to investigate the latter himself: ''It is no more right to suppose that the mental life develops and works *solely* by the expanding articulation of a 'whole,' or of many 'wholes,' than it is to suppose that it grows and operates *solely* through the gradual accretion of originally distinct elements'' (p. 308, emphasis added).

Bartlett, while not himself a Gestaltist, had like-minded critiques to make of associationism. Köhler's metaphor for associationist perception as "an incoherent mosaic" (1930b, p. 175) is strikingly similar to Bartlett's metaphor for associationist memory as "a passive patchwork" (1932, p. 201). And, to an even greater extent than the Gestaltists, Bartlett's ideas have been taken seriously by social psychology—particularly by social cognition investigators, who have not only resurrected the schema notion but have also made it a dominant theoretical construct in modern social psychology.

3. E. E. Smith's Organizational Model

E. E. Smith is a modern cognitive theorist whose work calls into direct question certain assumptions of the neo-associationist models. With respect to structure, Smith is in substantial agreement with neo-associationists that knowledge may be stored in the form of associative networks. In Smith's model, the elements of a related set of information are connected with other elements by means of inferences made both at the time of encoding and at the time of recall. Since all the propositions are interconnected, there is a direct path to any one element from any other. As a result of this assumption, the structure of memory in Smith's model is considerably more tangled than that of the nicely logical, hierarchical model of Anderson (1980). But unitization occurs in both models and in both, unitization has facilitating effects on recognition.

As Smith (1980) points out, the fan effect that is predicted by associationism is something of a paradox in practice. It makes sense from within a neo-associationist framework that the verification of a proposition (e.g., a canary is an animal) will be slower the greater the number of associated facts fanning out from its component terms, since associative models postulate blind search processes. However, the fanning phenomenon belies common sense. We all know that the more we know about a topic the more readily we can answer questions about it. Smith provides an account of this paradox in the light of *organizational* mechanisms, which permit the representation, storage, and retrieval of multiple facts about a topic without loss of efficiency. According to Smith (1980), organizational processes operate in at least three types of circumstances: (1) when facts can be subdivided into distinct classes (e.g., animal, vegetable, mineral); (2) when facts can be integrated by prior knowledge; and (3) when facts contain "perfectly correlated" predicates (e.g., "The banker *cleaned the wall*"; "The lawyer *cleaned the wall*").

Smith, Adams, and Schorr (1978) demonstrated that when a set of new propositions can be integrated by prior knowledge, recognition interference (the fan effect) does not occur. In this study, subjects learned either two or three propositions about a target individual. In one condition the propositions were unrelated to one another and were not readily integrable—for example, "The banker was asked to address the crowd" and "The banker broke the bottle." In another condition the propositions were easily related to some organizing script like ship christening—for example, "The banker was chosen to christen the ship" and "The banker broke the bottle." In a subsequent recognition test, subjects showed a fan effect only when presented with the sets of unrelated propositions, but not when the propositions were related to a common script.

Smith (1980) explains these results by contending that the subjects who learned related statements used prior world knowledge about ship christenings to integrate these propositions into a unitary whole which facilitated later recognition. As evidence for this use of prior knowledge, Smith points to the fact that subjects who had learned the script-related statements falsely "recognized" script-consistent distractor statements (e.g., "The banker broke the champagne bottle") more frequently than subjects who had learned the sets of unrelated sentences. Smith concludes that subjects in his study did not passively and blindly carry on a search-and-match process, but actively comprehended the material when they first learned it, drew inferences about it, organized it on the basis of prior world knowledge, and then utilized these inferences to guide their memory. The fact that the fan effect has *not* been found under conditions specified by Smith, by Hayes-Roth, and by Anderson presents a serious challenge to the universality of the associative and spreading activation mechanisms postulated by neo-associative theories.

Smith argues strongly for the active nature of memory, particularly through his emphasis on the role of comprehension in memory. Comprehension is seemingly a more active theoretical process than frequency or recency of activation, and Smith (1980) insists on the importance of comprehension and inference processes in memory, going so far as to suggest that comprehension has primacy over passive memory, or that a subdivided network is merely the "natural consequence of our comprehension processes" (p. 206), with associative networks being only the minimal "kind of representation you get out of comprehension processes when your input is sparse on relations" (p. 206). Smith suggests that associative network models may have proliferated at least in part because of the stripped-down nature of the stimuli studied in the past (e.g., the nonsense syllable of Ebbinghaus, paired associates, even simple sentences): "we may have underestimated the extent to which memory phenomena are dependent on comprehension, by consistently using materials that lack the stuff that makes comprehension go" (p. 206).

Smith's emphasis on the active organization and integration of knowledge has made its way into the thinking of social cognition researchers, particularly among investigators who are themselves examining the functioning of higher-order cognitive units.

4. J. R. Anderson's Unitization Model

Recently, Anderson (1980) has revised and refined his original (Anderson & Bower, 1973) theory, creating what he calls a "unitization" model. In this model Anderson examines the possibility that higher-level schemas or scripts (e.g., the set of propositions about dining in a restaurant) may also function as cognitive units alongside lower-level concepts (e.g., the idea of ordering from a menu). A central feature of this model is the specification of criteria for deciding whether cognitive complexes can be considered to operate as *units*; these criteria are all-or-none learning and all-or-none retrieval. In other words, if all the elements of a proposition or schema act as one (via associative links) when learned or recalled, then the proposition or schema is functionally a cognitive unit.

According to Anderson (1980), "unitization occurs when a set of elements in working memory can be put into correspondence with an existing knowledge structure" (p. 26). At unitization a new node is created (a "chunk" node) which links elements that were previously unconnected. An index tag is added to the new chunk node, linking it to the prior knowledge structure and allowing direct access to the chunk via the index tag without the necessity of individually examining the elements of the chunk.

Among the consequences of unitization predicted by Anderson are all-or-none encoding and retrieval of units, an increased rate of encoding and retrieval of units, and the elimination of interference or fan effects within a unit. Reder and Anderson (1980) found empirical support for these predictions. Their subjects were quickly able to reject foils that were not related to a ship christening (or other) script. With unitization via scripts the fan effect was reduced, a result previously produced by Smith, Adams, and Schorr (1978). On the basis of these results, Anderson (1980) concurs with E. E. Smith (1980) that "the individual propositions can be unified into a schema and that subjects can treat this schema in an unanalyzed fashion" (p. 20).[5]

---

[5]Like Collins and Loftus, who postulated the existence of two networks, a lexical (dictionary) network and a semantic (meaning) network, Anderson's (1980) model includes two kinds of traces, a word string trace and a proposition/meaning trace. Both formulations attempt to address the vitally important issue of the relationship between language and meaning. Anderson was led to this sort of thinking by the results of priming research which used multiple proposition sentences, such as this one: "The Arab approached the actress [proposition 1] who drank in the disco [proposition 2]." The finding in such studies is that there is better recognition/recall of words cued by words *within* the same proposition than by words *across* propositions, which might imply that the sentence taken as a

It will be remembered that in 1973 Anderson and Bower began with a neo-associationist theory in which memory was thought to be represented via a linguistically structured network of associations among concepts and propositions. By 1980, however, Anderson's cognitive structures had expanded from concepts and propositions to higher-order units such as schemas and scripts. Thus in the more recent formulations, there is both *more* organization and a *different kind* of organization than there was in the earlier formulations. Once again, the simple pairwise associations or stimulus–response (S–R) chains of associations postulated by traditional associationism have given way to hierarchically organized structuring (Anderson & Bower, 1973; Anderson, 1976, 1980) and even to heterarchical structuring (Hayes-Roth, 1977). (In *hierarchical* structuring, higher-order structures are thought to govern lower-order elements, whereas in *heterarchical* organization, structures operate reciprocally upon one another. In other words, there is no single highest level in heterarchical structures, but instead a "whole family" of recursive networks "tangled up, calling each other and themselves like crazy" [Hofstadter, 1979, p. 134].)

With regard to the question of how old knowledge is brought into correspondence with new information, that is, whether it is by means of passive, blind associative processes or by means of more active and constructive processes, many modern theorists are growing more eclectic. The implication is strong in the writing of Anderson and Hayes-Roth that the processes are essentially automatic or passive, depending heavily on mere frequency of exposure. However, Anderson (1976) has come to admit of higher cognitive processes interacting with memory processes, changing his earlier (1973) position that memory is passive and independent of such processes as inference, comprehension, and problem solving. In his elaboration proposal (1976), Anderson postulates that at encoding, people may make inferences based on the stimulus information and that these inferences may later facilitate memory for that input. In noting certain disparities between his elaboration proposal (1976) and his unitization hypothesis (1980), Anderson (1980) comes to the conclusion that no single theoretical mechanism can explain all memory phenomena, much less all cognitive processes. In the end, Anderson decides that he must "consider both hypotheses [elaboration and unitization] as necessary to account for the complexities of human memory" (1980, p. 36).

The history of J. R. Anderson's thought is strikingly representative of the progression of theorizing within cognitive psychology and social cognition. In both there has been a convergence of associative principles with principles of formerly opposing constructionist traditions.

---

whole is not a cognitive unit. However, Anderson disputes such an interpretation, arguing that word strings may be recalled in a fragmentary manner, while the deep structure propositions are acquired and recalled in an all-or-none fashion.

D. COMPARISON OF ASSOCIATIONIST AND
    CONSTRUCTIONIST PRINCIPLES

In view of the complexity of these formulations, it is difficult and unsatisfy-
ing to attempt to extract a limited set of their features for special consideration.
Nevertheless, we will now recapitulate what we judge to be either central aspects
of the associationist and constructionist theories we have discussed, and/or aspects that have been put to test within the area of social cognition. Another
criterion in selecting features of these theories for comparison is discriminability;
features that distinguish associationist from constructionist approaches will be of
particular interest.

At this time the structural concepts of constructionist and neo-associationist
approaches are quite similar, but the processing assumptions held by the two
perspectives remain divergent. With respect to structure, both approaches now
postulate similarly large and complex higher-order mental units built up from
smaller units. J. R. Anderson (1980) and E. E. Smith (1980) agree that prose is
likely to be encoded and stored in the form of associative networks, with concept
nodes linked to other concept or feature nodes by associative links. Some neo-
associationists have even begun to assert the Gestalt principle that under some
conditions, complex cognitive units become qualitatively different from their
constituents—for example, that these higher-order units are more readily recognized as a unit than as combined parts, or are not readily decomposable (Hayes-
Roth, 1977).

For our present purposes, the distinguishing features of neo-associationist
theories include the following: (1) *elementaristic representation* via independent
links among more or less atomistic elements and (2) *processing* that proceeds
passively from element to element, by means of mechanistic and quantitative
principles of association like frequency, recency, and contiguity. Constructionist–unitization–schema theories, on the other hand, postulate (1) a type of
higher-order representation in which once-independent elements may lose their
independence, having been unitized into qualitatively different higher-order cognitive modules and (2) a type of *processing* that proceeds actively by means of
qualitative principles such as assimilation, accommodation, simplification, and
distortion. These characteristics of structure and process can be found in most of
the models discussed, though there are noticeable differences from one to the
next.

Associationist theories are typically "bottom up" in orientation, assigning
greater functional importance to stimulus features than to processor features.
Associationists have traditionally espoused the view that perception, memory,
and other cognitive activities are built up from the features of the input, or are
more "data driven" than "theory driven" in their formation. This is, of course,

in contrast to the "top-down" view of the Gestalt school, Bartlett, and others who assert that form is imposed on input by the perceiver, or that thought and memory are informed by what is already in the head of the processor. The differing structural emphases, with the associationists stressing elements and the constructionists stressing integrated units of elements, are in accordance with these differing stances on the direction of cognitive processing. The units of cognition in associationist models are generally less integrated than those of constructionist or unitization models. Whatever their scope, the elements in associationist theories remain ultimately independent in their functioning, while in constructionist theories a number of formerly independent elements may come to function together as a unit, losing some of their autonomy in the process.

Associationists have always preferred passive or automatic mechanisms of processing to the more active principles endorsed by constructionist or unitization theorists. The memory component of HAM, for example, proceeds entirely passively. In a "strategy-free" (Anderson & Bower, 1973, p. 186) manner, HAM's memory "does passively accept whatever is sent to it by the parsers and does indiscriminately proceed to encode links in that input. During decoding it generates output trees in response to probe trees in a similarly automatic manner" (p. 186). In associationist accounts, perception and memory operate independently of more active processes such as comprehension, inference, or problem solving. Thus Anderson and Bower make the strong assertion that "there is a *strategy-free* memory component" (Anderson & Bower, 1973, p. 141, emphasis added)—that is, a part of memory which operates independently of "executive" activities such as problem solving and inference.

In contrast with the passive processing assumptions of associationism, constructionist approaches stress active, "top-down" processing. Bartlett cogently argued for the importance of top-down factors like expectation, interest, and emotional involvement in memory. Implied in this viewpoint is the corollary assumption that so-called lower cognitive processes, or processes that seem more immediately tied to the real world, such as perception and recognition, do not take place in isolation from so-called higher cognitive processes such as comprehension, inference, and problem solving. In constructionist approaches, structural interdependence is concomitant with processing interdependence.

The distinguishing features of associationist theories (element-by-element structural organization, passive and bottom-up processing) correspond to the kind of question posed earlier in this chapter: How do elements of the social world get combined? Constructionist models, characterized by integrated structures, active and top-down processing, are more likely to be brought to bear to answer the other question posed earlier: How does the perceiver construct ideas about the social world? In general, the associationist orientation emphasizes the object, while the constructionist approach emphasizes the subject.

III.   Application of Associationist and Constructionist
Principles in Social Cognition

Although associationist and schematic approaches began as distinct, even opposing, theories, in the area of research that goes by the name of social cognition the two traditions have begun to merge and even to become nearly synonymous. However, a few reasonably pure representatives of each of these formerly dichotomous approaches do exist, and it is with these that we will begin our examination of social cognition and its theories.

A.   ASSOCIATIONIST PRINCIPLES IN SOCIAL COGNITION

Associative models have been applied to a number of interesting questions about social cognition, including the following: (1) whether the frequency and/or recency with which information is presented affects the impressions we form of others; (2) whether the impressions we form of others can be affected by information of which we are not consciously aware; (3) whether our mood can have an impact on what we perceive and recall about ourselves and others.

1.   *Frequency, Recency, and Similarity Effects*
   in Social Cognition

The most longstanding of the associative processing principles are those of frequency, recency, and similarity introduced by Aristotle. The power of recency to affect everyday thinking is illustrated by the child's joke that goes something like this:

Hey, Dad, how do you pronounce M-A-C-B-E-T-H? "Mac-Beth."
Right. So how do you pronounce M-A-C-D-O-N-A-L-D? "Mac-Donald."
Okay. How do you pronounce M-A-C-H-I-N-E?

In a sophisticated version of this tradition Higgins, Rholes, and Jones (1977) carried out a study demonstrating that recently activated concepts are likely to be utilized to form impressions of others. In this study subjects were first exposed to one of two sets of paired associates in which the response words were similar in content but opposite in evaluative tone (e.g., self-confident–conceited; bold–reckless). Later, these subjects engaged in a putative reading comprehension task in which they read evaluatively ambiguous paragraph descriptions about a target person. When subjects were asked how well they liked the target person described in the paragraph, they tended to evaluate the person more positively when they had originally been exposed to relevant favorable words in the priming task than when they had been presented with relevant and unfavorable priming words. These subjects also tended to describe the ambiguous behaviors in terms of trait concepts that were closely related to the priming concepts (e.g., rash, crazy).

A spreading activation–network model may be used to explain these results. Concepts that have been recently activated (through the priming task) are expected to be more accessible than concepts activated longer ago. In addition, semantically associated, or similar, concepts are expected to be more accessible than unrelated concepts, due to the operation of spreading activation. Higgins did not maintain a strict associationist explanation of these results; more recently he proposed an energy cell metaphor to account for them (Higgins & King, 1981). Higgins and King note, however, that their energy cell model "fits nicely with the spreading activation model" (p. 79).

Wyer and Srull (1980) have reported additional results that are quite congruent with those observed by Higgins *et al.* (1977). These investigators had subjects first perform a sentence construction task in which they underlined 3 out of 4 sets of words in order to form a sentence. Some word sets were hostility related (e.g., leg break arm his) and others were not (e.g., paint box the pack). Both the absolute number (30 or 60) and the proportion (20 percent or 80 percent) of hostile items were varied. Then these subjects participated in a second, supposedly unrelated, experiment with a different experimenter and a different cover story immediately after the priming manipulation, 1 hour later, or 24 hours later. In this portion of the experiment, subjects were given a paragraph to read concerning events in a target person's life, and they were asked to form an impression of the target person. Some events in the stimulus paragraph could be interpreted as either neutral or hostile (e.g., refusing to pay the landlord the rent until the apartment was painted). Subjects then rated the target person along a number of trait dimensions, some of which were directly related to hostility (e.g., hostile, kind) and some of which were not directly related to hostility (e.g., boring, intelligent).

The greater the number of hostile items there had been in the priming portion of the experiments, the more hostile the subjects rated the target person. The more recent the priming portion, the higher the hostility rating. The results of this experiment support the importance of frequency and recency of activation of a trait concept in the process of forming impressions about another person.

Even more clearly supportive of associationist assumptions about passive processing are the recent results obtained by Bargh and Pietromonaco (1982). These investigators tested whether trait concepts that are presented below the threshold of conscious awareness can affect impression formation. Words were flashed very briefly on a cathode ray tube (CRT) screen, and subjects pressed a button as soon as they detected the flash. Hostile words (e.g., hostile, unkind, beat, stab) made up 0%, 20%, or 80% of the set of words presented; the rest of the words were unrelated to hostility but equivalent in length and frequency to the hostile words. After engaging in this detection task, subjects read a paragraph describing the behavior of a target person; the behavior presented had been previously rated as ambiguous with respect to whether it was hostile or appropriately assertive. (These stimuli were the same as those used by Wyer and Srull, 1980.) In control conditions, subjects were compelled to guess each word upon its presentation or to choose from among three alternatives the word to which they had just been exposed.

Results indicated that, although subjects were not consciously aware of the words flashed, the higher the proportion of hostile words presented during the priming phase, the more negative the impression of the stimulus person and the more extreme the ratings on hostile dimensions. These results represent rather strong support for the operation of a passive frequency-based principle of association.

2. Mood Effects and Associative Network Theory

In a journal entry made on his dying mother's birthday, Roland Barthes evokes a poetic sense of moods as ever-changing, disturbing, even exhausting human urges which interact with thought and with external reality (Barthes, 1982, p. 486):

> Moods, in the strong, Schumannian sense: a broken series of contradictory impulses: waves of anxiety, imaginations of the worst, and unseasonable euphorias. This morning, at the core of Worry, a crystal of happiness: the weather (very fine, very light and dry), the music (Haydn), coffee, a cigar, a good pen, the household noises (the human subject as caprice: such discontinuity alarms, exhausts).

Not only writers but also scientists have speculated that one's mood has an effect on one's thinking and vice versa. This supposition depends on a definition of cognition that is broader than the definition with which we have been working. Such a definition was advanced by Descartes in the seventeenth century: "What is a thing which thinks? It is a thing which doubts, understands, [conceives], affirms, denies, wills, refuses, which also imagines and feels" (1952, p. 79, brackets are translator's). In their book *Cognition,* Glass, Holyoak and Santa (1979) called for research in the area of state-dependent learning and memory, an area with roots in a Cartesian view of cognition. Specifically focusing on mood/cognition connections, Glass, Holyoak and Santa (1979) asked, "Does state-dependent learning extend to emotional states, so that it is easier to remember happy experiences when we are happy and sad experiences when we are sad?" (p. 107). This largely unknown territory has recently begun to be explored in cognitive psychology (e.g., Bower, 1981) and in social cognition (e.g., Clark & Isen, 1982) and to be articulated in associative network terms.

State-dependent recall involves superior memory for events or information when the mood at learning is the same as the mood at recall. State-dependent effects differ from what Bower (1981) terms *mood-congruity* effects, in which the functionally significant match is between mood at learning and mood-tone of the stimulus material. Thus, regardless of the mood at recall, mood-congruent learning can be said to occur when people learn and/or recall more about material consistent with their mood at the time of exposure than about mood-inconsistent information. Bower (1981) reports evidence for both state-dependent and mood-congruent effects on learning, memory, imagination, social inference, and self-perception. Clark and Isen (1982) show that these effects extend to the realms of social judgment and even behavior.

In a series of recent experiments, Bower and his collaborators (e.g., Bower, Monteiro & Gilligan, 1978) induced in hypnotizable subjects the emotional state of happiness or sadness, instructing subjects under hypnosis to put themselves into a particular mood by remembering or imagining happy or sad events. When free recall was tested under either the same- or opposite-mood condition, these investigators found state-dependent effects: subjects showed better recall of the same-mood list and worse recall of the opposite-mood list. Bower has also observed state-dependency effects in the recall of real-life personal events or childhood incidents. Similarly, Clark and Isen (1982) summarize a good deal of evidence supportive of feeling-induced judgments and behavior. Many of the effects cited by these authors have been demonstrated in naturally occurring contexts like shopping malls and tennis courts or soccer fields (Clark, 1982). In a well-known paradigm, shoppers are made to feel good by giving them free gifts before asking them to help someone or to rate their car's repair record (e.g., Isen, Shalker, Clark, & Karp, 1978). Shoppers in whom positive feelings are induced are more likely to engage in helping behavior and to rate their car favorably than shoppers in whom positive feelings are not induced.

The constructs and principles of associative network models have been explicitly applied to these and other mood-related phenomena (e.g., Bower, 1981; Clark & Isen, 1982). In these formulations, propositions and concepts are assumed to be linked with mood or emotion nodes by associative pathways, with activation spreading throughout the memory–emotion structure according to the usual neo-associationist principles of associative strength, node intersection, and summation of activation to threshold. Bower's associative network model accounts for state-dependent effects by construing mood reinstatement as a search cue to be used in the absence of other strong or adequate cues. The main innovation in Bower's framework, as well as in that of Clark and Isen, is the idea of emotion nodes, or cognitive (in the broader Cartesian sense of the term) units that bring together "many other aspects of the emotion that are connected to it by associative pointers" (Bower, 1981, p. 135). Some of the aspects of the emotion postulated to be linked with an emotion node are verbal labels, evoking events, expressive behaviors, and autonomic responses. Clark and Isen (1982) propose two different ways in which feelings might be processed within an associative network framework: in one conception the *emotion* nodes serve as major organizing hubs around which behaviors, objects, or situations might be linked, while in the other, the behaviors, objects, or events themselves are the central organizing elements around which emotions are linked.

To explain mood-congruency effects, Bower (1981) introduces a mechanism involving reverberating patterns of activation. The idea here is that while a happy person (i.e., a person with the happiness node in long-term memory activated) is reading happy material, the emotion node will be reactivated again and again, strengthening the associations within the newly formed stimulus node as well as strengthening the associative links between the mood and the stimulus node. In like manner, Bower explains other effects of mood on social cognition, such as the bias toward interpreting ambiguous interpersonal situations in line with one's mood (Roth & Rehm, 1980). For example, he and his collaborators have found that subjects who feel socially incompetent as a result of hypnotic induction judge themselves as engaging in more negative, socially unskilled behaviors than positive behaviors. This perceptual bias seems to generalize even more when the individual feels socially skilled, so that persons who have undergone this positive mood induction not only judge themselves to have committed more positive than negative acts, but they also evaluate their partner's behavior in this rosy light.

These formulations diverge from traditional associationism in at least one crucial way. The very fact that feeling states and emotions are included in the scheme represents an expansion of the narrower conception of cognition usually found in associative theories. The inclusion of emotion in the model brings with it a concomitant assumption that one kind of processing (e.g., memory) goes on in conjunction with another (e.g., emotion), rather than in isolation. The interdependence assumption, of course, has not been typical of associationist theorizing. Overall, however, Bower's work fits squarely within the neo-associationist tradition established by Anderson and Bower in 1973, positing a network structure, and passive processing by means of activation spreading from node to node along pathways that might be either facilitative or inhibitory in their (fixed) nature, and stronger or weaker, depending on frequency of activation.

Clark and Isen (1982), on the other hand, specify conditions under which mood effects might operate quite actively. They employ the distinction between automatic and controlled processing (Schneider & Shiffrin, 1977) to account for various mood effects that are otherwise difficult to explain. For example, circumstances such as stress, depression, old age, or very young age may be associated with relatively diminished levels of controlled processing, so that in these cases automatic processing, and thus less effective coping strategies, may be expected to predominate.

Although probably only one of the investigators just discussed would identify himself as an associationist (i.e., Bower), nevertheless, what these various studies of social cognition have in common is their reliance on certain associationist principles. This is particularly true of the priming research reported by Higgins and his colleagues (1977) and by Bargh and Pietromonaco (1982), which demonstrates that the processing of information about others is capable of being carried out passively, and by dint of frequency or recency of activation of the concepts in question. The work on mood and emotion reported by Bower (1981) and by Clark and Isen (1982) stresses an associative network model of representation and processing, adding emotion nodes to the usual network and specifying in detail the manner in which activation might spread from emotion nodes to other concept nodes or vice versa.

B. CONSTRUCTIONIST PRINCIPLES IN SOCIAL COGNITION

As we have seen, associationist applications have recently come into play in the study of social cognition, and we will later argue that associationist and constructionist constructs have tended to combine into a new hybrid in the study of social cognition. Still, insofar as social cognition is identified with any single conceptual approach, it is most clearly identified with a constructionist perspective, and particularly with the schema theory that Bartlett initiated.

1. Schemas: Definitional Issues and Research

According to one broad and generally accepted definition, a schema is an "abstract, general structure that establishes relations between specific events or entities" (Hastie, 1981, p. 41). Another "noncontroversial" and "minimal" definition describes schemas as "cognitive structures of organized prior knowledge, abstracted from experience with specific instances" (Fiske & Linville, 1980, p. 543). A third formulation also emphasizes the general–specific dimension of knowing in its conceptualization of a schema as:

a cognitive structure that consists in part of the representation of some defined stimulus domain. The schema contains general knowledge about that domain, including a specification of the relationships among its attributes, as well as specific examples or instances of the stimulus domain. (Taylor & Crocker, 1981, p. 91)

So far, then, there seems to be agreement on these features of schemas:

1. schemas are cognitive structures;
2. schemas represent both general and specific knowledge, in a single higher-order unit;
3. schemas have an impact on cognitive processing.

These features and definitions of schemas do indeed appear rather innocuous, so that the question arises as to why the concept evolved. "Schema" as opposed to what? As we have seen, social psychologists like Bartlett felt that such a concept was necessary to explain the idiosyncracies of memory for complex material. Others have employed the schema concept to help explain comprehension of complex stimuli or written texts and the solving of complex problems, or other phenomena that are difficult to explain by means of simple associative models.

The distinction between schemas and older associationist notions is highlighted when one considers more controversial definitions such as that of Fiske and Linville (1980) who view schematic thought as:

an active constructive process, rather than a veridical copy;
abstraction over instances rather than a collection of raw data;
structure based on experience, rather than determined wholly by genetic factors or by the current environment; and
elicit[ing] affect as well as inference. (p. 552)

Let us examine each of these four criteria in turn to get an idea of just how controversial this particular schema definition is. Note that the first three features of this definition enunciate what has been termed the "top-down" nature of schematic thought. The first, constructionist, clause of this definition rejects the so-called copy theory in which knowledge (perception and memory) is postulated to be a copy of sensation. Instead of a passive copy theory, this schema concept rests on epistemological assumptions in which knowledge is a matter of active construction. Hence, schema theorists who accept this definition are taking a stand in favor of constructionist principles of cognitive processing.

The criterion of abstraction over instances is only deceptively straightforward. Minsky's exemplar hypothesis illustrates the problem:

Does one know specifically that a silent Piggy Bank is empty, and hence out of money (I think, yes) or does one use general knowledge that a hard container which makes no noise when shaken is empty? . . . Logically the "general principle" would suffice, but I feel that this misses the important point that a specific scenario of this character is engraved in every child's memory. (1975, p. 244)

Minsky, of course, is not alone in stressing the importance of specific and concrete (episodic) events over that of general and abstract (semantic) inference in everyday thought (Adorno, 1978b; Tulving, 1972).

Regarding Fiske and Linville's third feature of schemas, there is less than perfect concurrence among cognitive and social psychologists concerning the point at which and the degree to which schematic thought remains true to raw data, as well as when and to what extent inferential processes actively operate on data. For example, a recent symposium on "Social Knowing" revealed an emerging "counterrevolution" to the "cognitive revolution." The members of this counterrevolution stress direct pick-up of raw data a la J. J. Gibson (1966, 1979) rather than inferential or schema-driven perception (Baron, 1980; Harvey & Baron, 1980; McArthur, 1980; and Newtson, 1980). The proponents of direct perception also argue against the cognitivist de-emphasis of genetic and stimulus determination of thought (bottom-up cognition). The members of the counter-revolution base their objections to the schema approach on Gibson's view that the human sensory apparatus is capable of directly picking up structure that already exists in the environment, through the use of texture gradients, depth cues, etc. To date, this approach has not been developed to any great extent, perhaps because it is most difficult to apply Gibson's constructs in the social realm. Nevertheless, it is worth noting that among social cognition researchers, there are those who dispute the widely held top-down assumption of the con-structionist camp.

Finally, the inclusion of affect in the last clause is not accepted by some schema theorists such as Taylor and Crocker (1981) who prefer to limit the schema concept to the cognitive (in the narrower sense of the term) domain.

The schema concept, at least in its extended formulations (e.g., Fiske & Linville), is innovative and perhaps even revolutionary. The problem of defining it with generality disciplined by precision remains, for the schema concept has become something of an umbrella concept or a "metaconstruct" (Fiske & Linville, 1980) subsuming a number of other hypothetical cognitive modules (e.g., scripts, stereotypes, prototypes). Consequently, the definitions of schemas have tended to be nearly all-inclusive. One schema expert accepts at least eight con-cepts as closely related to schemas, including "abstract hypotheses, expecta-tions, organizing principles, frames, implicational molecules, scripts, plans, or prototypes" (Hastie, 1981, p. 39). Likewise, Taylor and Crocker (1981) accept frames, prototypes, scripts, and Neisser's schemas as compatible with their own schema concept.

In the following section we examine how four of these hypothetical higher-order cognitive modules have been conceived in social cognition work—namely, stereotypes, scripts, prototypes, and the schema itself. With respect to our pre-vious historical discussion, we wish only to point out that these higher-order modules are more congruent with the constructionist approach than with associa-tionist perspectives. Schemas, stereotypes, scripts, and prototypes are constructs that were created to model various aspects of top-down thinking, or thinking that is significantly and actively influenced by what is in the head. Indeed the fact that schema-like constructs are proliferating in cognitive psychology and social cog-nition attests to the growing popularity of the constructionist framework.

Among the questions to which constructionist accounts have been applied are these: (1) How are one's self-perceptions organized? (2) How does the cognitive organization of one's self-knowledge influence the processing of social information? (3) Is social information capable of cognitive organization and reorganization resulting in the development of higher-order cognitive structures (e.g., schemas) that are qualitatively different from the original aggregation of elements? (4) How do socially constituted expectations about social groups (e.g., stereotypes) affect the processing of information about members of these groups? (5) How do socially shared expectations about situations or events (e.g., scripts) affect the processing of information about these events? (6) How are social stimuli categorized, and how do social categorizations (e.g., prototypes) affect the processing of social information? Besides explicating the constructionist aspects of each of these cognitive constructs, we compare the constructs with one another, and discuss how research on these cognitive constructs has begun to offer answers to some of the questions just listed.

Markus (1977) made one of the first attempts to measure individual differences in schematic structuring and processing. Among a sample of female students she distinguished three groups that differed along the dimension of independence–dependence. Based on the content of their self-descriptions and the importance they attached to such traits as independent–dependent, individualist–conformist, and leader–follower, Markus identified women with dependent and independent self-schemas, along with a group of aschematics, or people for whom these dimensions were not important.

Markus (1977) found that people classified as schematics categorize themselves more quickly on schema-consistent dimensions than on schema-inconsistent or irrelevant dimensions, and that schematics are able to list more examples of schema-consistent behaviors than aschematics. These results demonstrate the impact of self-schemas on cognitive processing. Similar results were obtained in a subsequent study using the Bem Sex Role Inventory to differentiate schematics from aschematics on the dimension of gender identification (Markus, Crane, Bernstein, & Siladi, 1982).

In addition to schema effects such as these, some social cognition researchers have begun to examine the possibility that schemas are not only complex cognitive modules, but also are qualitatively different from other aggregations of cognitive elements. Sherman and Titus (1982) conducted three experiments that addressed the influence of covariation information on memory for an implied causal agent. These investigators first had subjects study 32 paragraphs containing an initial statement concerning the affective relationship between a person and an object (e.g., Fred likes/dislikes the car), as well as three statements containing information about the degree of consistency, consensus, and distinctiveness of this relationship. Within each paragraph the implied causal agent was either the person or the object. One of the dependent measures was a recognition test in which subjects were presented with probe words (person or object) and were asked to identify as quickly as possible whether each word had appeared earlier. Reaction time was employed as a measure of the accessibility of the person/object concepts. When the order of presentation of consistency–consensus–distinctiveness information was one that is known to account for a high proportion of the variance in causal attributions (from which it can be inferred that subjects were in fact making causal attributions), subjects took longer to verify/reject implied causal agents than noncausal agents.

The authors explain this result in terms of Hayes-Roth's unitization and decomposition hypothesis. When the person or object is an implied causal agent, it is embedded into a more complex, unitized, higher-order structure than when it is not seen as a causal agent. Consequently, if a subpart of the unitary causal structure (a causal agent) is presented in a recognition test, that causal element is more difficult to access because the unitary structure must first be decomposed in order to match the subpart with the probe, whereas the noncausal probe has remained an isolated, independent element which is more quickly accessed.

As Sherman and Titus note, there is another study within the social cognition literature that relates to the unitization phenomenon. Sentis and Burnstein (1979) employed a variant of Sternberg's memory probe procedures (e.g., 1966) to test the prediction that information that can be integrated into a meaningful whole is more easily retrieved than non-integrable information (cf. also Moesher, 1979; Reder & Anderson, 1980). Following from results reported by Smith, Adams, & Schorr (1978), Sentis and Burnstein (1979) hypothesized three things:

1. a balanced set of interrelationships functions as a gestalt, acting as a cohesive unit, or as a "balance schema," in cognition; but an imbalanced set of interrelationships continues to function as a number of discrete elements;

2. information from a balanced set of interrelationships is more easily retrieved than information from an imbalanced set (Smith et al., 1978);

3. for imbalanced sets, the usual fan effect would occur, with slower response time the greater the number of relationships to be retrieved; but for balanced sets the fan effect would disappear, and response time would be the same regardless of number of relationships to be retrieved.

Balanced and imbalanced sets of information in Sentis and Burnstein's experiment consisted of Heiderian (1946, 1958) P-O-X triads, or scenarios interrelating two persons (P and O) and an attitudinal issue (X) on an affective dimension (like–dislike, agree–disagree). For example, in a balanced scenario Bill and John are good friends, and both strongly oppose the use of quotas in graduate school admissions. Subjects studied two scenarios (one balanced and one imbalanced) for two minutes. Then they were presented a probe of varying size (1, 2, or all 3 components of the triad) and were asked to respond "true" or "false" to the presented set of interrelationships.

Sentis and Burnstein's results confirmed only one portion of their response time predictions—that is, their prediction of a fan effect in the imbalanced set, and then only when "true" was the correct response. Under these conditions, a fan effect was observed, for subjects took longer to identify correctly the 3-part sets than the 2-part or 1-part probes. However, the prediction of a flat response-time slope for the balanced set of information (no set size effect on response time) was not supported. In fact, a negative slope was found for the balanced cases in which "true" was the correct answer. In other words, subjects recognized as true a complete set of 3 balanced interrelationships faster than they recognized probes containing 2 of the 3 balanced interrelationships and faster still than they identified only 1 of the 3 pieces of balanced information.

To explain this unexpected finding, Sentis and Burnstein (1979) combine Hayes-Roth's decomposition principle with her fan effect prediction. They postulate a 2-process operation in the recognition of balanced, or integrated, information, involving first retrieval from long-term memory to short-term memory or working memory, and then decomposition of the unitary schema in order to search for a match to the probe stimulus. Concerning the decomposition process, Sentis and Burnstein conclude, "there is a cost associated with the integrative function of the balance schema, namely, the integrated memory structure must be decomposed in order to access subsets of it" (p. 2207).

In this experiment, however, subjects had equal practice with the balanced and imbalanced sets, so Hayes-Roth's practice explanation cannot account for the results. Or can it? Perhaps people form and repeatedly utilize something like what Sentis and Burnstein call a "balance schema." For example, perhaps children repeatedly hear their parents make comments in the heat of political debate such as "If Agnew is for 'law and order,' then I must be against it." It is conceivable then that for adults, balanced sets of information, like the P-O-X triads in Sentis and Burnstein's study, may function like Hayes-Roth's over-learned cognitive units.

Taken together, the results of the experiments reported by Sherman and Titus (1982) and Sentis and Burnstein (1979) suggest that schematization or unitization in social cognition does not necessarily promote efficiency of functioning but in fact may impede the quick recognition of single components within the unitized whole.

In the face of these divergent effects, Taylor and Crocker (1981) conclude that schemas probably serve both functions, enabling people to "process some information faster and other information in more depth" (p. 103). Their explanation for the observed discrepancies in processing time centers on possible differences in the nature of the processing elicited by different kinds of information. Applying Schneider and Shiffrin's (1977) distinction between automatic (thus, faster) processing and controlled (slower) processing, Taylor and Crocker (1981) hypothesize that information that is redundant, central, affectively neutral, and/or evaluatively consistent with a schema might undergo faster, automatic processing. Conversely, novel, peripheral, affectively charged, and/or evaluatively inconsistent information might be processed more deeply and more slowly through controlled processing.

In these schema investigations, as well as in scores of others like them, a number of assumptions based on the constructionist perspective have received empirical support. There seems to be little doubt that at least some information is organized at a high level of unity and complexity, that such ways of organizing information are qualitatively different from a mere aggregation of elements, and that schematic thought proceeds from the top down and in combination with perceptual, memorial, inferential, and other processes.

2. Stereotypes

The schema, in the generic sense of the term, is not an entirely new sort of concept for social psychology. In addition to Bartlett's schema, *stereotypes* were another early schema-like construct developed in social psychology. Many years ago, Allport and Postman (1945) demonstrated the working of stereotype-driven cognition, finding that white college students, when passing information through a "communication chain," sometimes mistakenly described a razor as being in the hand of a black man, whereas in the cartoon that was used to initiate the communication chain, the razor had actually been held by a white man.

Classic conceptions of the stereotype concept have emphasized the role of individual and group psychopathology in the formation and maintenance of stereotypes. Other conceptions have focused on the "kernel of truth" hypothesis to account, at least in part, for beliefs about other groups. More recently, the emphasis on "bounded rationality" (biases and human limitations in the capacity for information processing) has suggested that the formation and maintenance of stereotypes may be importantly affected by purely cognitive considerations. The earlier emphasis on the emotional and defensive aspects of stereotyping gave way in the 1960s to a rather sanitized conception of a stereotype as simply a "categorical judgment that is relatively oversimplified and resistant to change" (Jones & Gerard, 1967, p. 140). By 1980 all traces of affect had been removed from most conceptualizations of stereotypes (for an exception, see Brewer, 1979), so that stereotypes came to be defined in cool Bayesian terms as "probabilistic definitions based on group membership" (McCauley, Stitt, & Segal, 1980, pp. 197–198) or as "correlational beliefs" that are subject to "information-processing biases" (Hamilton & Rose, 1980, p. 833). As documented by the title of a recent article by McCauley, Stitt, and Segal (1980), the stereotype concept has over the course of this century undergone a transformation "from prejudice to prediction." This evolution parallels a general thrust in psychology away from motivational or psychodynamic explanations and toward purely cognitive accounts (Dawes, 1976; Nisbett & Ross, 1980).

In the modern sense of the term, stereotypes fit the generic definition of a schema in that they are higher-order gestalts that guide cognitive processing. Taylor and Crocker (1981) include "stereotypic conceptions of social groups like blacks or women" (p. 91) in their class of social role schemas, and Hastie (1981) lists group stereotypes as one kind of schema (p. 60). A third example of the equation of stereotypes and schemas occurs in the theorizing of Linville and E. E. Jones (1980), who refer to prior knowledge about in-groups and out-groups as "cognitive schemas" (p. 691). These authors explain that this definition serves to emphasize the "structural and organizing features" (p. 691) of in-group and out-group stereotypes.

Tajfel was one of the first to highlight the critical importance of the distinction between ingroup and outgroup—the differences we generally see between those who are members of our "own group" as opposed to those who are not. In an influential program of research, he has shown that there is a general and strong tendency to favor "our own" (i.e., to reward them disproportionately, and to perceive them as more virtuous than others), even when the initial in-group-outgroup partition reflects a trivial or arbitrary grouping. For example, in one study (Billig & Tajfel, 1973), subjects were divided into groups on the basis of arbitrarily assigned code numbers. When subsequently asked to divide rewards among the other people in the experiment, subjects discriminated in favor of their "own" group members (the ingroup) at the expense of the outgroup. It is important to note that this form of bias does not simply derive from self-interest, for it has repeatedly been observed in settings in which the reward-allocator cannot affect the outcomes to him- or herself.

While Tajfel's research on categorization has focused on people's tendency to downgrade the outgroup relative to the ingroup, Park and Rothbart (1982) have emphasized the matter of *outgroup homogeneity*. Their basic hypothesis is that while people readily perceive individual variations among the members of their "own group," they believe that the outgroup is rather homogeneous, showing only minor differences from one person to the next. This generalization is forcefully captured in the American folk-wisdom concerning Chinese waiters, who are commonly regarded as "looking alike." In an ingenious series of experiments, Park and Rothbart have demonstrated the ubiquitous character of this type of assumption, which extends to our view of the opposite sex. Thus, men assume that as a group, women are more homogeneous than themselves (they assume that there is limited variability in the personality characteristics of women); women, on the other hand, assume the reverse (i.e., that men are relatively similar to one another).

Linville (1982) and Linville & Jones (1980) have explored a related hypothesis, contending that the outgroup normally seems *less complex* than the ingroup. According to this conception, familiarity with the ingroup leads us to recognize that individual group members may vary from one another in many ways (i.e., with respect to a variety of dimensions), while outgroup members are seen as relatively simple in this regard, varying on relatively few attributes.

One of the clearest examples of the purely cognitive approach to stereotyping may be found in a series of studies by Hamilton and Gifford (1976). These investigators sought to assess the proposition that distinctive (infrequently encountered) features of the social world might naturally seem to "go together," even in situations where such a belief was unwarranted. More particularly, they were concerned with the possibility that minority group members might be thought to engage in atypical behaviors simply because, *by definition*, they shared the property of distinctiveness (infrequency). In one experiment, they had a group of college students read a series of sentences; each sentence described the behavior of a different individual who was identified by first name and by his or her membership in one of two groups (group A or group B). Most sentences concerned the members of group A (the majority group) and described desirable behaviors rather than undesirable ones. Membership in group B and undesirable behaviors were thus relatively "distinctive" by virtue of the infrequency with which they were presented. It is important to note, however, that there was *no relationship* between these two characteristics. That is, in both group A and B, 69% of the group members were described as engaging in desirable behaviors, while 31% were presented as performing undesirable acts. After reading the entire list of sentences, subjects were provided with a list of the behavior descriptions. For each behavior, they were to identify from memory the group membership of the person who had engaged in that behavior.

Results indicated that the average subject had perceived an "illusory correlation" between undesirable behavior and membership in group B, although there was, in fact, no correlation between these variables. Similarly, in describing the two groups on a series of trait scales, the members of group A were rated more favorably than the members of group B. In a follow-up study, Hamilton and Gifford demonstrated the generality of their findings by showing that through a similar cognitive mechanism, the members of the minority group might be remembered as having displayed a disproportionate number of *desirable* behaviors, if desirable acts were infrequently presented in the context of the experiment. Clearly, we may sometimes fail to appreciate an individual's unique personal characteristics because of his or her membership in some group toward which we hold stereotyped beliefs. Misjudgments of this sort are thought to be a regrettable but common consequence of the stereotyping process; in a society like our own, the fairest types of judgments are normally regarded as those in which each person is judged on individual merits.

In contrast to this individually oriented approach, however, Bayes' theorem suggests that when attempting to evaluate an individual, or when predicting someone's behavior (e.g., Is he or is he not likely to attempt suicide?), we will minimize our errors if we take account of the base-rate frequencies that are involved—the relative frequency with which suicide is attempted, in the illustration posed here.

Base-rate information represents a type of stereotypic knowledge, for it consists of aggregate group statistics. According to Bayes' theorem, for example, all other things being equal, an individual who comes from a social group or geographic area where the suicide rate is relatively high should be recognized as having a greater likelihood of making a suicide attempt than a second individual *who has virtually the same psychological makeup* (so far as we can tell), but who comes from a group with a substantially lower suicide rate. Bayes' theorem also tells us that this base-rate component should be weighted in inverse proportion to the goodness (diagnosticity) of the individuating information that is available. If individuating information is perfectly diagnostic (i.e., if the individual's psychological profile is invariably associated with suicide attempts, and is never found among those who are nonsuicidal), then we might safely ignore the base rate for suicide in attempting to predict a particular individual's behavior. However, given the limited diagnosticity of psychological data in virtually every domain (e.g., the limited predictive validity of attitudinal information or of psychological tests), Bayes' theorem suggests that our capacity to make accurate predictions and appraisals will be enhanced through an appropriate blending of individuating data (based on the characteristics of the particular individual in question) and base-rate information (based on knowledge of his or her group and the relative frequency with which they engage in relevant behaviors).

A growing research tradition has sought to evaluate human judgments and decision making by comparing spontaneous impressionistic responses with a "normative" response pattern derived from Bayes' theorem. This work was initiated by W. Edwards and his co-workers (Edwards, Lindman, & Phillips, 1965; Peterson & Beach, 1967), and has recently been imaginatively developed by Kahneman and Tversky (e.g., 1973). Kahneman and Tversky have noted a number of critical discrepancies between naive human judgment and the normative model provided by Bayes' theorem. Most importantly for our present purposes, they have shown that people often appear to be relatively insensitive to base-rate considerations when making decisions under conditions of uncertainty, and are unduly affected by individuating information. This has been explained by reference to the representativeness heuristic—the tendency to base our judgments or predictions about a particular individual on the extent to which he or she resembles our conception of the prototypical case (e.g., the typical suicide attempter), while largely ignoring the frequency of occurrence (base rate) of the behavior in question. Note, however, that Kahneman and Tversky's contention here seems in direct contradiction to the widespread belief that human judgments are often unduly affected by stereotypes, based on the judge's expectations and beliefs concerning the individual's *group*.

Kahneman and Tversky's ideas concerning the relative importance of base-rate vs. individuating information have stimulated a great deal of interesting research, but the results have been rather diverse (e.g., Ajzen, 1977; Bar-Hillel & Fischhoff, 1981; Manis, Avis, & Cardoze, 1981; Manis, Dovalina, Avis, & Cardoze, 1980; McCauley & Stitt, 1978; Nisbett & Borgida, 1975; Wells & Harvey, 1978). Nonetheless, a number of conclusions seem warranted:

1. Despite occasional studies in which base-rate information is virtually ignored (e.g., Nisbett & Borgida, 1975), there is ample evidence that the average person can and does respond to base-rate data in making many social judgments. Indeed, the base-rate effect appears to be a fairly robust phenomenon that often results from automatic or unintentional cognitive processes (Manis *et al.*, 1981).

2. Base-rate information is particularly influential when it is causally related to the predictive judgment at hand (Ajzen, 1977), but causal linkage is not *essential* in the demonstration of base-rate effects.

3. Although base-rate data frequently affect people's social judgments, this type of information is not as influential as it "should be" when compared with a Bayesian standard. This is not necessarily the result of a grave cognitive deficiency, however, for there is a substantial body of information that indicates that subjective probability judgments are also insufficiently influenced by individuating information. Edwards and his colleagues (Edwards, Lindman, & Phillips, 1965) have shown that people's judgments are often quite conservative, in that they are reluctant to take sufficient account of accumulated "case data" when forming a probabilistic opinion.

It is possible that these seemingly contrasting phenomena—people's conservatism with respect to case data and their relative insensitivity to base-rate information—may both derive from common methodological weaknesses in this area (e.g., from respondents' reluctance to use extreme rating categories, despite supporting base-rate or individuating information). In cases in which base-rate information is underutilized, it may be at least partially due to the base-rate data's being hidden in a forest of other information that appears to the respondent more compelling for the decision at hand. In other cases, it is possible that base rates are ignored because respondents may feel that they are violating the experimenter's implicit demands if, instead of proceeding to decode individuating cues "intuitively," they base their predictions on "colder" statistical considerations. As it stands, the conflict between older conceptions that stress the problems deriving from stereotyping, and the newer literature that focuses on logical deficiencies deriving from the underutilization of base-rate data, awaits further clarification (but see McCauley & Stitt, 1978).

Although some social cognition theorists equate stereotypes and schemas, the two concepts are of course not synonymous. Like others have done, we have represented stereotypes as a sub-class within the general schema category. However, some features of stereotypes that differentiate them from schemas are these:

1. stereotypes refer to persons as members of a group;
2. stereotypes undoubtedly include a greater degree of affective and/or motivational involvement than other kinds of schemas; and
3. stereotypes embody the importance of the social constitution of private thought even more directly than do other post-Bartlett schema concepts. As Husserl phrased it, "all prejudices are obscurities arising out of a sedimentation of tradition" (1954/1970, p. 72).

3. Scripts

Unlike the stereotype, the *script* is a schema-like construct that is novel for social psychology. The script concept grew out of artificial intelligence work in which attempts to model the human process of story comprehension by computers brought to the fore the need for more complex, more dynamic and less "rationalistic" cognitive units (Abelson, 1976).

A script is defined as a "coherent sequence of events expected by the individual, involving him either as a participant or as an observer" (Abelson, 1976, p. 33). For example, there is a script, or set of shared expectations, for wedding ceremonies in Western societies. A little-used script track for the wedding ceremony of royalty includes colorful variants on the prototypical script, like trips to and from a cathedral in horse-drawn glass coaches, having the Archbishop of Canterbury officiate, and making the promise to share the wealth of an honest-to-goodness kingdom.

Research on scripts carried out by Graesser and his colleagues suggests that information that faithfully reflects a familiar organizing scenario may be represented by a combination of a "pointer" plus a "tag" (or correction which reflects irregularities or atypical aspects of the material to be remembered) (Graesser, Gordon, & Sawyer, 1979; Graesser, Woll, Kowalski, & Smith, 1980; Smith & Graesser, 1981). For example, typical elements in a restaurant script might include the patron's being seated by a hostess and ordering a meal; the fact that the waiter speaks with a Polish accent and has piercing eyes would constitute atypical elements with respect to the restaurant script. Several experiments indicate that in recall tests administered after relatively brief retention intervals (e.g., 30 minutes), atypical or unscripted actions are better recalled than typical ones, a pattern that is reminiscent of the results of studies by Srull (1981) and by Hastie & Kumar (1979), using a very different methodology. Graesser's research also shows differential forgetting; after a 1-week retention interval, typical script actions are better recalled than atypical acts.

Like schemas, scripts are hypothetical knowledge structures. Indeed, both Abelson and Graesser consider a script to be a type of schema; Taylor and Crocker (1981) classify scripts as a type of event schema; and Hastie (1981) includes the script in his category of linguistic schemas. Like schemas, a script interrelates the particular and the general, since in it, concrete events are organized by context into generic scenarios. And like schemas, scripts influence cognitive activities, functioning, for example, as a "bundle of expectations" (Abelson, 1981, p. 6), or as a "cognitive structure which when activated organizes comprehension of event-based situations" (p. 8). In accordance with Fiske and Linville's (1980) and Hastie's (1981) conceptualizations of schemas (and unlike that of Taylor and Crocker, 1981), scripts are postulated to be at least potentially affective in nature. For example, Abelson (1981) entertains the possibility of tantrum scripts and of a meta-script of "rage against authority" (p. 727).

A final way in which the script concept parallels the schema notion is in its postulation of an internal hierarchical structure with levels of abstraction ranging from the level of particular attributes, instances, or actions through the intermediate level to the most abstract level. Abelson (1976) classifies scripts into three types or stages of development. An *episodic* script is a single, specific vignette; *categorical* scripts are ensembles of related concrete vignettes; and *hypothetical* scripts are generalized event groups in which critical features of a situation have been abstracted. According to Abelson, the schema concept is most closely allied with the class of categorical scripts, in that they are based on actual concrete events grouped to maximize internal similarity and external distinctiveness. (From a very different perspective, T. Adorno, a theorist of the hermeneutic approach to social psychology, concurs with Abelson's emphasis on the categorical level of abstraction, as opposed to the hypothetical level. Adorno [1978b] asserts that social and physical "laws" operate "only in the particular" [p. 461].)

Schemas and scripts share a number of important elements. However, they also differ. Temporal order is an element of scripts usually missing from schemas and stereotypes; indeed, in the "strong" form of scripts, order is an invariant part of the script itself (Abelson, 1981). Scripts have also been more directly linked with behavior than is true of many schema conceptualizations. According to Abelson (1981), a person may choose to become a participant in scripted behavior under three conditions: the person possesses a cognitive understanding of the script, the evoking context is present, and an "action rule" is satisfied. Thus a couple may choose to enter a wedding ceremony script if they themselves have observed wedding ceremonies, if they plan to get married anyway, and if they wish to have a communal celebration of their marriage. Unless the action rule is satisfied that requires royal birth of at least one of the marriage partners, the *royal wedding* script will not be a behavioral option for a given couple.

If a script is not exactly a schema, for our present purposes it is even more pertinent to note that a script is not a propositional network. For one of Abelson's goals in developing the script idea was to challenge the associative network models of cognition, which he characterizes as preoccupied with "formal operations on abstract materials.'' By contrast, script theory is focally concerned with the ''concrete processing of episodic and situational material'' (1976, p. 36). Also in comparison with what Abelson refers to as the ''overly elementaristic'' (p. 33), ''noncommittal, formal, surface-oriented, and contextless'' (p. 36) assumptions of associative network models, script processing is hypothesized to be more complex, non-rationalistic, informal, elaborated, and embedded in a real-world context.

4. Prototypes

A third type of abstract knowledge structure that has begun to receive theoretical and empirical attention in social psychology is the *prototype,* a concept that found its way from cognitive psychology to personality and social psychology. Like schemas and scripts, prototypes are thought to be higher-order cognitive structures that represent and interrelate information at general and specific levels, and that influence cognitive processing. Prototypes are a kind of category that express the central tendency (Hastie, 1981) or ''core consistencies'' (Cantor & Mischel, 1979, p. 31) of a class.

Hofstadter refers to a ''prototype principle,'' whereby ''the most specific event [or instance, etc.] can serve as a general example of a class'' (1979, p. 352). Indeed, as Hofstadter notes, the power to generalize is a distinctly human ability: ''Our facility for making instances out of classes and classes out of instances lies at the basis of our intelligence, and it is one of the great differences between human thought and the thought processes of other animals'' (1979, p. 360).

Current thinking about the psychology of classification systems has been importantly influenced by Rosch's work on prototypes. Earlier work on conceptual categories had emphasized the role of critical cues that served to demarcate the instances (exemplars) in one category from those in another. Studies in this tradition normally used *arbitrarily* defined conceptual categories. In a typical study, respondents might be informed that their task was to place each of a series of wooden blocks into one of two categories that might be labeled DAK and VEC. The blocks would vary in shape, size, and color. The experimental session might proceed as follows: blocks would be presented one at a time, and the subject would attempt to label each one appropriately (DAK or VEC). The experimenter would reinforce the subject when his or her response conformed to some preselected rule—for example, red blocks=DAK; other blocks=VEC.

Following Hull's lead (1920), the conceptual categories that were studied in this fashion were typically organized in a *conjunctive* fashion in that all the exemplars of a given conceptual category shared a single common attribute (e.g., all red blocks) or several common attributes (e.g., all large red blocks). Researchers focused on such questions as the speed with which various category systems could be learned, and on the consequences of such concept learning for the acquisition of other category systems (i.e., transfer of training).

Rosch and her colleagues (Rosch & Lloyd, 1978; Mervis & Rosch, 1981) have approached the study of conceptual categories from a very different point of view, emphasizing real-world categories (e.g., furniture, musical instruments, etc.) in contrast to the arbitrarily defined "artificial" concepts that had previously been studied so intensively. This shift reflects Rosch's belief that conceptual categories derive, at least in part, from objective characteristics of the outside world, rather than reflecting arbitrary labeling rules that have developed through historical and cultural happenstance.

A related contrast between Rosch's work and that of her predecessors revolves about the sorts of stimuli used in their respective investigations. Most earlier studies involved exemplars that were constructed through a carefully chosen combination of *orthogonal* stimulus dimensions. For example, if a respondent was presented with a series of blocks which were to be classified into two or more categories, the colors, shapes, and sizes of the different exemplars were typically *unrelated* (e.g., there were just as many red squares as green ones).

Rosch notes, however, that the real world does not present us with this sort of orthogonal universe. Instead, stimulus sets often reveal a clear, correlational structure. For example, while it is readily apparent that the animal kingdom involves both two- and four-legged creatures, as well as some species with feathers (and others without), these two dimensions are highly correlated, in that there do not appear to be any feathered quadrupeds. Hence the category of feathered bipeds emerges as a sort of special "node" that demands attention and is ultimately recognized in our language (and other languages) as a separate conceptual category. Rosch and her colleagues contend that structured constellations like this may importantly affect our "natural" system of categories.[6]

Rosch's work also contrasts with earlier investigations of the categorization

----

[6]This emphasis on the nonarbitrary, environmental determination of conceptual categories is consonant with recent developments in the study of color systems. Anthropologists had previously regarded the color spectrum as a relatively undifferentiated continuum that was divided (by different cultural groups) into discrete color categories (e.g., red, blue, green, etc.). The emphasis in this earlier tradition was on the arbitrary placement of these conceptual boundaries, and on the resulting differences between groups in the color-regions for which they had explicit names. More recently, however, there has been a rethinking of this question, for several researchers have reported an unexpected degree of convergence between the labeling systems which different cultural groups apply to the color continuum (Berlin & Kay, 1969). This reevaluation has been derived in large part by a recognition that intergroup comparisons can be made most effectively between cultures that operate with color systems of *similar complexity* (i.e., involving the same number of color categories). In brief, more recent studies indicate a heretofore undiscovered convergence between cultures in the placement of color boundaries.

process on the matter of *criteriality*. As noted above, previous studies typically involved clearcut cues that were usually unequivocal indicators of category membership: e.g., the blocks in the DAK category might all be red, while none of the VEC blocks were red. Rosch, however, has emphasized the idea that many important conceptual categories cannot be defined in this clearcut fashion. What, for example, are the defining characteristics of *chairs* (as opposed to couches, benches, stools, etc.)? Rosch argues that it is often impossible to reach explicit agreement on issues like this. Consider a more complex example from the realm of social relations—the concept of *fairness*. What are the criteria we employ in judging whether or not a given act constitutes an example of fairness? Instead of looking for critical (necessary) features that unequivocally define the boundaries of such complex concepts, Rosch's analysis suggests that a more fruitful approach might be to recognize the essential "fuzziness" of many categories in which the constituent exemplars share only a "family resemblance." In this view, conceptual categories are often organized around *prototypes,* typical or highly representative cases of a general class which the perceiver uses to structure the world.

Besides positing a horizontal dimension to categorization (i.e., exemplars may be more or less prototypical members of a category), Rosch and her colleagues also hypothesize that categorization can occur at any one of three vertical levels of inclusiveness or abstraction, ranging from the most abstract *superordinate* level through the intermediate *basic* level to the most concrete or *subordinate* level. Examples of each of these vertical levels are musical instrument (superordinate level), cello (basic level), and quarter-size Japanese cello (subordinate level). Rosch has found that in everyday categorizing, people tend to find the basic level most useful, because of its particular combination of specificity and generality.

In the 1979 edition of this volume, Cantor and Mischel report a series of investigations designed to test the generality of Rosch's theory in the domain of social cognition. Operationally, a person prototype is derived by asking subjects to describe the attributes of a "good example" of a class of persons, such as the class of extraverts or cultured people. Cantor and Mischel (1979) found that person categories are organized around prototypical exemplars; prototypicality can be reliably rated; prototypes are characterized by richness of description as well as by distinctiveness from similar prototypes; and degree of prototypicality influences the ease with which information is processed. In general, they conclude that prototype principles that operate in the realm of nonsocial categories can be extended to the social domain.

In addition to the work of Cantor and Mischel, Brewer's work has helped to establish the importance of prototypes in social cognition. Brewer and her associates (Brewer, Dull, & Lui, 1981) observed that people sort photographs of elderly persons into groups that correspond closely to a priori prototypes of "grandmotherly type," "elder statesman," and "senior citizen." The category "elderly person" seems to function like Rosch's superordinate level category, which is subdivisible into basic level categories like "elder statesman." In other words, people seem to organize their thoughts about the elderly into prototypelike packages.

Brewer, Dull, and Lui (1981) also demonstrated that social prototypes have processing implications. In one study in their set, college-age subjects were exposed to slides of photographs of young and old persons. Within the set of photos of elderly persons, some had been previously categorized as grandmotherly types and others as senior citizen types. While each slide was presented, subjects also read behavior statements which were presented one at a time— e.g., fusses over children, likes to give advice. Subjects were asked to try to form an impression of the person depicted on the slide, using the available behavioral information. After engaging in a 5-minute distractor task, these subjects were given an unexpected recall test in which they were shown each slide and were asked to write down as many of the behavior statements as they could remember. The subjects correctly recalled more information about the young stimulus persons than about the elderly persons. Furthermore, the pattern of incorrect recall or intrusions was prototype-based. Most of the intrusions were for the elderly stimulus persons and most were prototype-consistent (i.e., consistent with the stimulus person's appearance). These results indicate that when people cannot remember a specific piece of information about a member of a group, they tend to fill in the missing information with stereotype- or prototype-consistent default values.

How then does the prototype concept compare with the other higher-order cognitive modules we have discussed? Taylor and Crocker (1981) and Hastie (1981) assert that the prototype concept is similar to and compatible with the notion of schemas. Taylor and Crocker point out the similarity in hierarchical structuring: in person prototypes, traits (e.g., extraversion, intelligence) occupy the highest levels of abstraction, while specific behaviors or specific attributes occupy the lower levels. Like Taylor and Crocker's (1981) and like Fiske and Linville's (1980) conceptions of schemas, and unlike Hastie's (1981) schema notion, prototypes are of necessity content-specific.

There is also a direct parallel between the prototype and the script concepts. Abelson (1981) asserts that a prototypical script is one that possesses "more of the most commonly experienced events" (p. 33), just as a prototypical depressive, for example, embodies more of the common attributes and behaviors of depression. Abelson hypothesizes that the degree of prototypicality of scripts, like that of other cognitive units, can be reliably rated. Script prototypicality produces prototypicality effects like the "gap-filling" phenomenon in which people mistakenly "recognize" elements of a script that are expected but that were not actually presented or experienced. Indeed, as Mervis and Rosch (1981) note, Abelson's computer model "treat[s] categories and categorization processes as inseparable from world knowledge and the inference processes used in such knowledge" (p. 104).

Cohen (1981) has brought the prototype and the stereotype concepts into direct contact with one another, using the terms "person categories" and "occupational stereotypes" synonymously. Similarly, in their discussion of stereotyping, Jones and Gerard (1967) identify a possible functional similarity between the stereotype and the prototype: "Assimilation to the *typical* instance should be especially marked when the object being judged is highly complex and there is uncertainty regarding many of its attributes" (p. 140, emphasis added). Of course, persons—even if members of an "outgroup"—are highly complex objects of judgment. Thus the evaluation of outgroup members tends to remain anchored near the middle of the distribution (i.e., the typical instance, or prototype) and to lack variability and complexity (Linville, 1982; Linville & Jones, 1980; Park & Rothbart, 1982). However, although the prototype and the stereotype constructs share certain features, the prototype concept seems to lack the affective charge of the stereotype.

C.   CONVERGENCE OF ASSOCIATIONISM
AND CONSTRUCTIONISM IN SOCIAL COGNITION

Despite their antagonistic beginnings earlier in the twentieth century, the tenets of associationism and constructionism have been merging in the latter half of the twentieth century. As we have seen in earlier sections of this chapter, this state of affairs began in cognitive psychology (e.g., Anderson, 1976, 1980; Hayes-Roth, 1977; Smith, 1980) and is now being carried on in social cognition research. A set of experiments reported by B. H. Ross and G. H. Bower (1981) exemplifies this type of merger within the area of cognitive psychology. Ross and Bower differentiated a schema model from an associationist model, specified each in mathematical terms, and tested one against the other in a series of three experiments. The results of these experiments suggest that even when differential predictions of associationism and schema theory are quantitatively spelled out, the data often fail to distinguish the two models.

Similarly, there are a number of cases of social cognition research that do not fit neatly into either the associationist or the constructionist camp but employ the language and constructs of both approaches. For example, S. Bem (1981) and H. Markus et al. (1982) merge associationist and schema language in their respective formulations concerning gender schemas. Both sets of investigators use the BSRI as a basis for selecting groups of persons thought to differ in their sex-typing (Bem), or gender-related self-schemas (Markus et al). Both find evidence of gender-related schematic processing. And what is most pertinent to our concern with theory is the fact that both researchers wed associationist and schema constructs in their theoretical explanations. According to Markus and her colleagues (1982), a gender schema may be conceived as a "network of knowledge relevant to masculinity or femininity" (p. 39). Likewise, Bem's (1981) gender schema is a "substantive network of sex-related associations" (p. 362). With regard to process, Bem hypothesizes that gender schemas produce a "generalized readiness to process information on the basis of the sex-linked associations that constitute the gender schema" (p. 355).

Research by Gilovich (1981) is also illustrative of the way associationist and constructionist approaches have converged in the area called social cognition. In this research Gilovich was investigating the manner in which associations influence social and political judgments. In one of these experiments the associations of interest were those elicited by descriptions of hypothetical college football players. The player profiles were varied in content to be more or less similar to that of an illustrious pro player by way of similarity in position played, college attended, award given, or home town. Gilovich found that when sportswriters were asked to rate the pro potential of these hypothetical football players, the players who were associated most closely (though irrelevantly) with a professional player were rated higher than players whose associated characteristics were less similar to those of a pro.

In another experiment, Gilovich (1981) found evidence for the influence of historical associations on foreign policy decisions. Undergraduates in a political science–international relations class read one of three versions of a hypothetical foreign-policy crisis. In one version a World War II/Munich script was suggested via information irrelevant to the decision (the invasion was called a "blitzkrieg," the U.S. President was from New York state). In one scenario a Viet Nam script was suggested (the invasion was called a "quickstrike," the U.S. President was from Texas). And in a third version, no analogy was suggested (neutral terms were used). Subjects were asked whether the U.S. should keep hands off or should intervene, and were also asked how similar the situations were to Viet Nam or to World War II/Munich. Subjects who read the description containing World War II associations made more interventionist recommendations than subjects who read the Viet Nam script or the neutral scenario. Interestingly, after the experiment subjects either were not aware of or denied that the descriptions bore any similarity to Viet Nam or Munich.

In explaining these results, Gilovich blends associationist and constructionist language and perspectives. First of all, the title of Gilovich's (1981) article is strongly associationist: "Seeing the past in the present: The effect of associations to familiar events on judgments and decisions." Secondly, the author concludes that "judgments about individuals are made by associating the person in question with others with whom one is more familiar" (p. 806). On the other hand, Gilovich's account calls upon constructionist notions—for example,

"The present research is consistent with recent work on the schematic bases of social information processing" (p. 807). Elsewhere in the report the constructionist approach is even more strongly endorsed: "The schematic viewpoint is nearly identical to the one presented here" (p. 807). Finally, the convergence is unmistakeable in this statement: "associations are formed or schemas are activated" (p. 807).

As Gilovich points out, the schematic approach has the advantage of being better able to account for the fact that subjects went beyond the data given when they concluded that two persons or situations similar in one way must be similar in other ways. Schema theory accounts for this by hypothesizing all-or-none retrieval of a schema with the filling in of unknown information by means of default values. However, this advantage for schema theory over associationist accounts disappears when the concept of spreading activation is considered. Associationists account for the same phenomena in terms of activation spreading from one concept to similar ones. Still, the fact remains that Gilovich melds the formerly antagonistic associationist and schematic principles in a single theoretical rationale.

In addition to these investigations concerning gender self-schemas and the role of historical or sports associations in social judgment and decision making, other phenomena have been addressed by the combined application of associationist and constructionist principles. For example, the following questions have sparked a good deal of research interest: (1) whether people better remember schema-consistent or schema-inconsistent information and (2) how people combine pieces of information about another person to form a unitary impression of that person.

1. Associative Schemas in Person Impressions and Memory

The title of a controversial set of studies reported by Hastie and Kumar (1979) suggests a unitization or top-down approach to person memory: "Person memory: Personality traits as organizing principles in memory for behaviors." However, in their report of this research, Hastie and Kumar's primary emphasis is on an associative network model in conjunction with depth-of-processing conceptions.

Hastie and Kumar (1979) reported three experiments designed to examine the recall of information that is either consistent or inconsistent with an original impression about the personality characteristics of another individual. First, subjects read aloud eight trait adjectives, all of which were synonymous with a single personality trait—for example, intelligent, or honest, or friendly. By this means an expectancy (or schema) was induced in subjects regarding a personality characteristic of the target individual. Next, subjects studied a number of items

(14 to 20, varying with experiment) of behavioral information about the target person. The proportion of behavioral information that was consistent, inconsistent, or neutral with respect to the expectancy was varied across conditions. Subjects were told to form an impression of the individual and also to remember the information. On free recall tests subjects remembered a larger proportion of the behavioral descriptions that were inconsistent than consistent with the initial trait expectancy. This effect was found in all three experiments and was influenced by the size of the set of incongruent items—the smaller the incongruent set, the greater the probability of recalling items from that set. Contrary to expectations derived from a schema model, there was no tendency for subjects to cluster their free recall of behaviors by trait-relevant categories (congruent, incongruent, neutral).

The Hastie and Kumar (1979) research has proved controversial for a number of reasons. First, the results are not what early schema theories would seem to predict. Although Bartlett (1932) did not specifically discuss memory for schema-*inconsistent* information, he did note that unfamiliar and/or seemingly trivial details are sometimes well remembered, and he explained this by surmising that "the familiar is readily accepted; the unfamiliar may hold us" (p. 19) and "the trivial is in fact often striking, and . . . as such it is likely to be retained" (p. 90). However, Bartlett's emphasis on the assimilation of incoming information to pre-existing schemas suggests that there might be a memory advantage for schema-consistent information. And in fact, other investigators of social cognition have found better recall or recognition of expectancy-consistent information (e.g., Cantor & Mischel, 1979; Cohen, 1981; Rothbart, Evans, & Fulero, 1979; Synder & Uranowitz, 1978).[7]

Hastie and Kumar's failure to find recall clustered in schema-relevant (trait) categories is also not what many schema theories would predict, although again Bartlett himself did not specify such a prediction.

Although these two sets of results are not supportive of earlier schema models, Hastie and Kumar assert that the data are compatible with an associative network model in which memory is thought to be organized as a network of associative links and idea nodes, with trait labels serving as intermediate level nodes subsuming behaviors at lower levels. For example, the trait concept "hon-

---

[7]Rothbart (personal communication, 1982) has suggested that some of the apparent inconsistency here may derive from the fact that respondents in the Hastie and Kumar research were provided with information that presumably pertained to a *single individual*. Under these circumstances inconsistent information might be especially jarring, and there might well be a concerted effort to integrate the unexpected elements with the respondent's prior expectations (i.e., deeper processing). Rothbart's research, by contrast, had as its target a group of *different individuals*, some of whom did not act in accordance with the group stereotype provided by the experimenter. Under these circumstances, nonfitting elements might be less eye catching, for most people are well aware that individuals may deviate from the behavior patterns that are common in their group. Srull's results (1981, see Table 2) are in general accord with this analysis.

est'' would be linked with instances of honest behaviors. Hastie and Kumar posit the usual associative processing assumptions of a blind and probabilistic search beginning at the highest level (in this case, at a trait node) and proceeding down until a remembered behavior node is reached, at which point the search starts over at a trait node.

However, as Hastie and Kumar note, their data are not entirely congruent with an associative network model. As we have discussed, neo-associative models predict a set-size effect, so that the smaller the number of items (e.g., behaviors) connected with a concept (e.g., trait label) the greater the probability of recognizing any single item (behavior). Although this effect did occur for the sets of incongruent items, there was no set-size effect for congruent items in any of the three experiments reported by Hastie and Kumar. It is possible that this deviation from the usual fan effect may be explained in terms of task characteristics. Hastie and Kumar's subjects were engaging in a free recall task rather than the recognition or identification task employed in studies yielding the fan effect. Consequently, the associationist account was not directly tested by Hastie and Kumar's set of experiments, at least with respect to the fan effect.

Hastie and Kumar's data fail to support associative network predictions in another way. Though the model predicts equal recall of congruent and incongruent items when set sizes are equal, in experiments 2 and 3 incongruent items were recalled better than congruent items, given equal set sizes.

Because of these failures of their data to conform to a simple associative model, Hastie and Kumar (1979) add depth-of-processing concepts to help explain their results. The depth-of-processing model (Craik & Lockhart, 1972) posits deeper processing at encoding for more distinctive information, with more deeply processed information being less susceptible to forgetting and more easily retrieved (by the usual network processing and search principles). As applied to Hastie and Kumar's experimental task, the depth-of-processing model would predict that distinctive (incongruent) behaviors would be more informative and thus would be processed more deeply than congruent or neutral items. Hence, the differences in recall found by Hastie and Kumar are just what depth-of-processing models would expect.

Hastie and Kumar's set-size effects are also explicable in depth-of-processing terms. The smaller the set, the more distinctive the items and thus the better the recall. By this reasoning, the incongruent items in a small set should have a double memorial advantage, being both qualitatively and quantitatively distinctive. As we have seen, there was just such a set-size effect for the incongruent items (and not for congruent items).

In their theoretical account of person memory, Hastie and Kumar (1979) were thus among the first social cognition researchers to reject schematic concepts in favor of associative ones. In the end they opt for a hybrid theory that favors depth-of-processing principles of encoding and associative principles of retrieval, and discounts schematic processing principles.

However, Hastie did not abandon schematic assumptions altogether. In a later chapter (1981) entitled "Schematic Principles in Human Memory," he weds associationist and schematic principles in an effort to explain results such as Hastie and Kumar's, as well as opposing results (better memory for schema-congruent than for schema-incongruent information). It is important to note, however, that Hastie's very definition of a schema incorporates both kinds of constructs: "the critical features of the concept of a schema are that it is an abstract, general structure that establishes relations between specific events or entities" (p. 41). More specifically, Hastie posits three possible approaches, all of which integrate associationist and schematic constructs: (1) *different types of links* for schema-congruent and schema-incongruent information; (2) different *numbers of links* for the two cases (e.g., greater number of links for important and unexpected events than for expected events); (3) different overall *configurations* of associations for the two types of information (e.g., an anomalous event linked with a less crowded schema complex). Here, Hastie has explicitly attempted to join associationist and schema principles, so that schemas may themselves be linked with other schemas, or may be embedded in other schemas or in larger associative networks. Hastie concludes that schemas are "necessary in any perceptual act" (p. 44), and indeed that "despite valiant efforts to preserve the associationist position (e.g., Anderson & Bower, 1973), there seems to be an emerging consensus that schematic principles are necessary to provide economical accounts for inference and memory task performances" (p. 53).

Srull (1981) has also recently explored the question of whether memory for persons operates according to neo-associationist principles or schematic principles. Srull predicted better free recall for information that is incongruent with an initial expectancy than for information that is expectancy-congruent. This prediction follows Hastie's associationist–depth-of-processing rationale (Hastie & Kumar, 1979; Hastie, 1980) in that incongruent items, because unexpected, are assumed to require a greater depth of processing than congruent items. This deeper processing is thought to result in the formation of a greater number of associative paths linking incongruent items to the initial person node and to one another; in free recall the greater the number of associative paths available to be retraced, the higher the probability of retrieving the information. Srull added to this account predictions concerning recognition that differ from those for recall— that is, he predicted no difference in recognition of congruent versus incongruent information. Srull's reasoning is that the recognition process may bypass the retrieval process in which associative pathways are searched in free recall. Srull (1981) tested these predictions in a series of four experiments which used the following general procedures.

Subjects were first told that an individual (or group) was more friendly–sociable (or unfriendly–unsociable) than average. Srull told some subjects to form an impression of the target and told others to try to remember the information that was to be presented about the target. Subjects then read a list composed of 30 behavior statements that were congruent, incongruent, or irrelevant with respect to the initial expectancy. The proportion of each of these three types of statement was varied across lists. Subjects' free recall of the behavior statements was measured either immediately after reading the list or 48 hours later. After a 12-minute interpolated distractor task, subjects then rated the confidence with which they recognized 30 old and 30 new ("lure") items.

In Srull's (1981) experiments a greater proportion of incongruent than congruent items was recalled; that is, behavior descriptions were recalled best if they conflicted with subjects' expectations. However, when subjects were compelled to engage in a task designed to prevent the formation of interitem associative links for incongruent items, the superior memory for incongruent items disappeared. There was, moreover, no difference in the confidence with which congruent and incongruent items were recognized. Other results showed that there was no significant degree of clustering; that is, items were *not* recalled in thematically related groups. Finally, recall was better under the impression set than under the memory set, a result that is congruent with a schema model and with other findings (Hamilton, Katz, & Leirer, 1980; Hamilton, 1981) and inconsistent with purely associative predictions (Wyer & Gordon, 1982).

Although these results do not consistently support any single theory, overall they seem to agree more with Hastie's (Hastie & Kumar, 1979; Hastie, 1980) eclectic theory than with either a neo-associative theory like HAM or a pure schema theory. Of course, the whole concept of congruence-with-initial-expectancy is itself more readily handled in a top-down constructionist framework, but schema theories have not precisely specified the role of schema-congruence in memory. Srull calls upon Hastie's associationist/depth-of-processing theory, which accurately predicts better free recall of incongruent than congruent information. The fact that engaging in a distractor task elminated subjects' superior memory for incongruent information further supports the hypothesis that associative linking was an essential mechanism underlying the original effect. The lack of significant clustering of free recall by congruence or relevance is also a result that more closely meets associationist predictions than schema predictions, since clustering is usually thought to indicate unitization or the operation of an organizing schema. However, the finding of better free recall with instructions to form an impression than in memory set conditions is usually explained in schema terms.

2. Themes as Associative Networks in Impression Formation and Memory

Another set of investigations that weds associationist and schematic constructs is the research reported by Ostrom, Lingle, Pryor, and Geva (1980) in the area of impression formation. These investigators call upon a largely associationist framework in attempting to answer questions about how people combine cognitive elements representing information about another person into a unitary impression. Indeed, the framing of this question itself presupposes the elementarist assumption that "a person impression is composed of a heterogeneous collection of elements" (Ostrom et al., 1980, p. 56). The theoretical response adopted by these investigators relies on concepts and principles of associative network theory, particularly the concept of nodal grouping of person features according to principles of interelement association. As in the theory of Collins and Loftus (1975), the process of person impression is construed as a process of activation spreading from node to node by way of pathways.

Ostrom and his colleagues conceive of person impressions as built up from an orderly interconnection of the cognitive elements they call person nodes and theme nodes. A person node is a higher-order center of associations concerning a target person. Similarly, a theme node is a central organizing metafeatural node connected both to its superordinate person node and to "a large percentage of the other feature nodes by relatively short pathways" (Ostrom et al., 1980, p. 62). To borrow an example from the work of Ostrom and his coauthors, a "belligerent" theme might develop that would unite a number of similar behaviors. Since a theme node is connected to a person node, activation of the person node spreads to the theme node together with the theme's component feature nodes. The notion of theme nodes may perhaps best be likened to Anderson's (1980) schema in that it is a higher-order cognitive unit composed of sets of interrelated propositions. Moreover, the theme nodes concept of Ostrom et al. recapitulates Anderson's assertion that thematic relatedness facilitates the bringing into correspondence of old and new information.

One of the special contributions to theory made by Ostrom et al. is their specification of various possible ways in which higher-order cognitive structures may be acquired. (The difficult subject of schema acquisition is also addressed by Eccles and her colleagues [e.g., Eccles, 1981; Parsons & Ruble, 1977].) Ostrom, Lingle, Pryor, and Geva (1980) outline three modes of development of a theme node. First, a theme may be based on specific instances, events, behaviors, or items of information about a target person. Alternatively, a theme node may be more actively produced by the perceiver out of two sorts of generalized cognitive activity. In one case a theme is itself based on an abstraction that has developed routinely out of repeated activation of a particular feature node along with its associated person node. In the final case, Ostrom et al. have a theme node forming as a result of judgments, decisions, or inferences actively produced by the perceiver. In their own investigations Ostrom and his collaborators focus on the role of the first, stimulus-based themes, and the third, inference-based themes.

How do themes affect memory? This question was addressed in a series of studies reported by Ostrom, Lingle, Pryor, and Geva (1980). In these investigations, subjects first read a list of 8–11 traits about a hypothetical target person. Then subjects were asked to make a judgment about the target person's proficiency at some activity or occupation, an operationalization of the concept of an inference-based theme representing the suggested occupation or activity. The traits had been selected on the basis of pretesting so that half of them were relevant to the occupation theme and half were not relevant. After a delay of varying duration, subjects' recognition or recall for theme-relevant versus theme-irrelevant traits was tested. The prediction was that the act of making the judgment about the person would result in the formation of a theme node around which the previously presented traits would be associated and remembered, with theme-relevant traits being remembered better than theme-irrelevant features upon later reactivation of the theme node.

Results of two memory studies performed by Lingle, Geva, Ostrom, Leippe, and Baumgardner (1979) support the prediction. Subjects did recognize and recall more theme-relevant than theme-irrelevant traits. Duration of delay did not, however, have the predicted effect of increasing the discrepancy between memory for relevant and irrelevant information. The fact that 96–97% of subjects showed perfect or nearly perfect recall of their prior occupational inferences suggests that, as the authors theorize, the subjects' memory may have been organized around the inference-based theme rather than according to the specific trait items themselves.

Themes do seem to affect memory. The question is how. Do themes influence people's subsequent search for remembered *facts* relevant to the theme, or do people rely on the remembered *theme* itself when making later judgments or decisions? In a series of decision-time studies Lingle and Ostrom (1979) explored this question. Their results lend support to the memory-for-themes model, since (1) subjects took longer to make a second dissimilar (theme-irrelevant) judgment than to make a second theme-relevant judgment and (2) no fan effect was found, indicating that subjects were not dependent on searching through individual trait items when they made the second decision, but used their memory for their first (unitized) judgment instead.

As Ostrom *et al.* note, however, this is not to say that people *never* use their memory for specific facts when making judgments about other people. Lingle (1978, cited in Ostrom *et al.*, 1980) found that when people knew they would be asked to justify or explain their inferences, they were able to retrieve the original specific stimulus traits on which the inferences were based. People's cognitive strategies thus seem to depend on their goals. They may fall back on their own inferences when this method is sufficient to meet a particular goal, for example, merely to identify a stimulus. But they can also keep in mind the original evidence for their inferences when they expect to have to justify a later judgment.

Ostrom *et al.* (1980) employ a generalized associative network model as a working theory to account for a variety of social cognition phenomena, specifically the formation and use of personality impressions. However, in some ways their theory is not entirely compatible with associationist approaches. Structurally, themes are higher-order units that seem to take on properties that differ from those of other aggregations of cognitive elements. According to these authors, person impressions "have a unity and coherence which distinguishes them from other cognitive arrays" (p. 55). Indeed, a person impression comes to function in their formulation as a gestalt or a "meaningful whole" (p. 56).

It is also difficult to construe the process of forming and using themes in the more passive, mechanistic, and atomistic terms of the associative network models. Insofar as themes are actively constructed, they begin to look less associationist and more constructionist. Finally, in that higher cognitive processes are construed to be interdependent on lower cognitive processes, the approach is more constructionist than associationist. Once again, in the study of social cognition we find the merging of associationist and constructionist explanations.

IV.   Historical and Theoretical Considerations

In this concluding section we ask difficult questions about the newness and quality of theory in social cognition. We are particularly interested in how the theories employed by social cognition fare when evaluated against three of the canons by which theories are frequently evaluated: definitional specificity, parsimony, and comprehensiveness. At the same time we also examine some metatheoretical implications of associationist and constructionist assumptions for the study of social cognition.

A.   HOW NEW IS THEORY IN SOCIAL COGNITION?

Let us now step back a bit and reconsider a question with which we began this exploration, that is, whether social cognition represents a significant theoretical advance or an elaboration of an established paradigm (Anderson & Bower, 1973). In other words, how new is social cognition?

The easy answer to this question is "not very." The cognitive approach is of course far from new, nor is it regarded as new by its proponents. Even some S–R theorists accepted this general formulation. For example, Osgood (1953), writing in the 1950s, championed a mediating response approach that emphasized the idea that external stimuli affect overt behavior by means of the mediating internal responses that they elicit. In fact, social psychology has a long history of cognitively oriented endeavor (see Zajonc, 1980a). Lewin (e.g., 1951) contended that behavior was a function of the actor's *psychological field* (his or her cognitions), which in turn was partly determined by the "foreign hull" (the objective world of external stimulation). For Lewin, the mind was a structured system of cognitive–dynamic "subwholes" (1938, p. 261) in which "needs and cognitive structures are interwoven" (1942/1951, p. 81).

A number of personality theorists also contributed to an early cognitive orientation in psychology. For example, different kinds of "schematizing modes" were identified by Klein and Schlesinger (1949), with these modes representing varying degrees of flexibility–rigidity in the frame of reference that a person tended to bring to judgment tasks of various kinds.

The work of Kelly anticipated the focus of current social cognition approaches on self-schemas. According to Kelly, a top-down theorist par excellence, "all thinking is based, in part, on prior convictions" (1955, p. 6), which he called *personal constructs*. Reacting equally against what he called "push" theories (among which might presumably be numbered associationism) and "pull" theories (e.g., psychoanalysis), Kelly insisted on the activity of the individual in constructing "personal versions" of reality (p. 135). The fundamental postulate of Kelly's personal construct theory underlined this emphasis on the contribution of the self to cognition: "A person's processes are psychologically channelized by the ways in which he anticipates events" (p. 46). Similarly, Bruner's (1957) concept of "perceptual readiness," or the differential accessibility of various categories for different individuals, anticipated social cognition's schema concept and its priming paradigm.

As we have gone to some pains to demonstrate earlier in this chapter, the modern study of social cognition owes theoretical debts to two major orientations within psychology—the associationist and the constructionist. By and large, the representatives of social and personality psychology whom we have just discussed fit into the constructionist camp. However, associationist formulations, which until recently were only nominally cognitive and not at all social, have also begun to influence the study of social cognition. Clearly, social cognition (or at least the portion of social cognition research which we have examined) has not sprung forth as an entirely new and different creation. It is the offspring of parents who were originally quite different from one another, perhaps downright incompatible. Nevertheless, in spite of these differences, associationism and constructionism did marry one another and did produce offspring. In fact, social cognition is not an only child of this rather unexpected union, but social cognition is a brood of children, with some of them seeming to have inherited mainly their aging father's associationist features, while others look very much like their constructionist mother, and still others combine the characteristics of both parents.

As we have previously stated, it is fairly easy to identify elements of social cognition that have been borrowed. However, it is also true that in some ways social cognition is quite new. Most obviously social cognition, like cognitive psychology in general, represents a radical departure from the behaviorist paradigm that dominated experimental psychology for much of this century. The very subject of inquiry of the social cognition approach was anathema to behaviorism—that is, the mind, indeed the mind as it apprehends its social world. Furthermore, the stimuli favored by social cognition investigators (e.g., stories, script scenarios, filmed interactions, etc.) are richer than those formerly used by verbal learning researchers working within the behaviorist framework.

While similar to traditional concepts such as expectancy, set, attitudes and attributions, the cognitive modules hypothesized by social cognition investigators (schemas, stereotypes, scripts, prototypes) are both more general and more specific in their formulation than the former concepts. As we have seen, the schema concept is a generic concept or metaconstruct that is capable of subsuming all the above concepts. At the same time, in the course of social cognition research and thinking, the structural and processing features of each of these constructs have been more specifically enunciated than was the case for most of the earlier constructs.

An innovative concept that has received some attention in social cognition research is the notion of nondecomposable mental units. In the past, it was assumed that an aggregation of elements behaved no differently from each of the independent elements. In cognitive psychology (Hayes-Roth, 1977; Mervis & Rosch, 1981) and in social cognition (Sentis & Burnstein, 1979; Sherman & Titus, 1982), however, evidence has been gathered that indicates that cognitive aggregates may be qualitatively different from their constituent elements in their manner of operation. For example, the elements of unitized cognitive modules may be less accessible than nonunitized elements. In general, where older theories (particularly associationist formulations) tended to emphasize atomistic, univocal, passive, and formal processes operating according to quantitative principles, the theoretical formulations favored by social cognition researchers tend to emphasize holistic, multiple, active, and less formalized processes operating according to both quantitative and qualitative principles. In our view, this pattern of development toward greater complexity of theory represents a significant theoretical advance.

There are a number of interesting ideas being developed in artificial intelligence (AI) research which may be applicable to theory in social cognition, for example, the concepts of heterarchical organization and procedural knowledge. Most neo-associationist models emphasized hierarchical types of cognitive organization in which ideas are assumed to be arranged in neat and logical systems, with memory search proceeding from one level to another in turn. However, some cognitive theorists (e.g., Hayes-Roth, 1977; Hofstadter, 1979; Holyoak & Gordon, in press) are now postulating that information may be organized heterarchically, in the form of families of recursive, tangled networks. As Holyoak and Gordon (in press) point out, the concept of heterarchical organization is particularly likely to be pertinent in *social* cognition, due to the fact that the object of social cognition typically plays multiple and overlapping social roles. A person who is the target of another's cognitive activity may be at the same time a woman, a mother, a spouse, a daughter, an athlete, an employer, etc. It seems likely that knowledge about such a social object may be arranged in tangled heterarchical systems rather than in neat hierarchical patterns.

The concept of procedural knowledge (Minsky, 1975) is another novel concept arising from cognitive psychology and AI research. Procedural knowledge is distinguished from declarative knowledge, which is information that is encoded and stored locally and explicitly—for example, facts, "small passive packets of data" (Hofstadter, 1979, p. 615). In contrast, procedural knowledge is encoded and stored globally and implicitly—for example, programs, melodies, implicit personality theories. Hofstadter (1979) explains that procedural knowledge is a "global consequence of how the program works, not a local detail" (p. 363). The linguistic, societal, and cultural underpinnings of schematic, scripted, and stereotype-based thought would seem to operate in implicit and global fashion rather than as packets of explicit data. Hence, it seems quite possible that the concept of procedural knowledge might be particularly relevant to *social* cognition.

B.   HOW GOOD IS THEORY IN SOCIAL COGNITION?

Research and theorizing in both social and nonsocial cognition has been accompanied by the serious reconsideration of certain canons by which theory is generally assessed—for example, definitional specificity, parsimony, and comprehensiveness.

1.   Definitional Specificity

Precision has long been considered an essential aspect of good theory. Anthropologist Clifford Geertz (1973) speaks for many when he contends that scientific advancement depends on improving theoretical precision: "progress is marked less by a perfection of consensus than by a refinement of debate. What gets better is the precision with which we vex each other" (p. 29).

Both Bartlett's schema theory and the Gestalt hypotheses were criticized in the past as too vague to serve as a real challenge to associationist theories (Anderson & Bower, 1973; Hastie, 1981). Cognitive theories in general, as well as theories of social cognition, and particularly schema theories, have also been widely criticized for a lack of conceptual, operational, and predictive precision (Anderson & Bower, 1973; Fiske & Linville, 1980; Hastie, 1981; Mandler, 1981; Taylor, 1981). Hastie (1981), for example, charges that the schema's "basic meaning is indefinite, its usage by theorists is highly individualistic, and its operational connection to empirical events is tenuous" (p. 79). In some ways the strength of the renewed interest in the specificity criterion reflects a change in subject matter that has taken place within psychology—from fixed and separate *entities* (e.g., physical stimuli or discrete behaviors) to active and overlapping *symbols* (Hofstadter, 1979; Mandler, 1981). Because it is inherently more difficult to define empirically mental constructs and processes than physical or behavioral ones, the specificity criterion has become something of a bête noir of the social cognition approach.

In the past, charges of theoretical imprecision or vagueness have been regarded as extremely damaging, particularly by mainline experimental psychologists. On the other hand, there are certain dangers of premature precision that might be weighed against the benefits of precision. Kaplan (1964), for example, comes to the conclusion that openness of meaning and of definition is the usual situation in science and not necessarily a sign of immaturity: "I have never known an empirical term, even from the most exact sciences, in which I could not, when pressed, bring to light a shadow of vagueness" (p. 66). This is true, Kaplan says, because specific theoretical constructs are embedded in larger theoretical systems which must themselves remain open if they are to approximate reality and accommodate new data. Conceiving of science as a process and not as a product, Kaplan cautions against premature precision. Not only is some degree of vagueness inescapable in science, Kaplan (1964) argues that it is also desirable: "The demand for exactness of meaning and for precise definition of terms can have a pernicious effect, as I believe it often has had in behavioral science . . . Tolerance of ambiguity is as important for creativity in science as it is anywhere else" (pp. 70–71). Festinger, one of the pioneers in the cognitive approach to social phenomena, agrees with Kaplan. In *Retrospections on Social Psychology,* Festinger (1980) warned that an insistence on theoretical and empirical precision may abort important ideas and may produce research that is "barren" (p. 252).

To return to the domain of social cognition, if it is still true, as Jenkins claimed in 1974, that "many of us confuse the dicta of associationism with the grounds of empirical science itself" (p. 796), then nonassociative constructs like schemas, scripts, and prototypes may require special protection from premature rejection. Moreover, much research in social cognition shows evidence of making significant improvements over both its constructionist and its early associationist forebears in the specificity and precision of its theoretical statements. Recent developments in the study of schemas and related constructs have, occasionally with the help of computer simulations, gone beyond earlier formulations such as Ebbinghaus's and Bartlett's in attempting to specify more concretely the information-processing mechanisms that might be involved in bringing global background information to bear on the processing or recall of some current input.

There is as yet no consensus among social cognition scholars regarding the resolution of the conflict between openness and precision in theory, but this very lack of consensus is itself new to the experimental disciplines of cognitive and social psychology. The very fact that the issue is being debated, rather than prejudged, is itself a sign of a growing tolerance for ambiguity that may promote greater creativity in social cognition research and thought.

A related theoretical debate is likely to appear in the near future in the context of theory evaluation in social cognition. Out of the artificial intelligence tradition, a high-tech version of the specificity criterion has begun to emerge that holds that a good theory must have constructs and processes that are spelled out with sufficient specificity that they can be simulated by a computer. In fact, in 1980 J. R. Anderson added *simulability* to his list of the characteristics of good theory. In view of the tendency of social cognition investigators to borrow heavily from cognitive psychology, it is probably only a matter of time before this new criterion is applied to theory in social cognition. Therefore, now is a good time to begin to scrutinize the simulability criterion rather closely.

The criterion of simulability follows directly from the assumption of some theorists (e.g., Hofstadter, 1979) that the mind is structured and operates like a computer program. But this view of the mind is itself open to question. Searle (1982) finds the computer = mind equation mistaken because "as far as the computer is concerned the symbols don't *symbolize* anything or *represent* anything. They are just formal counters" (p. 4, emphasis in original). According to Searle, the mind is not like the computer, because only the mind is capable of transcending the mere manipulation of signs in order to achieve real understanding: "no formal program by itself is sufficient for understanding, because it would always be possible in principle for an agent to go through the steps in the program and still not have the relevant understanding" (p. 5).

Not only is there disagreement with respect to the proposition that the mind works like a computer, there is also debate concerning the simulability criterion. As an *absolute* criterion by which to evaluate theory, simulability seems inappropriate, although its use as a rule of thumb might benefit theory building in social cognition. Because of the flexibility of the computer, it is likely that it can be programmed to mimic certain aspects of mental functioning *no matter how* these mental processes actually work. Computer models can help us to see the many sets of processing mechanisms and effects that are congruent with a general verbal formulation. Computer models may also be helpful in articulating the important consequences of "minor" details that must be decided in the implementation of a general theory.

Nonetheless, despite the virtues of simulability or computability, there remain dangers of premature closure. Just as we caution against the blind acceptance of any particular *operationalization*, we should also be cautious about the virtues of any particular program-theory for at least three reasons. First, modern philosophers of science dispute the requirement that theories be formal or ax-iomatic systems. In place of this view, Suppe (1977) and others advance a conception of theories as convenient abstractions, approximations to truth, or conceptual devices. It is possible that unquestioned allegiance to the simulability criterion might yield the kind of "empty formalism" that Lewin warned against with respect to mathematical models in psychology (1942/1951, p. 1). Secondly, a given computer realization of a general model may yield predictions not de-rived from another plausible computer version of the theory in question. In this case, too, we would not want premature closure on the properties of a given theory. Finally, we would not want to lose theoretical contributions from those who do not speak "computerese." Everyday social observations may lead to some worthwhile theoretical propositions. If we shut ourselves off from such input by demanding computability, we may well eliminate much that is of value.

2. *Parsimony*

When one notes the massive borrowing from cognitive psychology by in-vestigators of social cognition, the question arises: Is it valid for social cognition to import theory derived from the study of nonsocial phenomena? Do people know about one another the same way they know about sounds, geometric shapes, chairs, or animals?

The assumption has often been that the processes are not different. Writing about social cognition from within the framework of cognitive psychology, Holyoak and Gordon (in press) point out that "it would be a parsimonious outcome to find that cognitive principles that apply in other domains can account for social phenomena as well" (p. 3). Fiske and Linville (1980) recommend that social cognition should continue to operate under the assumption of similar processing in the social and nonsocial realms, in the interest of parsimony. These social cognition theorists buttress their recommendation with a functionalist ar-gument: "it is unlikely that in the process of evolution, qualitatively different knowledge structures or procedures developed for social and nonsocial classes of stimuli" (p. 548). Likewise, Mervis and Rosch (1981) cite a number of studies of social categorization that seem to be congruent with Rosch's conceptualization of nonsocial categorization. Cantor and Mischel (1979), while not taking a dogmatic stance, tend to agree with Mervis and Rosch that the "categorization rules and conceptual structures used in person and object perception may not be fundamentally different" (p. 8).

Although the business of studying social cognition has often gone on under the assumption of identity between nonsocial and social cognition, there are those who reject this assumption. Zajonc (1980a) asserts that social cognition is different from nonsocial cognition in a number of ways. First of all, there is a potential lack of stimulus consistency when the stimulus is a person rather than an object. If a person knows he or she is under scrutiny by another, that person may well attempt to change his or her self-presentation, whereas a lunar rock has no such capability.

A second way in which the study of social and nonsocial phenomena diverge, according to Zajonc, is that in the case of social phenomena it is often difficult or impossible to find measures that are independent of the phenomenon itself. While it is possible to measure people's body temperature independently of their own subjective judgment (or consensual judgments), it is another thing to try to measure a person's intelligence or degree of extraversion independently of cognitive judgments about these attributes. Fiedler (1982) makes a related point by way of criticizing the concept of the causal schema. According to Fiedler, the schema concept is a useful explanatory concept, but one that is difficult to identify independently of the experimental responses being explained.

As Zajonc also points out, the role of the self and of emotion is probably larger in social judgments than in nonsocial ones. Finally, according to Zajonc, social phenomena are different from nonsocial ones in that social phenomena cry out for causal explanation more than nonsocial phenomena because "the demands of everyday life make it much more important for us to know the causes of the behavior of other humans than to know the causes of the physical aspects of our environment" (p. 202). Zajonc (1980a) ends his comparison of nonsocial and social cognition by turning the tables on the assumption that nonsocial cognition subsumes social cognition:

> The conclusion that forces itself upon us is that social perception and social cognition are *not* special cases of perception and cognition . . . For social cognition is not the special case. It is experimental cognition which is the special case. It is social perception that represents the general case (pp. 203–204).

This is a very intriguing assertion and one that is similar to certain ideas prominent in the hermeneutic tradition. Max Horkheimer, a member of the Frankfurt School of thought, argues, like Zajonc, for the social and cultural determination of all knowing: "The perceived fact is . . . codetermined by human ideas and concepts, even before its conscious theoretical elaboration by the knowing individual" (1937/1976, p. 214). (Horkheimer is speaking here not only of the person-on-the-street but also of the scientist, which is an interesting sub-topic in its own right.) According to Adorno (1969/1978), another member of the Frankfurt School, "society is immanent in experience" (p. 503)—*all* experience, including the ostensibly nonsocial. The fact that language and thought do not arise in a social–cultural vacuum is also stressed by many modern linguists. In his book, *Roots of Language*, linguist Derek Bickerton (1982) emphasizes the operation of a "bioprogram" in language acquisition; at the same time, however, he *denies* that it is the case that:

when we were ready to talk [or to think], all the things in the universe stood there waiting—
rock and river, dodo and elephant, storm and sunrise, thirst and evil, love and dishonor—all
waiting patiently for their labels (p. 218, cited in Bruner & Feldman, 1982, p. 36; phrase in
brackets added by present authors).

In other words, reality (both social and nonsocial) is at no time knowable in and
of itself; the perception and communication of reality is shaped by cultural
experience.[8]

The debate about whether or not nonsocial and social knowing operate
according to the same principles arises out of an underlying metatheoretical
assumption that parsimony is both a desirable and a feasible characteristic of
psychological models (Anderson, 1978; Anderson & Bower, 1973; Fiske &
Linville, 1980; Hastie & Carlston, 1980). However, there are those who question
the feasibility of developing parsimonious models of cognitive functioning.
Newell (1973) and Minsky (1975), for example, both argue against setting up
parsimony as an absolute standard by which to judge cognitive theory: they feel
that human cognition is so complex and interactive that it demands relatively
complex, nonparsimonious theories.

Minsky's (1975) concept of procedural knowledge illustrates the need for
nonparsimonious theories. For Hofstadter, if declarative information is like a
town (a stationary metastructure), procedural knowledge is like a trip (a dynamic
process). Hofstadter (1979) points out that there may be alternate routes to the
same destination, or to the same cognitive outcome. Indeed, one of the main
theses of his book, *Gödel, Escher, and Bach: An Eternal Golden Braid* (1979),
is that, while hardware (physiological, neurological) rules are rigid and un-
changeable, "software [cognitive] rules on various levels can change" (p. 686)
and that in fact intelligence is due to the flexibility of its governing principles.

If we take the trip metaphor further, we see that, besides being an active
process, a successfully executed trip requires the operation of multiple levels in
concert. At the mechanical and electrical levels, the car must work; at the
physiological level, the driver must be awake and healthy enough to operate the
car; at the cognitive level, the driver needs to have and to follow a working plan
for getting where she or he wants to go. There is little reason to assume that the
same principles explain the process at each of these levels. Thus, Minsky (1975)
warns against the tendency to "minimize the variety of assumed mechanisms,"
arguing that "parsimony is still inappropriate at this stage" (p. 215) of theory
construction.

Similarly, both Smith (1980) and Anderson (1980) argue that no single
theoretical mechanism is sufficient to explain various phenomena of memory or

---

[8]This perspective is different from but not incompatible with the Roschian emphasis on the
contribution of reality itself to its categorization. Just as culturally based conceptualizations influence
one's thinking about objects, so may features of the objects themselves.

of cognition. Smith argues for the necessity of at least three different mechanisms to account for cognition: (1) spreading activation through subdivided networks, (2) organization of information by higher-order cognitive units such as scripts and schemas, which then serve to guide memory search, and (3) the formation and processing of multiple interconnections among elements due to processes of comprehension and inference. Anderson (1980) has added to his original associative network account (Anderson & Bower, 1973) two other mechanisms, both of which he feels are required to explain memory: elaboration (inference-based interconnection) and unitization (the formation of higher-order cognitive units such as schemas through linking of old and new knowledge). Like Anderson (1980), Smith (1980) concludes in a rather nonparsimonious vein that "no one mechanism is going to cover all organizational conditions" (p. 204).[9]

3. Comprehensiveness

In addition to specificity and parsimony, another criterion by which theory is often assessed is *comprehensiveness* (e.g., Krech, 1949). But comprehensiveness and parsimony may be to some extent incompatible goals. Any theory that attempts to address comprehensively the issue of how people know their social world takes on a heavy burden with respect to the criterion of parsimony. If it hopes to approximate the complex reality, such a theory must deal with everything from perception, memory, and inference to emotion, motivation, personality, and even culture. But social cognition has been criticized for neglecting one or the other of these aspects of cognition.

Taylor (1981) describes the social perceiver operationalized by social cognition investigations as "something out of a Camus novel: alone, bereft of language, *without emotion*" (p. 205). Taylor (1981) was not alone in recognizing the neglect of emotion in the early approaches to social cognition; Neisser (1980) warned that "social psychology should not be too quick to take detached perceivers and knowers as models for human nature" (p. 604). Fortunately, an important paper by Zajonc (1980b) has sparked a surge of empirical interest in the interaction of affect and cognition. Even more, Zajonc has mounted a direct challenge to the standard cognitive position by arguing that the affective system may operate independently of cognition. We feel that it is no longer accurate to indict social cognition for neglecting emotion. Indeed, affect, mood, and emotion are flourishing concerns in current social cognition research and thought (e.g., Bower, 1981; Clark & Fiske, 1982; Clark & Isen, 1982).

---

[9]The evolution of Wittgenstein's thinking about language shows a similar change from an early view of language as a "monolithic system of representations for picturing reality" to a less parsimonious view of language as a "melange of small language games, each with its own family of preconditions and applications and contexts" (Hacking, 1982, p. 43).

As we have seen, the study of social cognition has been greatly influenced by cognitive psychology and its favorite theories, particularly associationist theory. One result is that the study of social cognition has tended to be rather impersonal in its approach, neglecting the contribution of the individual's personality characteristics, emotion, and personal experience to social knowing. As Higgins, Kuiper, and Olson (1981) expressed it in the title of a recent chapter, social cognition needs "to get personal." Fortunately, social cognition is in fact getting personal. There is a growing body of research that establishes that people differ in the way they structure their thinking about themselves (Cantor & Kihlstrom, 1981; Kelly, 1955; Kuiper, 1981; Markus, 1977; Markus & Sentis, 1980; Markus & Smith, 1980) and that these differences affect the way they perceive others (Higgins, King, & Mavin, 1982; Schneider, 1973; Schneider, Hastorf, & Ellsworth, 1979).

Besides being relatively flat and impersonal, the phenomenon of social cognition, as it appears in social cognition research, has up to now tended to be only nominally *social*. In a typical social cognition or person perception paradigm, an individual subject is exposed in isolation and in the laboratory to sets of trait or behavior words or sentences presented via slides or printed lists. Although social cognition research has relied heavily on Bartlett's schema construct, it has tended to minimize the social and cultural context in which such schemas must be formed, as well as the truly social–cultural content of schemas.

Of course, whenever cognition is singled out for emphasis, there is the danger of neglecting interpersonal, social, and cultural factors. This is one of the legacies left us by Descartes, the first of the great subjectivists, and the problem has plagued all the heirs of this perspective, from Kant through Hegel to cognitive psychology and social cognition. In cognitive psychology the reality of interest has up to now been the reality constructed by the individual rather than reality as socially constituted. In a recent critique of cognitive psychology, Sampson (1981) points out that cognitive psychology grants primacy to the mind of the individual subject and in so doing shortchanges the role of the object (the world). One of the present authors recently came upon this very criticism expressed in graffiti form in a campus-area public facility: "The problem with Western thought is that it seeks to find a starting place within thought itself." According to Sampson, one effect of this orientation of cognitive psychology (and possibly of Western thought) is to serve the interests of maintaining the status quo instead of challenging the status quo. Whether or not one agrees with this latter conclusion, Sampson's characterization of cognitive psychology as overly individualistic[10] should be taken seriously by investigators of social cognition.

[10]Geertz (1973) charges cognitive approaches in anthropology with falling into the similar error of promoting "privacy theories of meaning" (p. 12), instead of recognizing that both culture and meaning are public.

All in all, these sorts of critiques of the theory and methods of social cognition research add up to a formidable set of demands for greater comprehensiveness. If they were met, the social knower under investigation could no longer be accused of looking like something out of Camus (Taylor, 1981), but might instead look more like someone we actually know—someone who is fairly articulate, emotional, and an active participant in vital social, familial, and cultural groups.

Scientific theories provide us with systematic attempts to account for regularities observed in the natural world. Historically, the most successful of these formulations are simultaneously parsimonious and comprehensive. This implies that explanatory principles should ideally be few in number, and they should adequately account for the phenomenon in all its breadth and richness. However, in practice there may be a trade-off between parsimony and comprehensiveness, and also between theoretical specificity and openness—at least for theories that attempt to deal with complexly determined phenomena such as social knowing.

In *The Miracle Worker* (Gibson, 1970), Annie Sullivan attempts to teach the deaf, blind, and mute child Helen Keller to communicate using hand signals. Her method involved placing Helen's hand on an object or person while simultaneously forming the manual sign for the object or person in Helen's other hand and naming the object orally. In perhaps the most dramatic scene of the play, Helen struggles to form the word "water" as Annie Sullivan pumps water into Helen's hands. Suddenly, Helen runs ecstatically from object to object, naming each with her hand signals and laughing. "She *knows!*" Miss Sullivan cries.

This drama may be seen as a powerful portrayal of the two opposing epistemologies with which we have been concerned. (To be quite fair, the example illustrates a primitive version of both associationist and constructionist perspectives; but in view of the necessarily abstract nature of theoretical discussions like this, a concrete example may provide some balance.)

Before the scene at the water pump, Helen had been exposed to repeated associations of signs with particular objects. Annie Sullivan was using the associative principles of contiguity and frequency to try to teach Helen language, repeatedly and simultaneously connecting sign with object. We, the audience, have the conviction throughout this early portion of the play that Helen was the passive partner in these experiences: for Helen does not learn. After many exposures, Helen remains ignorant and cut off from truly human communication.

At the water pump, however, we see a dramatic change take place in Helen. Suddenly she understands, has insight, actively makes the connection for herself—"She *knows!*" And it seems to us, the audience, as though Helen now knows from the "top down" not from the "bottom up." *She* knows; *Helen* knows. In forming the concept of language, Helen's mind is qualitatively different than it was before; *she* is different. We have no doubt that after that crucial insight, Helen will never be the same. Now she can understand, she can communicate.

It is a triumph of the mind. At the same time it is a triumph of the stimulus. Helen could not *know* had the connections not been made for her first. And she could not *know* had she not restructured the connections in a drastically new way for herself. Both must operate: association and construction, bottom-up and top-down processing. Nearly a century ago, William James (1890) anticipated the need for both types of processes and articulated what it would take for the reconciliation of associationism and "its rivals" (p. 362) to occur: "There need never have been a quarrel between associationism and its rivals if the former had admitted the indecomposable unity of every pulse of thought, and the latter been willing to allow that 'perishing' pulses of thought might recollect and know" (p. 362). As we have seen, this is just what has happened in theories of cognitive psychology and social cognition. In Hayes-Roth's knowledge assembly theory, for example, associative processing is hypothesized to be capable of producing nondecomposable higher-order cognitive units. In much social cognition research, associative cognitive and emotional elements are given credit for persisting and automatically influencing thought.

In the light of actual human cognition and in the light of James's insight, perhaps it is not so surprising to find that when psychology studies social cognition, it draws upon both types of theory, associative and constructionist. It is not only Helen Keller whose thought (and language) seems to require nonparsimonious explanations that include both associative and constructionist processes, both bottom-up and top-down activities. It seems likely that social knowing in general requires not only multiple mental processes but diverse ones. We suspect that the merging of associationist and constructionist theories in the current study of social cognition has happened because it had to happen if the theories were to approximate the complex reality of social cognition.

Finally, we believe that the consequences of the merging of these formerly antagonistic approaches are themselves salutary. In merging with constructionist approaches, certain deficiencies of associationism are corrected—for example, its tendency to produce explanatory accounts that are perhaps overly simple, overly impersonal, and overly mechanistic. On the other hand, by merging with associationist approaches, certain deficiencies of constructionism are corrected—for example, its tendency to produce explanatory accounts that are perhaps overly global and unspecified. This has the effect of curing the "holistic paralysis" (Isen & Hastorf, 1982, p. 45) which has sometimes afflicted constructionist theorists in the past. When the clarity and robustness of associationism are wedded with the richness of constructionism, as they often are in the investigation of social cognition, we can't help but feel that the phenomena of social knowing are better served than before.

ACKNOWLEDGMENTS

We are grateful to Nancy Cantor, Geoffrey Fong, and Myron Rothbart for their astute comments on an earlier version of this manuscript.

REFERENCES

Abelson, R. P. Script processing in attitude formation and decision-making. In J. S. Carroll & J. N. Payne (Eds.), *Cognition and social behavior.* Hillsdale, New Jersey: Erlbaum, 1976.

Abelson, R. P. Psychological status of the script concept. *American Psychologist,* 1981, **36,** 715–729.

Adorno, T. W. Subject and object (1969). In A. Arato & E. Gebhardt, (Eds.), *The essential Frankfurt School reader.* New York: Urizen Books, 1978. (a)

Adorno, T. W. The sociology of knowledge and its consciousness. In A. Arato & E. Gebhardt (Eds.), *The essential Frankfurt School reader.* New York: Urizen Books, 1978. (b)

Ajzen, I. Intuitive theories of events and the effects of base-rate information on prediction. *Journal of Personality and Social Psychology,* 1977, **35,** 303–314.

Allport, G. W., & Postman, L. J. The basic psychology of rumor. *Academic Science,* Series II, 1945.

Anderson, J. R. *Language, memory, and thought.* Hillsdale, New Jersey: Erlbaum, 1976.

Anderson, J. R., Arguments concerning representations for mental imagery. *Psychological Review,* 1978, **85,** 249–277.

Anderson, J. R. Concepts, propositions, and schemata: What are the cognitive units? NTIS Report. Pittsburgh, Pennsylvania: Carnegie-Mellon University, May 1980.

Anderson, J. R., & Bower, G. H. *Human associative memory.* Washington, D.C.: V. H. Winston & Sons, Inc., 1973.

Aristotle. On memory and reminiscence. *Great Books of the Western World.* Chicago, Illinois: Encyclopedia Brittanica, 1952.

Bar-Hillel, M., & Fischhoff, B. When do base rates affect predictions? *Journal of Personality and Social Psychology,* 1981, **41,** 671–680.

Bargh, J. A., & Pietromonaco, P. Automatic information processing and social perception: The influence of trait information presented outside of conscious awareness on impression formation. *Journal of Personality and Social Psychology,* 1982, **43,** 437–449.

Baron, R. M. Contrasting approaches to social knowing: An ecological perspective. *Personality and Social Psychology Bulletin,* 1980, **6,** 591–600.

Barthes, R. Deliberation. In S. Sontag (Ed.), *A Barthes Reader.* New York: Hill and Wang, 1982.

Bartlett, F. C. *Remembering: A study in experimental and social psychology.* London: Cambridge University Press, 1932.

Bem, S. L. Gender schema theory: A cognitive account of sex typing. *Psychological Review,* 1981, **88,** 354–364.

Berlin, B., & Kay, P. *Basic color terms.* Berkeley and Los Angeles, California: University of California Press, 1969.

Bickerton, D. *Roots of language.* Ann Arbor, Michigan: Karoma Publishers, 1982.

Billig, M., & Tajfel, H. Social categorization and similarity in intergroup behavior. *European Journal of Social Psychology,* 1973, **3,** 27–52.

Bower, G. H. Mood and memory. *American Psychologist,* 1981, **36,** 129–148.

Bower, G. H., Monteiro, K. P., & Gilligan, S. G. Emotional mood as a context of learning and recall. *Journal of Verbal Learning and Verbal Behavior,* 1978, **17,** 573–585.

Brewer, M. B. In-group bias in the minimal intergroup situation: A cognitive–motivational analysis. *Psychological Bulletin,* 1979, **86**, 307–324.

Brewer, M., Dull, V., & Lui, L. Perceptions of the elderly: Stereotypes as prototypes. *Journal of Personality and Social Psychology,* 1981, **41**, 656–670.

Bruner, J. S. On perceptual readiness (1957). In D. C. Beardslee & M. Wertheimer (Eds.), *Readings in perception.* Princeton, New Jersey: Van Nostrand-Reinhold, 1958.

Bruner, J., & Feldman, C. Fleisher. Where does language come from? (Review of *Roots of language* by D. Bickerton.) *New York Review of Books,* June 24, 1982.

Cantor, N., & Kihlstrom, J. F. (Eds.), *Personality, cognition, and social interaction.* Hillsdale, New Jersey: Erlbaum, 1981.

Cantor, N., & Mischel, W. Prototypes in person perception. In L. Berkowitz (Ed.), *Advances in experimental social psychology,* 1979, **12**, 3–52.

Chase, W. G., & Simon, H. A. Perception in chess. *Cognitive Psychology,* 1973, **4**, 55–81.

Clark, M. *Effects of arousal on mood, memory, and interpretations of positive and negative statements.* Paper presented at the meeting of the Society for Experimental Social Psychology, Nashville, Indiana, October 1982.

Clark, M. S., & Fiske, S. T. (Eds.), *Affect and cognition: The 17th Annual Carnegie Symposium on Cognition.* Hillsdale, New Jersey: Erlbaum, 1982.

Clark, M. S., & Isen, A. M. Toward understanding the relationship between feeling states and social behavior. In A. Hastorf & A. M. Isen (Eds.), *Cognitive social psychology.* New York: Elsevier, 1982.

Cohen, C. E. Person categories and social perception: Testing some boundaries of the processing effects of prior knowledge. *Journal of Personality and Social Psychology,* 1981, **40**, 441–452.

Collins, A. M., & Loftus, E. F. A spreading activation theory of semantic processing. *Psychological Review,* 1975, **82**, 407–428.

Collins, A. M., & Quillian, M. R. Retrieval time from semantic memory. *Journal of Verbal Learning and Verbal Behavior,* 1969, **8**, 240–247.

Craik, F.I.M., & Lockhart, R. S. Levels of processing: A framework for memory research. *Journal of Verbal Learning and Verbal Behavior,* 1972, **11**, 671–684.

Dawes, R. M. Shallow psychology. In J. S. Carroll & J. W. Payne (Eds.), *Cognition and social behavior.* Hillsdale, New Jersey: Erlbaum, 1976.

Deese, J. *The structure of associations in language and thought.* Baltimore, Maryland: Johns Hopkins Press, 1965.

Deese, J. Association and memory. In T. R. Dixon & D. L. Horton (Eds.), *Verbal behavior and general behavior theory.* Englewood Cliffs, New Jersey: Prentice-Hall, 1968.

Descartes. Meditations (1641). *Great Books of the Western World.* Chicago, Illinois: Encyclopaedia Brittanica, 1952.

Ebbinghaus, H. *Memory.* Translated by H. A. Ruger & C. E. Bussenius. New York: Teachers College, Columbia University, 1885/1913.

Eccles, J. Parsons. Expectancies, values, and academic choice: Origins and change. In J. T. Spence (Ed.), *Assessing achievement.* San Francisco, California: Freeman, 1981.

Edwards, W., Lindman, H., & Phillips, L. D. Emerging technologies for making decisions. In T. M. Newcomb (Ed.), *New directions in psychology: II.* New York: Holt, 1965.

Ericsson, K. A., & Simon, H. A. Verbal reports as data. *Psychological Review,* 1980, **87**, 215–251.

Festinger, L. Looking backward. In L. Festinger (Ed.), *Retrospections on social psychology.* New York: Oxford University Press, 1980.

Fiedler, K. Causal schemata: Review and criticism of research on a popular construct. *Journal of Personality and Social Psychology,* 1982, **42**, 1001–1013.

Fiske, S. T. Schema-triggered affect: Applications to social perception. In M. S. Clark & S. T. Fiske

(Eds.), *Affect and Cognition: The 17th Annual Carnegie Symposium on Cognition.* Hillsdale, New Jersey: Erlbaum, 1982.

Fiske, S. T., & Linville, P. W. What does the schema concept buy us? *Personality and Social Psychology Bulletin,* 1980, **6,** 543–557.

Geertz, C. *The interpretation of cultures.* New York: Basic Books, 1973.

Gibson, J. J. *The senses considered as perceptual systems.* Boston, Massachusetts: Houghton Mifflin, 1966.

Gibson, J. J. *The ecological approach to visual perception.* Boston, Massachusetts: Houghton Mifflin, 1979.

Gibson, W. *The Miracle Worker.* In E. A. White (Ed.), *Understanding literature.* Boston, Massachusetts: Ginn, 1970.

Gilovich, T. Seeing the past in the present: The effect of associations to familiar events on judgments and decision. *Journal of Personality and Social Psychology,* 1981, **40,** 797–808.

Glass, A. L., & Holyoak, K. J. Alternative conceptions of semantic memory. *Cognition,* 1975, **3,** 313–339.

Glass, A. L., Holyoak, K. J., & Santa, J. L. *Cognition.* Reading, Massachusetts: Addison-Wesley, 1979.

Graesser, A. C., Gordon, S. E., & Sawyer, J. D. Recognition memory for typical and atypical actions in scripted activities: Tests of a script pointer and tag hypothesis. *Journal of Verbal Learning and Verbal Behavior,* 1979, **18,** 319–332.

Graesser, A. C., Woll, S. B., Kowalski, D. J., & Smith, D. A. Memory for typical and atypical actions in scripted activities. *Journal of Experimental Psychology: Human Learning and Memory,* 1980, **6,** 503–515.

Hacking, I. Wittgenstein the psychologist. (Review of *Remarks on the philosophy of psychology* by L. Wittgenstein.) *New York Review of Books,* April 1, 1982.

Hamilton, D. L. Cognitive representations of persons. In E. T. Higgins, C. P. Herman, & M. P. Zanna (Eds.), *Social cognition: The Ontario Symposium* (Vol. 1). Hillsdale, New Jersey: Erlbaum, 1981.

Hamilton, D. L., & Gifford, R. K. Illusory correlation in interpersonal perception: A cognitive basis of stereotypic judgments. *Journal of Experimental Social Psychology,* 1976, **12,** 392–407.

Hamilton, D. L., Katz, L. B., & Leirer, V. O. Organizational processes in impression formation. In R. Hastie, T. M. Ostrom, E. B. Ebbesen, R. S. Wyer, D. L. Hamilton, & D. E. Carlston (Eds.), *Person memory.* Hillsdale, New Jersey: Erlbaum, 1980.

Hamilton, D. L., & Rose, T. L. Illusory correlation and the maintenance of stereotypic beliefs. *Journal of Personality and Social Psychology,* 1980, **39,** 832–845.

Harvey, J. H., & Baron, R. M. Contrasting perspectives on social knowing: An overview. *Personality and Social Psychology Bulletin,* 1980, **6,** 502–506.

Hastie, R. Memory for behavioral information that confirms or contradicts a personality impression. In R. Hastie. T. M. Ostrom, E. B. Ebbesen, R. S. Wyer, D. L. Hamilton, & D. E. Carlston (Eds.), *Person memory.* Hillsdale, New Jersey: Erlbaum, 1980.

Hastie, R. Schematic principles of human memory. In E. T. Higgins, C. A. Herman, & M. P. Zanna (Eds.), *Social cognition: The Ontario Symposium* (Vol. 1). Hillsdale, New Jersey: Erlbaum, 1981.

Hastie, R., & Kumar, P. A. Person memory: Personality traits as organizing principles in memory for behaviors. *Journal of Personality and Social Psychology,* 1979, **37,** 25–38.

Hayes-Roth, B. Evolution of cognitive structures and processes. *Psychological Review,* 1977, **84,** 260–278.

Head, H. *Studies in neurology.* London: Oxford Medical Publications, 1920.

Hebb, D. O. *Organization of behavior.* New York: Wiley, 1949.

Heider, F. Attitudes and cognitive organization. *Journal of Psychology*, 1946, **21**, 107–112.

Heider, F. *The psychology of interpersonal relations*. New York: Wiley, 1958.

Higgins, E. T., & King, G. Accessibility of social constructs: Information-processing consequences of individual and contextual variability. In N. Cantor, & J. F. Kihlstrom (Eds.), *Personality, cognition, and social interaction*. Hillsdale, New Jersey: Erlbaum, 1981.

Higgins, E. T., King, G., & Mavin, G. Individual construct accessibility and subjective impressions and recall. *Journal of Personality and Social Psychology*, 1982, **43**, 35–47.

Higgins, E. T., Kuiper, N. A., & Olson, J. M. Social cognition: A need to get personal. In E. T. Higgins, C. P. Herman, & M. P. Zanna (Eds.), *Social cognition: The Ontario Symposium* (Vol. 1). Hillsdale, New Jersey: Erlbaum 1981.

Higgins, E. T., Rholes, W. S., & Jones, C. R. Category accessibility and impression formation. *Journal of Experimental Social Psychology*, 1977, **13**, 141–154.

Hofstadter, D. R. *Gödel, Escher, and Bach: An eternal golden braid*. New York: Vintage Books, 1979.

Holyoak, K. J., & Gordon, P. C. Information processing and social cognition. In R. Wyer, T. Srull, & J. Hartwick (Eds.), *Handbook of social cognition*. Hillsdale, New Jersey: Erlbaum, in press.

Horkheimer, M. Traditional and critical theory (1937). In P. Connerton (Ed.), *Critical sociology*. Middlesex, England: Penguin Books, 1976.

Hull, C. L. Quantitative aspects of the evolution of concepts: An experimental study. *Psychological Monographs*, 1920, **28**, No. 123.

Husserl, A. [*The crisis of European sciences and transcendental phenomenology*] (D. Carr, Trans.). Evanston, Illinois: Northwestern University Press, 1970. (Originally published, 1954.)

Isen, A. M., & Hastorf, A. H. Some perspectives on cognitive social psychology. In A. H. Hastorf & A. M. Isen (Eds.), *Cognitive social psychology*. New York: Elsevier, 1982.

Isen, A. M., Shalker, T., Clark, M., & Karp, L. Affect, accessibility of material in memory and behavior: A cognitive loop? *Journal of Personality and Social Psychology*, 1978, **36**, 1–12.

James, W. *The principles of psychology* (Vol. I). New York: Henry Holt & Co., 1890.

Jenkins, J. J. Remember that old theory of memory? Well, forget it! *American Psychologist*, 1974, **29**, 785–795.

Johnson, N. F. On the function of letters in word identification: Some data and a preliminary model. *Journal of Verbal Learning and Verbal Behavior*, 1975, **14**, 17–29.

Jones, E. E., & Gerard, H. B. *Foundations of social psychology*. New York: Wiley, 1967.

Kahneman, D., & Tversky, A. On the psychology of prediction. *Psychological Review*, 1973, **80**, 237–251.

Kaplan, A. *The conduct of inquiry*. San Francisco, California: Chandler, 1964.

Kelly, G. *The psychology of personal constructs*. New York: W. W. Norton & Co., 1955.

Kintsch, W. *The representation of meaning in memory*. Hillsdale, New Jersey: Erlbaum, 1974.

Klatzky, R. L. *Human memory: Structures and processes*. San Francisco, California: Freeman, 1975.

Klein, G. S., & Schlesinger, H. Where is the perceiver in perceptual theory? *Journal of Personality*, 1949, **18**, 32–47.

Koffka, K. Special features of mental growth (1924). In R. W. Marks (Ed.), *Great ideas in psychology*. New York: Bantam Books, 1966.

Köhler, W. Human perception (1930a). In M. Henle (Ed.), *The selected papers of Wolfgang Köhler*. New York: Liveright, 1971.

Köhler, W. The nature of intelligence (1930b). In M. Henle (Ed.), *The selected papers of Wolfgang Köhler*. New York: Liveright, 1971.

Kraut, R. E., & Lewis, S. K. Person perception and self-awareness: Knowledge of influences on one's own judgments. *Journal of Personality and Social Psychology*, 1982, **42**, 448–460.

Krech, D. Notes toward a psychological theory. *Journal of Personality,* 1949, **18,** 66–87.

Kuiper, N. A. Convergent evidence for the self as a prototype: "The inverted-U RT effect" for self and other judgment. *Personality and Social Psychology Bulletin,* 1981, **7,** 438–443.

Lewin, K. *The conceptual representation and the measurement of psychological forces.* Durham, North Carolina: Duke University Press, 1938.

Lewin, K. *Field theory in social science.* (1942). D. Cartwright (Ed.), New York: Harper & Brothers, 1951.

Lingle, J. H., Geva, H., Ostrom, T. M., Leippe, M. R., & Baumgardner, M. H. Thematic effects of person judgments on impression organization. *Journal of Personality and Social Psychology,* 1979, **37,** 674–687.

Lingle, J. H., & Ostrom, T. M. Retrieval selectivity in memory-based impression judgments. *Journal of Personality and Social Psychology,* 1979, **37,** 180–194.

Linville, P. W. The complexity-extremity effect and age-based stereotyping. *Journal of Personality and Social Psychology,* 1982, **42,** 193–211.

Linville, P. W., & Jones, E. E. Polarized appraisals of out-group members. *Journal of Personality and Social Psychology,* 1980, **38,** 689–703.

Mandler, G. Association and organization: Facts, fancies, and theories. In T. R. Dixon & D. L. Horton (Eds.), *Verbal behavior and general behavior theory.* Englewood Cliffs, New Jersey: Prentice-Hall, 1968.

Mandler, J. M., & Mandler, G. *Thinking: From association to gestalt.* New York: Wiley, 1964.

Mandler, G. *What is cognitive psychology? What isn't?* Paper presented at the American Psychological Association convention, Los Angeles, California, 1981.

Manis, M. Cognitive social psychology. *Personality and Social Psychology Bulletin,* 1977, **3,** 550–566.

Manis, M., Avis, N. E., & Cardoze, S. Reply to Bar-Hillel and Fischhoff. *Journal of Personality and Social Psychology,* 1981, **41,** 681–683.

Manis, M., Dovalina, I., Avis, N. E., & Cardoze, S. Base rates can affect individual predictions. *Journal of Personality and Social Psychology,* 1980, **38,** 231–248.

Markus, H. Self-schemata and processing information about the self. *Journal of Personality and Social Psychology,* 1977, **35,** 63–78.

Markus, H., Crane, M., Bernstein, S., & Siladi, M. Self-schemas and gender. *Journal of Personality and Social Psychology,* 1982, **42,** 38–50.

Markus, H., & Smith, J. The influence of self-schemas on the perception of others. In N. Cantor & J. Kihlstrom (Eds.), *Personality, cognition and social interaction.* Hillsdale, New Jersey: Erlbaum, 1980.

Markus, H., & Sentis, K. The self in social information processing. In J. Suls (Ed.), *Social psychological perspectives on the self.* Hillsdale, New Jersey: Erlbaum, 1980.

McArthur, L. Z. Illusory causation and illusory correlation: Two epistemological accounts. *Personality and Social Psychology Bulletin,* 1980, **6,** 507–519.

McCauley, C., & Stitt, C. L. An individual and quantitative measure of stereotypes. *Journal of Personality and Social Psychology,* 1978, **36,** 929–940.

McCauley, C., Stitt, C. L., & Segal, M. Stereotyping: From prejudice to prediction. *Psychological Bulletin,* 1980, **87,** 195–208.

McGee, R. Imagery and recognition memory: The effects of relational organization. *Memory and Cognition,* 1980, **8,** 394–399.

Mervis, C. B., & Rosch, E. Categorization of natural objects. *Annual Review of Psychology,* 1981, **32,** 89–115.

Miller, N. E. Liberalization of basic S-R concepts: Extensions to conflict behavior, motivation and social learning. In S. Koch (Ed.), *Psychology: A study of a science* (Vol. 2). New York: McGraw-Hill, 1959.

Minsky, M. A framework for representing knowledge. In P. H. Winston (Ed.), *The psychology of computer vision*. New York: McGraw-Hill, 1975.

Mischel, W. On the interface of cognition and personality: Beyond the person-situation debate. *American Psychologist*, 1979, **34**, 740–754.

Moesher, S. D. The role of experimental design in investigation of the fan effect. *Journal of Experimental Psychology: Human Learning and Memory*, 1979, **5**, 125–134.

Moreland, R. L., & Zajonc, R. B. Is stimulus recognition a necessary condition for the occurrence of exposure effects? *Journal of Personality and Social Psychology*, 1977, **35**, 191–199.

Moscovici, S. *The coming era of representations*. Paper presented at Aix-en-Provence, July 1981.

Neisser, U. *Cognition and reality*. San Francisco, California: Freeman, 1976.

Neisser, U. On "social knowing." *Personality and Social Psychology Bulletin*, 1980, **6**, 601–605.

Newell, A. You can't play 20 questions with nature and win: Projective comments on the papers of this symposium. In W. G. Chase (Ed.), *Visual information processing*. New York: Academic Press, 1973.

Newton, D. An interactionist perspective on social knowing. *Personality and Social Psychology Bulletin*, 1980, **6**, 520–531.

Nisbett, R., & Borgida, E. Attribution and the psychology of prediction. *Journal of Personality and Social Psychology*, 1975, **32**, 932–943.

Nisbett, R., & Ross, L. *Human inference: Strategies and shortcomings of social judgment*. Englewood Cliffs, New Jersey: Prentice-Hall, Inc., 1980.

Nisbett, R. E., & Wilson, T. D. Telling more than we can know: Verbal reports on mental processes. *Psychological Review*, 1977, **84**, 231–259.

Norman, D. A., & Rumelhart, D. E. *Exploration in cognition*. San Francisco, California: Freeman, 1975.

Osgood, C. E. *Method and theory in experimental psychology*. New York: Oxford University Press, 1953.

Ostrom, T. M., Lingle, J. H., Pryor, J. B., & Geva, N. Cognitive organization of person impressions. In R. Hastie, T. M. Ostrom, E. B. Ebbesen, R. S. Wyer, D. L. Hamilton, & D. E. Carlston (Eds.), *Person memory*. Hillsdale, New Jersey: Erlbaum, 1980.

Palmer, S. E. Fundamental aspects of cognitive representation. In E. Rosch & B. B. Lloyd (Eds.), *Cognition and categorization*. Hillsdale, New Jersey: Erlbaum, 1978.

Park, B., & Rothbart, M. Perception of out-group homogeneity and levels of social categorization: Memory for the subordinate attributes of in-group and out-group members. *Journal of Personality and Social Psychology*, 1982, **42**, 1051–1068.

Parsons, J. Eccles, & Ruble, D. The development of achievement-related expectancies. *Child Development*, 1977, **48**, 1075–1079.

Peterson, C., & Beach, L. F. Man as an intuitive statistician. *Psychological Bulletin*, 1967, **68**, 29–46.

Quillian, M. R. The Teachable Language Comprehender: A simulation program and theory of language. *Communications of the ACM*, 1969, **12**, 459–476.

Reder, L. M., & Anderson, J. R. A partial resolution of the paradox of interference: The role of integrating knowledge. *Cognitive Psychology*, 1980, **12**, 447–472.

Rosch, E., & Lloyd, B. B. *Cognition and categorization*. Hillsdale, New Jersey: Erlbaum, 1978.

Ross, B. H., & Bower, G. H. Comparisons of models of associative recall. *Memory and Cognition*, 1981, **9**, 1–16.

Roth, D., & Rehm, L. P. Relationships among self-monitoring processes, memory, and depression. *Cognitive Therapy and Research*, 1980, **4**, 149–158.

Rothbart, M., Evans, M., & Fulero, S. Recall for confirming events: Memory processes and the maintenance of social stereotypes. *Journal of Experimental Social Psychology*, 1979, **15**, 343–355.

Russell, B. *Philosophy.* New York: Norton, 1927.

Sampson, E. E. Cognitive psychology as ideology. *American Psychologist,* 1981, **36,** 730–743.

Schneider, D. J. Implicit personality theory: A review. *Psychological Bulletin,* 1973, **79,** 294–309.

Schneider, D., Hastorf, A. H., & Ellsworth, P. C. *Person perception* (2nd ed.). Reading, Massachusetts: Addison-Wesley, 1979.

Schneider, W., & Shiffrin, R. M. Controlled and automatic human information processing: I. Detection, search, and attention. *Psychological Review,* 1977, **84,** 1–66.

Schustack, M., & Anderson, J. R. Effects of analogy to prior knowledge on memory for new information. *Journal of Verbal Learning and Verbal Behavior,* 1979, **18,** 565–583.

Searle, J. R. The myth of the computer. (Review of D. R. Hofstadter & D. C. Dennett's *The Mind's I: Fantasies and reflections on self and soul.*) In *New York Review of Books,* April 29, 1982.

Sentis, K. P., & Burnstein, E. Remembering schema-consistent information: Effects of a balance schema on recognition memory. *Journal of Personality and Social Psychology,* 1979, **37,** 2200–2211.

Sherman, R. C., & Titus, W. Covariation information and cognitive processing: Effects of causal implications on memory. *Journal of Personality and Social Psychology,* 1982, **42,** 989–1000.

Skinner, B. F. *Science and human behavior.* New York: Macmillan, 1953.

Smith, D. A., & Graesser, A. C. Memory for actions in scripted activities as a function of typicality, retention interval, and retrieval task. *Memory and Cognition,* 1981, **9,** 550–559.

Smith, E. E. Organization of factual knowledge. *Nebraska Symposium.* Lincoln, Nebraska: Univ. of Nebraska Press, 1980.

Smith, E. E., Adams, N., & Schorr, D. Fact retrieval and the paradox of interference. *Cognitive Psychology,* 1978, **10,** 438–464.

Synder, M., & Uranowitz, S. W. Reconstructing the past: Some cognitive consequences of person perception. *Journal of Personality and Social Psychology,* 1978, **36,** 941–950.

Solso, R. L. (Ed.), *Information processing and cognition: The Loyola Symposium.* Hillsdale, New Jersey: Erlbaum, 1975.

Solso, R. L. *Cognitive psychology.* New York: Harcourt, 1979.

Srull, T. K. Person memory: Some tests of associative storage and retrieval models. *Journal of Experimental Psychology: Human Learning and Memory,* 1981, **7,** 440–463.

Sternberg, S. High-speed scanning in human memory. *Science,* 1966, **153,** 652–654.

Suppe, F. The search for philosophic understanding of scientific theories. In F. Suppe (Ed.), *The structure of scientific theories* (2nd ed.). Urbana, Illinois: Univ. of Illinois Press, 1977.

Taylor, S. E. The interface of cognitive and social psychology. In J. Harvey (Ed.), *Cognition, social behavior, and the environment.* Hillsdale, New Jersey: Erlbaum, 1981.

Taylor, S. E., & Crocker, J. Schematic bases of social information processing. In E. T. Higgins, C. A. Herman, & M. P. Zanna (Eds.), *Social cognition: The Ontario Symposium.* Hillsdale, New Jersey: Erlbaum, 1981.

Thorndike, E. L. *The fundamentals of learning.* New York: Columbia Univ. Press, 1932.

Tulving, E. Episodic and semantic memory. In E. Tulving & W. Donaldson (Eds.), *Organization and memory.* New York: Academic Press, 1972.

Watson, J. B. *Behavior: An introduction to comparative psychology.* New York: Holt, 1914.

Wells, G. L., & Harvey, J. H. Naive attributors' attributions and predictions: What is informative and when is an effect an effect? *Journal of Personality and Social Psychology,* 1978, **36,** 483–490.

Welty, E. *The collected stories of Eudora Welty.* New York: Harcourt, 1980.

Winograd, T. *Language as a cognitive process.* New York: Academic Press, 1972.

Wyer, R. S., & Carlston, D. E. *Social cognition, inference, and attribution.* Hillsdale, New Jersey: Erlbaum, 1979.

Wyer, R. S., & Gordon, S. E. The recall of information about persons and groups. *Journal of Experimental Social Psychology,* 1982, **18,** 128–164.

Wyer, R. S., & Srull, T. K. The processing of social stimulus information: A conceptual integration. In R. Hastie, T. M. Ostrom, E. B. Ebbesen, R. S. Wyer, D. L. Hamilton, & D. E. Carlston (Eds.), *Person memory.* Hillsdale, New Jersey: Erlbaum, 1980.

Zajonc, R. B. The process of cognitive tuning in communication. *Journal of Abnormal and Social Psychology,* 1960, **61,** 159–167.

Zajonc, R. B. Cognition and social cognition: A historical perspective. In L. Festinger (Ed.), *Retrospections on social psychology.* New York: Oxford Univ. Press, 1980. (a)

Zajonc, R. B. Feeling and thinking: Preferences need no inferences. *American Psychologist,* 1980, **35,** 151–175. (b)

PARADIGMATIC BEHAVIORISM: UNIFIED THEORY FOR SOCIAL–PERSONALITY PSYCHOLOGY*

Arthur W. Staats[†]

SOCIAL SCIENCE RESEARCH INSTITUTE
UNIVERSITY OF HAWAII
HONOLULU, HAWAII

*The author wishes to express appreciation to Donald Topping, Director of the Social Science Research Institute, for the support that enabled this paper to be written.
†Present address: Department of Psychology, University of Hawaii, Honolulu, Hawaii 96822.

125

ADVANCES IN EXPERIMENTAL
SOCIAL PSYCHOLOGY, VOL. 16

I. The Problem of Disorganization

In inviting me to write this chapter, Leonard Berkowitz's letter indicated that "contemporary social psychology is to a very considerable extent an applied cognitive psychology. Stimulus–response conceptions are, in my view, unduly minimized." Several points in this statement coincide with my views in a manner that is relevant to the position I will present in this chapter. Berkowitz's statement can be viewed to involve metascientific, or methodological, questions concerning the nature of social psychology—for example, what is the role of stimulus–response (S–R) theory in social psychology? In the past several years, especially, I have focused some of my interests on the methodological aspects of psychology, in characterizing what psychology is as a science, and it is productive to use these interests in the consideration of social psychology in the present context.

As Berkowitz implies, social psychology is largely an applied cognitive psychology. But in what sense can we consider social psychology to be applied? Not in the traditional sense—that is, that its work consists of professional, problem-solving use of basic science knowledge to deal with practical problems—for our area is largely academic in nature. The sense in which the field could be considered applied is that social psychology *utilizes* a "background" theory, a conceptual body, that we can call general cognitive theory. And in our science of psychology the general study of cognition—perception, images, memory, thought, and so on—traditionally lies in another field, that of experimental psychology. I have alluded to social psychology's cognitive conceptual framework as a background theory, because it is not a precisely stated body of general principles that is developed in a systematic, integrated way. Also, social psychologists do not systematically derive their particular concepts and principles from the cognitive theory that is developed and investigated in experimental psychology, in the manner that would occur if experimental psychology were the basic field and social psychology the applied field. Rather, the basic underlying cognitive conception in social psychology has "grown like Topsy," on the basis of materials largely indigenous to social psychology and to other "applied" areas of psychology. Many diverse and unrelated conceptual developments have contributed to the background theory of social psychology, including developments from various areas of psychology and from common knowledge. The cognitive conceptual framework of social psychology is not a systematically developed theory. It is an "understood" general framework, rather than one that is punctiliously stated. Thus, the human being is considered to have internal structures and processes that determine her or his behavior. For example, a person is thought to have cognitions of various kinds such as causal attributions, awareness of situation demands and contingencies, cognitive dissonances, perceptions, themes, information-processing attributes, attention processes, roles and role characteristics, self-perceptions, and so on, and motivations of different kinds such as various types of attitudes, depression resulting from helplessness, intrinsic and extrinsic rewards, reactance, arousal, individual and collective interests, emotions, effectance motivation, and so on. An unlimited number of internal cognitive–motivational processes can be, or have been, introduced into the field on the basis of naturalistic and systematic observations and theorization. Moreover, the background theory of social psychology includes a myriad of personality theories, and their concepts, any element of which can be employed in projecting an experimental study—and the variation of approaches in personality theory is legend, each accepted as equally pertinent (Rychlak, 1968, p. 454).

Journals of personality and social psychology publish many studies of various phenomena of a personal and social sort. And the experimentally manipulated behavioral phenomena will be considered in terms of the multitude of concepts and principles available in the loosely stated body of "cognitive" theory. How the various concepts and principles and theories that are accepted in the field of social psychology are related to each other and, hence, how the findings of the various studies are related is not known, nor is this generally a topic of concern. The fact is that the underlying conceptual system, the underlying theory that constitutes the cognitive-personality theory of social psychology, is not systematically or precisely stated. It is an understood but unarticulated background theory that accommodates a multitude of concepts and principles ranging from those of a common sense cast to those with a basis in systematic, but restricted theories. The underlying framework is loose and elastic, giving freedom to encompass various beliefs; religious, humanistic, theoretical, and experimental. We can see acceptance of this state of social psychology in various statements that at least implicitly refer to the conceptual disorganization of the field, for example: "Theory construction in social psychology is in such a state of flux that it is not an exaggeration to say that last year's model often gets recalled" (Wrightsman, 1977, p. 7). Wrightsman, however, attempts to rationalize the problem state of theory in social psychology, defending the abundance of unrelated theories with the following philosophy: "The question is: which theory should be used? No one theory adequately accounts for all social phenomena. . . . This problem is not limited to social psychology; Kaufman, 1973, notes that there is no all-encompassing theory that can be used throughout the science of physics (Wrightsman, 1977, p. 7).

The analogy with the state of theory unification in physics is quite wide of the mark, actually, for the natural sciences are immeasurably more unified than is social psychology. The point that I wish to make, however, is that there is growing awareness that something is wrong with the disorganized state of knowledge in social psychology—even though there has not been a clear and succinct understanding of what is involved. We can see this puzzled dissatisfaction in various other expressions, such as the following statement from Michael Argyle.

"American psychology and especially social psychology . . . tends to move in fashions. One year there will be a lot of people working on one or another aspect. Two years later something else. . . . By the time the stuff starts getting published, probably everybody's given up doing it . . . and nobody is remotely interested" (Evans, 1978, p. 7).

Moscovici states essentially the same thing. "From time to time the interests of the research are mobilized by themes or areas which appear new and important at the moment; but sooner or later these prove to be sterile or exhausted and they are abandoned" (Moscovici, 1972, p. 32). Berkowitz describes the state of social psychology in the following terms. "We seem to be in, or at least approaching, a 'crisis' stage [to use Kuhn's (1962) term] in which diversity is paramount" (1970b, p. 299). The general dissatisfaction is captured in the following, in a statement indicating that the problem extends beyond social psychology into the field of psychology in general.

> Social psychologists once knew who they were and where they were going. The field's major scientific problems were obvious, and means to solve them were readily available. . . . Exciting new research discoveries were often reported, and theoretical developments seemed to promise dramatic advances in understanding of human behavior. . . .
>
> During the past decade, . . . many social psychologists appear to have lost not only their enthusiasm but also their sense of direction and their faith in the discipline's future. Whether they are experiencing an identity crisis, a paradigmatic crisis, or a crisis of confidence, most seem agreed that a crisis is at hand. . . .
>
> These widespread self-doubts about goals, methods, and accomplishments are by no means unique to social psychology. Similar doubts have been expressed recently within many other areas of psychology, particularly the closely related fields of personality research . . . , developmental psychology . . . , and clinical psychology. (Elms, 1975, pp. 967–968)

These observations are expressions of a criticism of social psychology in particular and psychology in general. But the criticism has had little effect. Psychology continues on its way, doing the same things it has always done, under the guidance given to it by its mission of becoming a science (see Staats, 1983). Psychologists proliferate experiments and theories, in fact at a greater rate than in the "golden age" described above. In the present view, however, there is something awry in psychology that is so general and so basic that our science will keep spinning its wheels until that basic problem is solved. Psychology is in a crisis that is felt but not known. This crisis requires systematic treatment and understanding, so that it can be remedied, which in turn calls for a major change in the nature of the science (Staats, 1983). While it is not possible to give the topic full treatment herein, the framework involved undergirds the present work.

To continue, however, what has been described as traditional "applied cognitive psychology" is a loosely articulated theoretical body (consisting of many, varied elements) that is generally accepted, but whose basic principles are not systematically isolated for study in the field, or in some more basic field such as experimental psychology. Moreover, this theoretical body is employed to project many studies that are also loosely related. Now the concern of the present paper is with S–R, or behavioral, formulations, and it is thus relevant at this point to ask how such formulations fit into this picture. Wrightsman, in attempting to characterize the profusion of theoretical elements in social psychology, has suggested that there are five theory types: psychoanalytic theory, role theory, S–R (or behavioral or learning) theory, Gestalt theory, and field theory (1977). Such a schema is oversimplified, however. Where would the implicit personality theory of Kim and Rosenberg (1980) fit, or the learned helplessness conceptualizations and findings such as the sex differences in learned helplessness (Dweck, Goetz, & Strauss, 1980), or conformity theory and findings such as the stimulus meaning conception of Allen and Wilder (1980), Russell's circumplex model of affect (1980), information and stress relationships (see Baum & Fisher, 1981)? Primarily, thus, Wrightsman's five-theoretical-types appears to be more of a categorization scheme by which to organize the contents of a classic textbook, than a conceptual analysis having theoretical or empirical implications.

Berkowitz, albeit in the informality of a letter addressing another purpose, mentions a distinction between S–R approaches and what he calls applied cognitive psychology. Let me elaborate such a distinction in the present context. Although there are differences amongst the various theories in traditional social psychology (applied cognitive psychology), and although they are not articulated into a general theory, and although they are too numerous to be categorized in a handful of ways, the various theories do not directly challenge one another. In basic terms they are accepting of one another, and they are considered to be of the same general nature. The same cannot be said of behavioral approaches. There are distinct and strong issues that make it difficult for the behavioral approaches and orthodox social–personality approaches to live amicably with one another, or to be coherent and mutually productive. This is an important concern of the present analysis, since the achievement of unity of science in the field of social–personality is to be a central concern. Let me broaden this to say the present chapter considers (1) the general nature of social psychology with respect to its disunity-unity, (2) the S–R conceptions that have penetrated this field, (3) the effect these theories have had on the field's unification, (4) a general methodology for producing unified theory, and (5) a particular approach that aims to provide the unifying articulation the field desperately needs.

II. S–R Conceptions in Social Psychology

In contemporary times there are a number of learning theories in social psychology, each with a separate empirical foundation and each considered to be a separate theory. It is relevant to characterize a few of these, at least partially and briefly, as a means of indicating something about the place of this orientation in the resolution of the problem under consideration.

A.   THE RISE AND CHARACTER OF BEHAVIORISTIC
     APPROACHES

To understand in a general way the character and role of S–R approaches in social psychology it is necessary to have an understanding of the characteristics of behaviorism. (Excellent works describing the evolution of behaviorism have been made by the eminent Spanish psychologist Mariano Yela, 1974, 1979). An important consideration lies in the general context of the second generation learning theories (or behaviorisms). The first generation of behaviorism consisted of such individuals as Pavlov and Thorndike and Watson. The focus of their work involved the experimental isolation of the principle of learning through contiguity (classical conditioning) and the principle of learning through reinforcement (instrumental conditioning), and the elaboration of these principles in the context of human behavior, at least in an incipient way.

The second generation of behaviorism took on a different character. Faced by the two principles of conditioning, and the extensive experimental literature that had developed based upon the two principles, the central task of the second generation theorists became that of composing general theories of animal learning that would incorporate the various experimental findings and would rationalize the relationship of the two conditioning principles. The puzzle of this relationship was solved differently by the various theorists and the differences became hallmarks of the theories and the stimulus for some of the research generated by the theories. For example, a second generation theorist, Edwin Guthrie, considered all of the experimental findings on conditioning to be explainable via one principle, that of contiguity (classical conditioning). Clark Hull, on the other side, also theorized that there was only one conditioning principle, but that the principle was reinforcement. B. F. Skinner seemingly took another position in saying that there were two different and separate conditioning principles, classical conditioning (which he renamed respondent conditioning) and instrumental conditioning (which he renamed operant conditioning). In actuality, Skinner was a one-factor theorist: classical conditioning, in his theory, was essentially an epiphenomenon, something that had nothing to do with behavior. For Skinner, behavior was governed solely by instrumental conditioning.

These theories were competitors, that is, separate theoretical bodies. They did not support each other, but rather contested one another, each trying to be *the* learning theory with its special theory–construction methodology, its special theoretical principles, methods of experimentation, and so on. These characteristics of second generation behaviorism are relevant here, because the extension of the learning theories into the human areas of study—social psychology in the present case—was affected by these characteristics, as will be indicated. Several things may be noted for later discussion: (1) the theories were competitors, and (2) the nature of the basic conditioning principles was a key issue in the contest.

1. Doob's Analysis of Attitudes and Osgood's Analysis of Meaning

The second generation of behaviorism was centered in the animal laboratory. The emphasis through the 1950s was not on human research or the human implications of learning theory. Instead, the main interests were in composing systematic theories of animal experimental findings and in projecting animal learning research to test and elaborate those theories. The theories were animal learning theories. Around 1950, however, interest in human implications of animal learning theory began to revive (see, e.g., Doob, 1947; Dollard & Miller, 1950; Miller & Dollard, 1941; Mowrer, 1950, 1954; Rotter, 1954; Osgood, 1953), at least on a theoretical level, for behaviorism did not have methods of research for studying complex human behavior. Most pointedly here, Doob formulated an analysis of attitudes in the framework of Hull's learning theory. According to Doob, attitudes were fractional anticipatory goal responses that could be elicited by a situation and that themselves could produce stimuli that would guide overt goal-oriented instrumental responses. Osgood used the same theoretical principles by which to define the similar concept of word meaning, including evaluative meaning (which he equated with attitudes), in a manner that was very much in agreement with Doob's analysis. It is significant to point out that these theoretical efforts generally followed the characteristics of the second generation of behaviorism—that is, they tended as in the above cases to select one or the other learning theory as *the* theory by which to approach the study of human behavior. They were applied theories in the usual sense of the word, formed by taking generally basic theories and applying them to a more complex realm of events. Another significant point is that these were theoretical analyses within the basic theories, which rested upon animal learning studies, and which did not for the most part involve human experimental findings. While Osgood developed the semantic differential for measuring word meaning, for example, he did not investigate the conditioning principles involved in his theoretical statement, nor did Doob. The next section, however, describes some of the human research and theory that arose within the second generation behavioristic framework and considers a sampling of some major achievements relevant to the direction of development to be followed herein.

2. Experimental and Theoretical Elaboration of Conditioning Principles in Social Psychology: Lott and Lott, Staats

Bernice Eisman Lott (1955) conducted a study that very explicitly attempted to provide experimental underpinning for the basic principles of the analysis formulated by Doob. Her work may be considered to be a basic experimental definition of Doob's concept of attitudes. In Lott's very complicated study, which followed Doob's complex Hullian analysis, children were rewarded for choosing a block with a particular color name. Later it was found that the children's behavior in various choice situations was mediated by the color name. Lott and Lott (1960) extended this approach by conducting a more straightforward and understandable study of the behavior of group cohesiveness mediated by an attitude. The attitude was defined as an implicit anticipatory goal response having cue and drive properties (1960, p. 297). The theory applied to the social interaction was that if a person was rewarded in the presence of another individual, the person would experience a goal response that would be conditioned to the individual. The learned anticipatory goal response would constitute the person's attitude toward the individual. As a consequence, the person would prefer being with the individual more than another person would who had not had the experience of reward with the individual. Lott and Lott tested this theoretical analysis by having "three-member groups of children [play] a game in which some members were rewarded and others were not. On a later sociometric test, outside of the game situation, rewarded *Ss* chose a significantly greater proportion of their fellow group members than did the nonrewarded *Ss* (Lott & Lott, 1960, p. 300). Lott and Lott continued their experimental analysis of interpersonal attitudes in a series of studies (see Lott & Lott, 1968, 1972; Lott, 1977). Importantly, the work involved a straightforward application of Hullian principles, and not the introduction of a new learning theory or new human learning principles and mechanisms or new theoretical concepts.

The present author, also in the early 1950s, began a systematic program, the goal of which was the empirical study of human behavior within the context of conditioning principles but including the formulation of a general theory of learning and a theory of human behavior as well. As will be seen, this development did not follow one particular second generation theory of learning. Moreover, the work involved in this effort was directed towards various aspects of human behavior (for example, behavior relevant to clinical psychology, child development, educational psychology, and experimental psychology) not just social psychology. Examination of the part of this work relevant to the present concerns follows.

While still a graduate student in 1953 the present author was interested in language and attitude formation and function. It is relevant to note that the first experimental exploration of the principles of his growing analysis involved testing the principles of classical conditioning in the context of how a pet cat could learn to respond to verbal stimuli. The cat was punished in the process of its toilet training, and the punishment was paired with the pronunciation of a word, "no." According to the theory involved—and in agreement with the analyses of Osgood (1953) and Mowrer (1954)—the word "no" should in this procedure come to serve as a conditioned stimulus for a negative attitude (emotional) response. The author applied the conditioning systematically, and systematically observed the effects of the word on the cat's behavior. The author and associates (see Staats, Staats, & Crawford, 1972) later formally conducted a study in the middle 1950s that confirmed the principles that were found, using human subjects. People could be considered to learn the emotional properties of words through classical conditioning.

During the same period the author extended the conception involved to consideration of the learning of attitudes in humans through "vicarious" means. The above experiment (and that of Eisman Lott, it may be noted) involved primary conditioning principles taken directly from animal learning theory. The present author, however, reasoned that attitude learning with humans more generally occurs in ways that are not really analogous to the animal laboratory, and that these ways involve higher learning processes not available to the animal, particularly cognitive or language processes. The theory behind these studies was that emotional words (of which there are many in our language) are those that have come, through primary and various forms of vicarious conditioning, to elicit an emotional response (positive or negative). These words, as a consequence of their emotional properties, could make any new stimulus object, event, or person either positive or negative simply through being paired with that stimulus, or through being attached to that stimulus, as in naming a stimulus. The author, in an extensive exploratory effort, worked out an experimental procedure for producing attitudinal conditioning to a new stimulus through pairing emotional words with that stimulus. Following the author's first experimental validation of the language conditioning method and principles, two replicative experiments were carried out by the author's wife in her dissertation study, to verify his theory additionally (see Staats, C. K., & Staats, A. W., 1957). At the same time he projected a study to demonstrate that attitudes towards social stimuli could be learned via language in this way (Staats & Staats, 1958). Many studies employing these language conditioning methods and principles have been conducted (see, for example, Early, 1968; Hekmat, 1972, 1973; Leduc, 1980a, 1980b; Parish, 1974; Parish, Buntman, & Buntman, 1976; Parish & Fleetwood, 1975; Sachs & Byrne, 1970). Of special note is the productive theoretical–empirical work of the group headed by Leduc in Quebec (see also Leduc, 1976, 1978; Henry and Leduc, 1982; Morissette and Leduc, 1981). These studies investigate the acquisition of social attitudes and the behavior that is exhibited towards the object of the attitudes.

The Lott and Lott and the present author's lines of work have been selected for description first because they constitute a basic, analytic use of learning principles. The social psychology theories involved are closely derived from a set of basic learning principles developed to deal with the facts of animal learning. The principles are stipulated and defined in the social context and expectations at the human social level are derived from the principles. The two approaches include early experimental developments of such learning theories in the social context (Berkowitz's and Byrne's theories, to be described in the next section, are also learning theory-based, theoretical–experimental formulations in the field of social psychology). In addition, the first studies constituted beginnings of systematic programs of research and theoretical elaboration, the theories involved have been followed by others' experiments that validate the theoretical bodies involved, and finally there are both similarities and differences in the theoretical bodies and methodology of these two approaches, as will be indicated. In general, in terms of similarity, both approaches began in the context of Hull's basic theory of learning. This must be qualified, however, in the case of Staats' theory. Even at the beginning, this theory only utilized parts of Hull's theory, and these parts were combined with parts of other basic learning theories. Furthermore, as will be indicated, in addition to the selectivity and integratory nature of the theory, new features were formulated at the basic learning-theory level, such that the outcome was a new learning theory. Bernice Eisman Lott began in the Hull–Doob tradition and with Albert Lott consistently developed their learning theory of interpersonal attitudes within this theoretical framework. This circumstance has made for the similarities and differences between these two theories, even at the level of basic principles. We can see this in the summary of the learning theory of interpersonal attitudes of Lott and Lott, using their own words.

1. Persons may be conceptualized as discriminable stimuli to which responses may be learned.
2. A person who experiences reinforcement or reward for some behavior will react to the reward, i.e., will perform some observable or covert goal response (R_G or r_g).
3. This response to reward will become conditioned, like any other response, to all discriminable stimuli present at the time of reinforcement.
4. A person . . . who is present at the time that Individual X, for example, is rewarded thus becomes able in a later situation to evoke R_G, or, what is more likely, its fractional and anticipatory component, r_g-s_g. This latter response, which Hull has called "expectative" (1952, Ch. 5), was earlier interpreted by Doob (1947) as the underlying mechanism of attitude (Lott & Lott, 1960, pp. 366–367).

It may be added that the anticipatory response was considered by Hull to be a mediating response that would tend to elicit overt responses instrumental in attaining the actual goal stimulus, and Doob followed this principle in his analysis of attitudes, as did Lott and Lott (1968). It should be noted that there is an animal learning model that is an essential part of this theory. That model consists of an animal–maze situation that involves the animal subject making a response and receiving a bit of food. This food elicits the Goal Response (R_G), and the anticipatory goal response (r_g) is conditioned to the goal box and is elicited by it and ultimately on later trials to earlier portions of the maze or runway. The important thing is that the theory is imbued with certain characteristics because of its use of this model of animal learning. For one thing, the model is clear for the positive case of reward, but it is not so clear for the negative case. We must ask, what is the counterpart, on the negative side, of the Goal Response? For Hull, all learning took place through the reinforcement of drive reduction. In the negative case, then, for example, in which the animal learns an escape response from shock, the reinforcement is the drive reduction of cessation of the shock. The Goal Response, it should be noted, is in this case still positive. What is a negative attitude, then, within this theory? We thus see as a consequence, I would suggest, that theories such as that of Lott and Lott deal with attraction, the positive case, but do not indicate clearly how their principles are related theoretically to negative attitudes and negative social behaviors. More generally, the social (paradigmatic) behaviorism position is that the classic learning theories were each composed some 45 or more years ago, with other purposes in mind, as will be indicated further on, and none of them is a good basic instrument with which to deal with human behavior. The social behaviorism basic theory of learning will be described in a later section. Here it only will be said that the theory of Staats (see Staats, 1957, 1963, 1964, 1968b, 1975; Staats & Staats, 1957, 1958), in being derived from the tradition of second-generation behaviorism in relevant parts, has common features with the theories of Doob, Osgood, Mowrer, and Lott and Lott, all of whom took their departure from Hull's theory. However, the present author's approach from the beginning was not that of adopting one or the other of the second generation theorists, for example, Hull's, Skinner's, or Tolman's. Parts of each of those preceding theories were employed, but others were rejected, and new principles and concepts were added, the result being the new three-function learning theory, one that employs *different learning models* from those of the animal learning laboratory.

3. The Learning Theories of Berkowitz and Byrne

Berkowitz has been conducting over the years one of the most systematic and extensive learning-oriented analyses in social psychology. The tradition in which this work arose was also that of Hull's theory of learning but not the primary learning theory as it was developed by Hull, or even Doob. Rather, Berkowitz first used Hull's theory one step removed, as it was joined with psychoanalytic theory in the development that has been called neobehaviorism (see Berkowitz, 1962). Miller and Dollard (see especially Dollard & Miller, 1950) attempted to construct a learning-oriented theory of human behavior by combining some of the features of Hull's learning theory with some of the

features of psychoanalytic theory. The learning principles were those of Hull—
for example, that all learning occurred on the basis of reinforcement—but simplified a great deal. The first basic principle was that the subject must experience
a *drive* which impels the subject to respond. The cues of the situation, which
include the drive stimuli, elicit various responses in the subject. If one of the
responses is rewarded (reinforced) in the situation by reducing the drive, the
subject will learn to make that response in that cue situation (Miller & Dollard,
1941). Additional principles were tacked on to that set of basic principles, for
example, that the drive would be conditioned to the cues with which it was
associated, that drive and responses learned to one cue would generalize to
similar cues, and that drives could be negative as well as positive (Miller, 1948;
Berkowitz, 1962). Dollard and Miller (1950), as an example of the manner in
which the learning theory was combined with psychoanalytic theory, explained
defense mechanisms in terms of reinforcement. Projection is one example.

> Circumstances . . . tend to cause the individual to think that others are motivated in the
> same way that he is. Freudians have noted that there is often a "kernel of fact" in the
> motivation attributed to someone else and have supposed that the "projector" could detect
> such unconscious motivation in the other person. . . . But this behavior is usually called
> projection only when the others are not obviously motivated in the same way. Often in
> projection the individual not only labels others' motives incorrectly but also fails to label his
> own correctly. Such behavior is reinforced by the reduction in anxiety that occurs when the
> blame is shifted to the other person. (Dollard & Miller, 1950, p. 182)

These authors exemplify the principles by a case of a man who has homo-
sexual drives, elicited by another man, that elicit anxiety in the former. He
represses the ideas that give rise to the anxiety, but is unhappy in the presence of
the other. He does not know why he dislikes the other person and the "thought
that the other person disliked him and was presecuting him occurred and was
reinforced by the reduction of in anxiety it produced through providing a logical
explanation" (Dollard & Miller, 1950, p. 183), and so on.

Berkowitz's work has developed in this tradition, in the context of making
an analysis of anger and aggression that has also included a vigorous experimental treatment of the theory's concepts and principles. For Berkowitz, aggression
"is defined as behavior whose goal is the injury of some person or object"
(1964, p. 104), following the treatment given this concept by Dollard, Doob,
Miller, Mowrer, and Sears (1939). Anger is regarded as the drive produced by
frustration that instigates aggressive behavior and is reduced by the injury to the
other that is produced and which acts as the reinforcement. Berkowitz has been
concerned especially with whether displaced or sublimated aggression can have a
cathartic effect (Berkowitz, 1970a), and with the effects of additional aggres-
sion-provoking stimuli (Berkowitz, 1973). In addition to this theory tradition,

Berkowitz also introduced to his theory the principles of classical conditioning, including conditioning through language. As an example of an experiment in this series, Berkowitz and Knurek (1969) conditioned subjects, via the language conditioning procedures, to have a negative attitude towards a name. The subjects were also either insulted or were not, by the experimenter. Later the subjects were introduced to an individual (confederate) who bore that name, or a different name, but who did not know the experimental condition of the subject. Subjects who had been insulted by the experimenter displaced their anger, as measured by a hostility–friendliness rating, on to the confederate regardless of his name, but more so if his name was the same as that for which they had a conditioned negative attitude. Moreover, these findings agreed with the ratings the confederate made of the subjects' behavior toward them. "In addition to demonstrating the generalization of a negatively conditioned attitude, the Berkowitz-Knurek . . . experiment had tried to show that persons having certain stimulus properties are particularly likely to be the 'scapegoat' victims of 'displaced hostility' following anger arousal: persons having characteristics the angry individual had previously learned to dislike" (Berkowitz, 1973, p. 117).

In the above experiment, besides its clear social significance, one of the concerns was with the effects of symbols (names) on aggression. (It may be noted that independently Staats and Higa [1970] completed another very similar study that showed the effect of occupational names, positive or negative, on interpersonal attitudes.) Berkowitz (1974) has also been concerned with the effects of other symbolic stimuli on the instigation of aggression. Thus, for example, Berkowitz and LePage (1967) found that subjects who had been made angry were more aggressive than nonangry subjects when there were stimuli present that had aggressive symbolic value (i.e., guns). Berkowitz's program for the study of aggression may be considered to be learning based, originally utilizing a simplified version of Hullian learning theory combined with concepts and principles from psychoanalytic theory, with later developments including additional learning principles and analyses—for example, those involving the emotional qualities of words (cognitions). This approach has been extended increasingly to a wider and wider set of phenomena in this area of study, along with the systematically advancing experimental series of studies. In later papers Berkowitz has come to stress the principle of classical conditioning of emotional responses in the elicitation of aggression, along with the drive inducement to aggression. The result is an imposing theoretical–experimental body that is well related to preceding and contemporary developments.

The Byrne–Clore–Griffitt program of study bears methodological features that are similar to the three programs already described in terms of its systematic investigation of an area of social psychology. Like the Lott and Lott's investigation, the focus has been on attraction. The contribution of the program has been of an experimental nature; its theoretical principles being those of the other learning theories of social psychology. Although commencing in a more traditional theoretical framework that emphasized the effect of similarity of attitudes on attraction (Byrne, 1961, 1962), Byrne's work has progressively adopted principles coincident with the three-function learning theory approach. The first study in this program was that of Golightly and Byrne (1964) in which it was found that statements that agreed with one's own attitudes were reinforcing, and a number of later studies were conducted to demonstrate the reinforcement value of attitude similarity on attraction (Byrne & Griffitt, 1966; Byrne, Griffitt & Clore, 1969; Byrne & Nelson, 1965). Stalling (1970), more specifically working in the context of three-function learning theory, showed that it was not the agreement in attitude statements itself that was the reinforcing stimulus, but rather the emotional value of the stimuli involved. Later studies in this program (which, incidently, supported a number of experiments hypothecated theoretically, see Staats, 1964, pp. 329–326) began working with this more general view of attitudes as emotion-eliciting stimuli that as incentives could affect the behavior of the subjects. For example, Byrne, Ervin, and Lamberth (1970) tested the effect of physical beauty on attraction. Male and female subjects after spending 30 minutes together demonstrated that beauty influenced such behaviors as standing close together, remembering the other's name, talking after the experiment, ratings as a desirable partner, and desire to date. This study supported the primary principles of the three-function learning theory that positive emotional responses tended to elicit a whole hierarchy of approach behaviors. Pandey and Griffitt (1974) showed that subjects with positive attitudes toward a person will help (perform work for) that other person more than subjects who have neutral or negative attitudes. Griffitt and Veitch (1971) showed in the negative direction, in a manner that supplements Berkowitz's concern with the effect of negative emotional responding on "negative" behaviors, that a hot and crowded physical atmosphere produced measures of dislike towards another person.

Byrne (1971) has addressed himself to some extent to general questions of theory construction and it is interesting to note in the present context that he considers the body of learning principles to serve the role of an abstract model that can be used in an analogical sense. That is, from his view, there is no suggestion that human behavior generally involves learning of the type demonstrated in the animal laboratory, but only that the principles of conditioning are productive models when applied to certain social situations. This is a different and far more restricted view than that which is involved in the present approach. Byrne's theory may be considered to use learning principles, but only as a tool, for specific purposes. His theorizing, thus, has not made contact with the basic field of learning theory, but has involved the employment of principles that others have found useful in working with human behavior. The experiments conducted in this program have been highly valuable however.

III. Types of Learning Theories of Social Psychology

Within the scope of this paper it is not possible to represent the richness of the learning theories in the field or the empirical products they have stimulated. Rather, the theories of Lott and Lott, Berkowitz, Byrne–Clore–Griffitt, and social behaviorism were selected because of their importance and because they are most closely related to the foundation that is of importance in the present analysis. That is, the major goals of the present chapter involve consideration of a general methodology for the construction of unified theory in social psychology (and psychology generally). Characterization of the four learning theories will provide examples for beginning this methodological consideration.

A. THE REDUCTIONISTIC APPROACH

Traditionally, behavioristic theories in social psychology as in other areas of study have followed the methodology employed by Doob. Doob (1947) adopted one of the extant second generation learning theories (that of Hull)—lock, stock, and barrel—and used principles from the theory to make an analysis of attitudes, at least in the abstract. That was the methodology that was implicitly espoused by his theoretical article. Lott and Lott's program of study has been in this tradition. In their program, attitudes, attraction, and group cohesiveness have been analyzed employing the principles of Hull's theory. Weiss' important program of study (see, for example, Weiss, 1971; Weiss, Boyer, Lombardo, & Stich, 1973; Weiss, Buchanan, Alstatt, & Lombardo, 1971) has in the same manner been based upon Hull's theory. We see a similar strategy in the work of Bem (1967, 1968) and McGinnies (1970; McGinnies & Ferster, 1971), only the theory they selected to employ was that of Skinner (1938). This approach assumes a classic reductionist posture which, implicitly or explicitly, is part of the logical positivism that underlay the learning theories of the second generation behaviorists. This classic reductionism assumes that there are animal learning theories that include principles of a higher-order (more basic) sort, and that lower-order human behavior fields are to be reduced to those higher-level principles. The focus in this view is on constructing the higher-level theory (the theories of learning); the reduction task (human learning theory) then follows from this basic development.

Only two levels of theory construction are recognized in this methodology. And the learning theorists such as Hull and Skinner concentrated their efforts almost exclusively at the first level, that of animal learning. It was in this area that their research was centered, within which their theory efforts were systematic and precise and closely connected to experiments. In the second level—the human behavior level—their theory was sparsely developed and conjectural, in a manner that was not of the same quality as that involved in their work on animal learning theory. They formed systematic theory in one particular area of psychology and simply assumed that everything else was thereby explained, or was capable of being explained. Their actual extensions to the human level was not of the sort that directly, closely gave direction to empirical works on the human behavior level of study. (This was true of behavior modification also, where it was necessary to break away from the Skinner box methods before meaningful work was conducted.) Importantly, their research on the human level had no impact upon their animal learning theories; movement was only in the other direction. Thus, there was no recognition that construction of the basic learning theory might profit from a concern with human behavior phenomena, or that additional principles of learning would have to be introduced at the basic level if an animal learning theory was to be applicable in a general way to human behavior. In the present view there are many studies that can be conducted within this framework that are very valuable. Those that have been described already number among those. However, it is equally apparent that the framework will not be capable of producing the various works that are needed for a theory of human behavior that deals successfully with the broad range of phenomena concerning humans that attract the attention of the psychologist.

B. THE SELECT-A-MODEL APPROACH

As has been indicated, Byrne's methodology has been adapted from that of the model builders, as seen in the strategy of mathematical-learning theorists. Thus, Byrne (1971) considers the task to be one of selecting the most appropriate learning theory available for use as a model in approaching topics of study in social psychology. This approach, it should be noted, is different from one that assumes there is an elementary continuity of learning phenomena from the animal learning laboratory to complex human behavior of all types. In the model building view the model is an abstract structure that is adopted because it is useful; there is no concern that there are fundamental relationships between the phenomena from which the model was derived and the phenomena to which the model is applied. Byrne's methodology is thus separatistic in the sense of giving little attention to the basic-principle level of study. We do not see in Byrne's approach an interest in the origin of the basic principles he employs, or in their validity in the area of basic research. He is interested in adopting principles that seem suited for specific applications on the human level. That the human level of study might have to develop principles in addition to the original principles or might have itself implications for the basic field of study would not derive from this select-a-model approach. Although one source of the principles that Byrne employs is the basic animal laboratory, his theory-construction strategy has the effect of separating the basic and the human level theory development, putting the focus on the field of application rather than on basic principle development. (This strategy may be functional in one sense in present-day social psychology since it makes Byrne's theory appear less behavioristic, thus avoiding the general hostility to behaviorism that exists.) Byrne's theory, in focusing on the lower-level human phenomena, is opposite to that of the reductionists in the sense that their focus is on the basic principles themselves, while he is interested in the basic principles only as a model to apply. As later indicated, it is essential to develop a methodology that gives equal status to the development of the basic principles and to the development of the principles in theory concerned with human behavior. Moreover, it is important to achieve continuity and heuristic value in both directions relevant to the different realms of empirical events involved. Finally, the model-using approach shows no interest in a general unifying theoretical endeavor.

C. THE GENERAL-LEARNING APPROACH

There are many theorists in social psychology who are convinced that human behavior is acquired at least in part through experience—that is, that human behavior is learned—but who only loosely connect their conceptions of learning to the systematic theories that have emerged from the basic laboratory. For example, McGuire (1968) includes reference to how attention to a message affects the influence–value of the message, and learning principles are involved. But the learning principles are not stated precisely in a way that is related to basic learning principles or theories. Greenwald (1968) refers to cognitive learning as a principle in explaining attitude change in persuasion, but in a general way, rather than as a basic principle itself or as one that has been closely derived from a basic principle. Baron (1968) deals with concepts like attractiveness and hedonic value, but again without relating them to basic principles. We see the same approach in the work of Cialdini and Kenrick (see Cialdini, Darby, & Vincent, 1973; Cialdini & Kenrick, 1976; Kenrick, Baumann, & Cialdini, 1979). We find other examples in the work of Aronfreed (1968), Janis and Mann (1968), Bandura and Walters (1959, 1963), as well as others who have called themselves social learning theorists. This is to say that there is a tradition that realizes the importance of learning as an influence on human behavior, but that utilizes general, sometimes common-sense, conceptions of learning, without requiring a systematic basic theory structure or systematic relationship to the work on learning in the basic, animal laboratory.

Again, this learning approach to social phenomena is probably more acceptable to social psychologists because of its distance from the animal laboratory and behaviorism, even though its principles are those of learning. But the approach also does not solve the problem of separatism between cognitive and learning theory knowledge. And this approach loses the value of the detailed study of animal learning and the rich set of analytic principles it offers. Furthermore, the eclectic approach may lack heuristic value for either the animal or human in a general way, as Woll has indicated in criticizing Bandura's social learning theory (1978).

Several strategies have been described whose aim has been to employ learning concepts in the context of problems of significance to social psychology. These methodological strategies have been described in good part to provide a basis for the systematic consideration of the general character of this work—as a means for projecting advancement in that character. With this discussion, for example, we will have a foundation for considering another methodological program that has a basis in learning theory. This program has been systematically developed over several decades of theoretical, experimental, clinical, and methodological work. It includes interest in topics that are not usually central in social psychology, but that in the present opinion should be, for reasons that will be apparent in the work. For example, although the social psychologist is not usually systematically concerned with theories of language, much social interaction is on the basis of language, and understanding those aspects of social interaction may demand a theory of language. In any event, the remainder of the present paper will be devoted to the characterization of a methodology for creating unified theory in psychology, including social psychology, and a characterization of the particular theory—paradigmatic behaviorism—that has been the vehicle by which to arrive at the general statement of the methodology.

IV. The General Unified Theory Methodology of Paradigmatic Behaviorism

It was said in the introduction that cognitive theory in social psychology is loosely articulated. That statement was actually euphemistic. When one examines psychology in general or social psychology in particular one finds that the bodies of knowledge involved constitute a chaos. There are various theories, large and small, that are unrelated. There are different and unrelated problems of study, experimental procedures, and methods of analysis. There are different areas of study that remain unrelated. The result of the many dimensions of difference is the existence of innumerable islands of knowledge unrelated to or competitive with other islands of knowledge. No wonder that there is no experience in our science of a growing, progressively powerful, unified, and thus cumulative body of knowledge and method and apparatus. This preparadigmatic state of psychology has been referred to (Mackenzie, 1977; Staats, 1968b, 1975; Yela, 1979) and a recent work has systematically dealt with this state of our science and its disadvantageous characteristics (Staats, 1983). A few summary remarks on this topic are relevant here.

A. PHILOSOPHY OF UNIFIED THEORY

As has been indicated (Staats, 1983) the separatistic zeitgeist that has served psychology has been that of a preparadigmatic, or disorganized, science. This characterization has been made on the basis of observing the artificial diversity that exists in our science, and on the basis of the serendipitous experience of attempting to construct a unified theory that flies in the face of the reigning zeitgeist. As a dominant characteristic psychology is not and has never been oriented toward the creation of unity of knowledge. There is not a powerful effort devoted to this goal. When one works within this zeitgeist, as most specialists would, the nature of psychology in this respect does not become apparent. The serendipity in my own experience was due to the fact that my work mission brought me into confrontation with the separatistic and disorganized—pre-paradigmatic—nature of our science. In trying to promulgate a unified theory, a primary aspect of my work, I experienced how important the divisions of the science were, how the divisive nature of psychology overrode and actually prevented progress towards unified theory. Typically, psychologists in one area of psychology will not even know about highly relevant conceptual or empirical findings that occur in another area of psychology, or in the language of another theory. Usually each psychologist is interested and knows about her or his own approach in a restricted area and rejects other approaches and their products.

Without any consensually accepted problems, theoretical structures, methods and apparatus, social psychology is not able to build much that is of lasting—that is, cumulative—value. The result is a multiplicity of small, empirical endeavors with sparse and specific theory development, whose excellence is judged by their ability to pique one's interest because the endeavors have some face-value relationship to a human concern, because they appear to be new and different, and because the methodology is suitably scientific. Since such works are not derived from general principles or constructed with generality in mind in any way, they can only be explored within a narrow range that has little general significance. The research involved is bound to expend its potential in a relatively brief time, and work must then move to another new, small, isolated problem of study. So we have the malaise occasioned by social psychology's fickle nature, disorganization, superficiality, and aimlessness, as already indicated by reference to the statements of others. This is not an efficacious way for a science to operate. No basis is provided for the construction of generality, unity, and hence meaning.

When we look systematically at the nature of our science, and its disorganized efforts and products, with an understanding of the history of scientific development and a comparison to the unified natural sciences when they were still preparadigmatically disorganized (Staats, 1983), we can see just how primitive and inefficient disorganization is. Moreover, such a study tells us that a central goal of science is generality and unity of knowledge. That is a central characteristic that gives power to scientific knowledge and to the endeavor to gain knowledge. No matter how much psychology tries to enter the pantheon of real sciences, it can never do so solely by improving its scientific technique and through the production of multitudes of scientifically reputable experiments and theoretical statements. As long as these products, however numerous, are in conflict with one another, or are simply unrelated, psychology will never be able to present that unified body of knowledge that advanced sciences display in such good and powerful quantity.

Some critics of scientific psychology contend that psychology has tried to advance through the development of grand theories of learning and that this approach has failed. On this basis it is said that general theory and unification are false goals (Koch, 1978, 1981). This pessimism is misplaced, however, for the classic learning theories were not unified or unifying theories. They did not have the goal of the unification. In fact they did everything possible to distinguish themselves as separate and competitive (Mackenzie, 1977; Yela, 1979). Although having a very common subject matter, and although being very similar except in a few points, they constituted themselves into warring camps and all semblance of unification was lost (see Hilgard, 1948, pp. 457–458). Moreover, this characteristic of separatism was imparted to the applications of learning theory in human behavior fields. Thus, in social psychology there are various different and competitive learning theories, usually based on one or the other basic learning theory. Even when they have much similarity and could be unified into one cohesive framework they are not.

When one considers this aspect of psychology in detail it becomes apparent that turning the science onto the path of unification is the most central need of the science (Staats, 1983). These matters concern a philosophy of psychology. In addition, psychology needs to have unified theories, large and small, as well as a methodology for producing those results, which is the topic of the following sections.

B.   METHODOLOGY FOR UNIFIED THEORY FORMULATIONS

Behaviorism—actually, scientific psychology in general—has been concerned with the philosophy of science for its value in contributing to the task of constructing good theoretical–empirical knowledge. The classic learning theories were closely related to the philosophy of science that has been variously called positivism, logical-positivism, scientific empiricism, operationism, and so on. Such philosophy, in the present opinion (Staats, 1983), contributed and contributes a great deal of sophistication to psychology. But the model for such theory was the works of the great theories of the advanced, organized sciences. It has been a long time since the natural sciences were in the same state of disorganized (preparadigmatic) knowledge (see Kuhn, 1962) as psychology is at present. Thus, natural science cannot be used as a model with which to understand preparadigmatic science (Staats, 1983). Nor can a philosophy that uses natural science as its model produce the methodology that is needed to transform the disorganized science into an organized science. This requires an indigenous philosophy of science (Staats, 1983).

Methodology by which to unify psychology constitutes a large study that can only be hinted at here. It will be suggested, however, that much of the diversity and disorganization of knowledge in our field is artificial. That is to say the diversity does not spring from the nature of human behavior but from how we conceive of human behavior. In the present view the manifold differences that we see in our science are largely a function of the fact that different psychologists study different phenomena, using different methods, apparatus, analyses, and theories. We study one part of a phenomenon and someone else studies another part. Because of this, and the different theoretical languages and different methods that we use, and because of the confusion that prevents us from seeing how the parts are related, we cannot realize that parts of a puzzle are involved. We cannot see that our task is putting the parts together and the solution is building organized wholes out of unrelated parts, picking and choosing throughout the range of psychology's interest. Our science tells us that discovering something pristinely new is the goal, even though we are already being drowned with the plethora of elements that have been found already. We continue to set in opposition the various knowledge elements of our science. We have, thus, a methodology for producing differences, separatness, disorganization. What we need is reduction of disorganization, and this requires a new methodology. Some aspects of this methodology (see Staats, 1983) will be described.

1.   Schism Resolution

Social behaviorism, as has been indicated, arose in the context of first and second generation behaviorism. Behaviorism has traditionally eschewed non-behavioral sources and methods of accruing knowledge. An equal and opposite force has been evident in the rejection by traditional psychology of the findings, theories, and methods of behaviorism. The consequence of this separation is that there are many psychologists of a cognitive orientation who will not really peruse anything published by a behaviorist, and vice versa, except if they wish to criticize the work. And this stance is maintained even in the many cases where there are actually overlaps in interest, and similarities in the substance of the separated bodies of knowledge. I know of a number of cases in which, for example, a cognitive psychologist will see something of value in a behavioristic analysis, and will actually employ the concept, finding, or method, but will not refer to its behavioristic origin. Rather than recognize the similarity and the mutuality of interest, the researcher will develop the observation or idea as something typically cognitive and new. And the same thing occurs in the other direction.

The result is at least inefficient. The two major bodies of knowledge continue to develop as independent domains. Worse, they even weaken each other through mutual criticism and competition. As a consequence, conceptions and areas of study that could be complementary and supportive are divided. In the present view the separation of behaviorism from the traditional–cognitive approaches to psychology developed on the basis of schisms between the lines of thought. The existence of those schisms, unresolved, perpetuates the general division—promulgating separations into smaller islands of knowledge that do not have to exist apart from each other in view of their actual similarity (Staats, 1975, chapter 13; 1981).

Thus, we should bring together knowledge elements that are artificially separated by seemingly divergent approaches. In addition, we should deal with the underlying schisms that work to affect those separations. As will be indicated in a later section, one such significant schism involves the differing and opposed conceptions of what is personality. This example will indicate how elements of both traditional psychology and behaviorism can be integrated. The present view is that there are various schisms in psychology that can be productively resolved by interlevel theory that takes elements from each position, or level, uniting them in a conceptual formulation appropriate for the phenomena in each area of concern.

> In the present view, however, productive concepts, findings, and methods typically exist on both sides of each schism. This is not to suggest an eclecticism that simply takes two antagonistic positions and places them within the same framework, without resolving the differences involved. . . . This does not mean the total incorporation of each side [into the unifying theory] but rather the incorporation of essential aspects of each side. Such a theoretical framework must be heuristic in each area and in this manner show the framework's intrinsic theoretical value. Eclectic combinations do not accomplish this, and the schism ultimately breaks out again, as is demonstrated in current heredity–environment arguments, which [the eclectic combination called] the interactionist position in no way resolves. (Staats, 1981, pp. 240–241)

Behaviorism has traditionally solved the problem of unity by exclusion. It has rejected all forms of knowledge that are not its own. By contrast, the present approach is that when psychological scientists have been engaged in the study of a given topic for some time so that there has been the production of a large body of knowledge, the knowledge is very likely to contain much that is valuable. The task of unified theory work is to select the valuable elements from the total that has been constituted—the elements that are valuable in the sense that they can be combined with valuable elements from other bodies of knowledge in the construction of a larger knowledge structure.

2. Collapsing Theories and Resolving Issues

Similarly, there is the problem of what I have called the separatism amongst individual theories in our science. Psychology is very complex in including many types of subjects, many types of behaviors, various problems, many methods, theories, and so on. It is thus inevitable that different members of the science can work on problems and formulate conceptions that actually have a great deal in common, yet the difference in their idiosyncratic aspects may cloak the commonality. The same principles may be present in theories that appear to be different because the subjects are different, the experimental tasks and methodology and apparatus are different, the principles are imbedded in different theoretical frameworks, and so on.

As a result, the power of a set of principles may go unrecognized. Although the principles may be very general, and very significant as a consequence, applying across a wide variety of subjects, situations, problems, methods, apparatuses, and so on, this power may be unseen because the principles are presented only within idiosyncratic formulations that apply uniquely to individual areas of study. We can see an example in what social behaviorism has called three-function learning principles. As has been indicated (Staats, 1963, 1964, 1968a, 1968b, 1970, 1975, 1981), in the classic learning theories the relationship of classical and instrumental conditioning was not well handled. The three-function learning theory of social behaviorism states that these forms of conditioning are interrelated and interact in affecting behavior. The important point here is that theories with similar notions of the interaction of classical conditioning and instrumental conditioning have arisen, although from different areas of study. Overmier and Lawry (1979), for example, have advanced a theory with the same principles in their analysis of transfer of control in animal learning, as has Bindra (1978) in the context of animal motivation. Each of the theories has certain specifics that are idiosyncratic, no doubt because of the backgrounds from which the efforts arose. But the underlying principles of learning are the same. Would it not be important for psychology to realize that the basic principles of interaction between the forms of conditioning are important in a broad range of phenomena ranging from basic animal behavior to complex human behaviors? The divisions within our science impede the recognition of such generality, which in this and other cases would help link experimental psychology and social psychology.

This is but one example; there are also cases in which there are differences between theories even though the theories are in the same areas of study and the principles in the theories have a great deal of overlap. This has already been exemplified in my discussion of second generation learning theories (see Staats, 1983). Although the principles of conditioning they employed were very similar, different and competitive theories were constructed, and the differences were enhanced by the use of different experimental designs (group versus single-organism research methods), different apparatuses (runways and mazes versus the operant conditioning chamber), different general methodologies (hypo-thetico–deductive versus experimental analysis methods), and so on. The same divisions continue in areas that utilize the learning theories in human areas of study. Thus, in the present case, the learning theories in social psychology have for the most part been developed as separate and different theoretical structures. The impression one gets is that there is one learning theory in the work of Byrne on attraction, another theory in the Lotts' work, still another in the work of Berkowitz on aggression, an additional theory that pertains to social psychology in social behaviorism, as well as various theories of learning in the conceptions advanced by Bem, McGinnies, and others.

Thus, separate but overlapping theories can emerge because the theories have arisen in different areas of study, employing different subjects and pro-cedures, and so on. There may also be separate but very similar theories even within the same area, because of idiosyncracies involving less-central charac-teristics. Separation of theories can also arise on even less-justified bases. Re-cently, as an example, the author showed, on the basis of a full documentation comparing principles, concepts, and analyses (see Staats, 1978b), how there could be an extensive but unnoted overlap between two theories, even though the two theories are considered to be quite separate and independent. A manuscript (Staats, 1978b) describing the problems that arise for the science when this occurs was accepted for publication by one of our APA journals. The article was intended to serve as the foundation for a special issue of the journal that was to include other commentaries by a prominent sociologist of science, a prominent philosopher of science, and an historian of psychology, among others. This article noted the deficiencies in citations that resulted in inadequate recognition of the overlap between theories. Ultimately, however, the implication of ques-tionable scholarship engendered opposition to publication of the issue so that the planned publication was cancelled. My point here is that there is more similarity and overlap in our theories than is often realized, partly because we have accept-ed a methodology of separatism, one aspect of which involves very slack citation standards.

Several types of separatism have been exemplified. Because there are dif-ferent phenomena studied, in different fields, using different subjects, and es-pecially because the theories involved have arisen in different traditions, the theories—although with similar principles—may not be seen as similar because they couch their principles within different theoretical contexts. Most of the unrecognized relatedness in psychology is probably due to this circumstance— that our science is very complex and it is difficult to recognize the "forest" of common principles amongst the multitude of different theory "trees." In addition, however, theories, although similar, may be developed as separate and competitive because their authors are in a competitive relationship, do not attend to each others' work, and attempt to differentiate their works as much as possible and ignore the similarities. And there are cases where commonality goes unrecognized seemingly purposefully, cases in which a theorist should have cited the similarity of his theory to another but has neglected to do so, presumably in the service of enhancing the originality of his or her own theory. Whatever the circumstances involved, the result is additional disorganization for our science.

We face the task of creating organization from the existing chaos. An important part of this task involves the recognition of the commonalities behind what seem to be differences but actually are not. The field of learning, for example, would have been helped if the commonalities in the second generation learning theories had been noted in the early days of their development—so that the competition and disorganization of that field would had been reduced by collapsing the theories at their extensive points of overlap. Rather than the nonproductive, self-defeating diversiveness and divisiveness, there would have been a much more unified and valuable body of knowledge to present to the rest of psychology.

Much the same comment could be made regarding the development of learning theories in social psychology, or in any other area of the study of human behavior. The differences between social psychology learning theories are those that stem from the differences that existed between the second generation learning theories. These differences are much smaller than the very large amount of commonality that also exists. The fact is that the work that has been done thus far in social psychology under the aegis of the various learning theories actually constitutes a unified body of knowledge when the unnecessary and erroneous idiosyncracies of the anachronistic learning theories, and their elaborations, are stripped away. Social behaviorism has attempted to demonstrate this (Staats, 1963, 1968a, 1975, 1981). Presently, the learning-based findings in social psychology, at least potentially, are the most coherent body of knowledge that exists in social psychology, having knowledge of the type that stems from systematically stated, empirically derived, elementary principles that have the characteristics of a formal theory. A good many areas and topics in social psychology have been successfully dealt with in learning principle terms—a much larger number than could be mentioned here. This is actually a very clear and unambiguous indication of the power and potentiality of a learning theory approach to human behavior. But this power and potential is masked by the seeming diversity of theoretical vehicles that have been employed in the various learning studies of human behavior so that the underlying unity is not visible. This apparent diversity also contributes to the disorganization endemic in the traditional field of personality–social psychology. The primary message of the learning theory endeavor is lost in the separation that has been described (Staats, 1967, 1968b, 1975, 1978a, 1978b, 1979, 1980, 1981, 1983). Without this message of unity, the several learning theories merely contribute to the disorganization of the field.

This is not to say that there are no actual points of difference in the various learning theories in social psychology. Differences do exist, as has been partly indicated by the discussion in the previous section of the general types of learning theories in this field. As another example, McGinnies and Ferster (1971) explicitly reject the three-function learning theory analysis of attitudes. They prefer Skinner's learning theory that totally separates the classical conditioning of emotional responses and the instrumental conditioning of behavior. Their theory considers the overt behaviors of responding positively and negatively to a social stimulus to be the attitude, with the internal emotional response (or attitude) being a non-causative, non-important occurrence. As they put it:

> Staats has suggested that the measure of the strength of an attitude is the physiological, "emotional" response that the subject makes. Actually, if we take a behavioral approach toward attitudes, recognizing them as comprising an operant repertoire, then the physiological signs to which Staats points are concomitants or symptoms rather than the attitude itself. Thus, the strength of an attitude is reflected in the frequency of the component performances. It only incidentally happens to be true that high frequency behaviors that are either positively or negatively reinforced also tend to be accompanied by physiological changes. (McGinnies and Ferster, 1971, p. 367)

This constitutes one point of issue between the learning theories in social psychology. As such, it is one disagreement that must be considered systematically and resolved in the service of creating a unified, organized body of knowledge. That is, there are many findings relevant to a learning theory of social psychology. Whether three-function learning theory or operant learning theory better handles these findings must be systematically evaluated. We must also determine which theory serves better as a heuristic vehicle for unifying knowledge in the field as well as for projecting research that adds knowledge and unifies that which exists. Through these endeavors the variations in the learning theories can be simplified in the quest for greater unification. This type of active resolution of issues can help create unity as can the demonstration of the commonalities in the theories. (It may be noted that notwithstanding the above issue, McGinnies and Ferster's learning theory of social psychology and social behaviorism's theory have much in common, as do all the learning theories.)

The fact is that the learning theories of the first and second generation behaviorists did not have an understanding of the need for unified theory in their field, and they did not develop programs for attaining unified theory. This lack has been the characteristic of each of the theoretical efforts that have attempted to use one of the learning theories as a vehicle for approaching the study of social psychology. Resolving schisms, issues between theories, and collapsing the unrecognized similarities between theories, it is suggested, should become major concerns of theorists who are interested in contributing to the development of a learning approach to social psychology. As a group of separate structures, the learning theories have a certain significance for the field. There would be much greater significance, however, if the various theories were collapsed into one, to show their potentiality as a basic theory for confronting the phenomena in the field. The relatively minor differences would continue to be points of issue and development.

The preceding discussion has described two ways of constructing unity from elements that are presently separated and frequently conflicting. There are other methods for obtaining unity of theory, method, apparatus, and findings (Staats, 1983) that cannot be treated here. These are ideologically neutral methods, it should be noted. There are sub-varieties in *all* of the major theoretical approaches that exist in psychology, and the methodology for organizing psychology's knowledge should have relevance across the various approaches. In addition, however, the philosophy that sets unification of our science as its goal establishes also a high place for the creation of comprehensive, unified theories of large scope. Again, the philosophy is ideologically neutral (Staats, 1983), suggesting that each major theoretical approach should attempt to construct its own unifying theory that covers the range of psychology's interest. It will be in part through such endeavors that we will be able to see what potential the different varieties have for serving as very general theories.

The next section will be devoted to describing a methodology for constructing broad, unified theories in general. This will be done, however, employing one theory—paradigmatic behaviorism—as the exemplar. The methods of schism resolution and collapsing theory have been employed in formulating that theoretical structure, as well as other methods for establishing unified theory.

V. The Multilevel Theory Methodology of Paradigmatic Behaviorism

While there have been theories in psychology that have had the goal of generality within a unified set of principles, the methodology by which this was to be accomplished across the various fields of psychology was not explicitly stated. The methodology that was implicit, however, can be seen from the nature of the theories constructed. The typical methodology in the general theories that we have known is to take the basic ideas that have been developed in some particular aspect of psychology, in the context of particular phenomena, and to project the ideas hypothetically in a general way to a much larger set of psychological phenomena. This methodology has always proved unsatisfactory to psychologists whose interests are not primarily in the particular theory.

Behaviorism in constructing its general theories also followed the same methodology and this is one reason why behaviorism is so widely rejected. As has been indicated, behaviorism has followed a two-level theory construction strategy. Its actual study was animal learning, its hypothetical projection was to general human behavior. Following the traditional ways of preparadigmatic psychology, behaviorism too has simply assumed that areas of knowledge that come from unfamiliar approaches can be rejected out of hand because the problems studied are silly, because the methods and apparatuses used are poor, and because the findings involved are thus invalid. So, as an example Skinner (1953, 1971) could bypass all of psychology's efforts and products and go directly to the raw consideration of human behavior, depending solely upon his own operant learning theory methods and findings. In general, this is an exemplification of the radical behavioristic strategy of projecting from the animal maze, problem box, or lever-press apparatus directly to the most complex of human behaviors, sidestepping the vast research and knowledge in personality, personality measurement, child development, cognitive psychology, and so on. There are no references to this type of knowledge in Skinner's works. This is not a strategy that takes seriously the vast theoretical task of unification, since there is such an abundance of findings in the various areas of psychology. The following sections will sketch out the paradigmatic behaviorism methodology that stipulates it must provide theories that utilize and unify the various areas (levels) of the science.

The basic concept of the methodology is that of interlevel theory (Staats, 1983). The methodology assumes that there are bodies of knowledge in separated fields that contain much that could be linked through the construction of suitable interconnecting (interlevel) theoretical structures. Generally this is a theoretical task that involves the examination of the two separated areas of knowledge with the purpose of organizing the contents of each and abstracting their principles. When this has been done it is then the task of relating the principles from each area in a close derivation that can yield empirical hypotheses in both directions. In the present case, that of constructing a general theory based upon learning principles, the task is one of relating the set of learning principles (and derivatives) to the principles, concepts, findings, and methods of the various fields that are included in the unification. As will be seen there is also a hierarchical manner of joining the fields through the interlevel theory, since the fields of psychology have a basic-to-advanced relationship, one field being basic to another that in turn is basic to yet another.

A.   THE BASIC LEARNING THEORY LEVEL OF THE THEORY

Paradigmatic behaviorism is a behaviorism in the sense that it sees principles that are studied in their elementary form in the field of animal learning to be basic in the theory construction task. But the term paradigmatic indicates that this is not done in the way that was construed in traditional behaviorism. The difference resides in the fact that the traditional learning theories did not see their mission to be the construction of a general, unified theory—with a task, thus, of finding in the field of animal learning the *subset* of principles that were valuable for the general theory of human behavior. The field of animal learning, like every field of psychology, is a buzzing confusion of different theories, methods, apparatuses, problems, and findings. In its raw form it is not a useful tool for constructing a theory of human behavior. The classic learning theories, as has been noted, were constructed to account for the field of animal learning. But this goal is not that which can be expected to yield the best basic level of theory for a theory of human behavior. This goal actually ensures that the classic animal learning theories included things that were irrelevant and did not include things that were necessary. For example, the extensive development of the intervening variable and mathematical structure of Hull's theory is extraordinarily complex and irrelevant for a unified theory of human behavior. And the endless preoccupation of Skinnerians with schedules of reinforcement produces a morass of knowledge that in the same way is irrelevant. Much of the field of animal learning is similar in this respect. In addition, the classic learning theories also contained much that was in error and they had gaping lacunae as well. One example of error, in the present view, is Skinner's statement that emotions have no causative effect upon behavior (see McGinnies and Ferster, 1971; Skinner, 1975). This is based upon his animal learning theory. However, in the context of human behavior this aspect of his theory makes no sense. Obviously the individual's emotional response affects his or her instrumental behavior. The field of behavior therapy shows this in systematic detail. Treatment of fear responses through desensitization, for example, has the effect of solving problems of overt behavior. To elaborate, the individual who strongly fears flying will not be able to board an airplane, a problem of instrumental behavior. Reduction of that fear can alleviate the problem. A learning theory that is to be the basis for a general human behavior theory must take account of such things. Thinking that the basic learning theory can be fitted solely to animal data made sense in the 1930s and 1940s, but it no longer does so, when we have so much solid knowledge of human behavior.

Paradigmatic behaviorism has systematically constructed its basic learning theory for the purpose at hand, that of obtaining the theory structure that can then be applied generally to human behavior. Recognition of the demands that it must serve in this regard have been involved in the basic theory construction methodology. Thismethodology has been different from that of the original behaviorists, and it has lead to a different basic learning theory. Paradigmatic behaviorism's learning theory is based upon the elementary principles of animal conditioning as are the other learning theories. But classical and instrumental conditioning interact in human behavior and the basic theory has been constructed so that the human behavior knowledge is utilized.

This can be exemplified since important principles are involved. That is, the interaction is shown by focusing on the functions that a stimulus can have in classical and instrumental conditioning. Thus classical conditioning, to begin, can impart an emotion-eliciting function to a new stimulus. When a new stimulus is paired with a stimulus that already elicits an emotional response, the new stimulus will come to do so also. Second, instrumental conditioning can give a new stimulus the power to elicit an instrumental response. When an instrumental response is rewarded in the presence of a stimulus situation, that situation will come to elicit the instrumental response. Such stimuli, because they elicit approach instrumental responses are called incentive, directive, or discriminative stimuli. The stimulus situation may then be said to have acquired that type of eliciting function. Third, it can be pointed out that not all stimuli can serve as rewards (that is, strengthen behaviors they follow), and this is thus a third function that some stimuli have or can acquire. One of the interactions between the two types of conditioning is that stimuli that elicit an emotional response will also have the reinforcing (rewarding or punishing) function. Thus, classical conditioning that makes a stimulus elicit an emotional response will also make the stimulus a positive or negative reinforcer, as the case may be. And, because of a process that will not be stipulated here, if a stimulus has the emotion-eliciting function, and hence the reinforcing function, it will also have the other function, that of eliciting approach or avoidance instrumental behaviors directly. This can be thought of in general terms by saying that organisms, including humans, learn to approach stimuli that elicit a positive emotional response and that have the rewarding function. And organisms learn to avoid and escape from stimuli that elicit a negative emotion and that have the punishing function.

There are a number of reasons why it is important that the basic theory recognizes that the three functions of stimuli—emotion-eliciting, reinforcing, and incentive-providing—are interrelated. One of them is the realization that changing the emotion-eliciting value of a stimulus, through classical conditioning, will change the manner in which that stimulus can affect instrumental behavior, both as a reinforcer and as a positive or negative incentive. The principles involved here are very important at the human level of theory, especially because there are many ways emotional responses are changed for humans. It is necessary that there be experimentation at the animal learning level of study that supports this elaboration of principles. This support has been indicated in presenting these principles (see Staats, 1968b, 1970, 1975).

Table 1 presents a summary of the various levels of the multilevel theory structure of paradigmatic behaviorism. A few words will be presented here about the various levels, to illustrate a little of the content of the theory development. More detailed treatments are available in the several works that have dealt with the theory, as listed in the references.

B.   THE HUMAN LEARNING LEVEL OF THE THEORY

It has been said that traditional behaviorism follows a two-level theory strategy. Behaviorism constructed basic, animal-learning theories which were then to explain all of human behavior phenomena. Paradigmatic behaviorism has progressively come to recognize the shortcomings involved in this general methodology and theory-construction approach. This has included a progressive recognition that the various fields of psychology represent original sources of stipulated phenomena, methods, findings, and theory that represent important types of systematic knowledge. A philosophy, such as behaviorism, that legislates out of the science large areas of work and achievement on the basis of a superficially based charge of lack of behavioral objectivity has not taken the task seriously. Moreover, a two-level theory that considers all of the basic theory to reside in the field of animal learning is shortsighted.

Rather, the present position is that general, unified theory—although it may base itself in conditioning principles—must realize that these elementary principles constitute only the foundations of what must become a building structure that successively incorporates the theory needs of the various areas of psychology. The principles of conditioning, by themselves, are not an adequate instrument for dealing with the wide range of phenomena of human behavior, and behaviorists such as Watson and Skinner have been wrong in taking the position that the principles were sufficient. The principles of conditioning, suitably formulated, constitute the basic part of the theoretical task, but this theory must be elaborated in successive levels such that the principles entailed are capable of dealing with progressively more complex phenomena.

Let me begin to illustrate the theory construction task involved by indicating that the conditioning principles derived from the animal laboratory do not even provide the full complement of learning principles that are necessary for understanding human behavior. Actually, one of the objections to learning theory approaches is that many psychologists find it difficult to see how human behavior involves either Pavlovian or Thorndikian conditioning. No one goes around putting food powder in our mouths while we listen to a political speech, so that

TABLE 1

THE MULTILEVEL THEORY OF SOCIAL BEHAVIORISM

Fields	Areas (examples)
Biological mechanisms of learning	Sensory psychology
	Brain and central nervous system
	Response systems
	Evolution of learning structures
Basic learning theory	Conditioning principles
	Generalizing principles, in stimuli, response systems, and species treated
	Motivation principles
Human learning principles	Complex stimulus–response learning with humans
	Cumulative-hierarchical learning principles and others unique to humans
	Vicarious learning mechanisms
Child development principles	Language development, intelligence, and language-mediated modeling
	Sensory–motor development and imitation
	Emotional development through learning
Personality	Personality theory
	The personality systems—language–cognitive, emotional–motivational, and sensory–motor
	Personality and environmental interaction
Personality measurement	Theory relating behavior principles and personality measurement and assessment
	Integrating tests with theory (clinical, etc.)
	Constructing tests and behavior assessments
Social psychology	Attitudes and social cognition
	Interpersonal relations and group processes
	Personality processes, individual differences, and cross-cultural psychology
Abnormal personality	Deficits in the personality systems
	Inappropriate aspects of personality systems
	Diagnostic categories in terms of personality systems
	Interaction of personality and social systems
Clinical psychology	Behavior modification of simple problems
	Personality change and personality measurement
	Language–cognitive methods of treatment
	Children's problems and treatment
Educational psychology	Learning theories or school subjects
	Intelligence and readiness in school learning
	Problems of school learning
	Motivation and school learning
Organizational psychology	Personnel selection
	Motivation in organizational settings
	Behavioral analysis of jobs
	Organizational conditions and problems

we will be positively conditioned to a candidate, a social policy, or an international analysis. No one provides food rewards for attending church, or removes electric shock when that behavior occurs, and the same is true for the individual's "approach" to religious principles and way of life, and so on.

The theorist who wishes to extend learning principles to human behavior thus has a task of indicating how conditioning principles function on the human level, as well as the task of showing how there are human level learning principles and mechanisms of learning—both of which do not emerge from the animal laboratory. As an example of the first need, one of the early experiments in the author's program of theory construction demonstrates that primary classical conditioning can take place with humans in a manner that produces emotional learning to essential human stimuli (Staats, Staats, and Crawford, 1962). The unconditioned stimulus was electric shock and a loud noise. The conditioned stimulus was an auditorily presented word. The emotional response was a physiologically measured GSR. The conditioning took place in a complex verbal learning task that disguised the emotional conditioning. It was shown that pairing the conditioned stimulus with the unconditioned stimulus resulted in the word eventually eliciting the emotional response. The important thing here was in advancing the primary conditioning principles to account for one of the central aspects of language—that is, the fact that language stimuli come to have a very general and very profound effect on humans in arousing emotions. The language arousal of emotions is significant in every type of human action and interaction.

But this example has been given also to illustrate the theory construction strategy involved. To elaborate, it has been said that most human learning does not occur on the basis of direct, primary conditioning. We must then ask how it does occur, by what additional principles or by what mechanisms. The experiment just cited was one of those in the present line of study that showed that words can come to elicit emotional responses (positive and negative) through primary conditioning experiences. But the observation of human behavior tells us that we also *learn* new emotional responses on the basis of vicarious language experience. When the religious figure, for example, says that abortion is murder, the adherents to the religion come to have a very negative emotional response to abortion. As we advance our theoretical understanding of human learning we must come to understand how language can be a mechanism for producing emotional learning as well as emotional experience. The present author and his associates and others have conducted a series of studies whose aim has been to study how new emotional learning is produced through the mechanism of language. Thus, for example, it was shown that groups of subjects could learn positive and negative attitudes towards social stimuli through presenting emotional words of a positive or negative type in conjunction with those social stimuli (Early, 1968; Sacha and Byrne, 1970; Hekmat, 1972, 1973; Lohr and Staats, 1973; Staats and Staats, 1958; Staats, Staats, and Biggs, 1958). Primary conditioning was thus shown not to be necessary in the learning or unlearning of emotional responses. Language provides very extensive vicarious learning mechanisms that function ubiquitously. Another study showed that the emotional property of words could be enhanced by general motivation-inducing conditions (Staats and Hammond, 1972) and it was further shown that this motivation operation increased the power of the emotional words to produce new emotional learning to additional stimuli (Staats, Minke, Martin, and Higa, 1972). But the importance of the individual's language repertoire for producing new learning is not limited to emotional responding. Emotional words serve a centrally important role in reinforcing and punishing overt, instrumental behaviors. When positive emotional (and hence reinforcing) words, descriptions, statements, and so on, are made contingent upon our behaviors, those behaviors are strengthened. The converse occurs with negative emotional language stimuli. Finley and Staats (1967) have shown this principle clearly. Harms and Staats (1978) have also shown that general motivational conditions enhance the reward effects of words—that is, when subjects had been deprived of food (missing one meal) food words had a greater reinforcement effect on learning than under no deprivation. When this finding is extended into the various types of motivational conditions that can effect the various types of emotional words, important individual and group differences in behavior can be understood. In addition, it has been shown that emotional words can have an incentive effect, and that motivational conditions will affect that incentive effect (Staats and Warren, 1974; Staats and Burns, 1981). Humans are widely affected by language that we describe as propaganda, advertising, governmental communications, education, news media, and so on, as well as in other social interactions involving language. Much of that effect is due to the emotional properties of the messages involved. It is important that we understand the basic principles by which these effects occur, as well as the language mechanisms involved. In the present discussion, however, the important point is that it is not possible to understand complex social interactions, involving communication—which means most interactions—without understanding the types of effects that can take place through language.

As was indicated in the present author's first general analysis of human behavior (Staats, 1963) language mechanisms, such as the repertoire of emotional words, constitute types of vicarious experience that are central in human learning. The range and versatility of learning through language far eclipse the extent to which learning occurs through simple, direct conditioning. This is not to say that the basic principles are not involved, however, for the language mechanisms were originally learned via those principles and continue to operate according to those principles (Staats, 1963, 1968a, 1971; Staats, Brewer, and Gross, 1970; Staats and Burns, 1981). But cognitive psychologists have seen clearly that conditioning principles themselves do not handle the complexities of human performance well. The answer, however, is not a retreat from the basic principles of learning in general, but rather the development of those principles in more advanced levels to link with the cognitive mechanisms and concepts that are useful in considering relevant cognitive activities. This requires a general psychology of language and knowledge of the way language functions in producing human learning (see Staats, 1963, 1968a, 1971, 1972, 1975; Staats and Burns, 1981).

The same thing is true of observational learning (or imitation or modeling) as was indicated early in constructing the theory of paradigmatic behaviorism (Staats, 1963, 1968a, 1971). Social learning theory (Bandura, 1969; Bandura and Walters, 1963) has generally assumed that humans naturally have imitation ability. Paradigmatic behaviorism takes the position that imitation ability is composed of skills (or repertoires) that are learned via conditioning principles and that function according to those principles. Some of these are language–cognitive skills, as the following early example indicates.

> Observing someone else's experience may provide an analogous type of experience. The person who has acquired the appropriate verbal habits may "learn from example." Thus, if a child is punished for striking another child and is told THAT WAS VERY MEAN AND BAD, this will constitute a learning trial for that child. In addition, however, another child observing this incident might acquire similar responses. He might make an [imitative] response to the words of the adult in the presence of the visual event including the sight of the blow being struck and the crying of the recipient of the blow. This would establish an association between these stimuli and the word responses MEAN, BAD, and so on. In the future if the child who was the observer strikes another child, the stimulus situation will be similar to that on the preceding occasion and according to the principles of stimulus generalization the similar stimulus situation should elicit the verbal responses WHAT I DID WAS MEAN AND BAD, and so on. These verbal responses should then function as aversive stimuli, the removal of which would be reinforcing. (Staats, 1963, pp. 315–316)

This is therefore an example of self- or cognitively induced emotionality, in a manner that affects the individual's own behavior. When this was written, Berger's work was unknown to the author. However, Berger (1962) had shown a very related form of vicarious conditioning. In his experiment, it was found that observation of the simulated pain response of a subject to a supposed electric shock acted as an "unconditioned" emotional stimulus. Subjects observing a person "expressing" pain learned a negative emotional response to a buzzer that was sounding at the time. Thus, the behaviors of others can elicit emotional responses in us, and the elicited emotional responses can be learned to new social stimuli. The example outlined above, it should be noted, includes self-mediation (via language) of the emotional response, which is a distinctly cognitive act. This is one type of "vicarious" experience (see Staats, 1963, pp. 315–316; 1975, pp. 192–193) that may involve mediating events consisting of self-language that is elicited by the situation, but that is also a function of what the individual has learned from the past. (It is in part through conceptualizing such mechanisms that the author has tried to bridge the behavioristic–cognitive schism.)

These are examples of a central concept of paradigmatic behaviorism. While the basic principles are those of conditioning, these principles by themselves *do not* constitute an adequate theory structure for dealing with most of complex human behavior. The basic principles must be elaborated in progressive theoretical development. Another such development involves the recognition of the differences in the learning studied in the animal laboratory and in dealing with human behavior. A central concern here is that human learning involves learning sequences that occur over years and years of time, whereas the behaviors studied in the animal laboratory are simple and of a "one-shot" variety. As was implicit in some of the previous examples, later learning of the individual may depend upon the individual having previously undergone previous learning that has resulted in the acquisition of certain complex skills. For example, the individual can learn new emotional responses based upon language, but this demands that the individual will have previously learned a repertoire of emotional words. Centrally, complex human performances of various kinds—artistic, musical, scientific, athletic, social skills, personality, and such—cannot be understood without a conception of cumulative–hierarchical learning. Cumulative-hierarchical learning principles are those that are involved in analysis of how complex human performances begin with the learning of relatively simple repertoires on the basis of primary conditioning. The principles then show how those repertoires provide the mechanisms by which more advanced repertoires can be learned, and how these then are basic to yet further learning, in very extended sequences. When we examine any complex human performance we must be prepared to analyze the cumulative–hierarchical learning involved.

Human learning principles thus constitute an essential level of theory development before we can venture very adequately into the treatment of realms that are most characteristic of humans and of great significance. To think that such phenomena could be handled with a few simple conditioning principles was overenthusiastic. Yet the stipulation of human learning principles and mechanisms has only been begun, opening a fertile field of study.

C.   THE CHILD DEVELOPMENT LEVEL OF THE THEORY

The human learning level of the multilevel theory has the purpose of describing in abstract form the advanced principles of human learning. With the basic principles and the human learning principles the method of paradigmatic behaviorism is to treat progressively the content phenomena in the field of human behavior in the building fashion that has been described. This begins with the analytic treatment of the basic behavioral repertoires that the individual commences to learn in childhood. Child developmentalists and others such as linguists and psycholinguists and personality theorists have described many of the important elements. But these must be analyzed within the principles of the advancing, building theory. Thus, a theory of the development of motor skills including imitation motor skills, as well as theories of intelligence, language, emotional learning, and many others, are necessary (Rondal, 1983; Staats, 1963, 1968a, 1971; Staats, Brewer, and Gross, 1970; Staats and Burns, 1981). This is not to say that this level of development (or any other level) is in any way complete. As has been indicated (Staats, 1981) the first multilevel theories will have to be presented in framework form, except for chosen points of detailed development, until a sufficient number of theorists join forces in completing the task to flesh out the skeleton.

D. THE PERSONALITY LEVEL OF THE THEORY

The methodology of the multilevel theory structure being described involves various instances of ''interlevel theory,'' that is, theory that conceptually relates formerly separated areas, fields, theories, and methods (Staats, 1983). The next level of the multilevel theory framework may be used as an example with which to describe a little more what is involved in interlevel theory. Let us begin by considering the two fields of learning theory and personality theory. Learning theory aims to establish the elementary laws of learning as basic to all behavior. The model followed is that of the natural, laboratory sciences. It seeks cause–and–effect laws with specified linkages. This demands simplification so that the independent variables of the environment can be manipulated to demonstrate the consequent effects upon behavior, the dependent variable. Animal subjects are employed, simple samples of the environment, and simple responses. There is precision of statement concerning what has been done and what are the effects. But the circumstances are highly artificial. How such findings relate to the complex phenomena of human behavior cannot be seen from such study.

The aim of the field of personality theory, on the other hand, is to describe the personality characteristics of humans by which to understand and predict human behavior and to treat problems of human behavior. The science tradition is shown clearly here in the seeking of basic, abstract causes of human behavior, not just its simple description. This process has taken the form of systematic observation of human behavior through a range of situations, comparison of behaviors, classification of types of behavior, and so on. Individual differences have been noted when individuals have been exposed to the same situation, and a central aim has been to account for such differences in terms of the inferred processes of personality. The model that tends to be most influential is that of the biological sciences: conceptually, the inherited differences of concern in evolution, as well as the taxonomic methods of biology. Objective stipulation and measurement has been a focus here also, primarily taking the path of isolating and measuring important aspects of personality through tests. Although such tests typically measure the manner in which the individual responds, interest usually is in the underlying trait that the responses are thought to index. Systematic isolation of the genetic or learning determinants of personality has been of secondary interest, although there have been widespread attempts to show personality is inherited.

Thus, the two fields under the aegis of their differing approaches have churned out innumerable studies, concepts, principles, findings, and methods. The two fields remain quite divergent (1) in general character, (2) in method, (3) in philosophy, (4) in goals, and (5) in substantive findings. On the one hand we can see that there should be a relationship between the field that studies the elementary principles of how the environment affects behavior and the field that studies the general characteristics that humans have that determine individual differences in behavior to the environment. Almost everyone would agree that important aspects of personality must be learned. But the funds of knowledge of the fields have been so divergent that unification has been almost nil.

There are those who have concluded that such schisms between fields such as learning theory and personality theory represent inherent and irreparable differences (Koch, 1981); I believe that the type of schism that has been described does not represent such a difference. Rather, what has been described calls for interlevel theory to form a bridge by which to join the two separated but actually related spheres of knowledge, a brief example of which can be given. The basic problem of joining the fields in this case is that of including a concept of personality that has the causal properties demanded by the field of personality theory, but one that also meets the demands of scientific determinism and objective specification of behaviorism. The problem is to stipulate what personality is in a manner that links the concept to the principles of learning and the methods of studying learning.

The social behaviorism solution to the problem has been to conceive of personality as composed of very complex, learned repertoires or systems. To elaborate, using things already developed herein, personality–social theorists widely refer to affective aspects of personality using terms such as attitudes, interests, needs, motivations, traits, values, cathexes, and so on. These personality characteristics are given causative properties. Typically, there is little theoretical–empirical specification of how individual differences in the affective aspects of personality arise, the emphasis being on how to measure the differences, and on the demonstration of the effects that the differences have on behavior, in a global way, without detailing the principles or processes involved.

The multilevel-theory task of joining personality concepts of emotion with the learning theory, however, demands that the personality characteristics must be indicated in a specific manner. The way in which the characteristics are learned also requires specification, as do the principles by which the characteristics determine behavior. These various specifications are necessary to meet the behavioristic operationalization the theory demands. In developing the example, already used, individual differences in personality can be seen to involve differences in characteristic ways of emotional responding. Individuals differ in the stimuli to which they respond emotionally. To the same stimulus one person may respond positively, another negatively, and another not at all. Individuals may differ in intensity of emotional response to a stimulus. Even when intensity is the same, the intensity relative to other emotional stimuli in the situation may differ and result in different behaviors. These differences in emotional response to stimuli involve very, very complex considerations, because there are thousands and thousands of stimuli that have emotional value for us. No two people can be alike in personality, because of the complexity of the elements involved.

But we have to break into manageable portions the specification of what we mean by the emotional aspects of personality. And this has occurred, albeit not by plan. That is, we see that some investigators have constructed tests to measure occupational interests, in the present terms, emotional responsivity to stimuli involved in work situations and activities. Other researchers have developed personality tests to measure values of a more general type, such as religious, economic, and political values, and so on. And still others have been concerned about attitudes towards social stimuli. Thus, when we examine the literature, we find that investigators have composed tests to measure peoples' emotional response differences to various classes of stimuli. Because there have been no generally accepted basic principles involved, different terms have arisen—such as interests, attitudes, and values—although each involves emotional responding. Ordinarily, also, such emotional personality traits are considered to be global characteristics. The analytic approach of paradigmatic behaviorism, appropriate to the objectivity of behaviorism, asks that the constituents of the global characteristics be specified.

To continue, since our objective is to unify the personality concepts of affect with the learning theory, it is necessary to specify also the objective determinants involved. It can be said briefly that paradigmatic behaviorism states that the *basic* principles that produce emotional differences in personality are those of classical conditioning. Some stimuli elicit emotional responses in us on a biological basis. But we learn to respond emotionally to a myriad of other stimuli because they have been associated with other stimuli that already elicit an emotional response (on an unlearned or learned basis). As has been indicated, however, this type of learning takes place in the typical vicarious ways of humans, and ordinarily involves language–cognitive mechanisms. A major reason for describing the language means of producing emotions was to illustrate one of those typically human mechanisms.

Here, however, it is important to indicate that the human learns a fantastically complex system of emotional stimuli. The human has a long, long learning history, during which an enormous number of learning trials occurs, mostly through the various language–cognitive mechanisms. The experience is so extensive and involves so many different stimuli that it could not be the same for any two individuals. Learned emotional stimuli may be social, for example, facial expressions, styles of dress, ways of behaving, manners, arguments, parties, physical features such as shape and sex and size and color. Learned emotional stimuli may be ideational, for example, beliefs, values, opinions, thoughts, creeds, images, delusions, dreams, literature, and so on. Learned emotional stimuli may consist of physical objects or events, cars, jewelry, paintings, books, houses, music, and so on. And there are other categories of learned emotional stimuli, for example, recreational activities, phobic and fear stimuli, foods, anxiety-producing situations, and so on. Different experiences determined by culture, race, ethnic, familial, educational, occupational, socioeconomic class, and other conditions produce differences in the multifaceted emotional system that the individual will learn.

Now when two people are faced with the same situation and they experience different emotional responses, we consider them to have different personalities. It is those kinds of differences that are measured by an interest test (Staats, 1963), for example. Thus, one individual indicates by his responses to the items on such a test that he or she has a system of emotional responses that is like those of successful librarians. Another individual by his responses is seen to have an emotional system like that of successful engineers. One general way that we separate people by personality type is on the basis of their differences in emotional response to the many significant types of stimuli that humans encounter in life.

But why have psychologists traditionally been interested in personality differences such as emotional characteristics. Using the above example, we are interested in differences in individuals' emotional personality systems, for one thing, because individuals who respond differently in an emotional way to situations will overtly behave differently to those situations. Thus, the interlevel theory linking the learning theory and personality theory must also specify the principles that account for the way that personality differences determine different types of behavior. Many personality theories simply assume that the personality characteristics of concern to them determine differences in behavior. That does not provide a pleasing theory for someone who insists on specification of principles. On the other hand, the behaviorist who bypasses the study of personality because its concepts are not objective in this and other ways does not have a sufficient approach. This does not account for such an observation as that a person with interests like those of successful librarians not only likes being a librarian better than a person with engineering interests, but also shows better performance in that job.

Let us take the example of religious values. A person can be classified by a test as having high religious values relative to her or his other values. It is assumed that this characteristic will somehow affect the person's behavior. And we may have validation studies that support our conviction—people with such values may attend church more than individuals who test low on religious values. But what are the principles involved, what are the mechanisms by which the characteristics of personality translate themselves into action? The social behavioristic methodology of specificity, as is being described holds that it is necessary to specify these mechanisms, that they are part of the definition of the concept of personality. An example is appropriate here. It has been said in the present theory that the emotional aspects of personality involve differences in the way that the myriad of stimuli that impinge upon the person have emotion-eliciting value. A person with religious values in this conception is a person who (among other things) has very positive emotional responses to stimuli that are of a religious nature. How the person learns such responses is important, as has been indicated, but we must also know the principles by which this difference in emotional responding to various stimuli translates into determination of the individual's characteristic behavior. The important point here is that the principles of the interlevel theory, as elaborated into the theory of personality, provide directives concerning the principles by which personality differences affect different behaviors. The basis for this theoretical development has already been indicated. To illustrate, the theory says that people with religious personalities have a positive emotional response to religious stimuli. This means that such stimuli will serve as reinforcers and affect the individual's behavior. The stimuli will also function as an incentive, that is, be directive. Such stimuli will attract the individual, so that the individual will have tendencies to approach positive emotional stimuli (and avoid negative emotional stimuli). The principles of reinforcement and incentive value have been identified in basic laboratory research. These principles, *in conjunction with the personality theory,* and a personality measuring instrument that stipulates the nature of the stimuli that elicit emotional responses in the individual, will tell us how he or she will behave (see Staats, Gross, Guay, and Carlson, 1973). Following the example, we would expect that a person with high religious values would learn to attend church because the experience received in church has reinforcement value. The cause is not in the reinforcement principles, which are the same for everyone, but in the individual's personality system of values. In addition, the other principle should work to achieve the same result: Since religious stimuli elicit a positive emotional response in the person, he or she will approach such stimuli—which is to say the stimuli will have incentive value. Thus, the person with high religious values who reads an announcement of a lecture on religion is more likely to "approach" the lecture than a person without such a personality characteristic. (A recent study, see Staats & Burns, 1982, shows this effect in the clarity of a laboratory study.) It should be noted that a traditional, global conception of a "religious personality" would not specify as clearly what mechanisms influence the behavior to be expected (a primary reason for the contemporary issue of whether attitudes do or do not determine behavior).

The central reason this elaboration has been made is to illustrate the type of bridging theory that is integral to the multilevel theory development. If we wish to tie the important knowledge of basic learning principles together with the vast and vastly important knowledge of personality, personality measurement, social psychology, abnormal psychology, and so on, it is necessary to have an interlevel theory that bridges the separated and antagonistic realms. This interlevel theory must do justice to the essential ingredients of each realm. Such a theory must develop a methodology that meets the objective, causative demands of behaviorism, with these demands requiring that the concept of personality be specified in terms of observables. Personality cannot be considered an unspecifiable, internal process or structure. Moreover, the principles by which the stipulated personality process comes to be, as well as the principles by which the personality process has its effects, must be stipulated. On the other side, the essential demands of personality theorists must be met. The multilevel theory must provide a framework for considering individual differences in personality. Moreover, the knowledge of proven validity that has been gained of personality must be utilized, as should the validated methods of study and measurement of personality. In addition, and centrally, the interlevel conception must include the focal aspect of the traditional concept of personality—namely that it is a causal process that determines how the individual will behave. Standard behaviorism rejects the concept of personality as a cause. The interlevel theory must thus recognize the process of self-causation (see Staats, 1963, 1968a, 1975, 1979, 1981).

E. THE PERSONALITY MEASUREMENT LEVEL
    OF THE THEORY

As has been indicated (Burns, 1980; Staats, 1975, 1977, in press), standard behaviorism has had no place for the study of personality measurement or the construction of personality tests. (The field of behavioral assessment does not fill that gap.) Paradigmatic behaviorism's introduction of the concept of personality and the specification of the personality repertoires, however, provides the basis for such study within a consistent set of principles in a manner that is closely derived from the theory developed in the level-by-level manner. An early study treated traits that had been established by factor analytic methods to be response classes that could be changed through learning (Staats, Staats, Heard, and Finley, 1962). Staats (1977) and Burns (1980) have indicated how the concept of personality and the analysis of the repertoires of which personality is composed provide a conceptual framework within which to understand different types of psychological tests. For example, interest and value tests can be seen to measure part of the individual's repertoire of emotional stimuli (Staats, 1968b, 1975; Staats & Burns, 1982; Staats, Gross, Guay, and Carlson, 1973), and intelligence has been analyzed in terms of the language–cognitive, sensory–motor, and emotional–motivational repertoires that constitute its elements (Staats, 1968a, 1971) and experiments have been conducted of an analytic sort based upon the theoretical analyses (Staats and Burns, 1981). This development constitutes a full, empirical theory of intelligence. A new analysis (Staats, in press) projects lines of development in the study of personality—linking behavioral assessment and personality measurement—as based upon this level of the theoretical development.

F.   THE SOCIAL PSYCHOLOGY LEVEL OF THE THEORY

As has already been indicated, there is considerable development of the application of basic learning principles in the context of phenomena of interest in social psychology. In the present view this is important work. But it nevertheless suffers from the restrictions, lacunae, and errors of the traditional behavioristic approach. This work is still based upon a two-level theory construction methodology. As such it can never be satisfying to the great body of psychologists whose interests require them to use concepts that only more advanced theory levels legitimate. Prominently, most social psychologists would not want to operate within a framework that did not include a concept of personality or personality measurement, abnormal personality, personality development, and so on. Paradigmatic behaviorism now provides the necessary levels of theory development. It has begun to conduct social psychology research to demonstrate the heuristic value of the theory (Staats, Gross, Guay, and Carlson, 1973; Staats and Burns, 1982). There is great potential for new theoretical and empirical work at this level. (Staats, 1975, chapt. 7, has analyzed a number of social psychology problem areas within the present theoretical structure. See also Leduc, 1976, 1978, 1980a, 1980b, 1980c.) Moreover, when it has been done it will yield a body of knowledge that is meaningful and lasting in that it will link to other levels of development both above and below. Social psychology has had difficulty finding this type of general meaning for its products, as have other areas of psychology.

G.   THE ABNORMAL PSYCHOLOGY LEVEL OF THE THEORY

This area of theory development was one of the early interests of paradigmatic psychology. The present author made one of the first analyses of a specific abnormal behavior in terms of the principles of reinforcement (Staats, 1957), providing one of the foundations for the development of the field of behavior modification. His taxonomy of abnormal behavior (Staats, 1963, ch. 11) was the first that was based upon a behavioral analysis. This account included an implicit personality level of study, but when that level of theory was developed explicitly (Staats, 1975, ch. 8) it provided the basis for an heuristic theory of abnormal behavior. That theory is now seeing both theoretical and empirical development. Thus, Staats and Heiby (in press) have made a detailed analysis of depression within the framework of paradigmatic behaviorism's theory of abnormal behavior. And the general theory has formed the conceptual background for a hospital treatment program (Leduc and Dumais, 1983; Levesque and Leduc, 1980). There are so many implications for theoretical and empirical development within the present framework, at this level, that many individual researchers are necessary for the work ahead.

H.   THE EDUCATIONAL PSYCHOLOGY LEVEL OF THE
      THEORY

Paradigmatic behaviorism has extended its theory and development in some detail at this level. An early series of studies dealt with reading acquisition (Staats, 1968a; Staats, Brewer, and Gross, 1970; Staats, Finley, Minke, and Wolf, 1964; Staats, Staats, Schutz, and Wolf, 1962; Wolf, Giles, & Hall, 1968). And a series of studies dealt with children with reading problems (Collette-Harris & Minke, 1978; Staats & Butterfield, 1965; Staats, Minke, & Butts, 1970). The author divised the token-reinforcer system for these two lines of work, and this system was employed in many other behavior modification studies in educational psychology and in other applied fields. Other studies have dealt with the child's learning of number concepts (Staats, 1968a; Staats, Brewer, & Gross, 1970; Staats & Burns, 1982) imitation skills in copying and writing (Staats, 1968a; Staats et al., 1970), reading for pleasure (Mainguy & Leduc, 1980), syntactic skills (Caron & Leduc, 1982; Sailor, 1971; Staats, 1963), concept learning (Staats & Burns, 1982), learning letters (Giasson-Lachance & Leduc, 1981; Therialt-Pitre & Leduc, 1979), alienation in school (Morissette & Leduc, 1981).

I.   THE ORGANIZATIONAL PSYCHOLOGY LEVEL OF THE
      THEORY

More advanced levels of study of human behavior remain to be linked to the multilevel, unified theory, levels that have not been dealt with yet in a detailed, systematic way, but ones that clearly deal with related phenomena. Staats (1975) spends one chapter indicating that the unified theory is to be extended to the social sciences (chapt. 14) and one chapter indicating in general form the strategy for linking the unified theory to the biological level of study (ch. 15). The organizational level of the theory shown in Table 1 indicates an area that, like the social sciences, contains related phenomena that would be expected to involve the principles developed in the various levels of the theory, in which the first theoretical unification efforts have yet to begin.

VI. Unification is Originality Too

In the contemporary preparadigmatic science of psychology originality tends to be equated with the pristinely new, or at least with that which can be presented in that manner (Staats, 1983). A new experimental method, psychological test, concept, theory of small or large scope, phenomenon, or whatever are considered to be marks of originality. Because the science has not yet developed the goal of unity in the way the advanced sciences have, and because so little has been accomplished with unifying contributions, the importance, originality, and value of the organization of knowledge through unified theory has not been recognized (Staats, 1983).

It is not possible to hint at the potentiality for that type of creativity in the type of theory development that is being described. The studies cited herein have mostly come from paradigmatic behaviorism's own line of work. Many others could be presented from other learning-oriented as well as nonlearning-oriented approaches. Of special mention is the work of Aimeee Leduc and her group, who have produced a broad range of social behaviorism works. The fact of the matter is that there are multitudes of studies and concepts and theoretical principles that can be unified within the one, meaningful theoretical framework that has been described. When one looks at this record of accomplishment by various learning-oriented investigators in its totality, one cannot help but feel astonishment. There is no question that a proposal for a general, unified theory in psychology appears at the outset to be the height of chutzpah, a grandiose leap, such that it is difficult to obtain serious attention for such a project. Yet when one examines what has been accomplished to date that could be unified into one structure, one can only be surprised at the substantive development that already exists. Why is there such a discrepancy between the actual record and what is commonly perceived? The answer is actually so complex it cannot even be hinted at here (see Staats, 1983). But there is one point that should be mentioned: One reason that the potentiality of a unified theory based on learning principles remains unseen is that necessary and essential levels of the structure are left out of the various theories. For one thing, the individual theories are each focused at only one level of concern. There are basic animal learning theories, using this orientation as an example, social psychology learning theories in particular areas, learning theories in child development areas, behavior modification learning theories, and so on. But they are separated, and in being insular, they have lacked the conceptual developments that are necessary to provide the more general characteristics that would make them appropriate for the purpose of unifying the several levels of study. In particular, the lack of a personality level of study in the classic learning approaches has meant that learning efforts in child development, personality, personality measurement, social psychology, abnormal psychology, clinical psychology, and educational psychology have not been believable. Even though learning approaches have produced important works in each of these areas, they have not been able to deal with the central topics of personality causation and personality differences. That inadequacy has made learning theory approaches to complex human behavior at odds with traditional approaches of all varieties. How can a cognitive psychologist, for example, accept an approach such as Skinner's operant behaviorism which says that cognitive processes do not affect the determination of the individual's overt behavior? This represents a schism that cannot be dealt with until the necessary interlevel theory has been established between the basic conditioning principles and the personality phenomena studied by the cognitive psychologists, with the schism bridged in the multilevel manner described. As an example, the basic learning principles must be elaborated to indicate how the child learns various language–cognitive repertoires. Language learning has been a traditional concern of behaviorists. But the study of language learning is not enough; the bridging step involves the recognition that the language repertoires (and other repertoires as well) that the child learns become part of the child's personality. In later situations the child responds not only to the learning characteristics of a situation (to reinforcement or other learning variable), but also to the characteristic language–cognitive processes the situation arouses within him or her. It is the cognitive function of language that has not been treated in standard behaviorism. As an example, two individuals may respond in entirely different ways based upon their different cognitions in the *same* situation. It is important to study how different cognitions lead to different behaviors. Cognitive psychologists have been concerned with this part of the task, that is, the specification of types of cognitions and their effects on behavior. But to bridge the knowledge of cognitive psychology with that of learning theory, the interlevel theory must indicate how cognitions are learned, and generally relate the two types of study. When we recognize the legitimacy of both types of study the task becomes one of solving the problem of how to bring them together in a productive (heuristic) unification.

The point is, however, that if the science will stop and look it will see that there is already one multilevel theory and that the empirical–theoretical works of many other psychologists fit into and support that theory. Although at present this unity cannot be seen, what appears to be divergence is due to artifical diversity. Kuhn (1962) has described exactly the same phenomenon of unrecognized unity in the natural sciences before they became paradigmatic. In describing one preparadigmatic area he states "During that period there were almost as many views about the nature of electricity as there were important electrical experimenters. . . . All their numerous concepts of electricity had something in common" (1962, p. 13). Psychology is in that preparadigmatic state, where it needs unifying theory to bring its vast stores of common knowledge together. Perhaps the multilevel theory described here is not the best that can be formulated. But that we need unified theory of large scope is quite clear.

VII. Conclusions

There has been a complex of purposes for the present chapter. A beginning aim was to indicate something about the progress of S–R approaches in the areas of social–personality psychology, as well as to contribute to progress of that general framework. Learning theory work in social psychology has been largely divided from the mainstream of the field. Leonard Berkowitz in his letter inviting me to do the chapter seemed to recognize this when he said that S–R conceptions in social psychology are unduly minimized (see also Berkowitz, 1970b, for a more complete analysis). In my view, a simple review of what S–R psychologists have achieved in their individual efforts will not correct the problem involved. This is true because the preparadigmatic state of disorganization is basic, as is the search only for new and different methods, findings, and theories. Social–personality psychology suffers from problems of disunity and disorganization. This is true in the cognitive parts of the field and it is true in the various S–R approaches. In the latter case, although there is much potential commonality and mutual support, since the various findings actually comprise a basically complementary body of knowledge, this strength is lost in the separation and even competition of the several approaches. Learning approaches are as ununified as are other approaches in social psychology. Behaviorism has contributed to psychology's disorganization in the same way that other approaches have. A review of the achievements that have been made by the major learning-oriented theorists in this field thus would not remove the disorganization that exists even within the S–R orientation. Nor would a review demonstrate the power that is yielded by unified theory.

The major thrust of the present chapter has been to focus on what is seen as the central problem of present day personality–social psychology: its lack of organization. This is the main problem that must be faced for the field to begin to make general progress past its present character. Although the topic demands much greater elaboration (see Staats, 1983), I have tried herein in the brief space available to awaken the field to the problem of disorganization. This awakening is the first essential need. The second is to work on the problem once it has been recognized. In the service of the latter, a methodology has been described to create organization and unity of theory. A general methodology to effect unification has been developed (Staats, 1983). Moreover, a comprehensive methodology of theory construction has been described, that called multilevel theory. This methodology was exemplified through reference to the particular theory involved in the development of this methodology, the theory of paradigmatic behaviorism. I feel this is the approach to be taken; at the present time it is the only such approach. However, the methodology is considered to have general moment, which is disconnected from the particular theory involved in its development. The general suggestion is that whatever theory is constructed to handle the breadth of material that has been gained in social psychology, it will have to follow the multilevel-theory construction methodology that has been described.

The first generation of behaviorism focused on the discovery and experimental stipulation of the basic conditioning principles. The second generation of behaviorism focused on systematizing the multiple principles and findings of the study of animal learning into general animal learning theories. In both instances there was not a systematic consideration of the problems of making the basic learning theory general with respect to the study of human behavior, including the incorporation of the vast knowledge that had been found by nonbehavioral psychologists. The multilevel theory methodology is offered as a third-generation development with which to construct a theory that is general to personality–social psychology and general to psychology. I hope this will encourage others to become interested in the same goals—within the present theoretical framework, or in another—for it is time that psychology begins the laborious movement toward unity that it has lacked.

> [Psychology] is a fund of knowledge and technique that with the concentration of a guiding framework—and the participation of a large number of the science's members—could enter into the first rank of sciences . . . . These possibilities are obscured by the elements of separateness and antagonism that characterize the field of psychology, and by the lack of comprehensive theory to unite the separate strivings. A common set of goals within a common theoretical framework could mobilize the immense strengths now hidden in the field. (Staats, 1970, pp. 234–235)

Berkowitz has made a supporting suggestion, in a work also addressed to contemporary scientific psychology, in terms very consonant with the integratory interests of social behaviorism. ''Social psychology may now have reached the stage in which it is important to acknowledge the contributions of the different theoretical approaches. We would do well, I believe, to seek out the conditions most appropriate to a given conception and then bring these different schemes together in an integrated analysis of human social behavior (Berkowitz, 1970b, p. 311).

Psychologists in other parts of the world similarly have recognized the importance of this goal of unification. In a eulogistic paper dealing with the unifying properties of social behaviorism, Luis Lara Tapia, the eminent Mexican psychologist, states, "Perhaps the best eulogy that one is able to make of Arthur W. Staats is that he presents an integrative model that surely will be the image of psychology 2000 when psychological science passes to a phase of paradigmatic development" (1978, p. 199, translated from Spanish). The noted French psychologist Paul Fraisse evaluates the unified theory of social behaviorism by asking, "Will this perhaps be the psychology of the future?" (1976, p. 282, translated from French). There is enormous power released in the process of turning from a preparadigmatic (disorganized) science to a paradigmatic (unified) science. The puerile and inchoate strivings of the scientific but undirected, noncumulative, nongeneral, goalless groping of the disorganized science changes to the efficacious strength of the advanced sciences. With the entrance of a number of theorists and experimentalists and methodologists into the task of making psychology paradigmatic, our science will embark upon the revolution to unity (see Staats, 1983), which in the present opinion will ultimately be one of the great revolutions of science.

REFERENCES

Allen, V. L., and Wilder, D. A. Impact of group consensus and social support on stimulus meaning: Mediation of conformity by cognitive restructuring. *Journal of Personality and Social Psychology*, 1980, **39**, 1116–1124.

Aronfreed, J. *Conduct and conscience: The socialization of internalized control over behavior*. New York: Academic Press, 1968.

Ayllon, T., and Michael, J. L. The psychiatric nurse as a behavioral engineer. *Journal of the Experimental Analysis of Behavior*, 1959, **2**, 323–334.

Bandura, A. *Principles of Behavior Modification*. New York: Holt, Rinehart and Winston, 1969.

Bandura, A., and Walters, R. *Adolescent aggression*. New York: Ronald, 1959.

Bandura, A., and Walters, R. *Social learning and personality*. New York: Holt, Rinehart and Winston, 1963.

Baron, R. M. Attitude change through descrepant action: A functional analysis. In A. G. Greenwald, T. C. Brock, and T. M. Ostrom (Eds.). *Psychological foundations of attitudes*. New York: Academic Press, 1968.

Baum, A., Fisher, J. D., and Solomon, S. K. Type of information, familiarity, and the reduction of crowding stress. *Journal of Personality and Social Psychology*, 1971, **40**, 11–23.

Bem, D. J. Self-perception: An alternative interpretation of cognitive dissonance phenomena. *Psychological Review*, 1967, **74**, 183–200.

Bem, D. J. Attitudes as self-descriptions: Another look at the attitude–behavior link. In A. G. Greenwald, T. C. Brock, and T. M. Ostrom (Eds.), *Psychological foundations of attitudes*. New York: Academic Press, 1968.

Berger, S. M. Conditioning through vicarious instigation. *Psychological Review*, 1962, **69**, 450–466.

Berkowitz, L. *Aggression: A social psychological analysis*. New York: McGraw-Hill, 1962.

Berkowitz, L. Aggressive cues in aggressive behavior and hostility catharsis. Psychological Review, 1964, **71**, 104–122.

Berkowitz, L. Experimental investigations of hostility catharsis. Journal of Consulting and Clinical Psychology, 1970, **35**, 1–7. (a)

Berkowitz, L. Theoretical and research approaches in experimental social psychology. In A. R. Gilgen (Ed.), Contemporary scientific psychology. New York: Academic Press, 1970. (b)

Berkowitz, L. Words and symbols as stimuli to aggressive responses. In J. F. Knutson (Ed.). Control of aggression. Chicago: Aldine, 1973.

Berkowitz, L. Some determinants of impulsive aggression: Role of mediated associations with reinforcements for aggression. Psychological Review, 1974, **81**, 165–176.

Berkowitz, L., and Knurek, D. A. Label-mediated hostility generalization. Journal of Personality and Social Psychology, 1969, **13**, 200–206.

Berkowitz, L., and LePage, A. Weapons as aggression-eliciting stimuli. Journal of Personality and Social Psychology, 1967, **7**, 202–207.

Bierstedt, R. The social order: An introduction to sociology. New York: McGraw-Hill, 1957.

Bindra, D. How adaptive behavior is produced: A perceptual-motivational alternative to response-reinforcement. Behavioral and Brain Sciences, 1978, **1**, 41–91.

Burns, G. L. Indirect measurement and behavior assessment: A case for social behaviorism. Behavior Assessment, 1980, **2**, 197–206.

Byrne, D. Interpersonal attraction and attitude similarity. Journal of Abnormal and Social Psychology, 1961, **62**, 713–715.

Byrne, D. Response to attitude similarity-dissimilarity as a function of affiliation need. Journal of Personality, 1962, **30**, 164–177.

Byrne, D. The attraction paradigm. New York: Academic Press, 1971.

Byrne, D., and Clore, G. L. A reinforcement model of evaluative responses. Personality: An International Journal, 1970, **1**, 103–128.

Byrne, D., Ervin, C. R., and Lamberth, J. Continuity between experimental study of attraction and real-life computer dating. Journal of Personality and Social Psychology, 1970, **16**, 157–165.

Byrne, D., and Griffitt, W. Similarity and awareness of similarity of personality characteristics as determinants of attraction. Journal of Experimental Research in Personality, 1969, **3**, 179–186.

Byrne, D., Griffitt, W., and Clore, G. L., Jr. Attitudinal reinforcement effects as a function of stimulus homogeneity-heterogeneity. Journal of Verbal Learning and Verbal Behavior, 1968, **7**, 962–964.

Byrne, D., and Nelson, D. Attraction as a linear function of proportion of posiiive reinforcements. Journal of Personality and Social Psychology, 1965, **1**, 659–663.

Caron, C., and Leduc, A. L'apprentissage d'une forme syntaxique complex selon la theorie du behaviorisme social: Aspects theoriques. La technologie du comportement, 1982, **6**, 53–60.

Cialdini, R. B., Darby, B. L., and Vincent, J. E. Transgression and altruism: A case for hedonism. Journal of Experimental Social Psychology, 1973, **9**, 502–516.

Cialdini, R. B., and Kenrick, D. T. Altruism as hedonism: A social development perspective on the relationship of negative mood state and helping. Journal of Personality and Social Psychology, 1976, **34**, 907–914.

Collette-Harris, M. A., and Minke, K. A. A behavioral experimental analysis of dyslexia. Behavior Research and Therapy, 1978, **16**, 291–295.

Cuber, J. F. Sociology: A synopsis of principles. New York: Appleton, 1955.

Dollard, J., Doob, L., Miller, N., Mowrer, O., and Sears, R. Frustration and aggression. New Haven: Yale University Press, 1939.

Dollard, J., and Miller, N. Personality and psychotherapy. New York: McMillan, 1950.

Doob, L. W. The behavior of attitudes. Psychological Review, 1947, **54**, 135–156.

Dweck, C. S., Goetz, T. E., and Strauss, N. L. Sex differences in learned helplessness: IV. An experimental and naturalistic study of failure generalization and its mediators. *Journal of Personality and Social Psychology*, 1980, **38**, 441–452.

Early, J. C. Attitude learning in children. *Journal of Educational Psychology*, 1968, **59**, 176–180.

Elms, A. C. The crisis of confidence in social psychology. *American Psychologist*, 1975, **30**, 967–976.

Evans, P. A visit with Michael Argyle. *APA Monitor*, 1978, **9**, No. 8, 6–7.

Finley, J. R., and Staats, A. W. Evaluative meaning words as reinforcing stimuli. *Journal of Verbal Learning and Verbal Behavior*, 1967, **6**, 193–197.

Fraisse, P. Psychologie generale. *L'Anne Psychologigue*, 1976, **76**, 280–282.

Giasson-Lachance, J., and Leduc, A. L'utilisation de la couleur daus la mise en relief de graphemes chez des enfants de classes de maternelle. *Reeducation Orthognonique*, 1981, **19**, 429–433.

Golightly, C., and Byrne, D. Attitude statements as positive and negative reinforcements. *Science*, 1964, **146**, 798–799.

Greenwald, A. G. Cognitive learning, cognitive response to persuasion and attitude change. In A. G. Greenwald, T. C. Brock, and T. M. Ostrom (Eds.), *Psychological foundations of attitudes*. New York: Academic Press, 1968.

Griffitt, W., and Veitch, R. Hot and crowded: Influences of population density and temperature on interpersonal affective behavior. *Journal of Personality and Social Psychology*, 1971, **17**, 92–98.

Harms, J. Y., and Staats, A. W. Food deprivation and conditioned reinforcing value of food words: Interaction of Pavlovian and instrumental conditioning. *Bulletin of the Psychonomic Society*, 1978, **12**, 294–296.

Hekmat, H. The role of imagination in semantic desensitization. *Behavior Therapy*, 1972, **3**, 223–231.

Hekmat, H. Systematic versus semantic desensitization and implosive therapy: A comparative study. *Journal of Consulting and Clinical Psychology*, 1973.

Hekmat, H., and Vanian, D. Behavior modification through covert semantic desensitization. *Journal of Consulting and Clinical Psychology*, 1971, **36**, 248–251. **40**, 202–209.

Herry, M., and Leduc, A. The principle of higher-order instrumental conditioning in Staats learning theory. *International Newsletter of social behaviorism*. 1981, **1**, 5–13.

Herry, Y., and Leduc, A. La privation et les trois fonctions des stimuli selon la theorie de l'apprentissage d'Arthur W. Staats. *La technologie du comportement*, 1982, **6**, 160–175.

Hilgard, E. *Theories of learning*. New York: Appleton, 1948.

Hovland, C. K., Janis, I. L., Kelley, H. H. *Communication and persuasion*. New Haven: Yale University Press, 1953.

Hull, C. L. *A behavior system*. New Haven: Yale University Press, 1952.

Janis, I. L., and Mann, L. A conflict-theory of approach to attitude change and decision making. In A. G. Greenwald, T. C. Brock, and T. M. Ostrom (Eds.), *Psychological foundations of attitudes*. New York: Academic Press, 1968.

Kaufmann, H. *Social psychology: The study of human interaction*. New York: Holt, Rinehart and Winston, 1973.

Kenrick, D. T., Baumann, D. J., and Cialdini, R. B. A step in the socialization of altruism as hedonism: Effects of negative mood on children's generosity under public and private conditions. *Journal of Personality and Social Psychology*, 1979, **37**, 747–755.

Kim, M. P., and Rosenberg, S. Comparison of two structural models of implicit personality theory. *Journal of Personality and Social Psychology*, 1980, **38**, 375–389.

Koch, S. Comment: Psychology and the future. *American Psychologist*, 1978, **33**, 631–647.

Koch, S. The nature and limits of psychological knowledge: Lessons of a century qua "science." *American Psychologist*, 1981, **36**, 257–269.

Kuhn, T. S. *The structure of scientific revolutions* (2nd ed.). Chicago: University of Chicago Press, 1962.

Lara Tapia, L. Psicologia 2000. *Ensenanza e Investigacion en Psicologia*, 1978, **4**, 198–199.

Leduc, A. Le behaviorisme et l'autonomie de la personne. *Revue de modification due commporte-ment*, 1976, **6**, 1–16.

Leduc, A. Vers un meilleur concept de soi. *Apprentissage et socialisation*, 1978, **1**, 23–37.

Leduc, A. L'Apprentissage et le changement des attitudes: L'approche interactionniste de Staats. *Canadian Journal of Education*, 1980, **5**, 15–33. (a)

Leduc, A. L'Apprentissage et la mesure des attitudes. Research project supported by the Ministere de l'Education, Government du Quebec, 1980–1983. (b)

Leduc, A. L'apprentissage et le changement des attitudes envers soi-meme: Le concept de soi. *Canadian Journal of Education*, 1980, **5**, 91–101. (c)

Leduc, A., and Dumais, A. Une innovation dans la programmation d' interventions aupres de beneficiaires du C. H. Robert Giffard. *Revue de modification du comportement.* 1983, **13**, 53–65.

Levesque, M., and Leduc, A. L'apprentissage du comportement anormal dans le cadre du behav-iorisme social de Staats. *Apprentissage et Socialisation*, 1980, **5**, 196–209.

Lohr, J. M., and Staats, A. W. Attitude conditioning in Sino-Tibetan languages. *Journal of Person-ality and Social Psychology*, 1973, **26**, 196–200.

Lott, A. J., and Lott, B. A learning theory approach to interpersonal attitudes. In A. G. Greenwald, T. C. Brock, and T. M. Ostrom (Eds.), *Psychological foundations of attitudes.* New York: Academic Press, 1968.

Lott, A. J., and Lott, B. The power of liking: Consequences of interpersonal attitudes derived from a liberalized view of secondary reinforcement. In L. Berkowitz (Ed.), *Advances in experimental social psychology.* New York: Academic Press, 1972.

Lott, B. Eisman. Attitude formation: The development of a color preference response through mediated generalization. *Journal of Abnormal and Social Psychology*, 1955, **50**, 321–326.

Lott, B. Stimulus-response theories in social psychology. In *International Encyclopedia of Psychia-try, Psychology, Psychoanalysis, and Neurology*, 1977, **10**, 459–462.

Lott, B. E., and Lott, A. J. The formation of positive attitudes toward group members. *Journal of Abnormal and Social Psychology*, 1960, **61**, 297–300.

Mainguy, E. and Leduc, A. En venir a lire . . . pour le plaisir, selon Staats. *Apprentissage et Socialisation*, 1980, **3**, 35–40.

MacKenzie, B. D. *Behaviorism and the limits of scientific method.* Atlantic Highlands, New Jersey: Humanities Press, 1977.

McGinnies, E. *Social behavior: A functional analysis.* New York: Houghton Mifflin, 1970.

McGinnies, E., and Ferster, C. B. (Eds.). *The reinforcement of social behavior.* Boston: Houghton Mifflin, 1971.

McGuire, W. J. Personality and attitude change: An information-processing theory. In A. G. Green-wald, T. C. Brock, and T. M. Ostrom (Eds.), *Psychological foundations of attitudes.* New York: Academic Press, 1968.

Miller, N. E. Studies of fear as an acquired drive: I. Fear as motivation and fear-reduction as reinforcement in the learning of new responses. *Journal of Experimental Psychology*, 1948, **38**, 89–101.

Miller, N. E., and Dollard, J. *Social learning and imitation.* New Haven: Yale University Press, 1941.

Morissette, D., and Leduc, A. Le sentiment de l'alienation scolaire: Une attitude apprise dans la famille et a l'ecole. *L'Orientation Professionnelle*, 1981, **17**, 9–36.

Moscovici, S. Society and theory in social psychology. In J. Israel and H. Tajfel Eds.). *The context of social psychology.* New York: Academic Press, 1972.

Mowrer, O. H. *Learning theory and personality dynamics.* New York: Ronald, 1950.

Mowrer, O. H. The psychologist looks at language. *American Psychologist,* 1954, **9,** 660–694.

Osgood, C. E. *Method and theory in experimental psychology.* New York: Oxford University Press, 1953.

Overmier, J. B., and Lawry, J. A. Pavlovian conditioning and the mediation of behavior. In G. H. Bower (Ed.), *The psychology of learning and motivation* (Vol. 13). New York: Academic Press, 1979.

Pandey, J., and Griffitt, W. Attraction and helping. *Bulletin of Psychonomic Science,* 1974, **3,** 123–124.

Parish, T. C. Conditioning of racial attitudes and color concepts in children. *Perceptual and Motor Skills,* 1974, **39,** 707–714.

Parish, T. S., Buntman, A. D., and Buntman, S. R. Effect of counterconditioning on test anxiety as indicated by digit span performance. *Journal of Educational Psychology,* 1976, **68,** 297–299.

Parish, T. S., and Fleetwood, R. S. Amount of conditioning and subsequent change in racial attitudes of children. *Perceptual and Motor Skills,* 1975, **40,** 79–86.

Rondal, J. L'Interaction adult-enfants et la construction du langage, Brussels: Pierre Mardaga Editeur, 1983.

Rotter, J. B. *Social learning and clinical psychology.* Englewood Cliffs, New Jersey: Prentice-Hall, 1954.

Russell, J. A. A circumplex model of affect. *Journal of Personality and Social Psychology,* 1980, **39,** 1161–1178.

Rychlak, J. F. *A philosophy of science for personality theory.* Boston: Houghton Mifflin, 1968.

Sachs, D. H., and Byrne, D. Differential conditioning of evaluative responses to neutral stimuli through association with attitude statements. *Journal of Experimental Research in Personality,* 1970, **4,** 181–185.

Sailor, W. Reinforcement and generalization of productive plural allomorphs in two retarded children. *Journal of Applied Behavior Analysis,* 1971, **4,** 305–310.

Skinner, B. F. *The behavior of organisms.* New York: Appleton, 1938.

Skinner, B. F. The steep and thorny way to a science of behavior. *American Psychologist,* 1975, **30,** 42–49.

Spence, K. W. The nature of theory construction in contemporary psychology. *Psychological Review,* 1944, **51,** 47–68.

Staats, A. W. Learning theory and ''opposite speech.'' *Journal of Abnormal and Social Psychology,* 1957, **55,** 268–269.

Staats, A. W. (with contributions by C. K. Staats). *Complex human behavior.* New York: Holt, Rinehart and Winston, 1963.

Staats, A. W. (Ed.). *Human learning.* New York: Holt, Rinehart and Winston, 1964.

Staats, A. W. Outline of an integrated learning theory of attitude formation and function. In M. Fishbein (Ed.), *Attitude theory and measurement.* New York: Wiley, 1967.

Staats, A. W. *Learning, language, and cognition.* New York: Holt, Rinehart and Winston, 1968. (a)

Staats, A. W. Social behaviorism and human motivation: Principles of the attitude-reinforcer-discriminative system. In A. G. Greenwald, T. C. Brock, and T. M. Ostrom (Eds.), *Psychological foundations of attitudes.* New York: Academic Press, 1968. (b)

Staats, A. W. A learning behavior theory: A basis for unity in behavioral-social science. In A. R. Gilgen (Ed.), *Contemporary scientific psychology.* New York: Academic Press, 1970.

Staats, A. W. *Child learning, intelligence, and personality.* New York: Harper and Row, 1971.

Staats, A. W. Language behavior therapy: A derivative of social behaviorism. *Behavior Therapy,* 1972, **3,** 165–192.

Staats, A. W. *Social behaviorism.* Homewood, Illinois: Dorsey Press, 1975.

Staats, A. W. Social behaviorism: Unified theory in learning and personality. In R. B. Cattell and R. M. Dreger (Eds.), *Handbook of modern personality theory*. New York: Wiley, 1977.

Staats, A. W. About social behaviorism and social learning theory. Unpublished manuscript, 1978. (a)

Staats, A. W. Science standards or separatism? Questions in the methodology of citations. Unpublished manuscript, 1978. (b)

Staats, A. W. Separatism in theory construction: Methodological problems exemplified by Bandura's social learning theory. Unpublished manuscript, 1979.

Staats, A. W. The three-function learning theory of social behaviorism: A third-generation unified theory. *Aprendizaje y Comportamiente*, 1979, **2**, 13–38.

Staats, A. W. 'Behavioural interaction' and 'interactional psychology' theories of personality: Similarities, differences, and the need for unification. *British Journal of Psychology*, 1980, **71**, 205–220.

Staats, A. W. Paradigmatic behaviorism, unified theory, unified theory construction methods, and the zeitgeist of separatism. *American Psychologist*, 1981, **36**, 240–256.

Staats, A. W. *Psychology's crisis of disunity: Philosophy and method for a unified science*. New York: Praeger, 1983.

Staats, A. W. Unifying personality measurement and behavioral assessment: Beyond the consistency versus specificity framework. In R. O. Nelson and S. C. Hayes (Eds.), *Conceptual foundations of behavioral assessment*. New York: Guilford Press, in press.

Staats, A. W., Brewer, B. A., and Gross, M. C. Learning and cognitive development: Representative samples, cumulative–hierarchical learning, and experimental–longitudinal methods. *Monographs of the Society for Research in Child Development*. 1970, **35** (8. Whole No. 141).

Staats, A. W., and Burns, M. L. Intelligence and child development: What intelligence is and how it is learned and functions. *Genetic Psychology Monographs*, 1981, **104**, 237–301.

Staats, A. W., and Burns, G. L. Personality specification and social behaviorism's interaction theory. *Journal of Personality and Social Psychology*, 1982, **43**, 873–881.

Staats, A. W., and Butterfield, W. H. Treatment of nonreading in a culturally-deprived juvenile delinquent: An application of reinforcement principles. *Child Development*, 1965, **36**, 925–942.

Staats, A. W., Finley, J. R., Minke, K. A., and Wolf, M. M. Reinforcement variables in the control of unit reading responses. *Journal of the Experimental Analysis of Behavior*, 1964, **7**, 139–149.

Staats, A. W., Gross, M. C., Guay, P. F., and Carlson, C. C. Personality and social systems and attitude-reinforcer-discriminative theory: Interest (attitude) formation, function, and measurement. *Journal of Personality and Social Psychology*, 1973, **26**, 251–261.

Staats, A. W., and Hammond, W. W. Natural words as physiological conditioned stimuli: Food-word elicited salivation and deprivation effects. *Journal of Experimental Psychology*, 1972, **96**, 206–208.

Staats, A. W., and Heiby, E. M. The social behaviorism theory of depression. In S. Reiss and R. Bootzin (Eds.), *Theoretical issues in behavior therapy*. New York: Academic Press, in press.

Staats, A. W., and Higa, W. R. Effects of affect-loaded labels on interpersonal attitudes across ethnic groups. Unpublished manuscript, 1970.

Staats, A. W., and Lohr, J. M. Images, language, emotions, and personality: Social behaviorism's theory. *Journal of Mental Imagery*, 1979, **3**, 85–106.

Staats, A. W., Minke, K. A., and Butts, P. A token-reinforcement remedial reading program administered by black instructional technicians to backward black children. *Behavior Therapy*, 1970, **1**, 331–353.

Staats, A. W., Minke, K. A., Martin, C. H., and Higa, W. R. Deprivation-satiation and strength of attitude conditioning: A test of attitude-reinforcer-discriminative theory. *Journal of Personality and Social Psychology*, 1972, **24**, 178–185.

Staats, A. W., and Staats, C. K. Attitudes established by classical conditioning. *Journal of Abnormal and Social Psychology,* 1958, **57,** 37–40.

Staats, A. W., Staats, C. K., and Biggs, D. A. Meaning of verbal stimuli changed by conditioning. *American Journal of Psychology,* 1958, **71,** 429–431.

Staats, A. W., Staats, C. K., and Crawford, H. L. First-order conditioning of meaning and the parallel conditioning of a GSR. *Journal of General Psychology,* 1962, **67,** 159–167.

Staats, A. W., Staats, C. K., and Heard, W. G. Denotative meaning established by classical conditioning. *Journal of Experimental Psychology,* 1961, **61,** 300–303.

Staats, A. W., Staats, C. K., Schutz, R. E., and Wolf, M. M. The conditioning of reading responses using "extrinsic" reinforcers. *Journal of the Experimental Analysis of Behavior,* 1962, **5,** 33–40.

Staats, A. W., and Warren, D. R. Motivation and three-function learning: Food deprivation and approach-avoidance to food words. *Journal of Experimental Psychology,* 1974, **103,** 1191–1199.

Staats, C. K., and Staats, A. W. Meaning established by classical conditioning. *Journal of Experimental Psychology,* 1957, **54,** 74–80.

Stalling, R. B. Personality similarity and evaluative meaning as conditioners of attraction. *Journal of Personality and Social Psychology,* 1970, **14,** 77–82.

Therialt-Pitre, J., and Leduc, A. Le phenomene d'acceleration dans l'apprentissage du nom et son lettres de l'alphabet. *Apprentissage et socialization,* 1979, **2,** 133–148.

Weiss, R. F. The drive theory of social facilitation. *Psychological Review,* 1971, **78,** 44–57.

Weiss, R. F., Boyer, J. L., Lombardo, J. P., and Stich, M. H. Altruistic drive and altruistic reinforcement. *Journal of Personality and Social Psychology,* 1973, **25,** 390–400.

Weiss, R. F., Buchanan, W., Alstatt, L., and Lombardo, J. P. Altruism is rewarding. *Science,* 1971, **171,** 1262–1263.

Wolf, M. M., Giles, D. K., and Hall, V. R. Experiments with token reinforcement in a remedial classroom. *Behaviour Research and Therapy,* 1968, **6,** 51–64.

Woll, S. The best of both worlds? A critique of cognitive social learning. Unpublished manuscript, 1978.

Wrightsman, L. S. *Social psychology* (2nd ed.). Monterey, California: Brooks/Cole, 1977.

Yela, M. G. *La estructura de la conducta.* Madrid: Real Academia de Ciencias Morales y Politicas, 1974.

Yela, M. G. La evolucion del conductismo. *Interdisciplinaria,* 1979, **1,** 43–65.

SOCIAL PSYCHOLOGY FROM THE STANDPOINT OF A STRUCTURAL SYMBOLIC INTERACTIONISM: TOWARD AN INTERDISCIPLINARY SOCIAL PSYCHOLOGY*

Sheldon Stryker

DEPARTMENT OF SOCIOLOGY
INDIANA UNIVERSITY
BLOOMINGTON, INDIANA

I. Introduction

The underlying and major premise of this paper, made explicit and elaborated in its penultimate section, is that the work of those approaching social psychology from traditional psychological perspectives would be better were it to take seriously theoretical and methodological lessons contained in a perspective rooted in a more sociological approach to the field. That perspective has been labelled a structural symbolic interactionism (Stryker, 1980); it emphasizes ''meaning'' as the critical dimension of humans' responses to both their physical

*This is a revised version of a paper initially prepared for and presented as a lecture in a seminar, *''Orientaciones y tendencias de la psicologia social contemporanea,''* José Ramón Torregrosa, Director, Universidad Internacional Menedez Pelayo, Santander, Spain, August 4, 1981. An abbreviated version was the basis for an address to Division Eight, American Psychological Association, Los Angeles, California, August 24, 1981.

ADVANCES IN EXPERIMENTAL
SOCIAL PSYCHOLOGY, VOL. 16

and social environments, the source of meanings in the social interactions and relationships of persons, the centrality of the meaning-system termed the self to theoretical accounts of those responses, and the constraints on responses that are a consequence of the embeddedness of persons in structures of roles and the further embeddedness of role structures in the larger organization of society.

My intent in arguing the validity of this underlying premise is not to vent a sociological chauvinism, but rather to promote a more interdisciplinary social psychology. Ideally, social psychology is an interdisciplinary endeavor, drawing mainly from psychology and sociology, but necessarily using the intellectual resources of various other fields from biology through linguistics through anthropology. In practice, though, there are two main social psychologies, each with important internal variants, one with a disciplinary base in psychology and the other in sociology. Throughout their existence, the relation of these two major social psychologies has been tangential to one another. Given the social structure of academe and related institutions—separate departments, separate professional meetings, separate journals, separate invisible networks, separate systems of honor and prestige—their practitioners have had minimal contact with one another and with the work and ideas of one another. As a consequence, the two social psychologies have developed essentially independently (Stryker, 1971; Stryker, 1977).

Short of a radical restructuring of universities, professional associations, and publication outlets that currently act to separate rather than to integrate social psychologists with differing academic heritages, it is unrealistic to expect even an approximation of the ideal; a truly interdisciplinary social psychology is unlikely to emerge under forseeable social organizational circumstances. The improbability of achieving the ideal, however, makes it no less important that the social psychologies maintain contact and learn from one another. This paper, in its intention at least, seeks to contribute to that goal.

The ultimate end of an interdisciplinary social psychology and the more immediate goals of maintaining contact and benefitting from one another obviously require that the separate social psychologies be open to mutual influence. Persons whose work has differing disciplinary backgrounds and who historically have tended to talk past one another must be willing to talk to and even listen to one another. To focus, as is done in this paper, on a one-directional flow seems to belie this requirement. As the disclaimer of sociological chauvinism was meant to suggest, this focus does not deny the importance and relevance of work being done from psychological perspectives in social psychology for work being done from more sociological perspectives. It reflects, rather, the vehicle in which the paper is published and its consequent major audience.

Admittedly, the concentration on a one-directional flow reflects, in some degree as well, my disciplinary background in sociology and the character of my own theoretical and research efforts in social psychology. The latter have been concerned with elaborating the ideas and extending the implications of the version of symbolic interactionism for which special virtues are claimed. These virtues, if granted, legitimate the thesis that psychological social psychology would be importantly enriched were it to adopt the ideas and implications of this framework.

Sociologically trained social psychologists generally have found a symbolic interactionist framework, at least in its essentials, most appealing, perhaps precisely because it provides a theoretically principled way in which to visualize the fundamental interdependency of person and society, giving at least as much attention to the latter as to the former. Psychologically trained social psychologists—certainly of the American variety; Europeans may constitute exceptions to this assertion (see the authors represented in Israel & Tajfel, 1972)—have not been likely to be much aware of this framework. If aware of it, they tend to be aware of only one elaboration of it. And, even if aware of this elaboration, they are not likely to have found it of any great use.

In significant degree, however, the situation just described may be changing. To offer a partial explanation of why this may be so, and, more importantly, to encourage continued change requires discussion of recent developments in symbolic interactionist concepts and ideas. Why is the framework now receiving respectful attention in quarters in which it was earlier ignored or disdained? The very question suggests that, factually, the current flow of information and influence across the line that separates psychological and sociological versions of social psychology is, importantly, from the latter to the former. In my judgment, that is the case. Whatever may be true historically, at the present time the major directional flow is that on which this paper is focused. That factual state, assuming it to be such, is in my judgment justified by the current state of psychological social psychology and its "needs." Specifically, the justification lies in the crisis of confidence that over the past decade or so has beset psychologists who do social psychology, the sources of that crisis of confidence, the unsatisfactoriness of "internal" solutions offered for that crisis, and the ways in which a more sociologically oriented social psychology may serve to restore confidence in the possibility of a reasonable science of social psychology, albeit not one that all envision or seek.

Thus, to explicate the major premise of this paper more fully necessitates not only a discussion of what is entailed in a structural symbolic interactionism, but it requires a discussion as well of why psychological social psychology may be receptive to the ideas and emphases of that frame. More generally, it will be useful to ask, against a background of relative mutual ignorance, what it is that permits even measured optimism that—whatever the extant "needs" and the validity of available "help" with respect to those needs—social psychologists of differing disciplinary background are listening or will listen to one another?

The explication begins by examining two social psychologies, the one emanating from psychology and the other from sociology, asking in particular why historically they have not been more open to one another. Then, the question of why there seems to be a new openness vis-à-vis one another is raised. This question is answered in terms of developments over recent years that have occurred in common to both social psychologies: specifically, the commonalities in attacks that they have faced, and the discovery that many of their practitioners are encountering very similar problems and finding solutions in similar or complementary frames of reference. It is also answered in terms of developments relatively peculiar to each of the two social psychologies: the emergent respectability of subjective experience and the sense of crisis in psychological social psychology; and a variety of theoretical trends both in and outside of symbolic interactionism in sociological social psychology. Next, one of these trends—the development of a structural symbolic interactionism—is appraised with respect to its potential in dealing with, in particular, the crisis in psychological social psychology and, more generally, important methodological and theoretical issues generated by work in that segment of the total social psychological enterprise. The paper ends with a brief coda articulating the key challenge facing contemporary social psychology.

II. Two Social Psychologies

Those whose intellectual interests are social psychological know that there is a social psychology whose disciplinary home is psychology, whose concerns have been defined primarily in terms of the impact of social stimuli on individual behavior, and whose methods are characteristically experimental. Many are at least dimly aware of another social psychology whose disciplinary home is sociology, whose interests are specified by a concern with the reciprocal impact of society and person, and whose research procedures have been primarily observational and survey. The spate of papers, from the late 1970s and early 1980s, invoking the image of multiple social psychologies (e.g., Stryker, 1977; Stryker, 1981; House, 1977; Gottlieb, 1977) does not represent a "discovery"; virtually every social psychology text from the invention of the genre by E. A. Ross (1908) to the present both announces that social psychology is rooted in psychology and in sociology, and pays virtually no attention to the contributions of the discipline other than that with which the author identifies.

Awareness of multiple disciplinary roots has not, then, led to widespread appreciation of mutual relevance in either major social psychology. Lip service is forever given the ideal of an interdisciplinary social psychology; exemplars of a real interdiscipline are rare. Why this is so is a sociology and social psychology of knowledge question, whose answer is relevant to understanding why a new willingness to listen seems to exist among both psychologists and sociologists.

Part of the answer lies in the social structure of academe alluded to earlier. Part also lies in the metaphysics characterizing earlier development of the parent disciplines. Durkheim's insistence on the independence of the social fact, indeed its causal priority vis-à-vis individual psychology, amounted to a manifesto warning sociologists against the perfidious psychologizing of their theory and research; the attitude implicit in that warning is still widespread in sociology and attenuates whatever inclination social psychologists trained in sociology may have to look to psychology for intellectual sustenance. From the other side, the dominant behaviorism of either the early Watson or later Skinner varieties translated to a vision of social psychology as an experimental discipline, the arena of inquiry being the laboratory, and the model social psychologist being the white-coated scientist. On the defensive internally, since they had to prove themselves as true scientists to experimental psychologists in the face of the humanistic taint of their subject matter, psychologically trained social psychologists in their relations with their sociologically trained brethren tended toward arrogance and condescension. They were inclined to dismiss the social psychology produced by sociologists as nonscience if not nonsense (perhaps more often the latter), because it characteristically abjured experimental methods in favor of direct observation of real-life situations to which the notion of control was foreign, or favored survey procedures in which controlled observations were achieved through post hoc application of statistical methods rather than through random assignment of subjects to conditions and manipulation of experimental variables. This inclination was reinforced by the characteristic predilection of a sociology-based social psychology for ''soft'' humanistic and subjectivist concepts like the self rather than more directly behavior-based conceptualizations, as well as by its propensity for theorizing in the absence of a strong research base.

Sociologically trained social psychologists, for their part, were likely to dismiss the social psychology produced by psychologists as irrelevant to the human condition, its characteristic behaviorism relegating the most distinctive and important facts about human beings—mindedness, the symbolic character of their worlds, their reflexivity—to a residual dung-heap of the non-observable, non-measurable, and, therefore, non-scientific. Further, from the standpoint of the sociologically trained social psychologist, the experimental situations favored by their psychological counterparts were biased away from a focus on interaction and toward a focus on the responses of individuals as individuals. Floyd Allport's (1924) view that other persons and social institutions are stimuli no different in principle from other (nonsocial) stimuli—a view that effectively denies the defining principles of a social psychology as conceived by most sociologists—seemed to be built into the experimental procedures of psychologists. While they may no longer dismiss experimental work, as they did thirty years ago, with the contemptuous remark that rats are not people, sociologists are still inclined to regard experimentation as antithetical to producing the knowledge they seek. Further, sociologists tended to see the social psychology produced by psychologists as atheoretical, even worse as uninterested in theory. Finally, there was an element of insecurity in the responses of sociologically trained social psychologists to their psychologically trained brethren. In part, that insecurity reflected the dominance in the culture at large of hard science vis-à-vis more humanistically oriented disciplines; in part, it reflected the fact that psychologists, nurtured by the image of their discipline as experimental science, were in general better trained mathematically and statistically than sociologists (a fact also reflected in the attitudes of psychologists toward sociological social psychology earlier noted).

The attitudes just recounted seem less in evidence today. There is indeed a new openness in the relations of the two social psychologies. Why? What has happened, against the background sketched, to make persons on either side of the division more receptive to the work of persons on the other side, and to make a difference in how social psychological issues are thought about and researched? Mutual receptivity must be grounded in appropriately prepared soil. Conditioning the soil have been a variety of relatively recent developments in one or the other, or both, of the two social psychologies.

III.   Developments in the Two Social Psychologies

A.   COMMON DEVELOPMENTS

Some developments have occurred in both social psychologies, rather than being particular to one, a not-surprising fact, given that they exist in the same world and respond to many of the same social and intellectual currents. Both have been, and are, under attack from a variety of sources; while the terms of the attack vary somewhat, there are strong commonalities in them and they have comparable consequences. Too, practitioners of the two social psychologies have discovered that they sometimes ask essentially similar questions and approach the answers to those questions with similar and/or complementary frames of reference. These common developments, very different in character and quality, make it more likely that each social psychology will attend to the other. With reference to the first, while there may be little sense of what kind of aid can be forthcoming, a typical response to being under attack is to look for allies among those experiencing comparable attack. With reference to the second, it becomes difficult to avoid a sense of responsibility for what the other has to say.

1.   Social Psychology Under Attack

The bases for the attacks on both social psychologies are varied: the demand for relevance; the sense that social psychological theory and methods are ideologies or serve ideological purposes; alleged deficiences in theoretical frameworks and theories; and the presumed inadequacies of the underlying operative models of science and of explanation.

a. The Demand for Relevance. Both social psychologies face the demand that they be "relevant." Just what that slippery term means is not clear, and one person's relevance is another's irrelevance. Nevertheless, the Marxist insistence on seeing all phenomena as largely the consequence of the structure of economic (productive) relationships is one influential basis for a judgment of relevance, and has been the premise of critiques of both psychological social psychology (Archibald, 1978; Israel, 1972; Janousek, 1972) and sociological social psychology (Gouldner, 1970).

Sociological social psychology over the past few decades opened itself to a radical critique by neglecting its motivating insight: that social structure and social person mutually constrain one another (indeed, symbolic interactionism insists that they presuppose one another and do not exist except in relation to one another). A significant proportion of sociologists who defined themselves as social psychologists or did social psychological work during the 1950s and 1960s especially, but to the present as well, dissipated that insight. Some did so by adopting operant conditioning principles, insisting that sociological work merely applied those principles (Homans, 1961; Hamblin, Buckholdt, Ferritor, Kozloff, & Blackwell, 1971) or elaborated them (Burgess & Bushell, 1969) and in this way denigrated social structure by ignoring its impact on social interaction and on persons. The operant conditioning scheme, as a social psychology, begs the question of the impact of social structure by failing to ask what it is that determines what can and cannot be used as reinforcers in particular social contexts, as well as how it is that some and not others control reinforcers and decide what behaviors to reinforce.

Other sociologically trained social psychologists found the appeal of the cognitive balance theories, especially Heider's (1958), or dissonance theory (Festinger, 1957) irresistable, perhaps because of the ingenuity with which those theories were formulated, their sometimes counter-intuitive implications, and their amenability to experimental test and/or demonstration. Under the siren spell of such theories, these investigators focused their attention on intrapsychic processes without essential reference to the structured situations in which balance or dissonance processes took place; in so doing, they too failed to capitalize on the insight motivating a sociologically oriented social psychology.

Not only those sociologists who took their theoretical cues from Skinner, Heider, or Festinger were led away from a serious concern with questions of the impact of social structure on social interaction and social person; many followed more indigenous paths to the same end. Some (e.g., Blumer, 1969) dissolved social structures into definitions of the situation by pushing to an extreme implications drawn from W. I. Thomas' (Thomas & Thomas, 1937) maxim, "if men define situations as real, they are real in their consequences." So doing, they converted the pregnant observation that humans live in symbolic environments to the denial that there are "real" social structures that constrain social interactions and products thereof appearing in the context of those structures. Others (e.g., Cicourel, 1973) moved in comparable directions by interpreting social structure as existing only in persons' cognitive sense of that structure. Either tactic elevates the reasonable assertion that social structure is created and recreated in interaction, and therefore a thoroughgoing sociological determinism is unacceptable, to the unreasonable assertion that social structures have no reality and therefore do not significantly affect the course of human conduct and interaction. Both have been used to justify the implicit assumption that since humans can define situations in widely divergent ways, there are no significant operative social structural constraints on how they will define situations.

Finally, some sociologically trained social psychologists, carrying out the injunctions of Mead (1934) and Cooley (1902) to see social life as process, committed themselves to observation as the valid method of gathering data and producing knowledge. They committed themselves, as well, to concepts grounded in their immediate observations and explicitly or implicitly denying the validity of concepts not so grounded (Glaser & Strauss, 1967; Lofland, 1978). A consequence of these methodological and metatheoretical decisions is to narrow attention to minutiae of face-to-face interaction or strategies of everyday behavior and to visualize that interaction or behavior as essentially free of institutional and large-scale social structural constraints (see, e.g., the various analyses in Lofland, 1978, especially Bernstein's on accounts used by students to justify not studying and Walum's on cross-sex door openings). Another consequence is that analyses remain at a low level of abstraction, moving little beyond description and classification. The methodological and metatheoretical sources of Goffman's (1959; 1961; 1974) work are somewhat different. In its deliberate focus on the momentary encounter and the episodic, however, it also tends to see social behavior in the context of frames or definitions of the situation constructed by participants in the immediate interaction under analysis rather than in the context of larger social structures whose existence is largely independent of such interaction.

The foregoing does not deny either the legitimacy or the social psychological interest and content of such work. Its point is to observe that insofar as sociologically trained social psychologists restrict themselves to such work or to work in the operant conditioning or cognitive dissonance/balance veins, or reduce social structures to cognitions, they fail to exploit the insight that person and society mutually constrain—even presuppose—one another. It is also to observe that such work has been charged with trivializing social psychology by rendering it irrelevant to the political-economic issues of our times (Gouldner, 1970). Finally, it is to observe that the demand for relevance that underlies this charge, in part but not totally emanating from the radical left, has reinvigorated the motivating insight of a sociological social psychology, making it more likely that social structural variables will be incorporated into explanations of social psychological events and behaviors. One way to meet this intellectual pressure is to become more sensitive to the social structures (economic, power, sex, age, etc.) impacting on more narrowly defined social psychological relationships.

The demand for relevance impacts on psychological social psychology in comparable ways. This part of social psychology has been strongly infused with one kind of relevance since the 1930s, under the influence of Lewin (1951). That relevance, however, tended to define problems at the individual level: how can persons be motivated to produce more, or to stop smoking, or to be less prejudiced. The relevance implied by the radical critique of social psychology is of a different variety; it concerns the potential of social psychology for designing, motivating, and implementing large-scale social change. The change called for is not in individual behavior; it is in social organization. Insofar as psychological social psychology accepts the demand for this kind of relevance, it too must incorporate social structural variables into its theories and research. Insofar as it seeks to meet that requirement, it is more likely to open itself to work done by sociological social psychologists whose parent discipline has as its core concept precisely the notion of social structure. Even should psychological social psychology decline to put itself in the service of radical social change, the intellectual thrust of the radical demand for relevance remains effective. That thrust asserts the importance of the way social relationships are organized for comprehending persons' behavior. The message is clearly that psychological social psychology must pay more attention to social structure than it typically has in the past.

b. Social Psychology as Ideology.   The attack on the theories and methods of contemporary sociological and psychological social psychology that asserts their ideological character follows closely from what has already been said about relevance. In the classic Mannheim (1936) sense, an ideology is a system of ideas defining or protecting the social status quo. With respect to psychological social psychology, the argument has been made (Moscovici, 1972) that the research done (e.g.) on worker motivation or worker output simply accepts the legitimacy of and protects the extant system of economic relationships by failing to incorporate into the research a critical probing of it. A comparable argument has been made concerning research in the social psychology of work done by sociologists (Braverman, 1974). It has been asserted (Tajfel, 1972) that the experimental methodology favored by psychological social psychology is ideological in taking for granted and failing to question or challenge conventional interactional frameworks; and it has been asserted (Gouldner, 1970; Smith, 1973) that a focus via observational studies on everyday interaction has equivalent ideological consequences. The claim has been made that the individualistic emphasis of theory in psychological social psychology constitutes an ideology through its implicit acceptance of existing social organizational arrangements (Moscovici, 1972); and it has been claimed that symbolic interaction theory is ideological since it neglects social structure as a consequence of its emphases on actors' definitions of situations, the immediate situation of action, and the emergent character of organized social behavior (Huber, 1973).

The most fundamental claim that social psychology is ideology, however, relates to the way human beings are conceptualized, a topic that blends into the next subsection of this chapter. Psychological social psychology, of both the behavioristic and the cognitive types, is seen by critics with a more sociological perspective (Cooley, 1902; Mead, 1934; Moscovici, 1972) as premising the person as an "individual" defined apart from, in contrast with, or in opposition to other human beings. Such a conceptualization, it has been said (Israel, 1972), serves as an ideology in defense of the competitive individualism of capitalistic society. (An alternative conceptualization of the human, to be discussed briefly in another context, is to see the person as in part constituted by other persons, in the sense that the person is the product of his or her interaction with others; the political-economic system for which this constitutes an ideology I will leave for others to suggest.)

   c. Inadequacies of Conceptualization and Theory.   A third focus of critics of the two social psychologies is on theory and conceptualization. The social psychologies have, of course, been criticized from a variety of metatheoretical perspectives implying very different conceptions of human beings, of social interaction, and of society. What has been said about an individualistic versus a social conception of the human being who is the fundamental unit of social psychological analysis need not be repeated. The version of social psychology that draws heavily on one or another reinforcement model has been criticized for its explicit or implicit view of human behavior as totally reactive, as occurring in response to external stimuli impinging on the human organism, and thereby ignoring or minimizing the active, creative potential in human behavior (Smith, 1974; Harré & Secord, 1973). The phrase "the human is an *actor* as well as a *reactor*" describes the essential character of this criticism, and, not incidently, is one of the underlying assumptions of symbolic interactionism (Stryker, 1964). On the other hand, cognitively oriented social psychology has been scored for positing totally rational actors, decision-making their way through life by accurately estimating the consequences of projected lines of action for meeting their needs or goals.

Not surprisingly, symbolic interactionism, conceptualizing humans as exercizing self-control in solving interactional problems, is also attacked for postulating overly cognitive, overly rational actors who play the part of scientists examining alternative hypotheses as they go about the business of meeting contingencies arising in everyday existence (Stryker, 1980). It is, on the other hand, symbolic interactionism that is a major source of a criticism of both social psychologies—that they fail to recognize sufficiently or even wholly ignore the "meaning" dimension in human behavior, while arguing that this dimension is crucial for comprehending how external, environmental circumstances impinge or fail to impinge on human action. Succinctly, the claim is that humans live in a symbolic environment constituted by meanings developing out of social interaction, that the human capacity to generate and to use symbolic systems (principally language) defines the human being, and that such "facts" demand a conception very different from the automaton, mindlessly and mechanically responding to external stimuli, that is presumed to be inherently the conception of the human that underlies experimental social psychology.

Another—influential—line of critical comment on work done from a sociological frame initially developed in response to a role theory derived from the anthropologist Linton (1936) and entering sociology primarily through the writings of Parsons (1951). This line seeks to reassert biological and deep psychological (in a Freudian sense) influences on human social behavior, arguing that these influences have been dimissed in a role theory that conceptualizes the human being as a quiescent role-player whose actions are determined by the normative expectations of society. These expectations are seen as built into the psyches of humans through socialization processes designed to maintain order and stability in the social system. Thus, persons are "motivated" in ways commensurate with the needs of their society: individual motivation reinforces societal motivation and meets societal needs. In Wrong's (1961) apt phrase, such thinking produces an "over-socialized conception of man," one he believes requires correction by the re-introduction of consideration of the dark side of human nature—the primitive, instinctual, and emotional.

If, to return to earlier observations, meanings are crucial to human behavior, quite different conceptualizations of social interaction and of society are required than if meanings are incidental. Not surprisingly, therefore, extant conceptions of social interaction and of society have drawn their share of critical comment.

Behavioristic social psychology has been attacked for its sense of social interaction as a complex stimulus-response system, with each interactant "merely" serving as a stimulus to others' reaction. Such a conceptualization, it is claimed, fails to grasp the implications of viewing humans as interpenetrating and of the symbolic nature of human exchanges. It also fails to provide for the emergent quality of interaction, to recognize that interaction unfolds and evolves out of the processes of interaction itself (Blumer, 1969), sometimes taking turns unpredictable from elements present at the beginning of the interaction. From the point of view underlying many of these criticisms, social interaction *is* the communication of evolving meanings; and human behavior (both individual and social) is to be understood in terms of symbolic exchanges, especially of meanings taking the form of social and personal identities. Cognitive social psychology, for instance, attribution theory, is criticized for an equivalent failure to incorporate the meaning dimension in its formulations, for not seeing interaction as the arena in which meanings are produced and changed, and for ultimately reducing others interacting with some focal person to that focal person's perceptions of the others (Stryker & Gottlieb, 1981).

The term ''social'' has a basic ambiguity: it refers to the processes by which particular human beings impinge on one another as they come together in physical or symbolic space; it also refers to the larger social organization(s)—from family group to total societies—that serve as the contexts within which interaction takes place. Sometimes the two are identified, as when Blumer (1969) defines society as symbolic interaction, arguing that society is comprised only of sometimes overlapping, sometimes independent circles of social interaction. Thus, Blumer effectively denies the reality of larger social systems (although he certainly recognizes the significance of the definitions people hold with respect to such larger systems).

A second possibility is to ignore those larger social systems. (A third is to grant the reality of these larger social systems, as well as the reality of social interaction and the persons who interact, taking as theoretically and empirically problematic precisely the nature of the relationships among the three. This possibility underlies what is said in section IV of this paper). This second possibility draws Moscovici's (1972) fire. He notes that in much social psychology, the indices of ''social'' translate to whether others are present when the behavior of an individual being studied takes place, and how many others are present. At best, he argues, the social so defined refers only to an interindividual interactional subsystem of society, and fails to incorporate the structure of society: its processes of production and consumption, its rituals, its symbols, its institutions, norms and values. It thus fails to recognize society as an organization; so failing, it permits a social psychology only partially, ambiguously, and inadaquately social. A comparable criticism has been leveled (Stryker, 1980) at the version of symbolic interactionism defined by Blumer (1969), practiced by many who restrict their analyses to interaction that they have directly observed and their conceptualizations to those ''discovered'' in that directly observed interaction.

Beyond conceptual inadaquacies, the two social psychologies have been and are under attack for alleged deficiencies in the form and content of their theories. Criticisms on this score include polar opposites. Psychological social psychology has been scolded for being a congeries of small-scale theories of particular phenomena (social comparisons, attitude change, choice shifts, self-awareness, causal attributions, equity judgments, etc.) without any overall theoretical framework to give these disparate theories coherence and to bring them into some sort of systematic relationship to one another (Harré & Secord, 1973). Sociological social psychology, quite differently, has been criticized for having an overall theoretical framework but having no theories with direct empirical implications that can be tested.

d.   Inadequacies of Underlying Models of Science and Explanation.   Although some aspects of a last focus of attack on the two social psychologies receive attention later, the issues and arguments contained or implicit in it are suggested in the following discussion. However, an adequate statement of this focus on presumed inadequacies of underlying models of science and of explanation requires more space than can be given here. In particular, I cannot address the large variety of questions that exist with regard to the legitimacy of the claims of inadequacies.

The most thoroughgoing and serious challenge to "mainstream" psychological or sociological psychology arises out of a radically phenomenological perspective. That perspective has somewhat different roots in the two disciplines and goes by different names—in sociology it is ethnomethodology and its roots are in Husserl and Schutz; in psychology, it is ethogeny and its roots are in Kant and in ordinary-language philosophy. The nature of the diagnoses of mainstream errors in views of science and of explanation as well as the prescriptions to eliminate those errors, however, have an essential resemblance, and I will not distinguish between them.

Both ethomethodology and ethogeny take as the villain positivistic images of science and of explanation that are said to be pervasive in mainstream social psychology, and both are used to draw strong theoretical and methodological implications. Harré and Secord's (1973) characterization of positivism in social psychology invokes three related elements: a mechanistic model of man requiring that behavior be explicated in terms of external stimuli, with internal sources of behavior minimized, and requiring a one-to-one relationship between particular causes and particular effects; a Humean conception of cause requiring that causal laws express invariant stimulus–response (S–R) correlations with the mode of connection between cause and effect not taken as part of empirical science, a naive determinism in which external stimuli approach being efficient causes, and either ignoring or reducing to the status of conditions organismic sources of behavior; and a logical positivist methodology requiring a verification theory of meaning, an operationalist theory of definition, and (by implication) restricting the role of theory to that of providing a logical organization in facts. While this image may caricature social-psychology-in-practice, it has provided an effective rallying ground for adherents of ethnomethodology and ethogeny.

As this language suggests, both ethnomethodology and ethogeny (especially the former) have had the character of social movements. Social movements, in seeking adherents, frequently exaggerate their differences from established patterns, particularly, perhaps, established patterns most closely resembling those they seek to promote. Thus, both ethnomethodology and ethogeny have a great deal in common with symbolic interactionism (more in common with certain versions of that framework than with others, to be sure), though there is resistance to recognizing those commonalities. At least some symbolic interactionists, however, retain a more conventional view of science and of explanation—by a conventional view, I do not mean the image of a positivism as outlined by Harré—that accepts the goal of social science as the development of empirical generalizations explained in terms of causal theory or theories tested under the most controlled observations possible. In contrast, ethogeny and ethnomethodology appear to deny the possibility of empirical generalizations and/or causal theory and/or controlled test. Research based on anything but naturalistic observation or examination of protocols produced in the course of everyday interaction (i.e., research introducing controls) is rejected; and causal explanation is abandoned in favor of understanding through deep contextual analyses.

Ethnomethodology (Garfinkel, 1967; Sudnow, 1972; Cicourel, 1964) is not a singular discipline; however, ethnomethodological work tends to have two implications. One is methodological and follows from viewing the conduct of science as no different from the conduct of persons going about their everyday business. Given this view, ethnomethodology argues the reactive character of all research that interferes in persons' everyday conduct. A research instrument, the argument goes, necessarily imposes without warrant the theoretical premises and concepts of the social scientist. In so doing, it shapes the behavior being observed and leads to findings reflecting the researcher's premises and concepts rather than those of subjects, distorting the reality of the experience of those subjects. Research is to be approached without presuppositions so that the methods people use to make sense of their own phenomenological worlds can be grasped.

A second implication is theoretical. Both following from the methodological implication reviewed and having additional methodological consequences, it is incorporated into Cicourel's (1973) call for a cognitive sociology. Cicourel invokes the methodological stance of ethnomethodology and ethogeny to argue the inapplicability of social psychologists' concepts such as role, norm, status, and social interaction to everyday experience and to the lay explanations of the persons whom social psychologists study. To replace such concepts, he calls for explicit attention to how actors recognize relevant stimuli in the course of their interactions and how they generate coherent responses recognized as relevant by those with whom they are interacting. The aim of his cognitive sociology is the discovery and analysis of fundamental interpretative procedures allowing actors to sustain a sense of social structure to organize their behavior in social settings. These interpretative procedures constitute a set of rules, by analogy a generative grammar, for the conduct of social life: an illustrative rule is the "reciprocity of perspectives," which enjoins interacting persons to assume that their experience would be the same were they to exchange positions in the interaction and were they to ignore personal differences. That assumption allows interactants to, for all practical purposes, attend to issues at hand in the same way. Interpretative procedures thus constitute a "deep structure" that interacts with a surface normative structure to produce social behavior. Cicourel further argues that theory failing to provide for deep structure interpretative procedures must fail, as must research premised on an assumption of the nonproblematic character of analysts' a priori conceptualizations.

Ethogeny has a comparable vision and offers a comparable program. Social psychologists, if the Harré and Secord (1973) argument is accepted, must treat humans as agents acting according to rules, and the research aim becomes to uncover rules formulated in lay explanations of social behavior. Further, Harré (1977) criticizes traditional social psychology as a parametric science that assumes the properties of variables used to describe a system are not internally related. The ethogenic approach is said to be structural: Components of social psychological systems take on meaning only in relation to one another. Drawing on molecular genetics and structural linguistics as models, he suggests that social psychology treat social interaction as a social product and seek out the templates or cognitive representations of the structure (the internally related componential system) that led to the product. Obviously, there are essential similarities among those taking their methodological and research cues from ethogeny, ethnomethodologists, sociolinguists, and microsociologists (a la Goffman) who adopt a dramaturgical perspective.

2. The Discovery of Commonalities

Social psychologists of differing disciplinary background have always been aware that they have overlapping (certainly not identical) sets of interests; relatively new is the sense that with respect to some interests there are questions and a frame of reference in responding to these that have considerable commonality. The commonalities linking ethogeny and ethnomethodology, already noted, or between ethogeny and the dramaturgical perspective, or between ethogeny and any framework that is in the symbolic interactionist tradition, are cases in point. However, the discovery of commonality has occurred where it has long been resisted—in mainstream portions of the two social psychologies. While other illustrations exist (for example, in work on equity and justice, or on exchange processes, or on the social psychology of self), it is the commonalities between attribution theory and symbolic interactionism that will be pursued here. The claim, it should be noted, is of commonalities and not identity; there are important differences between these frameworks (Stryker & Gottlieb, 1981), some of which are relevant to section IV of this paper.

While a cognitive emphasis has always marked psychological social psychology (Hilgard, 1980), cognitive processes have assumed an almost defining centrality in comparatively recent years. The prime emphases in recent and current work derive from Lewin (1935) and Heider (1944; 1946; 1958). The former's influence is more general, reflecting the field theoretic doctrine that forces underlying human action are wholly contemporary and wholly subjective, in the sense of being in the actor's life space, field of consciousness, or mind, and reflecting as well the treatment of cognitions as motivational. Heider's influence is more specific, as in the earlier flow of cognitive consistency and the more recent flow of attribution research.

Only a brief statement of attribution theory is necessary to ground subsequent comparisons with symbolic interactionism. The theory develops from Heider's concern with phenomena having meaning and phenomenological reality for actors: actions like "trying" or "wanting," ideas like "can." Heider focuses on perceptions in interpersonal relations, in which a perceiver perceives another perceiver, arguing that a perceiver's expectations, attributions, and actions are in part consequences of the fact that others with whom he or she interacts are also perceivers.

Attributions involve assigning qualities to the environment, including others and self. Persons make attributions to order and stabilize what otherwise would be an intolerably confused psychological environment. They develop and use their own naive psychologies to give meaning, coherence, and continuity to others' actions and ultimately to their own. Attribution theory is a theory of these naive psychologies seeking to describe and explain how people order their cognitions to give meaning to their worlds.

The fundamental commonality of attribution theory and symbolic interactionism is in their underlying phenomenological perspective, in particular their insistence on comprehending the subjective experience of the persons they study and the necessity of incorporating this comprehension in explanations of human behavior. Both argue that social conduct can be understood only through examining actors' perceptions of their physical and social environments. Heider's (1958) arguments parallel those of Mead (1934), from whom symbolic interactionism draws much of its inspiration. Paralleling Thomas' (1937) assertion that "if men define situations as real, they are real in their consequences" is Heider's (1958, p. 5) assertion, that "If a person believes that the lines of his palm foretell his future, this belief must be taken into account in explaining certain of his expectations and actions."

Mead's social psychology developed in reaction to Watson's behaviorism. Less explicitly, Heider's psychology of interpersonal relations developed in reaction to another behaviorism: Skinner's. Mead is part of a long philosophical tradition, conveniently marked as beginning with the Scottish Moral Philosophers (Hume, Smith, Ferguson) and developing through pragmatism, that gave mind and minded activities central place. Heider's links to Gestalt psychology and to Lewin locate him in a phenomenological tradition also giving priority to mind in explaining human behavior.

There are commonalities in attribution theory and symbolic interactionism other than their respective bases in phenomenological perspectives and their consequent emphasis on the subjective in human behavior. Both, albeit each within limits (Stryker & Gottlieb, 1981), adopt a view of the human as rational problem-solver whose cognitive activity follows logical and explicable norms. While some attribution theorists challenge Kelley's (1973) characterization of humans as analysts of variance, they (e.g., Fischoff, 1976) do not challenge the basic image of the human as intuitive scientist. A comparable idea is strongly embedded in the pragmatic tradition on which symbolic interactionists draw. Mead's social psychology focuses on activity in which blocked impulse requires reflection to set up hypotheses to guide action; characteristic human behavior is modelled on the research procedures of science (Stryker, 1956).

The two frameworks converge in their emphases on everyday life and everyday experience as both what they seek to explain and the source of the concepts required for explanations. These emphases are straightforward consequences of phenomenological orientations rationalizing interest in the subjective worlds of persons studied. For the attribution theorist, explanations of cognitive processes must correspond to the psychology of the "naive" actor, and that psychology is formed in real life experience. For the symbolic interactionist, explanations of human behavior are necessarily in terms of meanings entering persons' experience, and meanings emerge from everyday interaction with others.

Thus, attribution theory and symbolic interactionism hold in common that the subjective aspect of experience must be examined because it is persons' inferences and the subjective meanings they assign to things that organize their behavior. This assumption is the basic premise of symbolic interactionism; it is entailed in virtually all theoretical statements of attribution theory (Heider, 1958; Kelly, 1967; Jones & Davis, 1965). The two are thoroughly functionalist: attributions, and meanings, occur in the interest of prediction and control of behavior.

This observation leads to the last and most complex commonality of the two frames: their "meanings" of "meaning." What do persons infer, analyze and interpret as they live their everyday lives? Both frames assume that people engage in cognitive-symbolic processes to simplify and make manageable the worlds in which they live. Those worlds are too complex to be conceived and perceived in detail; they must be ordered to permit coherent responses. Cognitive-symbolic processes impose limited principles that organize things and occurrences in relatively simple, concise, and parsimonious form. Attribution theory has traditionally focused on a single principle—attribution of cause—while symbolic interactionism, viewing symbols (the meanings attached to things) as emergent from interaction, permits relations among objects in a virtual infinity of forms. More recently, their commonality is emphasized as attribution theory expands its search for relevant cognitive activities by introducing conceptions reminiscent of early symbolic interactionist thinking about the grammar (Burke, 1945) and vocabularies (Mills, 1940) of motives and of later thinking about accounts (Scott & Lyman, 1968) and disclaimers (Hewitt & Stokes, 1975) as interpersonal tactics.

The commonalities reviewed reflect similar assumptions, sometimes only implicit, about the nature of the human actor and of social interaction that lead to a domain of common theoretical interest. Discovering those commonalities, then, gives psychological social psychologists and sociological social psychologists hard-to-deny reasons for paying greater attention to one another than they otherwise might.

B.   DEVELOPMENTS IN PSYCHOLOGICAL SOCIAL
     PSYCHOLOGY

The discussion now turns to theoretically relevant developments that are relatively particular to each of the two social psychologies, first within the domain of psychological social psychology. Most of the developments have to do with the so-called crisis in social psychology. One represents a continuation of the preceding discussion; I will begin with it.

1.   The Respectability of the Subjective

As noted, psychological social psychology since its inception has had some cognitive focus. To an important degree, however, that focus was grudging, symptomatically cast in as behavioristic a form and language as possible. Thus, the subjectivistic implications of a focus on cognition tended to be hidden, and explicit recognition, acceptance, and exploitation of a phenomenological perspective implied by such a focus became muted. The major, and in many ways revolutionary, change in the content of psychological social psychology over the past few decades is that subjective experience has become respectable. It has become respectable both as object of explanation (as in attribution theory in most of its manifestations) and as it enters explanatory theories (Zajonc, 1968).

This new respectability of the subjective, its legitimacy particularly as it enters explanations of human behavior, is variously evidenced. There is the "back-door" respectability implied by the introduction of cognitive conceptualizations into behavioristically motivated theories (Berger & Lambert, 1968) in the attempt to give them more explanatory power. There is the fact that part of the underlying malaise termed "the crisis of social psychology" (discussed later) is a function of pursuing implications, real or only apparent, of introducing phenomenological elements into social psychological frameworks and theories. Further, there is the fact that suggestions offered in resolution of the crisis are premised on the importance of subjective experience in human behavior. There is, of course, the literal preeminence of attribution theory and research in recent years, and of cognitive consistency or balance theories and research in the decade before that. Finally, there is the rather remarkable surge of interest within psychological social psychology in that most subjectivistic and phenomenological of social psychological concepts, the self.

The concept of self is a keystone of the sociological social psychology inspired by Mead and Cooley. In psychology, the concept has a checkered history. The older behaviorism exorcized it. For a social psychology bent on scientific respectability, the self smacked too much of a deus ex machina, or the clinical claim of the uniqueness of the individual and the impossibility of valid generalization about human behavior, or the mysteries of the Freudian ego. Where interest in the self existed, that interest tended to be limited to self-esteem. Yet, periodically, a richer concept of self surfaced (Allport, 1954; Lecky, 1945), comparatively recently coincident with the appearance of cognitive consistency and attribution theories and in part motivated by theoretical problems in these theories. As Hilgard (1980) notes, recent work in various fields of psychology seems to imply executive control functions of the sort to which the concept of self has referred; as he suggests, contemporary psychology must learn to deal adequately with the concept. If the concept of self is not the linchpin of current psychological social psychology, it has a central role in the development of theory.

By whatever conceptualization or definition, the reality of the self is phenomenological. The constitution of self has long puzzled humanistically oriented philosophers, and concern with self is in part a product of the times in which social forces have raised uniquely defined individuality to a moral imperative (Turner, 1976). The phenomenal self constitutes one theoretical problem for social psychology; that is, such a concept raises the question of how we come to view ourselves in particular ways. Bem (1972) offers a self-perception theory in which actors are presumed to monitor their own behaviors to learn what kinds of persons they are. Kelly's attribution theory contains a theory of self-development, albeit residual and fragmentary, in the assertion that certain conditions lead people to make attributions to the external environment, and failure to meet those conditions results in internal attributions.

The self, however, is of theoretical interest in other ways than as something to be explained; if this were not true, the self could be taken as epiphenomenal and of no essential interest to social psychology. In relation to cognitive dissonance theory, the concept has been used to try to tie up a variety of theoretical loose ends. Thus Bem, accepting the counter-intuitive findings of dissonance theory, uses the concept to argue that persons observe their behavior to infer the kinds of persons they are and then use their inferences to produce responses to dissonant experimental conditions. Aronson (1969) argues that it makes sense of sometimes contradictory research findings to presume that dissonance and consonance are consequences of persons relating their opinions, attitudes, and behaviors to their underlying concepts of self. Schlenker (1975) offers a self-directed impression-management theory of dissonance research findings as an alternative to Festinger's intrapsychic theory. More generally, Hilgard (1980) argues that a concept of self is implied in an image of man as a hierarchical control system complete with feedback loops, a metaphor that relates work on the reflexive human organism and on complex machines.

More recently, the concept of self enters social psychological theorizing in a wide variety of ways: in terms of the processes by which one reflexively pays attention to oneself (Snyder, 1979); in terms of the sources and consequences of becoming self-aware (Duval & Wicklund, 1972; Hull & Levy, 1979) or self-conscious (Buss, 1980); in terms of the dynamics and impacts of self-presentations and impression management (Tetlock, 1980; Tedeschi & Reiss, 1980; Schlenker, 1980); in terms of the biases of self-attributions (Weary, 1978; Greenwald, 1980). But perhaps of most general theoretical importance is the work on self schema (Marcus, 1977; Rogers, Kuiper, & Kirker, 1977) offered as a concept that explains when and why persons' behavior across social situations is consistent and when and why it is inconsistent, or that organizes other responses of persons.

2. The Crisis in Social Psychology

Less is heard about a crisis in social psychology today than a few years ago, perhaps because the practicalities of academic existence require continuous research production. Based on a variety of indications, I judge that while overt talk about the crisis has subsided, the sense of crisis nevertheless remains. There is reason to doubt whether the concerns underlying the earlier, more overt expression of crisis have truly abated.

Insofar as there is a crisis, it is partly the result of methodological doubts traceable to the discovery of experimenter demand (Orne, 1962). "Everybody" knew, long before the 1960s, that interviewers in sample surveys tended to produce results consistent with their biases on value-relevant issues. The culture of at least some social psychologists (it may be that these persons were largely sociologists; I do not know) contained the notion of a role of "experimental subjects," whose operative expectation was to give experimenters what they appeared to want. Thus the idea that a researcher and experimental subjects are in a social relationship governed by norms, that various actions or verbalizations of the experimenter may convey expectations with respect to subject performances that demand (at least in degree) compliance, and that such demand exists as an explanation for hypothesized results alternative to an experimenter's theory, has considerable precedent. The implications of this idea, however, did not take hold in experimental social psychology until the mid-1960s. Then it became a challenge to the validity of the entire experimental social psychology enterprise, all the more serious given the almost total dependency of psychological social psychology on experimentation as a research method. At an extreme, the demand possibility in most social psychological research can be taken as warrant for dismissing the findings of all such research, and an edifice of apparently secure research findings and theory accounting for those findings evaporates.

Something of a counterrevolution with respect to experimenter demand has gotten underway. That is, doubts are being cast on the doubters by attacking the validity of the research purportedly demonstrating experimenter demand (Kruglanski, 1976). In my view, there is good reason to believe that experimenter demand does occur; there is also good reason to believe that experimenter demand cannot account for all experimental research findings. Neither complacency with respect to the issue nor the pessimism that results in challenging the validity of the entire experimental social psychology enterprise is warranted.

From a relatively narrow methodological point of view, the experimenter demand issue is not necessarily devastating in its implications, provided one recognizes where the problem lies. The issue is essentially one of the importance of subjective experience in accounting for behavior, in particular the definitions of the situation research subjects develop as they seek to make sense of or give meaning to their experience in experiments. When experiments are viewed, as they should be, as social situations having a social psychology, they cannot be treated as neutral conduits for experimental manipulations. The implication is not that valid experimentation is impossible, it is that a more subtle view of experimentation must condition experimental procedures. Experimenter demand will not always exist as a strong competing hypothesis relative to an experimenter's theory. Where it is, double-blind procedures can sometimes be used. More to the point, however, is that an experiment can be analyzed in terms of the social positions occupied by experimenter and subjects and the roles available in the experimental situation, and this analysis can be used to structure explicit positions and roles, cross them with other experimental variables, and control their effects. There are, then, at least some procedural means available to deal with experimenter demand and reduce its negative implications for knowledge gleaned through experimentation.

There are also theoretical means. The implications of viewing experiments as social situations can be put to theoretical use, as Alexander (e.g., Alexander & Knight, 1971; Alexander & Wiley, 1981) has done from a situated identity perspective which seeks to manipulate and to measure subject identities in various prototypical experimental designs, as Schlenker (1975) does in his impression management work, or as Rosenthal and Jacobsen (1968) do in the Pygmalion studies that manipulate teacher expectations and trace the effect of these manipulated expectations on pupil performance. The general implications of adopting this strategy will be noted in section IV of this chapter.

The crisis in social psychology relates not only to the relatively narrow experimenter demand issue, but to broad methodological arguments deriving from radical phenomenology and ordinary-language philosophy which, if accepted, have a devastating impact on the possibility of a generalizing science of social psychology. We return here to ethnomethodology and ethogeny, and to arguments offered by Cicourel and by Harré (although not in this precise form): (1) Categories developed in subjective experience guide behavior, and thus, an investigator must discover subject's cognitive categories in the context of an investigation itself; (2) Social life is constructed in the process of interaction, so that no social situation has fixed properties and dimensions; (3) Since an experiment is a social situation, investigators' a priori concepts and theory have no privileged status vis-à-vis those of their subjects; (4) Either investigators' categories are imposed on research results, making findings artifacts of their a prioris, or they are modified (reconstructed) in the research encounter and so are different in situ than they were prior to the encounter; and (5) In either event, causal interpretations of experimental results in the usual terms of independent and dependent variables are nonsense. No argument could undercut experimental social psychology more.

The most articulate statement of a profound disillusionment with mainstream social psychology is still that of Gergen (1973), in part premised on acceptance of the thrust of the argument just reviewed. Gergen despairs of social psychology as a generalizing science and rejects methods (e.g., experimental) whose goal is generalized knowledge that transcends particular historical moments. He assumes that the aim of a generalizing social psychology is the discovery of laws, and that laws can be discovered only if there are stable relationships among persons or among social psychologically relevant categories of events; but he denies such stability exists. Human interaction is unstable because it is essentially indeterminate. It is indeterminate because there is a feedback loop joining science and society. People see evaluational biases built into social psychological concepts (e.g., the authoritarian personality) and act to deny the bias, thus invalidating the concepts. Further, knowing social psychological principles, actors are liberated from the behavioral implications of those principles; their cognitions can serve to reorganize their behavior in ways contrary to the principles. Western values of autonomy and individuality lead persons to escape to freedom, i.e., to act in ways contradicting social psychological findings and theory. Gergen's conclusion: social psychology can be only an historical discipline providing a systematic account of contemporary affairs; it is not and cannot be a discipline providing general scientific principles. Whether Gergen's dirge is necessary, or even reasonable, is a question to which I will return. Clearly, however, it expresses in extremis the sense of crisis in social psychology.

Gergen denies the possibility of social psychology as science on "practical" grounds: its scientific aims cannot be accomplished. The sense of crisis in social psychology has also been fed by another, typically less complete, denial of science, based on humanistic values. Involved (see, e.g., Smith, 1974) is a deep concern with the ethics of experimentation, involving as it does the manipulation of human beings and (frequently) deceiving them. Involved as well is a critique of the achievement of methodological rigor at the expense of saying anything useful about the human condition, or about important conditions in the lives of human beings. And involved, even further, is the fundamental feeling that science poses more of a threat to human values than it offers by way of helping in the achievement of those values.

C.   DEVELOPMENTS IN SOCIOLOGICAL SOCIAL PSYCHOLOGY

In my judgment, the most significant current development in sociological social psychology is the attempt to meld elements of role theory into symbolic interactionism in order to develop a viable general theory that is sensitive to the variably constraining impact on human social behavior of an organized social structure as well as to the creative possibilities in that behavior (Turner, 1978; Stryker, 1980; Stryker & Statham, forthcoming). There are, however, other noteworthy developments, both outside and within a symbolic interactionist frame relevant to the purposes of this paper; these will be addressed first.

1.   Exchange Theory

Exchange theory in sociology (Emerson, 1981; Blau, 1964) is closely linked to, and one form it takes is derived from, a sociological behaviorism whose early inspiration is Homans (1961). That behaviorism reinterprets sociology in terms of principles of operant psychology, and seeks to extend those principles through a program of experimentation (Burgess & Bushell, 1969), thus rejecting Homan's contention that sociology can only apply known principles of behavioral psychology. Early versions of exchange theory closely followed the operant model; not surprisingly, these were heavily criticized for depending on individualistic hedonism, for being a psychological reductionism that denied the reality of society as a structure of norms, for being tautological in their explanations, for arguing more calculative rationality than exists in social behavior, and for failing to move beyond dyadic relationships.

Accepting these criticisms, Emerson (1981) charts changes in the theory, in particular two related developments: an increased awareness of the differences between economic and social exchanges, and between the theories needed to account for these; and theoretical expansions beyond the dyad to N-person corporate groups and network structures. The basic unit of economic theory, he notes, is the transaction; transactions are assumed to be independent events and are aggregated into markets, a concept giving economic theory its analytic power.

The basic unit of exchange theory is the exchange relation between specific partners; exchanges between partners are assumed to be related events occurring over time; these exchange relations are aggregated into exchange networks, a concept Emerson contends has analytic power comparable to that of the market. Developing these assertions, Emerson argues that exchange theory has a distinctively social, nonindividualistic character, is applicable to collectivities and networks larger than 2-person units, and is a special theory whose focus on the flow of benefits through interaction is complementary to symbolic interactionism's focus on the flow of information.

2. Social Structure and Personality

While social structure-person relations define sociological social psychology, most practitioners have limited their attention to microstructures: friendship pairs; small (dyadic, triadic) networks; families; work groups; etc. Yet there is a long-standing interest in the field in the relation of macrostructures (societies, classes, ethnic groups, etc.) and macroprocesses (industrialization, mobility, etc.) to personality. Traditionally, the bulk of work pursuing this interest has linked global characteristics of total societies to holistically conceived personalities of societal members.

A newer, revitalized version of this interest seeks to specify the impact of particular aspects of social structure on particular aspects of personality (House, 1981). The emergent theory strongly argues that the relationship between macrostructure and personality is mediated through the concrete interactional experience of persons giving meaning to the macrostructure, a theoretical claim that parallels developments in symbolic interactionism.

Illustrative of this newer genre of social structure-personality theorizing and research is that of Kohn (1977) and Kohn & Schooler (1978), which relates the structural condition of substantive complexity of work to the personality characteristic of intellectual flexibility, specifying earlier claims of the relation of social class and conformity. Also illustrative is work by Rosenberg (1979) specifying the relationship between large-scale structural variables, especially social class and ethnicity, and self-esteem by introducing interaction contexts such as the degree of class or racial homogeneity in classrooms to account for variation in effects of class or ethnicity on esteem. Rosenberg, incidentally, draws on an eclectic theory made up of elements from symbolic interactionism, attribution theory, self-perception theory, and social comparison theory to undergird his research.

3. Developments in Symbolic Interactionism

Two kinds of developments within symbolic interactionism merit discussion. The first involves specific theories, rooted in a symbolic interactionist framework, designed to deal with specific empirical issues. The second is much more general, and is in part intended to respond to criticism of the framework that it has been insensitive to the facts and import of social structure.

   a. Specific Theories. It has sometimes been said that symbolic interactionism is a framework without theories, that it provides no systematic propositions derived from a set of assumptions and concepts intended to explain some empirically observed phenomena. Whatever its validity historically, the remark is clearly less true now than it may have been. The development of three theories serves to illustrate the point. These theories are quite different in style and tone; their differences, however, should not mask their common symbolic interactionist premises.

   Symbolic interactionism has been criticized for ignoring affect in social interaction. This criticism is not precisely true, since persons working with the framework have dealt with the social construction in interaction of emotional responses. The charge derives from symbolic interactionism's traditional emphasis on cognition and reason at the expense of emotion as a determinant of other behaviors. Heise (1979), explicitly presenting affect control theory as a version of symbolic interactionism, argues that all common social actions have an underlying basis in the psychology of affect. Distinguishing between established feelings, or fundamentals, and more situationally induced feelings, or transients, he theorizes that persons act to maintain the former when events strain these feelings by creating transients which depart to some extent from them: persons construct new events that return transient feelings to the level of fundamentals. This dynamic is assumed to be subordinate to definitions of the situation. The latter provide a restricted set of cognitive elements used in recognizing and constructing events; they also specify what cognitive categories are salient in the situation and therefore what fundamentals are retrieved and compared with the transients particular to the situation. Heise's research program includes building mathematical models of the affect control process and examining these models under experimental conditions.

   Not typically recognized as kin to symbolic interactionism, expectation states theory (Berger, Connor, & Fisek, 1974) nevertheless is so related in its emphasis on self-conceptions, definitions of the situation, interaction as the source of expectations, and status characteristics as socially constructed realities. This theory evolved through the attempt to explain the research finding that stable power and prestige orderings quickly take shape in problem-solving groups composed of (initial) status equals. It postulates that persons develop self-conceptions of their performance capabilities with respect to the group task, and that others develop performance conceptions for those persons out of their interaction. Thus, expectations for future performances arise and determine subsequent task-related interaction such that the interaction depending on the expectations serves to confirm and maintain them. When inequalities on status dimension relevant outside the problem-solving group characterizes group members, the theory asserts that the status dimension provides beliefs and expectations that almost instantaneously become the basis for power and prestige orderings. "External" status characteristics, in other words, are taken by participants in group problem-solving processes to be relevant to the task at hand, with the burden of proving otherwise falling on anyone who asserts the irrelevance of the external characteristic. This burden of proof principle is one specification of how definitions of the situations are constructed (others being the length of the inferential chain linking a status characteristic and the group task, and a sequencing principle asserting that definitions constructed in pair interaction will continue to operate when one of the pair is replaced by another person). Expectations state theory has also been deliberately tied to mathematical models and experimental examination of these models.

Derivations of identity theory (Stryker, 1980) have been examined using structural equation models (Stryker & Serpe, 1981), but this theory has been more oriented to survey data than to that produced experimentally. This theory purports to deal with choices among behaviors expressive of more than one role (example: a man must choose between taking his child to the zoo and playing golf with friends on a weekend afternoon). Identity theory predicts such choices through specifying terms in symbolic interactionism's general explanatory formula: Self reflects society and self organizes behavior. It begins with a conception of the person as having a self comprised of multiple identities, internalized positional designations existing insofar as persons are placed by others as social objects, while appropriating for themselves the terms of such placement. Persons are assumed to have as many identities as structured sets of social relationships in which they are implicated. This conception of self follows from the premise that society shapes self and from the observation that contemporary society is a multifaceted mosaic of interrelated parts. The theory postulates that identities have varying probabilities of being invoked in given situations or across situations, and defines a salience hierarchy of identities in these terms. The theory further postulates that the location of an identity relative to others in that hierarchy is a consequence of commitment to roles; commitment is defined by the extensiveness and intensity of relationships to others premised on occupying a position and playing a role, and can presumably be measured by the costs of important relationships lost should one no longer occupy the position on which those relationships are based. Finally, the theory predicts that (other things—including structural determinants—being equal) behavioral choices will be a function of the location of identities in the salience hierarchy. Thus, the theory translates symbolic interactionism's general formula into "commitment affects identity salience, which in turn affects role performance."

These theories have in common not only their derivation from symbolic interactionist premises, but a methodological aspiration relatively novel in this tradition of social psychological work: they seek to build theories or models from which hypotheses can be derived and tested with a reasonable degree of precision and control. As this assertion suggests, symbolic interactionism historically tended to eschew formal theorizing and rigorous test in favor of developing conceptualizations from direct observations of ongoing interaction and using those conceptualizations to arrive at an understanding of why that interaction took the course it did. Such a symbolic interactionism is vigorously practiced today, frequently under the rubric of "the dramaturgical approach." Some taking this approach argue that "Dramaturgical theory . . . does not 'demonstrate truth' in some esoteric language whose validity can be judged by only a few experts, nor is it meant to make an empirical contribution to knowledge" (Scott, 1981). Less extremely, many taking this approach seem more concerned with cataloging possibilities in social interaction than in discovering regularities in behavior, explaining those regularities through constructing abstract theory, and testing inferences drawn from such theory. Work by Hewitt and Stokes (1975) on disclaimers, and Scott and Lyman (1968) on accounts, both concerning sociolinguistic devices sustaining organized social interaction, illustrates this genre of symbolic interactionism.

The orientation of these theories deriving from symbolic interactionism to more formal theorizing and rigorous test, so different from the orientation identified with "traditional" symbolic interactionism, may help account for the increased likelihood of the framework's being attended to by psychologists. It is only being partially facetious to suggest that the use of (for example) structural equation models, as yet more familiar to sociologists than psychologists, in examining these theories lends them authority they would not otherwise have.

b. General Developments. A major theme in critical appraisals of symbolic interactionists' work through the years in an allegation of indifference to social structure, especially structures of class and of power, which constitutes both a theoretical deficiency of considerable moment and an ideological bias (Huber, 1973; Meltzer, Petras & Reynolds, 1975; Gouldner, 1970). While the allegation of indifference to social structure has been denied (Maines, 1977), the genre of symbolic interactionism heavily influenced by Blumer (1969) had no principled theoretical way to accommodate aspects of social structure beyond those emergent from the immediate situation of interaction or beyond persons' perceptions of structure. The idea of a complexly organized society with structures of social class or power (or structures based on age or sex distinctions, etc.), existing prior to interactions and affecting the probabilities of certain interactions occurring as well as the probabilities of various interactional out-comes, is in fact severely attenuated in this version of the symbolic interactionist framework.

Two quite different responses to the alleged indifference to social structure have developed: One may be termed a processual and the other a social structural symbolic interactionism. The former is illustrated by the negotiated-order frame-work (Strauss, 1978), which assumes that all social structures continuously break down and are constructed as social orders via negotiation. The framework focuses attention on ongoing interaction, the actors involved, tactics and strat-egies of interaction, negotiation subprocesses (e.g., "trading off"), and conse-quences in the form of new or reconstituted orders that are the context for further negotiations. Contexts, linking interaction to social structure, are of two kinds: structural and negotiation. The former defines the parameters within which nego-tiations occur (e.g., a hospital setting with its division of labor); the latter defines the properties of immediate situations that bear on negotiations (e.g., nego-tiators' skills, whether issues are simple or complex, etc.). Anchored in a grounded-theory methodology (Glaser & Strauss, 1967) that emphasizes direct observation of interaction, the framework's major focus is on negotiation con-texts and it (as yet) leaves structural contexts relatively undeveloped. Perhaps for this reason, it seems more oriented toward understanding particular negotiations than developing general theoretical explanations.

The second response weds elements of role theory to emphases on self, the interaction process, and the creative potential in human behavior, in order to provide a structural symbolic interactionist framework that is sensitive to the constraining impact of social organization on self, interaction, and "construc-tion" behavior, as well as to the fluidity of social organization as a consequence of self and the constructed character of (much) social interaction (Stryker, 1980). The wedding of role theory and symbolic interactionism is facilitated by their fundamental compatibility—their common emphases on the meaning dimension of human experience, the importance of bringing into explanations the perspec-tives of those whose behavior is being studied, and their common reliance on the bridging concept of role.

Building a framework that combines role theoretic and symbolic interac-tionist emphases is the objective of current work by a number of sociological social psychologists (Stryker, 1980; Stryker & Statham, forthcoming; McCall & Simmons, 1978; Turner, 1978; Burke, 1980; Weinstein & Tanur, 1976) who differ in the degree to which they see normatively defined role expectations as constraining social behavior. They also vary on the explicitness with which they visualize how large-scale structural variations shape interaction by affecting what persons are brought together with what systems of meanings and what interac-tional resources in what settings with what possibilities for attaching meanings to self, other persons and nonhuman objects. My own terse statement (Stryker, 1968; 1977; 1981) of this emergent structural symbolic interactionist framework asserts that:

1. Behavior is dependent on a named world. Names or class terms attached to environmental features have meaning in the form of shared behavioral

expectations emerging from social interaction in which one learns how to classify objects in the environment and how one is expected to behave with reference to those objects.

2. Learned in interaction are symbols used to designate positions, relatively stable components of organized social structures, which carry shared behavioral expectations conventionally termed roles.

3. Persons acting in the context of social structure recognize one another as occupants of positions, name one another, and so invoke expectations for one another's behavior.

4. Such persons name themselves as well; their reflexively applied positional terms become part of the self, creating internalized expectations with regard to their own behavior.

5. Entering an interactive situation, persons apply names to it, to themselves and others in it, and particulars of it, and they use the resulting definitions of the situation to organize their behavior.

6. Early definitions constrain but do not determine the behavior that will occur. Behavior is the product of a role-making process initiated by early definitions and developing in a sometimes subtle, probing interchange among actors that can reshape the form and content of their interaction.

7. The degree to which roles are made and the elements entering their construction will depend on the larger social structures in which interactive situations are embedded. Some structures are open, some closed, with respect to altering behavioral expectations and novelty in role performances. All social structures impose some limits on the definitions called into play and on the possibilities for interaction as well, by bringing only certain people together in certain places at certain times under certain conditions.

8. To the degree that roles are made, changes in the character of definitions, the names used in those definitions, and in the possibilities for interaction can occur. Such changes can lead to changes in the larger social structures within which interactions take place.

This version of symbolic interactionism obviously gives considerable weight to social structures, including (potentially) those of class and power as they may operate in society, in a way that permits taking into account the complexities of the organized social worlds in which humans exist. It opens the way for serious theorizing about the reciprocity of self and social structure, of person and society. It requires that social behavior be seen in part as a consequence of where persons are located in the larger social structures that make up society.

It is the idea that persons must be located in role relationships embedded in a larger structure, as well as the more traditional symbolic interactionist idea that persons' behaviors are mediated by self and other meanings derived from social location and interaction, that contains theoretical lessons important to social psychology. This observation introduces the next section of this chapter.

IV. Structural Symbolic Interactionism and Psychological Social Psychology

Earlier discussion has noted the current flow of influence from sociological to psychological social psychology, that this directional flow derives from the crisis of confidence in the latter, the sources of that crisis, and how a more sociologically-oriented social psychology might relate to resolving that crisis. That discussion can now become more specific by suggesting that it is structural symbolic interactionism that contains the pertinent emphases and concepts; involved is the theoretical and methodological potential of the ideas of social structure and of self. While the crisis theme is a convenient vehicle for what is to be said, its reality is not necessary to the essential message.

The crisis in social psychology, particularly as articulated by Gergen (1973), has a number of sources. In part, it arises out of disappointment with a philosophy of science that calls for the discovery of laws governing human social behavior as the objective of the social psychological enterprise, the presumption that invariable regularities are the hallmark of such laws, and the assumption that only a completely deterministic universe can produce such regularities. That human experience is historical and the meanings that constitute symbolic environment are historically conditioned is virtually certain to produce disillusionment when accomplishments are measured against the aspirations implied by this philosophy. An available alternative view of the social psychological enterprise begins with the common sense observations that human behavior is not random, that humans must, can, and do continuously predict one another's behavior in order to live their lives. There is at least some order and regularity in human behavior; the task of social psychology is to discover such regularity as exists in behaviors to which its frameworks direct it, to invent theories parsimoniously explaining those regularities (rather than to discover laws), and to test those theories as best it can to sort out better and worse theories from the point of view of the range of behaviors they explain and how completely they explain them. To engage in this enterprise, it is unnecessary to argue a strict determinism in human life, only that particular circumstances affect the probabilities of certain behaviors' occurring. While the aspiration implied by this reformulation may be less grand than that implied by the philosophy of science that Gergen presumes underlies the practice of experimental social psychology, it has the virtue of being attainable.

To those nurtured on the work of Mead (1934), the idea that human behavior is only partially determinate is familiar and not upsetting. Gergen's disillusionment, however, it also premised on the inference that the failure of experimental social psychology to produce stable findings reflects a general indeterminacy of human behavior. He is sorely troubled by the "fact" of ephemeral or nonreplicable findings, either in the sense that the same experimental conditions have a low probability of producing replicated findings over time and over place, or in the sense that minor variations in experimental procedures produce wide and erratic swings in behavioral outcomes. The disillusionment is made still more profound by believing that "truths" thought to be the product of tracing behavioral consequences of theoretically informed variables that are manipulated by an experimenter turn out instead to be the produce of demand characteristics of experiments.

Before proceeding, it may be wise as well as useful to offer a caveat. The argument being developed is not premised on nor does it require the rejection of experimental social psychology, or a belief that findings of experimental laboratory research that fail to incorporate its message can have no external validity, or a denial of the possibility of replicable findings generalizable across time and space. Not only the possibility but the fact of external validity and generalizability of some research findings (Berkowitz & Donnerstein, 1982) are granted. The argument is premised, however, on the belief that social psychology requires a more general frame that can accomodate, under specifiable conditions, such "successes," and, at the same time, can provide reasonable correctives for equally apparent "failures."

If we consider the prototypic social psychological experiment, we can perhaps better glean the meaning of failures to replicate, or inexplicable wide variation in behavior under minor variations in experimental conditions. The goal of experimental design is, of course, to permit observations under controlled conditions. Thus, the ideal experiment is one that successfully purifies the experimental situation of "extraneous" factors, either by random assignment of subjects to conditions or by contriving an experimental situation to remove them. Only if random assignment is difficult or impossible to accomplish, or cannot be trusted to control some undesirable variation, and only if extraneous variation cannot be controlled by exclusion, are we likely to introduce some potentially contaminating factor as a covariate, and then our objective is to get rid of it statistically.

When we now add that conventional social psychological experimentation regards social structural variables as extraneous, we have a basis for estimating the consequences of these procedures. Experiments are run with same sex subjects and experimenters in order to avoid the contamination that cross sex experimenter-subject relationships would introduce. Experimenter-assistants are instructed to dress neatly and similarly in order to eliminate that potential disturbing source of variation in subject behavior. Strangers are brought together when research demands interacting subjects so that past history of relationships will not distort subject interaction and the consequences thereof. Subjects are drawn only from student populations to eliminate as much social class variation as possible. And so on.

It is not unreasonable to assert, as summary, that the prototypic social psychological experiment, in the sensible aspiration to observe under closely controlled conditions, removes subjects from the structured social relationships and their associated meanings that anchor persons in a social context and are an essential basis for stability in much of their behavior. We then wonder that their behavior can be erratic.

The moral to be drawn from the failures of experimental social psychology is not that persons' behaviors are unstable, however; it is that behavior of persons removed from 'social structure may well be unstable. A structural symbolic interactionism suggests why, through its insistence that society and person are defined only in relation to one another.

Embeddedness in a system of role relationships anchors human behavior and systems of role relationships are in turn embedded in larger social structures. If this is true of human social behavior, in general, it must be true of experiments; an important lesson we must learn from ethogeny and ethnomethodology is that experiments are not exceptions to this general rule. The implied lesson, however, is not to abandon the experiment. It is, rather, to build role and social structural variation into experiments insofar as it is feasible to do so; and it is to investigate, in the context of experiments themselves, the operative role expectations and their conditioning social structures.

To accomplish this, however, requires sensitivity to the relevance of role variables and social structure; a structural symbolic interactionism provides that sensitivity in a manner in fundamental compatibility with the current emphasis on cognition. The care psychologists often take in designing experiments—in building cover stories, in minutely controlling assistants' behavior, in introducing confederates to play necessary other parts in experimental scenarios, as well as in matching sex of experimenter and subject—suggests awareness of structural considerations. But that awareness is, in general, limited to methodological implications related to issues of control. It does not translate into an interpretive frame forcing the recognition that, for example, telling a female subject she will be judged by a male confederate can invoke sex role-related expectations, that the student role may generate an identity demanding subversion of the proceedings, or that experimenter dress carries social class meanings, and insisting that we cannot treat these simply as bothersome details necessary to control but as essential to understanding data produced in an experiment. It does not give such matters general meaning or suggest a strategy for dealing effectively with them.

A structural symbolic interactionism accords theoretical and not simply methodological status to such matters. Aware of that framework, one is more likely to think of building role relationships and social structural variables into designs and to think of how to do so; and one is more likely to locate individual cognitive processes (or choice behavior, or whatever) in contexts that give them reasonable stability and that open up ways to understand them.

Building role relationships and social structure into experiments, however, may not be possible for reasons that go beyond incomplete awareness or inability to design creatively experiments incorporating them. Herein lies the virtues of moving outside the laboratory, at least sometimes, and examining social behavior in its "natural" setting (whether one continues to use experimental designs in natural settings is incidental to the point being made). Work done outside the laboratory must increase one's sensitivity to facts of social structure, and is likely to reinforce the use of an interpretative frame that emphasizes role and social structure even when these are not or cannot be explicitly built into experiments.

The utility of such an interpretive frame is considerable. Gergen is disturbed by the nonreplicability of experimental research across time and space. The failure of work done in Spain to replicate work done in the United States, or the failure of work done in the United States in 1980 to replicate 1950 results, can be used to bemoan the instability of human behavior and to underwrite a judgment of the impossibility of a science of social psychology; it need not do so. Such "failures" may indicate only the poverty of frameworks that do not recognize the changed system of meanings attached to changed structural circumstances in the two time periods, or the different systems of meanings attached to different structural circumstances in various countries. A structural symbolic interactionism can protect against an inappropriate cynicism.

It is, I think, important to recognize that more is involved than sensitivity to social context; it is a matter of having a principled theoretical way to interpret contextual effects and to link contextual variation to wider systems of social organization: Social class affects interaction or even individual behavior and cognitions through the boundaries it erects to the interaction of particular kinds of people; or the limitations it imposes on the kinds of interaction persons can engage in; or the set of self, other and environmental meanings brought into interaction. In these ways, social class also makes a difference with respect to the kinds of social constructions likely to occur in and through interactions. Without a framework that permits—that requires—a structural concept such as class and a sense of how social class enters interaction, theoretical understandings must be impoverished.

More generally stated, the meanings persons attach to objects in their worlds, including themselves, are for the most part learned in interaction with others. Class, age, sex or other social structures affect group formation and maintenance, and consequent interactions, and in this way enter the systems of meanings actors use to organize their behaviors. Recognizing this opens the way for theoretical understanding of the social contexts of meanings and their impact.

It is also a matter of having a principled way of incorporating into our theories the essential interdependency of person and others, of "individual" and "society." If the person is even in part constituted by the responses of others, there clearly can be little social psychological justification for treating persons in isolation from others or for regarding mere co-presence as sufficient to define the social. This implies, for example, that perceptual and cognitive processes are not "private," but are to be examined as they are shaped in interaction with others. It implies that cognition of a person considered in isolation from others must differ from those cognitions considered in relation to others. Heider's social psychology would not only be enriched by recognizing that meanings persons attribute to their worlds are developed in and sustained by social interaction, and in turn sustain that interaction; it would also be enriched by more clearly envisioning attributional processes in their social contexts. Taking seriously the idea that meaning is a product of interaction might prevent social psychologists from sliding from an initial determination to study interaction and from initial theorizing about interaction to, first, focusing on perceptions of participants in interaction and then, ultimately, observing the perceptions of one party to an interaction, and using this last to characterize relationships—as, for example, in so much equity research.

Taking this idea seriously might also enlarge the pool of talent thinking about the problem of categorizing situational contexts that affect the production of meanings in ways going beyond the banality that situational variation occurs; we might even make significant inroads on this to date largely intransigent problem.

Finally, social structural symbolic interactionism offers, along with a more adequate sense of what the concept "social" requires of a social psychology, a rich conception of self, going far beyond the self-esteem (Rosenberg, 1979) to which most attention has been directed. Conceptually, it offers the self as reflexive activity and as the reflexive application of interactionally produced meanings. So doing, it offers a principled account of how the person is at once the product of his or her relationships with others and the creator of those relationships. It sees subjective experience as both created by and creating the external world. While it thus demands a departure from simple, unidirectional causal theories and their examination with methods assuming both simplicity and unidirectionality, it does not require that we accept an image of the human as free of external constraints in favor of one which pictures the human as the determinant product of external forces, or vice versa. It thus lends credibility to the humanistic idea of the person as something more than a quiescent product of conditioning processes, as an active participant in his or her own unfolding experiences, without dismissing those conditioning processes. Indeed, it demands that both images be brought into a single focus and it provides the theoretical means to make that possible.

V.   Coda

What has just been said has a ring of accomplishment to it. More realistically, it represents aspiration. There is considerable tension between the phenomenological perspective argued above and a desire to produce theoretical generalizations verified through empirical research. That tension suggests the terms of the key question or challenge facing the inter-discipline of social psychology. As stated elsewhere (Stryker, 1977), that challenge is to what degree will it prove possible to be true both to the demands imposed by taking the subjective seriously, and to the requirements imposed by science for replicable, generalizable results. In my judgment, we will come closer to meeting that challenge if the two social psychologies do in fact listen to and learn from one another.

REFERENCES

Alexander, C. N., Jr., & Knight, G. W. Situated identities and social psychological experimentation. *Sociometry*, 1971, **36**, 65–82.

Alexander, C. N., Jr., & Wiley, M. G. Situated identity theory. In M. Rosenberg & R. H. Turner (Eds.), *Social psychology: Sociological perspectives*. New York: Basic Books, 1981.

Allport, F. H. *Social psychology*. Boston, Massachusetts: Houghton Mifflin, 1924.

Allport, G. W. *Pattern and growth in personality*. New York: Holt, 1954.

Archibald, W. P. *Social psychology as political economy*. Toronto, Ontario: McGraw-Hill Ryerson, 1978.

Aronson, E. The theory of cognitive dissonance: a current perspective. In L. Berkowitz (Ed.), *Advances in experimental social psychology* (Vol. 4). New York: Academic Press, 1969.

Bem, D. J. Self-perception theory. In L. Berkowitz (Ed.), *Advances in experimental social psychology* (Vol. 6). New York: Academic Press, 1972.

Berger, J., Conner, T. L., & Fisek, M. H. *Expectation states theory*. Cambridge, Massachusetts: Winthrop, 1974.

Berger, S. M., & Lambert, W. W. Stimulus-response theory in contemporary social psychology. In G. Lindzey & E. Aronson (Eds.), *Handbook of social psychology* (2nd ed.). Reading, Massachusetts: Addison-Wesley, 1968.

Berkowitz, L., & Donnerstein, E. External validity is more than skin-deep: some answers to criticisms of laboratory experiments (with special reference to research on aggression). *American Psychologist*, 1982, **37**, 245–257.

Blau, P. M. *Exchange and power in social life*. New York: Wiley, 1964.

Blumer, H. *Symbolic interactionism*. Englewood Cliffs, New Jersey: Prentice-Hall, 1969.

Braverman, H. *Labor and monopoly capitalism*. New York: Monthly Review Press, 1974.

Burke, K. *The grammar of motives*. New York: World, 1945.

Burke, P. J. The self: Measurement requirements from an interactionist perspective. *Social Psychology Quarterly*, 1980, **43**, 18–29.

Burgess, R. L., & Bushnell, D., Jr. (Eds.), *Behavioral sociology: The behavioral analysis of social process*. New York: Columbia University Press, 1969.

Buss, A. H. *Self consciousness and social anxiety*. San Francisco, California, Freeman, 1980.

Cicourel, A. V. *Method and measurement in sociology*. New York: Free Press, 1964.

Cicourel, A. V. *Cognitive sociology*. Middlesex, England: Penguin, 1973.

Cooley, C. H. *Human nature and the social order*. New York: Scribner's, 1902.

Duvall, S., & Wicklund, R. A. *A theory of objective self-awareness*. New York: Academic Press, 1972.

Emerson, R. M. Exchange theory. In M. Rosenberg & R. H. Turner (Eds.), *Social psychology: Sociological perspectives*. New York: Basic Books, 1981.

Festinger, L. *A theory of cognitive dissonance*. Stanford, California: Stanford University Press, 1957.

Fischoff, B. Attribution theory and judgment under uncertainty. In J. H. Harvey, W. J. Ickes, & R. F. Kidd (Eds.), *New directions in attribution research* (Vol. I). Hillsdale, New Jersey: Erlbaum, 1976.

Garfinkel, H. *Studies in ethnomethodology*. Englewood Cliffs, New Jersey: Prentice-Hall, 1967.

Gergen, K. G. Social psychology as history. *Journal of Personality and Social Psychology*, 1973, **26,** 309–320.

Glaser, B., & Strauss, A. *The discovery of grounded theory*. Chicago, Illinois: Aldine, 1967.

Goffman, E. *The presentation of self in everyday life*. New York: Doubleday, 1959.

Goffman, E. *Encounters*, Indianapolis, Indiana: Bobbs-Merrill, 1961.

Goffman, E. *Frame Analysis*. New York: Harper and Row, 1974.

Gottlieb, A. Social psychology as history or science; an addendum. *Personality and Social Psychology Bulletin*, 1977, **3,** 207–210.

Gouldner, A. W. *The coming crisis of western sociology*. New York: Basic Books, 1970.

Greenwald, A. G. The totalitarian ego. *American Psychologist*, 1980, **35,** 603–618.

Hamblin, R., Buckholdt, D., Ferritor, D., Kozloff, M., & Blackwell, L. *The humanization process*. New York: Wiley-Interscience, 1971.

Harré, R. The ethogenic approach: theory and practice. In L. Berkowitz (Ed.), *Advances in experimental social psychology* (Vol. 10). New York: Academic Press, 1977.

Harré, R., & Secord, P. F. *The explanation of social behavior*. Totowa, New Jersey: Littlefield, Adams, 1973.

Heider, F. Social perception and phenomenal causality. *Psychological Review*, 1944, **51,** 358–373.

Heider, F. Attitudes and cognitive organization. *Journal of Psychology*, 1946, **27,** 107–112.

Heider, F. *The psychology of interpersonal relations*. New York: Wiley, 1958.

Heise, D. R. *Understanding events*. London and New York: Cambridge University Press, 1979.

Hewitt, J. P., & Stokes, R. Disclaimers. *American Sociological Review*, 1975, **40,** 1–11.

Hilgard, E. R. Consciousness in contemporary psychology. In M. R. Rosenzweig & L. W. Porter (Eds.), *Annual review of psychology* (Vol. 31). Palo Alto, California: Annual Reviews Inc., 1980.

Homans, G. C. *Social behavior: Its elementary forms*. New York: Harcourt Brace Jovanovich, 1961.

House, J. S. The three faces of social psychology. *Sociometry*, 1977, **40** 161–177.

House, J. S. Social structure and personality. In M. Rosenberg & R. H. Turner (Eds.), *Social psychology: Sociological perspectives*. New York: Basic Books, 1981.

Huber, J. Symbolic interaction as a pragmatic perspective: The bias of emergent theory. *American Sociological Review*, 1973, **38,** 278–284.

Hull, J. G., & Levy, A. S. The organizational functions of self: an Alternative to the Duval and Wicklund model of self-awareness. *Journal of Personality and Social Psychology*, 1979, **37,** 756–768.

Israel, J. Stipulations and construction in the social sciences. In J. Israel & H. Tajfel, (Eds.), *The Context of Social Psychology*. London: Academic Press, 1972.

Israel, J., & Tajfel, J. (Eds.). *The context of social psychology*. London: Academic Press, 1972.

Janousek, J. On the Marxian concept of *praxis*. In J. Israel & H. Tajfel (Eds.), *The context of social psychology*. London: Academic Press, 1972.

Jones, E. E., & Davis, K. E. From acts to dispositions: the attribution process in person perception. In L. Berkowitz (Ed.), *Advances in experimental social psychology* (Vol. 2). New York: Academic Press, 1965.

Kelley, H. H. Attribution theory in social psychology. In D. Levine (Ed.), *Nebraska symposium on motivation*. Lincoln, Nebraska: University of Nebraska Press, 1967.

Kelley, H. H. The processes of causal attribution. *American Psychologist*, 1973, **28**, 107–128.

Kohn, M. L. *Class and conformity*. Chicago, Illinois: University of Chicago Press, 1977.

Kohn, M. L. & Schooler, C. The reciprocal effects of substantive complexity of work and intellectual flexibility. *American Journal of Sociology*, 1978, **84**, 24–52.

Kruglanski, A. W. On the paradigmatic objections to experimental psychology. *American Psychologist*, 1976, **31**, 655–663.

Lecky, P. *Self-consistency*. New York: Island Press, 1945.

Lewin, K. *A dynamic theory of personality*. New York: McGraw-Hill, 1935.

Lewin, K. *Field theory in social science*. New York: Harper, 1951.

Linton, R. *The study of man*. Englewood Cliffs, New Jersey: Prentice-Hall, 1936.

Lofland, J. (Ed.) *Interaction in everyday life*. Beverly Hills, California: Sage, 1978.

Maines, D. R. Social organization in symbolic interactionism. In A. Inkeles, J. Coleman & N. Smelser (Eds.), *Annual review of sociology* (Vol. 3). Palo Alto, California: Annual Reviews Inc., 1977.

Mannheim, K. *Ideology and utopia*. New York: Harcourt Brace, 1936.

Marcus, H. Self-schemata and processing information about the self. *Journal of Personality and Social Psychology*, 1977, **35**, 63–78.

McCall, G. J., & Simmons, J. L. *Identities and interaction*. New York: Free Press, 1978.

Mead, G. H. *Mind, self and society*. Chicago, Illinois: University of Chicago Press, 1934.

Meltzer, B. M., Petras, J. W., & Reynolds, L. T. *Symbolic interactionism: Genesis, varieties and criticism*. London: Routledge and Kegan Paul, 1975.

Mills, C. W. Situated actions and vocabularies of motives. *American Sociological Review*, 1940, **5**, 904–913.

Moscovici, S. Society and theory in social psychology. In J. Israel & H. Tajfel (Eds.), *The context of social psychology*. London: Academic Press, 1972.

Orne, M. T. On the special psychology of the social psychological experiment. *American Psychologist*, 1962, **17**, 776–783.

Parsons, T. *The social system*. Glencoe, Illinois: The Free Press, 1951.

Rogers, T. B., Kuiper, N. A., & Kirker, W. S. Self-reference and the encoding of personal information. *Journal of Personality and Social Psychology*, 1977, **35**, 677–688.

Rosenberg, M. *Conceiving the self*. New York: Basic Books, 1979.

Rosenthal, R., & Jacobsen, E. *Pygmalion in the classroom*. New York: Holt, Rinehart and Winston, 1968.

Ross, E. A. *Social psychology*. New York: Macmillan, 1908.

Schlenker, B. R. Liking for a group following initiation: Impression management or dissonance reduction? *Sociometry*, 1975, **38**, 99–118.

Schlenker, B. R. *Impression management*. Monterey, California: Brooks/Cole, 1980.

Scott, M. B. Review of Schlenker, *Impression management*. *Contemporary Sociology*, 1981, **10**, 582–583.

Scott, M. B., & Lyman, S. M. Accounts. *American Sociological Review*, 1968, **33**, 46–61.

Smith, D. L. Symbolic interactionism: definitions of the situation from Becker and Lofland. *Catalyst*, 1973, **7**, 62–75.

Smith, M. B. *Humanizing social psychology*. San Francisco, California: Jossey-Bass, 1974.

Snyder, M. Self-monitoring processes. In L. Berkowitz (Ed.), *Advances in experimental social psychology* (Vol. 12). New York: Academic Press, 1979.

Strauss, A. *Negotiations*. San Francisco, California: Jossey-Bass, 1978.

Stryker, S. Relations of married offspring and parent: A test of Mead's theory. *American Journal of Sociology*, 1956, **62**, 308–319.

Stryker, S. The interactional and situational approaches. In H. Christensen (Ed.), *Handbook of marriage and the family*. Chicago, Illinois: Rand-McNally, 1964.

Stryker, S. Identity salience and role performance. *Journal of Marriage and the Family*, 1968, **30**, 558–564.

Stryker, S. Review symposium: The Handbook of Social Psychology. *American Sociological Review*, 1971, **36**, 894–898.

Stryker, S. Developments in 'two social psychologies': Toward an appreciation of mutual relevance. *Sociometry*, 1977, **40**, 145–160.

Stryker, S. *Symbolic interactionism: A social structural approach*. Menlo Park, California: Benjamin/Cummings, 1980.

Stryker, S. Symbolic interactionism. In M. Rosenberg & R. H. Turner (Eds.), *Social psychology: Sociological perspectives*. New York: Basic Books, 1981.

Stryker, S., & Gottlieb, A. Attribution theory and symbolic interactionism: a comparison. In J. H. Harvey, W. J. Ickes, & R. F. Kidd (Eds.), *New directions in attribution research* (Vol. III). Hillsdale, New Jersey: Erlbaum, 1981.

Stryker, S., & Serpe, R. T. Commitment, identity salience and role behavior: theory and research example. In W. J. Ickes & E. S. Knowles (Eds.), *Personality, roles and social behavior*. New York: Springer-Verlag, 1981.

Stryker, S., & Statham, A. Symbolic interactionism and role theory. In G. Lindzey & E. Aronson (Eds.), *Handbook of social psychology* (3rd ed.). Reading, Massachusetts: Addison-Wesley, forthcoming.

Sudnow, D. *Studies in social interaction*. New York: Free Press, 1972.

Tajfel, H. Experiments in a vacuum. In J. Israel & H. Tajfel (Eds.), *The context of social psychology*. London: Academic Press, 1972.

Tedeschi, J. T., & Reiss, M. Predicaments and verbal tactics of impression management. In C. Antaki (Ed.), *Ordinary language explanations of social behavior*. London: Academic Press, 1980.

Tetlock, P. E. Explaining teacher explanations of pupil performance: An examination of the self-presentation position. *Social Psychology Quarterly*, 1980, **43**, 283–290.

Thomas, W. I., & Thomas, D. S. *The child in America*. New York: Knopf, 1928.

Turner, R. H. The real self: From institution to impulse. *American Journal of Sociology*, 1976, **81**, 989–1016.

Turner, R. H. The role and the person. *American Journal of Sociology*, 1978, **84**, 1–23.

Weary, G. Self-serving biases in the attribution process: A reexamination of the fact or fiction question. *Journal of Personality and Social Psychology*, 1978, **36**, 56–71.

Weinstein, E. A., & Tanur, J. M. Meanings, purposes, and structural resources in social interaction. *Cornell Journal of Social Relations*, 1976, **11**, 105–110.

Wrong, D. The oversocialized conception of man. *American Sociological Review*, 1961, **26**, 454–466.

TOWARD AN INTERDISCIPLINARY SOCIAL PSYCHOLOGY*

Carl W. Backman

DEPARTMENT OF SOCIOLOGY
UNIVERSITY OF NEVADA, RENO
RENO, NEVADA

*A portion of this manuscript was completed while the writer was a visiting professor of social psychology at Catholic University, Nijmegen, The Netherlands. This support is gratefully acknowledged.

219

ADVANCES IN EXPERIMENTAL
SOCIAL PSYCHOLOGY, VOL. 16

I. Introduction

Following the wave of critical commentary on the state of social psychology in the 1970s, a second wave is upon us. This wave is concerned with the relation between the two social psychologies: the sociological and the psychological traditions in our field. Not only has there been a steady outpouring of journal articles on this topic (Blank, 1978; Cartwright, 1979; House, 1977; Quinn, Robinson and Balkwell, 1980; Stryker, 1977; Wilson and Schafer, 1978), but this subject has been a series feature in *The Society for the Advancement of Social Psychology Newsletter*. These two waves are interrelated. As I have argued elsewhere (1979), the first suggests the emergence of a new paradigm among psychologically trained social psychologists that contains many elements basic to symbolic interactionism, the most distinctive strand of sociological social psychology. These elements (shown more in what psychologists are actually doing than in what constituted the older paradigm that is still reflected in much of graduate training) include the idea of man as agent, an emphasis on meaning, and an emphasis on situational determinants of behavior.

This movement of research and theory in the direction of the sociological tradition has not occurred for the most part as a result of diffusion of knowledge between the fields. Until very recently the frequency of reference to the sociological literature on the part of psychologists was minimal, and when it occurred it seemed to reflect more an attempt at bibliographic completeness than an instance of real influence. Rather, this shift in assumptions, topical focus, and to a lesser extent, research methods appeared largely in response to internal developments within the psychological tradition. These developments include the concern for relevance, the growing awareness of the problems and limitations of knowledge based on the social psychological experiment, the cognitive revolution in psychology, and I suspect, either a sense of security that psychology was really a science and/or perhaps just less concern for its status as such.

Because this shift in paradigm in the direction of the sociological perspective has been largely an internal development, and also because psychologically trained social psychologists are still unduly wedded to experimental methods, the full impact of the sociological perspective has been blunted. While the rate of independent invention of sociological ideas and foci of interests has gone up, with the usual wastes of redundancy, promising developments are still missed or incompletely carried out. In this chapter I illustrate these deficiencies by reference to developments in three areas of social psychological research. In two of these areas the rate of research activity peaked before adequate consideration was given to the contributions that might be made from a sociological perspective. The first one is concerned with the behavior of actors as "subjects" in psychological studies. Here the full implications of a sociological approach to this problem—situated identity theory—which was developed over a decade ago by Alexander and others (Alexander and Knight, 1971; Alexander and Weil, 1969; Alexander and Wiley, 1981), is being applied to the reinterpretation of a number of bodies of experimental findings under the guise of self-presentation theory, of an even earlier sociological vintage (Goffman, 1959). The second area, broadly concerned with the relation between social norms and behavior, includes studies of harm-doing and aggression and their opposites, altruism and prosocial behavior, and has developed with only a partial appreciation of the full implications of the sociological view concerning the operation of social norms. This view, I argue, has gained increasing empirical support from recent developments in cognitive psychology and social learning theory.

A social psychological approach to stability and change in personality, based on the recent research on the development of relationships, is the final problem to be dealt with here. This area is the one that has benefited most from the interpenetration of the sociological and psychological traditions. Following a number of abortive attempts over the past quarter century, the time seems ripe for a successful revival of what has been from the beginning of social psychology a central though insufficiently developed focus of research. This is not to say that social psychologists have not dealt with a myriad of individual differences having significance for social behavior, but rather to assert that a truly social psychological approach to various issues in personality theory has yet to be developed and widely accepted in our field.

In what follows I plan to bring some further influences of the sociological perspective to bear on these topics. In doing so I hope first to add to the improvement of experimental methods in social psychology and to our understanding of some of the limits of this approach for the generation of social psychological data. Second, I hope to call attention to some lines of inquiry concerning moral behavior that an oversimplified view of the role of norms in human action has caused to be neglected. Finally, in sketching the core ideas of what appears to be an emerging social psychological approach to personality theory, relating this to what we currently know and suggesting where more work is needed, I would like to stimulate some further lines of research and theory that will contribute to the increasing synthesis of the work of sociologists and psychologists on this central problem in social psychology. In the following section a brief exposition of the sociological perspective will be combined with a discussion of the implications of this perspective for research methods in social psychology in general and the social psychological experiment in particular.

II.   The Sociological Perspective: Some Methodological
Implications

A.   PERSON AND SOCIETY

Fundamental to the sociological perspective is the interactional, or more recently termed, dialectic, character of the relationship between persons and their society. Persons are continually creating and being created by society. In interaction with others they create forms of thought and action which in turn become a part of the objective constraints and opportunities that influence their behavior. While few psychologists would quibble with what appears to have become accepted as a truism, the accompanying assumptions and implications of this basic sociological premise have not had as great an effect on psychological research as might be supposed.

What are some of these assumptions and implications? First, there is the assumption of human agency. While constrained by the influence of others, human behavior is not fashioned in a deterministic manner by the social stimuli that impinge upon it. Persons are in part at least masters of their own fate in that they participate in the creation of the social fabric that surrounds and constrains them, and at times in the pursuit of some end or another surmount these constraints. Second, these social constraints emerge out of processes of interaction and are constantly subject to modification in the psychic give-and-take that characterizes human interaction. Third, the substance of such constraints and opportunities consists of jointly constructed symbolic representations of reality. Social interaction and the products that arise from these processes (shared views of the world, of self and of others, social norms or approved patterns of behavior, values or shared evaluations of various states of affairs) are possible because man has the capacity for the joint construction of meanings through the use of language. This latter assumption lies behind the sociologists' emphasis on gaining an understanding of processes underlying what has been termed the social construction of reality (Berger and Luckmann, 1967).

B.   IDENTITIES AND THE SOCIAL CONSTRUCTION OF
     REALITY

While the phrase ''the social construction of reality'' was introduced in the context of the development of world views within the framework of the sociology of knowledge, I am using it in a more prosaic fashion to refer to persons' definitions of social situations which, while never identical, overlap sufficiently to allow them to pursue their respective goals in concert. Basic to the perceptual organization of such definitions of situations are the social or role identities of the participants. The concept of identity, until recently largely ignored by psychologically trained social psychologists, is a crucial sociological variable since it is central to contemporary sociological analyses of social interaction. A person's identity is a link to the constraints within social situations and also includes the element of active purposiveness characteristic of persons in interaction. As an aspect of self, identities share the reflexive character of that entity. In the carrying out of actions, persons not only take into consideration the responses of others to their acts, but because they can also respond to themselves as an object, their behavior is influenced by their own reactions. In imagination persons can plan their actions, and both as stage director and audience can control and react to their imagined performances. This capacity provides the basis for a system of self-control that guides behavior in accordance with internalized standards and knowledge of the world, including the potential responses of others.

Perhaps the most extensive treatment of the concept of identity has been that of McCall and Simmons (1966, 1978). They suggest that role identities can be thought of as the somewhat idealized conceptions persons have of themselves as occupants of a particular position or social category. These imaginations concerning the self take the form of vicarious role performances in the inner forum and include the reaction of others to these performances. As such they constitute both plans of action and standards of evaluation that help shape the person's behavior.

A wide variety of intraindividual and interpersonal processes underlies the construction of the meaning of situations, including the meanings of the identities of the participants. The intraindividual processes, which include these processes of person perception and attribution, have been a dominant preoccupation of psychologists in recent years. Those processes of a more interpersonal character include the social influence process, which was an earlier interest of psychologists; and various processes of identity negotiation, including self-presentation and altercasting, which until recently have been almost exclusively the interest of sociologists.

The latter interpersonal processes, while rounding out a more balanced interactional view of social perception (where due weight is given to the influence of others, particularly the target), unfortunately are frequently implicated in the production of data hitherto largely interpreted in terms of processes within the perceiver. A number of investigators have called attention to the role of negotiation in the creation of attributions in everyday situations. Prus (1975) has attempted to extend attribution theory in this direction, and others (Sagatun and Knudsen, 1977; Schlenker, 1980) have reinterpreted a number of the experimental findings from attribution research in this manner, particularly in terms of the process of self-presentation.

Not only is the recent research on attribution undergoing a reinterpretation in terms of the effects of identity negotiation, but as reflected in the recent writings of Schlenker (1980; 1982), Arkin (1980), and many of the contributors to the Tedeschi (1980) volume on self-presentation and impression management, other bodies of research findings are being reinterpreted in terms of these processes. These include, as Arkin (1980) suggests, work on sex roles; equity in exchange; attitude change, including the diverse findings concerning forced compliance, aggression, and prosocial behavior; audience effects on task performance, etc. While this development is another dramatic instance of the rapprochement between the sociological and psychological traditions in social psychology, it also stands as an example of the costs to the field of having all too frequently to reinvent the wheel.

C.   SITUATED IDENTITY THEORY

Much of this reexamination of earlier findings was anticipated by Alexander and others at the time of the development of situated identity theory (Alexander and Knight, 1971; Alexander and Weil, 1969). Even today, however, the full possibilities of a more sociological orientation are not fully exploited because there is insufficient appreciation of the normative background against which imputations and presentations of character emerge. While Schlenker (1980) in his recent work on self-presentation, as well as Jellison and Green (1981), incorporates elements consistent with the sociological emphasis on norms, others have not paid sufficient attention to this aspect.

Situated identity theory is in one respect similar to attribution theory in that it is concerned with attributed dispositions. However, it differs in a number of major respects because of its origin in the sociological tradition of symbolic interactionism. In keeping with their intrapersonal orientation, psychologists studying attribution have focused on questions concerning the person's attributions of causes of behavior of self and others based largely on how humans process information about the world. However, the symbolic interactionists' concern with the process of role taking in social interaction has led sociologists to focus on the determinants and consequences of the attributes others are thought to impute to the person. Role taking is seen as a central process by which actors take into account the potential responses of others as they attempt to achieve their goal in a given situation. While there are other bases for making inferences about one person's reaction to the behavior of another in the context in which it occurs, one very important basis is the normative backdrop: the shared perspective having both an expectational and a prescriptive quality that actors in interaction typically share. These shared perceptions of reality and of the social appropriateness of behavior make it possible for actors to anticipate both the behavior of others and the kinds of dispositional qualities and behavioral choices that others will impute to them. While Heider (1958) recognized that an actor needs to take into account not only the dispositional qualities of the others but the latter's perceptions concerning the actor's dispositions, he as well as most contemporary attribution theorists have concentrated on the former. At the same time, psychologists in the design of their research and as in the course of their everyday activities take into consideration the normatively structured perspectives of others.

Role taking is a basic process in experimental design. In a psychological experiment, the experimental scenario (including the manipulation) takes the particular form it does because experimenters are capable of imagining the likely interpretations and responses to their attempts to construct a particular social experience for their subjects. While all experimental social psychologists do this and many are aware of this fact, there is insufficient appreciation of the implication that others in the research situation, particularly the so-called subjects, are engaging in the same process, which in turn allows them to engage in negotiation with the experimenter concerning each's situated identity. The resultant attributions that constitute the situated identity of those in interaction are rarely if ever simply a product of internal perceptual and cognitive processes, but the outcome of conscious or unconscious processes of identity negotiation in which each is both an active perceiver and an active controller of information. Situated identity theory in particular emphasizes that where choices between alternative responses are possible, actors tend to choose that alternative that they anticipate will lead to the most socially desirable attributions. In fact, employing the same logic concerning the influence of social desirability on attitude and personality test results employed by Edwards (1957), Alexander and Wiley (1981) conclude from a number of studies that unless the alternative response possibilities provided to subjects in the typical experiment as the dependent variable are of equal social desirability, situated identity theory provides a more parsimonious explanation of the results than the diverse theoretical explanations these experiments were designed to test. Such reasoning suggests that much more attention must be given to developing ways of controlling for these effects. Their own work in testing predictions made from situated identity theory suggests the manner in which this can be done. Typically they describe the behavior of subjects in various experimental conditions in terms of their responses to measures of the dependent variable to a group with backgrounds comparable to these hypothetical subjects. These groups are then asked to make attributional judgments of the subjects. By using this procedure, an investigator can guess how subjects in an actual experimental condition might judge the attributional implications of their behavior. Were this to become a standard practice in pretesting for social desirability associated with responses of subjects, experimenters could estimate and control for these effects.

An excellent example of the application of situated identity theory that demonstrates both the above social desirability effect and its normative basis is a study by Sagatun and Knudson (1977). In contrast to some of the earlier findings concerning the tendencies of observers to make internal attributions and actors to employ explanations in terms of situational or external causes, they found evidence that persons in the role of observer attribute another's success to internal causes and the failures to external ones, while in the role of actor they make external attributions to both success and failure. In interpreting these findings they argued that different attribution norms exist for different persons in different settings. Persons in the role of observer felt obliged to show concern for others. Thus attributing the observed person's success to internal factors and their failures to external ones was in conformity to this norm, and showed the observers to be generous and concerned persons. Similarly they suggest that the social expectation for self-explanations of success and failure lead persons in the role of actor to make external attributions in both cases. In the case of success the objective fact of success is apparent and the actor makes a good impression by conforming to the norm of modesty and attributing his success to external factors. At the same time, conforming to expectations that persons should believe in their own abilities and not be thwarted by failure leads to the attribution of their failures to external circumstances which in these circumstances help maintain a favorable impression.

In the last few years psychologists, as mentioned earlier, are increasingly coming to the same conclusions concerning the determinants of attributions. Yet if much can be made from bibliographic citations, this appears to have occurred, with only an occasional exception (Schlenker, 1980; Snyder, 1979), without awareness of situated identity theory. Those making such interpretations, however, while acknowledging that attributions are influenced by tactics of self presentation, have, except for Schlenker, tended to view norms as operating in a somewhat global fashion irrespective of situational features (Jellison and Green, 1981), or when focusing on situational variations have viewed these in terms of whether the situation is such that persons engaging in self-enhancing tactics are likely to be believed or likely to be exposed to future disconfirmation of an unduly positive image (Bradley, 1978). However, as some of the earliest work on situated identity theory suggests, rather small differences from one experimental condition to another, as these interact with experimental manipulations and the resulting options for subjects' responses, result in marked differences in the kinds of character traits attributed to subjects in such situations (Alexander and Wiley, 1981). These considerations suggest that a much more complex conception of normative influence than psychologists, and many sociologists as well, have employed in the past might throw some light on some of the recent controversies in results and interpretations that have characterized the literature on attribution theory and other bodies of research findings in recent years. It is not my purpose to attempt such a sorting out in this chapter, in part because most of the interpretations of the identity implications of behavior in various experimental situations would be ad hoc on my part. However, there does exist another area of social psychological research in which a more complex theory of the influence of norms has been applied.

III. Social Norms and Moral Behavior

A. DEFINING SITUATIONS

While psychologists following the work of Sherif (1936) and Asch (1956) showed considerable interest in social norms several decades ago, in recent years this interest has waned, even though a number of areas of research activity might have benefited from greater attention to the role of norms in social life. These areas include the study of altruism, bystander intervention, harm doing, and the related area concerned with equity and other distributional norms.

While some researchers studying altruism and bystander intervention have found the concept of social norms useful (Berkowitz and Daniels, 1964; Schwartz, 1977; Staub, 1974), others have questioned its use (Darley and Latané, 1970; Hoffman, 1981) on the grounds that the concept has little explanatory value.

The variety of theories that emerged to explain both altruistic behavior and its absence or the obverse, as in the case of Milgram (1963) and destructive obedience, were characterized by a number of similarities despite the different emphases on the role of norms. All of these theorists explicitly or implicitly stressed the importance of situational definitions in explaining the behavior of subjects in these situations. Schwartz (1968a, 1968b) was most explicit on this point, arguing that norms influencing altruistic behavior only became operative when persons defined a situation as one in which their behavior had consequences for the welfare of another and in which they viewed themselves as responsible for their behavior and its consequences. Latané and Darley's (1968) explanation focuses essentially on these same two conditions in arguing that before persons respond in an emergency they must define the situation as a true emergency requiring them to act and accept responsibility for doing so. Milgram (1974) in his emphasis on the agentic state places particular significance on the latter variable. The various experimental situations employed to test these theories placed subjects in a state of conflict because of the mixture of costs and rewards associated with the response options they faced. Piliavin, Rodin, and Piliavin (1969) have devoted the greatest attention to this variable taken from exchange theory.

While all of these explanations were essentially situational in character,

Schwartz (1968a, 1968b, 1973, 1977), whose theory was the most sociological, included a focus on personality elements, both in terms of his emphasis on personal norms embedded in the self and his notion that there were individual differences in the degree to which persons tended to see their behavior as having consequences for others and to see themselves as being responsible for their behavior.

If we place these ideas in a more explicitly sociological framework, a theory emerges that is capable of accounting for a good bit of the findings of research generated by these earlier formulations, is consistent with a number of theoretical developments since, and directs attention to some unfinished business. These are promising lines of research that have not yet been fully explored. While a more detailed and systematic presentation of this theory has been presented elsewhere (Backman, in press), the version presented here is sufficient to accomplish these objectives.

B. NORMS, ACCOUNTS, AND SITUATED IDENTITIES

Definitions of situations are generally jointly constructed, negotiated products that reflect both the objective facts, the reality constraints and opportunities in the objective situation (including the influence of others), and the subjective resources that persons bring to bear on the development of such constructions. The relevant subjective resources in this context are accounts. These are widely employed and accepted explanations for behavior that relate a person's behavior in situations to norms in a manner that results in the creation and/or maintenance of favorable situated identities.

Scott and Lyman (1968) introduced the concept of accounts into the sociological literature, basing it on a classification of explanations of untoward behavior proposed by the ordinary-language philosopher John Austin (1961). More recently this conceptualization has entered the psychological literature, principally through the work of Schlenker (1980) on self-presentation. According to a typology of such devices described elsewhere (Backman, 1976), accounts fall into three classes: excuses, justifications, and conventionalizations. Excuses include explanations of conduct in terms of a denial of responsibility. Behavior contrary to a norm is explained as an accident, as not due to intent or foreknowledge of its consequences, or as in some manner beyond the control of the person. Justifications, in contrast, are accounts in which persons accept responsibility for their actions but deny their pejorative character in the proffered definition of the situation. Such devices include the denial or minimization of harm. The act is not defined as wrong because no harm resulted, or if it did, the injury was trifling. Thus the person who steals from a large corporation may justify his behavior on the grounds that the loss is covered by insurance or that compared to the large assets of the company the theft is of no consequence. A second cognitive device in this category takes the form of defining the victim as deserving of the harm. Attacks on drunks or homosexuals may be justified in terms of the moral depravity of such victims. Scott and Lyman labeled a third form of justification as condemnation of the condemners. In this instance the act is not bad because others are seen as having committed as bad or worse offenses. The petty thief who justifies his vocation by asserting that corrupt police and judges commit worse offenses illustrates this device. A fourth type involves the invocation of some higher priority. While the act may be contrary to one norm, it is not wrong because it is consistent with another, more important social expectation. Aggression on the part of an individual may be defined in terms of self-defense. The typology offered by Scott and Lyman includes two other forms of justification, the sad tale, where the persons define their behavior as resulting from a particular configuration of adverse circumstances, and self-fulfillment, in which an act is justified as necessary for complete development of the self. Drug users who justify their use of mind- or consciousness-expanding drugs would be an example of the latter. As I have suggested elsewhere (Backman, 1976), the latter type of account could be regarded as a variant of the higher principle justification and the former as a type of excuse. Lofland (1969) has added the last class of accounts to the typology presented here, conventionalization, where usually through some form of rhetorical transformation the act is defined as other than what it appears to be, thus calling in question the relevance of a particular norm. Embezzlement, a form of theft, may be defined as borrowing temporarily with intent to repay at some future time.

Finally, two further assumptions should be made explicit in any theory of norm violation. First, conformity to rules of the moral variety typically involves both rewards and costs arising in part from the nature of the behavior but also from the reactions of self and others. It is assumed that in situations involving the operation of norms, as in other social situations, persons are motivated by the goal of maximizing rewards and minimizing costs. This is, of course, a basic assumption from exchange theory. A second assumption comes from symbolic interactionist theory. A basic premise of this view is that persons' definitions are powerfully influenced by the goals of the actor; and while situated identity theory may overemphasize the goal of self-enhancement, it nevertheless is a prevalent goal in most situations.

With these ideas in mind, it is possible to understand the behavior of persons in the type of experimental situations contrived by experimental psychologists studying moral behavior, and the behavior of others in everyday instances of moral confrontation makes sense.

C. THE RESOLUTION OF MORAL DILEMMAS

Most scenarios in social psychological experiments dealing with norm violation place the naive participants in a choice situation in which they face incompatible demands. In one of the situations employed by Darley and Latané (1968), the subject is faced with a choice between possibly compromising his role as a good subject in an experiment and intervening in what could be a serious emergency. In the Milgram experimental paradigm (1963), a similar dilemma is faced by the subject between carrying out the experimenter's specifications of his role and inflicting possibly serious damage on another, or violating these expectations and refusing to continue the experiment. A variety of experimental scenarios employed by Berkowitz and Daniels (1964), Schwartz (1968a, 1968b), and others (Macauley and Berkowitz, 1970) studying helping behavior also placed persons in a conflict situation—either to violate the norm of social responsibility and, depending on the private or public nature of the breach, face sanctions from self or others, or engage in costly behavior. In situations where moral considerations are involved, as well as others in which some standard of self-worth applies (such as behavior relevant to standards of achievement), the implications of one's choice for one's situated identity become an important determinant of that choice. Given the pervasive goal of maintaining or at least salvaging a favorable situated identity, persons tend to fashion definitions of situations (including an account of their behavior) that permit the least costly behavior to be seen in as favorable a light as possible by themselves as well as others.

The ideal situation for persons facing these experimenter-imposed dilemmas is to construct a definition that permits them to have their cake and eat it too. Thus to the degree that the situation is defined so that their actions or failures to act do not have serious consequences for the welfare of the other—there is no emergency, the harm is trifling, others have probably already acted, or others are equally responsible, why should I stick my neck out?—the person avoids the costs associated with one of the alternatives with minimal damage to a favorable situated identity.

A basic element of the design of the experimental settings employed in such research is the attempt by the experimenter to provide a basis within the objective structure of the situation to encourage particular subjective definitions. In studies of bystander intervention, variations in the degree of ambiguity concerning the nature of the emergency provide varying degrees of leeway for persons to define the situation as not a serious emergency. Similarly, varying the number and characteristics of others and the behavior of confederates encourages or inhibits definitions concerning whether an emergency exists and whether the person is primarily responsible for action. In research on harm doing, varying the objective situation so as to either underscore or deemphasize the victim's suffering or the degree of responsibility of the subject and thus encourage or inhibit appropriate subjective definitions similarly affects the person's perceptions of the harm inflicted and the locus of responsibility for such harm.

While the type of theorizing I have outlined here implicitly seems to guide

experimenters in their research, making it explicit provides a theoretical framework that has a number of advantages. A typology of the definitional alternatives
available to subjects provides the researcher with guides to better-designed studies that capture the determinants of a particular experimental outcome and allow
them to classify these outcomes properly when they occur. Thus by systematically varying the degree of ambiguity of the lady in distress episode employed
by Latané and Rodin (1969), Warner (1976) was systematically able to increase
the proportion of subjects who intervened on the victim's behalf, further supporting the conclusion that given the ambiguity of the situation and the failure of
most others in the situation to confirm the existence of an emergency through the
reactions they displayed, persons tended to minimize the seriousness of the
emergency and the necessity to intervene.

While Latané and Darley (1968), for instance, were well aware that definitions of situations are in varying degress socially constructed (i.e., each person's
definition, particularly in physically ambiguous situations, is in part based on the
intentional or unintentional behavior of others), the full impact of others in
defining a situation appears to have been missed in Milgram's (1974) interpretation of his results. The emphasis that he placed on his subjects' diffusion of
responsibility to the experimenter, along with the confidence that most experimenters have that their definition of the situation as imposed by their experimental scenarios is the one accepted by subjects, seems to have led him to ignore the
possibility that many subjects may have defined the injury to the "victim" as
less serious than was intended. At least this is suggested by Mixon's (1972) role-
playing replication of the Milgram study. Reasoning that the lack of concern
evidenced in the behavior of the experimenter was incongruous with other features of the situation designed to emphasize the severity of harm, Mixon hypothesized that a succession of scenarios in which the experimenter showed increasing concern would be characterized by a corresponding increase in the percentage of subjects refusing to continue the experiment. This hypothesis was
confirmed in a series of role-playing episodes based on the Milgrim paradigm.
More recently Mantell and Pinzarella (1976) have provided further experimental
support for this interpretation of Milgram's results.

Finally, it should be noted that expanding the theory of norm activation
developed by Schwartz and implicit in the work of Latané and Darley to include
the concept of accounts suggests ways, in addition to denial of responsibility and
minimization of consequences, by which persons define situations to neutralize
the effect of particular norms. Some types of accounts are not easily subsumed
under the two types of mitigating circumstances delineated by these writers, such
as those that assert that while an act violates one norm it is in accordance with
some more important requirement in the situation, or those that cast the victim of
a harm as deserving of his fate either because of past depredations or because he

has somehow contributed to his victimization. Similarly the justification that others frequently commit the same or worse offenses is an additional type of account that is not covered in this twofold classification.

D.   SOME FURTHER DIRECTIONS FOR RESEARCH AND
     THEORY

Progress (Backman, 1976, in press) has been made in developing a theory of moral judgments that suggests the circumstances under which one or another of these neutralizing definitions will be employed. The theory relates characteristics of the person, both personal and social, those of the victim, the particular act, and the situation, to the liklihood that persons motivated both to maintain a favorable view of themselves and at the same time avoid the costs of adhering to moral dictates will employ one or another of these accounting devices. To illustrate, persons who by virtue of their positions in the social structure have low status and power may tend to employ and be more accepting of an account that denies responsibility, and the same might be expected of those characterized as externals on the (I–E) scale. The fact that the victim of a theft is a large corporation whose assets dwarf the amount of a petty theft encourages the thief's use of a justification that minimizes the harm. The fact that the amount or distribution of a type of norm violation is unknown (as in the case of income tax evasion in many countries) invites the justification that it is not bad because many people engage in it. These illustrations point up two bases that influence the construction of accounts, the actual facts concerning the situation and the participants, and characteristics of situations such as ambiguity that invite an invention or distortion of facts.

Because the actual facts of situations and the socially constructed and shared interpretation of these facts vary throughout the social structure, it is possible to explain, in part at least, the social distribution of norm violation in terms of this theory. For instance, blacks can with some justification in fact defend looting of ghetto business establishments in the belief that they had been the victims of extortionary practices. Sutherland's theory of differential association (Sutherland and Cressey, 1974) developed well over a quarter of a century ago, and one of the few theories of that vintage still widely accepted by criminologists, explained the distribution of crime throughout the social structure in terms of exposure to either definitions unfavorable or favorable to engaging in criminal behavior. Basic elements in the latter were rationalizations or what we have called accounts.

From the beginning research by Schwartz (1968a, 1968b), it has been clear that personality characteristics are involved in explaining the distribution of norm violation. His measures of the tendency for persons to be aware of the consequences of their behavior for others and the tendency of persons to accept or deny responsibility for their acts reliably distinguished between those more apt to conform to moral expectation and those less so. It is interesting in this context to note that the items in the scale employed to measure the latter tendency, to accept or deny responsibility, include not only those items that are logically related to the norm of responsibility for consequences of one's acts, but also items included in the expanded theory offered here, such as the tendency to justify a lack of consideration of another on the grounds that the other had behaved badly.

This focus on individual differences has implications for research on moral development. It could be argued that individual differences in the frequency of norm violations would be related to the learned tendency to employ various accounts. Sullivan (1953) recognized this long ago. The early work of Redl and Wineman (1951) and Sykes and Matza (1957) on disturbed and delinquent children suggested the value of such an approach. While the evidence has not been entirely consistant (Minor, 1980), a number of investigators (Ball, 1966; Ball and Lilly, 1971; Verlarde, 1978) have since demonstrated that delinquents compared to nondelinquents are more accepting of the kind of accounts first distinguished by Sykes and Matza and seem even more prone to attribute such acceptance to their peers. These include, among others, accounts that deny or minimize the harm done to a victim or assert that the victim deserved the harm. Our own unpublished work with children as well as that of Darley, Klosson, and Zanna (1978) suggests that children define situations in these terms at a very early age. Other work that suggests that research on the development of accounts in children might prove fruitful in understanding the development of internal controls is the large body of research on the relations between disciplinary techniques and conscience development. Hoffman's (1970) review of the literature concluded that the group of parental behaviors called induction, in which the parent attempts to reason with the child following his transgressions in terms of the consequences of the child's behavior for others, appears to be the disciplinary technique most highly associated with strong conscience development. It is possible that the explanation for this association is that such reasoning counters the development of habits of defining situations in a manner that facilitates norm violation. While Hoffman (1981) favors an interpretation of these results in terms of a theory that relies more on the influence of emotional empathic responses than cognitive ones, neither his approach nor the one advocated here are mutually exclusive. In fact, it is becoming increasingly clear that a tight separation between cognitive and motivational variables and theories is not warranted. Nevertheless, the emphasis on the operation of norms in the manner suggested does provide a framework for expanding our understanding of marked situational variability in conformity to moral norms, long recognized in the literature; to the manner in which individual differencs may contribute to individual differences in conformity; and finally to an explanation of subcultural differences, such as class differences in conformity to norms reported by Berkowitz and Friedman (1967) and Muir and Weinstein (1962).

E.   A NOTE ON THE CAUSAL STATUS OF NORMS,
     ACCOUNTS, AND DEFINITIONS OF SITUATIONS

Before concluding this section, a number of points frequently raised as objectives to an approach to prosocial or altruistic behavior that employs the concept of norms should be addressed. One objection is that the very diversity and complexity of the normative structure easily invites an endless series of ad hoc explanations with which any result can be explained either by inferring a new norm or asserting that one norm takes priority over another. The latter is not necessarily an ad hoc explanation. Sociologists have long recognized that norms are organized in hierarchies of priority and salience. As to the former objection, while the analogy of the discarded notion of instincts is often invoked, I believe it to be greatly overdrawn. Rather than being prone to excesses in this respect, psychologists have actually greatly underestimated the extent to which norms do in fact guide behavior.

More serious have been objections as to the causal status of norms and accounts. It has been suggested that norms and accounts are after-the-fact explanations that persons make to themselves and others in order to reduce guilt, restore self-esteem, and avoid external sanctions. Thus Schlenker (1981), one of the few psychologists to make extensive use of accounts, employs them largely as devices which after-the-fact of norm violation are employed to restore the person's favorable image. This objection frequently has been buttressed by the observation that in studies of bystander intervention, persons seem to act immediately without thinking, but cognitive processing in normative explanations takes time and thus is unlikely to precede such immediate reactions. Elsewhere (Secord and Backman, 1974) we have suggested that the short latency of response can be seen as support for the type of explanation offered here. If persons take time to think they will not intervene, particularly where the ambiguity of the situation and the behavior of others allows for the construction of a definition that completely absolves persons from the obligation to act or leaves them in a state of uncertainty, conflict, and vacillation that results in no action. It is also possible, as the recent work on schemata suggests (Schank and Abelson, 1977), that cognitive processing can occur at a much more rapid rate than hitherto supposed. This work, along with our previous comments on the development of individual differences concerning the tendency to employ various accounts, suggests that moral development may involve the learning of schemata that allow a person to classify situations rapidly in a manner that either encourages or inhibits norm violations. It could be argued that the routinization of emergency procedures through frequent drills that are typical in the training of emergency specialists (firemen, for instance) or those required to engage in potentially highly costly behavior (combat soldiers, as an example) has the effect of ensuring rapid, automatic, and unthinking behavior in accordance with schemas developed through this type of repetitive training.

In nonemergency situations requiring prosocial behavior, there is typically sufficient time to engage in the type of mental activities that the symbolic interactionists envisage as occurring prior to an act. As was noted earlier in our discussion of McCall and Simmons' (1978) conception of the function of role identities, imaginings of self are not just idle musings but serve as plans of action underlying imaginary rehearsals prior to an act. Since they include criteria for appraising one's performance, those actions inconsistent with one's imagination of self in a particular role will be accompanied by anticipated embarrassment that will lead to their discontinuation and the substitution of actions more in keeping with one's self-conception.

An examination of some of the recent writing on the role of scripts in the decision-making process in general (Abelson, 1976), and more particularly in the context of deciding to engage in prosocial behavior (Langer and Abelson, 1972), provides a distinct parallel to what has been argued here. While using different terminology, Abelson and others employing this concept are talking about essentially the same internal events. Scripts are learned definitions of situations. Some are particularly important for the identity of persons employing them as these scripts relate situational features to the invocation of accounts. The causal role of these mental events is also acknowledged by Abelson when he suggests that cognitively mediated social behavior depends on the joint occurrence of two events. These include the selection of a particular script to represent a given social situation and the taking of a role within that script.

Bandura's (1978) recent extension of social learning theory places him in the same camp. In language very much like that of symbolic interactionists, he suggests that because of the human ability to use symbols, persons can plan foresightful courses of action, react to these in terms of cognitive inducements, that is, of self-imposed rewards and punishments, and thus modify their own behavior. In fact, he notes in connection with man's capacity to react to anticipatory self-censure, that such anticipatory censure may be avoided by various disengagement practices that essentially involve the invocation of the types of accounts that have been previously described. In sum, the sociological emphasis on the causal role of situational definitions, including the norms and accounts that are a part of these definitions, seems to find increasing support in psychology, both within social psychology and elsewhere.

Finally, the findings reported by Duval and Wicklund (1972), Buss (1980), Scheier and Carver (1981), and Diener (1980) suggest that persons are particularly apt to conform to moral norms when attention is directed to self. This idea is consistent with the sociological interpretation of the causal role of norms, and in particular with theories such as those of Schwartz (1977) and Secord and Back-man (1974), that view the role of conformity to norms in terms of the mainte-nance of a favorable view of self. While support for the causal role of such internal mental processes is not as clear as might be desired, the convergence of evidence to support this view is impressive. In addition to the results of experi-ments by Bandura, Underwood, and Fromson (1975), studies of various forms of norm violation that have traced the sequence of events leading to either confor-mity or deviance suggest the causal priority of accounts. As an example, Cressey (1953) found in every instance of embezzlement that the development of ra-tionalizations for the act occurred prior to its occurrence. While admittedly these findings were drawn from interviews with convicted embezzlers and thus were necessarily retrospective in character, this evidence is consistent not only with the previously cited experimental evidence, which unfortunately was also retro-spective, but with other findings. Schwartz (1973, 1977) posits that a causal relation does exist between norms and behavior, arguing from the fact that the correlation between personal norms and behavior holds only for those who see their behavior as having consequences for others and accept responsibility for their acts. Finally, if one views norms as essentially attitudes toward various behaviors, then the research employing structural equation analysis (Bentler and Speckart, 1981) that concludes that attitudes do play a causal role provides another line of support for the position taken here.

IV. Social Psychology and Personality Theory

A.   RESEARCH ON THE SELF: SOME CURRENT TRENDS

While the previously discussed research on prosocial behavior was charac-terized by little interpenetration of the two traditions in social psychology, two other lines of research of growing interest to psychologists show increasing evidence of the diffusion of ideas from one discipline to the other. These include the burgeoning research on the self and related topics, and on the development of relationships based on attraction. Until recently at least, both of these topics have been of more concern to sociologists than psychologists. For almost half a century the area of marriage and the family has been a recognized teaching and research specialty in sociology. While interest in the self has had an even longer history in both fields, it has remained a more central focus of interest in sociol-ogy, particularly among symbolic interactionists. During the long hiatus created by the reaction in psychology against any form of mentalism, self theory was not in vogue among most psychologists. However, due in part to the cognitive revolution and the increasing disarray of personality theory, and perhaps encouraged by the narcissism of the "me" generation, self theory has enjoyed a renaissance, as attested by the spate of books that focus on the self written or edited primarily by psychologists (L'Ecuyer, 1978; Lynch, Norem-Hebeisen and Gergen, 1981; Mischel, 1977; Schlenker, 1980; Suls, 1982; Tedeschi, 1981; Wegner and Vallacher, 1980; Wicklund and Gollwitzer, 1982). An increase in the tempo of interest in the self on the part of sociologists is similarly reflected in the publication of a number of volumes on this topic, including those by Zurcher (1977), Rosenberg (1979), and Rosenberg and Kaplan (1982). While the self research in both disciplines bears the imprint of the distinctive current preoccupations of information processing (in the case of the psychologists) and the effects of social structure for sociologists, there is growing convergence between the two, largely in the direction long espoused by sociologists, who have conceived of the self both as a product of and as a force in interaction (Rosenberg, 1981). The work of Snyder (1979) on self-monitoring, that of Schlenker (1980) on self-presentation, and the volume concerned with both of these topics edited by Tedeschi (1981) reflects this trend. In contrast to most psychological research, which has largely concentrated on the self as a product of information processing in the service of the self-esteem motive, the self as a force in directing the course of interaction and in the development of relationships is increasingly coming to the fore, although much of this work is still tied to the self-esteem variable. The movement of self theory in this direction should pave the way to an integration of self theory and theories of relationship formation and perhaps provide the basis for further contributions from social psychology to personaltiy theory. As Marlowe and Gergen (1969) over a decade ago suggested, self theory holds considerable promise for integrating the social–personality area in psychology. But before attempting to suggest further lines of research that would lead in this direction, a few words on recent convergences between sociologists and psychologists in the study of developing relationships are in order.

B. DEVELOPMENTAL OR STAGE THEORIES OF RELATIONSHIPS BASED ON ATTRACTION

The changing style and focus of social psychological research on the part of both psychologists and sociologists over the past fifty years is reflected in the history of research on attraction. The early research of the 1930s and 1940s on the determinants of sociometric choice and on mate selection and marital satisfaction focused largely on individual characteristics, initially at least on those of one person in a group or dyadic relationship—characteristics of the overchosen in contrast to the underchosen, or characteristics correlated with some individual measures of marital adjustment. Somewhat later, during the 1950s and 1960s, characteristics of both members of the pair were studied, both in terms of their similarity and their complementarity. Toward the end of this period, stimulated in part by the emergence of exchange theories, the focus of research and theory shifted from the characteristics of partners to an examination of processes involved in the development of relationships. At this time there emerged a number of developmental or stage theories of relationships. While the earliest ones appeared in the literature on the family in sociology (Bolton, 1961; Reiss, 1960), later ones (Secord and Backman, 1964) and particularly those appearing in the 1970s (Altman and Taylor, 1973; Levinger and Snoek, 1972; Murstein, 1971) became prominent in the psychological literature, although to an increasing degree these stage theories incorporated ideas and research findings from sociology. Accompanying these developments has been a considerable broadening of exchange theory so as to incorporate sources of reward other than those typically included in the earlier versions. As Kelley and Thibaut's revision of their theory attests (Braiker and Kelley, 1979; Kelley, 1979; Kelley and Thibaut, 1978), rewards and costs are experienced not only as the direct result of the behaviors of the partners in a relationship, but also as a result of each person's responses to his own behavior and outcomes and those of his partner, and the responses of others outside the relationship.

The inclusion of the rewarding or punishing consequences inherent in persons' reactions to their own behavior as it supports or threatens their self-conceptions, as well as the imagined responses of others to the character of their relationships, increases the usefulness of exchange theory in the understanding of these phenomena and helps to counter the objections of many to its overly self-centered stance. Add to this the developments in social learning theory (Bandura, 1977) and the work on the role of empathy in prosocial behavior (Hoffman, 1981) that underscore the role of vicarious rewards, and the ground has been laid for a much richer motivational base than that previously supplied by exchange theory for understanding both the growth of relationships and the role of the self in this context. These developments, along with the paradigmatic shifts briefly noted at the beginning of the chapter and some further developments to be touched on later, should provide a basis for further contributions from social psychology to personality theory. One way to discern the direction that such contributions will take is to consider the ways in which earlier attempts by social psychologists to fashion personality theory might have been the same or different if these developments had occurred prior to those attempts.

C.   RECASTING SOME EARLIER SOCIAL PSYCHOLOGICAL
APPROACHES TO PERSONALITY

Major previous thrusts in the direction of a relationship approach to personality include the symbolic interactionist theory of the self based on the work of

Cooley (1902) and Mead (1934); Carson's (1969) creative synthesis of Sullivan's (1953) conception of personality with Leary's circumplex model (1957); and interpersonal congruency theory (Secord and Backman, 1961, 1965).

The basic social psychological premise in all these theories, that relationship formation and personality development are intrinsic to each other, should be retained. This premise seems particularly applicable to the development of social identities and other aspects of the self. While subsequent developments suggest that the emphasis placed by these theories on the role of others' views of the person on the development, maintenance, and change of the self-concept should also be retained, some modification of this thesis is in order. It has become clear from the voluminous research on this linkage and the latest research and theorizing on information processing and memory that there is many a slip between cup and lip, or perhaps to use the more appropriate metaphor employed by Shrauger and Schoeneman (1979), the self is seen through the looking glass darkly.

Certainly we are well along the way to understanding the manner in which adults, at least, process information about the self derived from information provided by others, as well as information provided by their own behavior, both in itself and in the context of comparison with others. What is not well known is how children process such information. What evidence there is suggests that young children give greater credence to information from others, particularly adults, than is the case for the college-age group of participants in most social psychological studies (Rosenberg, 1979). This may be due in part to the less rigid and well-developed self-schemas of the young, but also to less freedom to engage in selective interaction and evaluation, which were emphasized in interpersonal congruency theory as major ways in which individuals actively created and filtered information about the self in the process of forming relationships with others. Most studies of these processes have involved as subjects college students, who probably are less locked into institutionally structured patterns of association than young children or older adults. Certainly what research there is on the effects of consensus among significant others, in part created and maintained by these processes, suggests the importance of further research on factors related to the effectiveness of selective interaction and evaluation in self-maintenance and self-creation, particularly for groups other than young adults. The latter term, self-creation, suggests another way in which a new social psychological approach to personality theory will differ from these earlier formations.

Interpersonal congruency theory in particular had an unduly conservative emphasis in that much more attention was given to the determinants of stability than to those of change. The interpersonal processes included in this theory were viewed largely as they contributed to the stability of the self system. Persons were seen as creating an interpersonal environment and processing information concerning their own behavior and the behavior of others so as to maintain congruence, a state of consistency and mutual support between elements of the self, relevant aspects of their behavior, and the behavior of others. Much of the later research and theorizing concerning the role of self-presentation and self-disclosure in the process of relationship-formation suggests that these processes are employed not just to maintain but also to create new elements of self. Some of these elements of self are short-lived or transitory where they are created in the process of achieving short-range plans of action in a particular episode; others are more long term and stable as they are tied to long-term plans embedded in relatively enduring relationships. While these processes are generally employed to maintain favorably evaluated or socially desirable identities, it has become clear from recent work that unfavorable ones may also be maintained, more frequently in connection with short-term goals but sometimes for long-term ones as well (Schlenker, 1980).

In interpersonal congruency theory, sources of change were viewed as largely external to the individual. Shifts in one's own behavior and that of others occurred as a result of assuming new roles as a consequence of orderly passage through the social structure. Such changes were also posited to occur as a result of fortuitous events that altered the personnel and/or the behavior of those in the person's interpersonal environment.

The recent emergence of theories of relationship-formation, along with the assumption that the person is capable of instigating and guiding the development of new elements of self, has provided a basis for a more detailed understanding of the subinstitutional and institutional changes that influence the development of personality. This more dynamic view of the sources of structure in interaction and in the organization of the personality not only recognizes the person as an active source of self-creation, but shifts the focus of analysis to a truly social psychological level, the analysis of processes of interaction. Analysis at the level of social interaction should provide a conceptualization of regularities in each person's behavior in terms of syntheses arising out of dialectic processes inherent in interaction and relationship-formation. Human relationships and the parts of personality that constitute such relationships can be seen as unique products of both partners' attempts to create, maintain, and at times change themselves and the other in response to both short-term and long-term plans of action. This synthesis reflects not only these plans but a wide variety of factors that affect the process of joint creation of selves.

The term dialectic is used here to underscore the notion that the selves created in a relationship are a unique product of the history of interaction, the characteristics each brings to the relationship, and the circumstances surrounding its formation and growth, including the relationship each has with others and the larger social and cultural milieu that surrounds any two partners. In one sense the use of the term may be misleading. The emphasis on conflict in the connotation of this term could lead to a continued neglect of important processes of cooperation and accommodation, of teamwork and other-enhancement, which along with conflict and other oppositional processes are engendered in the development of a relationship and its constituent identities. Certainly a major weakness of the earlier interactional theories, both Carson's (1969) and our own, was this neglect. It can be hoped, however, that the recent broadening of exchange theory to include the effects of self-imposed rewards and the increasing acceptance of the importance of vicarious rewards and punishments will remedy this defect. At any rate, in the discussion that follows, a more-evenhanded treatment will be attempted with due space given to processes of accommodation and mutual support.

D.   A THEORY OF RELATIONSHIPS: SOME IMPLICATIONS
     FOR PERSONALITY THEORY

Elsewhere (1981) I have outlined a general theory of relationship formation based largely on the work over the past half-century or so on the relationships that exist between friends and lovers. Since the purpose of that discussion was to organize what was currently found in the research literature, it suffered from the limitations of that literature. Most of this research over the years has been based on samples drawn from a limited population, for the most part college students and young adults from white, middle-class backgrounds living in the United States. Not only are limits to our knowledge imposed by the sample of participants in this research, but also by the limited sample of relationships examined. Relationships based on attraction differ in a number of significant ways from those formed on other bases such as kinship or economic cooperation. In contrast to relationships based on kinship, for instance, those based on attraction can be entered or terminated at will. In addition, they seem to carry the imperative for growth: Relationships between friends and lovers are expected to increase in strength over time or fade into oblivion. Unlike those between kin or fellow workers these are less constrained by cultural expectations. Friendship and, to an increasing degree, the relationships between lovers and spouses are negotiable within broad limits. Finally, in contrast to the relationships between parent and child or teacher and pupil or employer and employee, they involve persons roughly equal in power. These features relatively distinctive of relationships based on attraction among young adults suggest that their study can be particularly valuable in furthering our understanding of the processes of identity negotiation that contribute to self-maintenance and creation. At the same time these distinctive features suggest that these processes may take a somewhat different form in other types of relationships. For instance, while there is increasing evidence (Lewis and Rosenblum, 1974) that children have considerably more influence on the parent-child relationship and the identities of both parent and child than had hitherto been presumed, their power and resulting influence is probably less than that existing between two adult partners. These considerations suggest that rather than generalizing to the entire life span, the most that social psychologists can aim for at this point is to contribute to an understanding of how elements of self are created, maintained, or lost as a function of the development of relationships in adolescents and young adults, particularly those relationships entered into by choice and based on sentiments of attraction. Explanations of this phenomenon may apply to populations other than young adults and for other types of relationships, e.g., the parent-child relationship, but any extrapolation is of necessity largely a matter of speculation at this point.

E.   PROCESSES OF RELATIONSHIP DEVELOPMENT AND
     IDENTITY FORMATION

Given the premise that relationship formation and personality development are highly interdependent phenomena, all of the processes affecting the initiation, development, maintenance, and/or dissolution of a relationship are relevant to an explanation of personality development, stability, and change. While many of these have been dealt with in more detail in the recent literature on relationships, for our purposes here we will focus mainly on processes of identity formation and those psychological, and in particular sociological, sources of the content of these relationship based elements of personality.

A number of factors and processes influence the liklihood that any two persons in a given population will have the opportunity and the motivation to initiate a relationship. These include the institutional structure, social processes, and personal characteristics that influence the liklihood and frequency with which any two persons in a population will at least become aware of each other's existence. Whether such awareness will lead to attempts to interact will involve a variety of processes of person-perception and self-presentation that allows each to estimate the value and the liklihood of obtaining various outcomes as a result of the relationship.

The effect of these early processes on the development of identity elements is for the most part conservative in that they tend to maintain previous identity elements. They directly or indirectly encourage interaction between persons who are similar both in terms of identity conceptions and relative power. The effect of such ecological processes as differentiation and segregation, along with norms of endogamy, on the patterns of contacts and the emergence of social networks insures similarity between partners in these respects. Similarly, the compromise processes (Backman, 1981; Backman and Secord, 1964) contributes to this state of affairs, functioning as it does to discourage the formation or the continuation of relationships between persons grossly different in power-related attributes. This results in a situation in which, in the long run at least, the contest over identities as a relationship develops is relatively equal and the resultant synthesis symmetrical in reflecting the contribution of each partner.

Where these initial processes affecting the liklihood of initiating a relationship lead to deeper levels of penetration, a variety of processes become involved in the formation of patterns distinctive to that relationship. Here the basic processes are those of identity negotiation, the results of which are influenced in part by what each brings into the relationship. These include identity elements, short-term and long-term plans, resources, dependencies and alternatives, along with interpersonal skills and interpersonal dispositions that influence the ability and motivation of each to modify the behavior of self and other in the direction of an initial synthesis.

This synthesis in turn will be maintained by various processes underlying commitment and institutionalization. It will be changed or possibly destroyed as a result of a variety of internal and external factors that modify or reverse these processes of growth and maintenance. Most of these processes have been at least touched upon in the various treatments of relationship formation that have emerged over the past two decades in the writings of Altman and Taylor, 1973; Backman, 1981; Bolton, 1961; Kelley, 1979; Kelley and Thibaut, 1978; Levinger and Snoek, 1972; Murstein, 1970; Reiss, 1960; Thibaut and Kelley, 1959; Turner, 1978. In the remainder of this section, however, I would like to concentrate on those processes most germane to the understanding of the uniqueness of each personality as a product of relationship formation. The processes central to this topic are those of identity negotiation.

1. Identity Formation: Processes of Accomodation

The process of identity negotiation can be divided into two subprocesses, self-presentation and altercasting (McCall and Simmons, 1978). The process of self-presentation was until recently largely a sociological preoccupation, with psychologists more interested in the related process of self-disclosure. Recently, however, interest in self-disclosure has waned, and psychologists, as I noted earlier (Section II, B), have displayed a marked increase in interest in self-presentation and the related process of self-monitoring (Snyder, 1979). Both of these concepts have been applied by these psychologists in understanding the carrying out of plans of action involving the achievement of particular short-term goals through the manipulation of others' views of the self. Most often the goals involved were to maintain a favorably valued situational identity or the achievement of some other short-term goal. Self-presentation as a basic process of identity negotiation within the context of the growth of an enduring relationship has not been the focus for research on this topic among psychologists. The work by psychologists on self-disclosure (Cozby, 1973) is more germane, since typically it has been studied in the context of longer-term relationships such as those between client and therapist or friends and others with some history of interaction beyond that typical of short-term episodes such as the social psychological experiment. Yet the term *disclosure* in itself implies one major limitation of current conceptions of this process. As the term suggests, there is an implicit assumption that what is disclosed is already there, or is at least thought to be so by the disclosing person. While the self-disclosure process does play a role in the maintenance of existing elements of the self-concept, it also plays an important function in self-creation, in the process of transforming nascent elements of the ideal self into the extant self (Rosenberg, 1979). Furthermore, most of the discussion in the psychological literature on self-disclosure fails to capture the contribution of each of the partners adequately in the joint interpretation of each of their disclosures, that is, in the joint construction of reality produced by this process. As the research on self-disclosure suggests, this occurs through the growth of trust; and as the following discussion of altercasting suggests, through the increasing supporting and interpretive role provided by each partner vis à vis the revelations of the other. This feature of self-disclosure is inherent in the interactional activity in which it occurs, namely, the continuing conversations that constitute a major activity of intimate pairs. Such conversation consist of the recounting of daily episodes, of the recalling of earlier significant life encounters, and the projection into the future of planned encounters. This constant replay or projections into the future before an appreciative audience undoubtedly encourages a bit of touching up or exaggeration that contributes to the building of elements from the ideal self into the extant self. As Berger and Kellner (1964) emphasize, these new elements represent a synthesis of the meanings contributed by both the speaker and the listener. And as the work (Morton, 1978) comparing the conversation between intimates with that between strangers attests, both intimates are very active in the conversation, frequently interrupting, correcting, adding elements, etc. In fact, comparison of partners' reconstructions of each other's biographies is apt to reveal cognitions that reflect the addition of elements beyond those each has self-disclosed that in time have become part of the jointly held view of each other. The result is a truly dialectical synthesis, as Berger and Kellner (1964) have suggested in the case of marriage. Marriage creates a new reality. Each partners' relationship with this new reality is a dialectical one. Each acts upon it in collusion with the other and it acts back upon both of them, wedding their reality.

While self-disclosure did receive, and self-presentation is now receiving, considerable attention from psychologists, the concept of altercasting, except for the work of Kelley (1979), has been almost completely ignored. Like self-presentation, its initial use was heavily freighted with the connotation of manipulation. The process basically was seen by Weinstein and Deutschberger (1963), who first introduced the term, as a tactic employed to bring to bear normative influence on its target. To the degree that persons are successfully cast into a particular role identity they become subject to the obligations of that role vis à vis other role partners. Thus casting another person into the role of friend makes that person amenable to requests for aid. This is essentially a manipulative strategy. Elsewhere we have noted that altercasting may also be a way of rewarding another (Secord and Backman, 1974), the attribution of a favorable identity to another serving as a form of ego enhancement. It also may be employed in the reverse fashion in which the casting of an invidious identity is a form of punishment. This may, as Kelley (1979) has suggested, also be a manipulative strategy. While he does not employ the term *negative altercasting*, he suggests that one interpretation that might be made of the tendency for persons to make invidious dispositional attributions to their partners when the latter are associated with a reduction in the quality of their outcomes is that persons are attempting to change their partners' behaviors. Accusing a partner of being a selfish person is possibly a way of forcing this person to either accept this undesirable identity or behave in a contrary fashion. Here again as in the case of self-presentation I would like to define this process broadly, not in terms of its motivational bases, which are diverse, but simply in terms of the impressions conveyed by the partners of their views of each other. This very general definition provides the basis for a consideration of a variety of motive states and other bases for the exchange of attributions that occurs in the development of a relationship and contributes to the self the elements created or maintained by the relationship. Most of the determinants of the content of these attributions operate both through processes of self-presentation and altercasting, although their influence may be more or less, depending on which process is involved.

Some of these determinants have recently been explored in great detail by psychologists influenced by attribution theory, others are of a more ancient vintage in psychology, and some have been largely of interest to sociologists. The relevant findings suggest that the effects of the growth of attraction in a relationship is to produce attributions directed by each partner to the other that are congruent with the tendencies attribution theorists have associated with self-attributions. Except possibly where negative altercasting occurs in an episode of conflict, positively evaluated outcomes are seen both by actors and role partners attracted to them as internal in origin whereas negative outcomes are viewed by both as situational (Regan, 1978). In this instance charity may begin at home but doesn't stay there. The effect of these tendencies is for persons, most of whom positively value many elements of their existing self-concepts (and when in doubt are susceptible to the self-enhancing definitions of others), to encounter definitions from partners that maintain already existing self-elements, and aid in the creation of new, favorable ones. These findings from attribution research reflect a more basic tendency, that of affective-cognitive consistency, long recognized as a basic principle of social perception (Ostrom, 1969). When one adds to this the general tendency to attribute to others traits having similar valence, the effect is to further the production of supporting definitions of self between members of a pair. Were this not countered by a certain amount of conflict in every relationship, these effects of attraction on self-maintenance and self-enhancement might be even greater. These mutual self-confirming and self-enhancing tendencies of the pair are apt to increase with the growth of their relationship for a number of reasons. First, as both become more dependent on the relationship, they become more motivated to provide the other with these rewarding responses. Second, increasing empathy between the pair that parallels the development of a relationship also can be expected to heighten the potency of vicariously experienced outcomes, encouraging both rewarding and cost-cutting behaviors associated with the confirmation and enhancement of each other's identity and the avoidance of disconfirming attributions.

While these processes of self- and other-attribution provide an explanation for the general positive and consistent tone of the elements created and maintained in relationships based on attraction, they fail to specify much in the way of content. Two additional influences go partway at least in this direction, the influence of central traits and that of master status, which serve to organize further the perception of self and other by members of a pair. A striking instance of parallel developments in psychology and sociology of somewhat similar concepts, but with each reflecting the distinctive focus of each discipline, was the introduction at about the same time of the concept of master status by Hughes (1945) and Asch's early work on person perception demonstrating that the attribution of certain characteristics called central traits powerfully affect the interpretation placed on other traits (1946). Those trait associations that are part of both partners' implicit personality theories influence the attributions made by each to the other. Similarly, how each is categorized in terms of appropriate social identity elements, social statuses, membership groups, social types, etc., delineated by Rosenberg (1979) in his discussion of the structure of self-concept, also encourages the attribution of some characteristics rather than others. Master statuses such as certain prestigious or invidious occupations, race, sex, and deviant statuses have, like central traits, all been shown to influence greatly the character of the attributions that persons make concerning each other and themselves.

A striking example of the effects of central traits has been demonstrated by Snyder, Tanke, and Berscheid (1977). Not only did their study further demonstrate powerful effects of persons' physical attractiveness in influencing the attributions and behavior directed by others to them, but also demonstrated the self-fulfilling prophecy effect (Merton, 1948). Subjects responded to these attributions, at least in a brief experimental episode, in a manner that confirmed these attributions. In still another study, Snyder and Uranowitz (1978) demonstrated that such a master status as the deviant status lesbian influenced later reconstruction by subjects of a target person's characteristics. The stereotypes associated with such master statuses influence memory formation in much the same way as schemata. This is consistent with the arguments of labeling theory

(Becker, 1963). These effects, evidenced in brief experimental episodes involving strangers, are undoubtedly magnified in the context of more long-term relationships.

While the concepts of central trait and particularly master status have tended to emphasize the shared character of attributions, there is evidence also, especially for central traits, of individual differences in the assumed linkages between traits. This suggests that the effect of these perceptual tendencies is to create both consistency and inconsistency between each partner's attributions to self and other in a particular relationship, as well as between these attributions and those encountered from others outside the relationship in question. Other sources of differences in the attributions that partners make to themselves and receive from others include the effects on attribution processes of short- and long-term plans. Included also in the case of lovers are what have been termed images of the ideal mate, which may in part be a reflection of unrealized elements of the ideal self as well as characteristics of role models and other influences related to the unique biographies of each person.

Finally our early discussion of role identities should be kept in mind. Just as most social roles are reciprocal in that they consist of interlocking and coordinated behavior between partners, the same is the case for role identities. A part of persons' role identities, in addition to the imagining of their own behavior, is the imagined confirming response of the other. The latter is an important and unique source of imputed identity elements.

While the emphasis in the preceding discussion for the most part has been on processes of accommodation leading to mutual support and maintenance of relationship-based identities, a variety of other processes and sources of differences in self-definition help account for the modifications in each self as a result of processes of conflict as the details of a relationship are hammered out.

2. Processes of Conflict and the Negotiation of Identities

Two approaches to identity negotiation in relationships throw some light on identity elements arising in this fashion. The first, which draws heavily on the sociological tradition, is a theory of role negotiation based on ideas developed by McCall and Simmons (1966) and modified by the addition of elements from theories of power and social influence by Secord and Backman (1974). A second approach is that of Kelley and Thibaut's (Kelley, 1979; Kelley and Thibaut, 1978) recent revision of their theory of interdependence. The latter investigators have conceptualized the structure of interdependence in terms of three levels. At the lowest, or first, level the structure consists of the stable patterns, routines, and combinations of behavior that constitute the day-to-day activities of the pair. The second, or normative, level of structure consists of the norms and shared understandings that constitute the somewhat unique role structure of the relationship. The third level consists of each partner's personality, attitudes, and elements of self that are embedded in the relationship. It is the third level that is of primary concern here. Thibaut and Kelley place particular emphasis on interpersonal dispositions, which are general tendencies on the part of persons in a relationship to resolve problems of interdependence that influence the outcomes that each experiences in a particular manner. These dispositions have a normative quality based on internalized rules and personally held values as to how the person is to weigh his outcomes and future obectives against those of his partner. As such they constitute central elements of that portion of the ideal self that Rosenberg (1979) has labeled the moral self. These tendencies, in part a product of socialization in previous relationships, in part an outcome of identity negotiation and attribution processes operating within the relationship, are particularly important identity elements. Like other elements of the self they are both forces and products of the twin developments of identities and relationships. Kelley (1979) and Braiker and Kelley (1979) have particularly emphasized the role of conflict in the production of identity elements. Disagreements at the behavioral level spread to the normative level when partners attempt to resolve problems of outcome interdependence by appeals to existing rules or the creation of new ones. When this fails, the conflict tends to spread upward to the personal level where attributions concerning the interpersonal dispositions of each are negotiated. Where such negotiation leads to a change, where one party as an example in rejecting the attribution of selfishness or dominance adopts a more conciliatory concern for the other partner's outcomes, changes are instigated at lower levels. Distributive rules such as those of equity or other notions of fairess may become more salient in the relationship, and at the behavioral level there may follow a change in the distribution of labor between the partners.

Secord and Backman's (Backman, 1981; Secord and Backman, 1974) theory of role negotiation includes a similar emphasis on the dialectical production of identity elements which in turn influence the behavior of the interacting pair, but the theory proceeds from a more sociological stance, by tying conceptions of identity to the social structure. Starting with the concept of role identity developed by McCall and Simmons described earlier, Secord and Backman view the negotiation process as influenced by a number of personal, social, and situational factors. Role identities, it will be recalled, are the person's somewhat idealized views of himself in particular role relationships. While tying identity to role and thus underscoring the contribution of shared categories of meaning and their cultural and subcultural origins to the content of the identities that persons create for themselves, the theory still allows for considerable variation on these cultural themes. The unique role configuration and its identity counterparts for each person in a relationship are seen to be the result of processes of identity negotiation as influenced by a variety of constraints. In addition to the content of role identities that reflect each partner's socialization experiences, these constraints include situational demands, properties of the social systems in which the roles are embedded that affect the intrusion of other roles, the influence of third parties on the bargaining process, and the power of each partner as determined by their respective resources, dependencies, and alternatives.

In addition to these factors identified earlier (Secord and Backman, 1974) two other, more recent additions to a theory of role negotiation are included here. These consist of interpersonal skills, including those related to assessing the constraints and opportunities in the interpersonal environment accurately, and Kelley's interpersonal dispositions arising out of previous socialization experiences, both of which will affect the ability and motivation to affect the emerging role structure and resultant identities of the partners.

Situational demands and opportunities entering into role negotiations and identity formation include situational features such as those that provide an opportunity for a particular kind of performance. These may be short-lived or episodic in character, as when temporary illness of one partner requires or allows a more solicitous version of the friendship or marital role. They also may be of a more long-run character, as when the wife's employment or a birth requires a new division of labor.

The latter example also illustrates another set of influences listed above, namely, the intrusion of other roles and corresponding identities. Role systems are never so well-integrated that persons are not subject to conflicting and competing role expectations stemming from their simultaneous commitment to more than one role.

Third parties are also involved in role identity negotiation, both directly where they intervene on behalf of one or the other party, or indirectly where they act as sounding boards and sources of advice as to how a person should behave in a particular relationship.

Enmeshed in these sets of influences, persons work out their respective role identities in each of their relationships, the product of such negotiations reflecting the above constraints and opportunities as well as each person's exercise of power, and its effectiveness. The latter depends in part on the resources, dependencies, and alternatives, but only in part. There exists considerable slippage for a number of reasons. First, persons may not perceive accurately their own and their partner's resources, dependencies, and alternatives. Many of the tactics of interpersonal negotiation revolve around altering these perceptions. Second, as suggested above, persons are influenced by interpersonal dispositions in the degree to which they exercise to their advantage the full extent of their power. These tendencies reflect the effects of internalized standards and images of self, agreed-upon rules previously worked out in the relationship, and the increasing empathic concern for the partner's outcomes as dependency develops between the members of the pair. Yet differences in power, predictable from an analysis of resources, dependencies, and alternatives, do help account for some of the unique features of each relationship. One study of the division of labor between married and cohabiting couples (Stafford, Backman, and Dibona, 1977) has demonstrated this. Among the married women in this study, those whose dating history and degree of commitment to the relationship suggested few alternatives and greater dependency conformed more to the traditional division of labor and performed at a higher level. However, the effects of power differences between members of the pair was less than the influence of role models on the role identities each brought into the relationship. The couple's division of labor appeared more influenced by the cultural form of the relationship exhibited by their parental families.

While this study underscores the importance of social structural and cultural factors in determining the content of role identities, I have argued elsewhere (Secord and Backman, 1974) that identity negotiation at the micro level does feed back on the macro structure in the historical long run, modifying the culturally prescribed and structurally allocated identity elements. In fact, the current breakdown in the traditional division of labor within the family illustrates the continuous effects that processes at the macro and micro levels of society have on each other. Changes that occur at the macro level in a society have the effect of changing power at the micro level which feeds back and modifies the cultural forms that are one of the determinants of role identities. Thus, a variety of changes in Western society, in which the changing economic role of the wife has been most important, has significantly increased the resources and alternatives of women in marriages and decreased their dependencies, while other social changes, such as increasing impersonality outside the family, have had the effect of increasing the male's dependency on the relationship. This, along with certain ideological movements that were both a product and a cause of these changes, has as a result of countless instances of negotiation on the micro level of analysis gradually modified the cultural forms for the marriage relationship and the role identities reflecting these forms. These changes should be reflected in the type of identity elements negotiated in later generations.

Our theory so far has emphasized how persons in the process of constructing a relationship create, support, and modify identity elements. The resultant synthesis reflects both forces toward accommodation and these toward conflict. Tendencies toward accommodation are rooted in the growth of attraction and the merging of selves that result in motivation affecting processes of attribution, self-disclosure, and altercasting, in a manner that facilitates mutual support and self- and other-enhancement. At the same time forces toward conflict inherent in interdependency and a certain inevitable amount of noncorrespondence of outcomes lead to modification of existing elements of identity and the joint construction of new ones, essentially as a result of the interplay of the processes of power and social influences within the relationship.

3. Congruency Processes Revisited

While the present focus has been on processes of self-creation and mainte- nance that have been of later concern among social psychologists, earlier work on other relevant processes should also be mentioned in any discussion of the role of social psychological processes in the development of personality. These include processes such as cognitive restructuring, selective evaluation, selective interaction, response evocation, and social comparison processes, earlier high- lighted by interpersonal congruency theory (Secord and Backman, 1961). While earlier reviews of the literature (Secord and Backman, 1965) provided support for the operation of these processes primarily in the service of maintaining existing elements of self, subsequent research provides further evidence for their operation not only in the service of self-maintenance but self-enhancement as well. Later work on the role of self-schemata in the processing of information about the self support earlier findings subsumed under the notion of cognitive reorganization by considering how persons selectively attend, accept, and recall information (Kuiper and Rogers, 1979; Markus, 1977; Rogers, Kuiper, and Kirker, 1977). Swann and Read (1981) have demonstrated in a series of experi- ments that persons seek out or at least spend more time attending to self-confirm- ing information, attempt to elicit or evoke self-confirming responses from others, and recall to a greater degree self-confirming over self-disconfirming informa- tion. Shrauger (1975) in a review of relevant literature concludes that persons are more apt to accept evaluations of their competence when these are consistent with their own self-assessments. His evaluation of findings concerning affective reactions to information about the self provides support for the idea that persons not only are attracted to and attempt to associate with those who see them as they see themselves (Backman and Secord, 1962), but where possible see them in a more favorable light. Greenwald's (1980) review also underscores the conserva- tive and self-enhancing tendencies in human cognition.

Interpersonal congruency theory also emphasized the role of social compari- son in self-maintenance. Persons tended to select others and to perceive in them characteristics that by comparison confirmed elements of their self-concepts. In one early study in support of this idea (Secord, Backman, and Eachus, 1964) it was found that when participants were led to believe that they were high in a trait they considered undersirable, this increased their estimate of the degree to which this trait was characteristic of their friends. The steady accumulation of literature on social comparison supports this earlier notion of a general tendency to use social comparison in the service of self-confirmation and self-enhancement (Suls, 1977; Tesser, 1980; Tesser and Campbell, 1980).

F.   SELF AND BEHAVIOR

Our emphasis on identity negotiation in the preceding discussion has been prompted by our objective of emphasizing a sociological approach that views the self as the central component of personality. We would be remiss, however, in not looking at an issue of much greater concern for psychologists in recent years, namely, the relation between self and behavior, the latter being more central to psychological conceptions of personality. A wide variety of issues concerning this relationship are currently being explored by psychologists. Some lines of research have focused on the manner in which information about behavior is employed by persons in knowing about themselves (Bem, 1972; Greenwald, 1980; Markus, 1977). Others have focused on the situational and individual difference variables that determine whether persons will behave consistently with various elements of self (Scheier and Carver, 1981), the ideal self (Duval and Wicklund, 1972), and the presented self (Schlenker, in press) among others. Finally, a number of investigators have addressed the relation between types of performance and related concepts of ability (Ballif, 1981; Coopersmith and Gilbert, 1981) as well as self-efficacy (Bandura, 1982). While obviously this work is relevant to the present line of argument in that it has contributed to our understanding of the dynamic relationship between self and behavior, I do not attempt to discuss it here. However, in keeping with the character of this chapter in emphasizing the sociological perspective, two comments regarding this litera-ture will be made. Researchers concerned with the relationship between self and behavior, particularly where this involves conformity to internalized standards of conduct, should keep in mind the points emphasized in the previous sections of this chapter. First, the relationship between self and behavior of this type is mediated by persons' definitions of situations. A failure to find a close relation-ship between elements of the ideal self and behavior can be expected where individual and situational variables allow for the construction of accounts, which as a part of a person's situational definition permit behavior–self inconsistency. Self–behavior consistency is of course also influenced by situated identity con-cerns as discussed in Section I, C. However, as we noted there, the increasing attention to the effects of self-presentation in experimental settings by psychol-ogists lessens the need for caution on this score. Second, there exists a certain amount of conceptual confusion in these areas of research that stems from the failure to develop an agreed-upon structural taxonomy of the self. Fortunately, such a taxonomy, reflecting in part an earlier attempt by James (1890) and subsequent work in the symbolic interactionist tradition, has recently been of-fered by Rosenberg (1979).

The neglect of such a taxonomy undoubtedly reflects the general ignoring by most psychologists of the determinants of the content of the self, particularly as affected directly and indirectly by the social structure.

G. THE INFLUENCE OF THE SOCIAL STRUCTURE ON THE
    STRUCTURE AND CONTENTS OF THE SELF-CONCEPT

The influence of the social structure on the self has been a continuing interest of sociologists concerned with research on the self, both in terms of role learning (Heiss, 1981) and also in terms of the relative influences of various roles on the structure of the self. Both Stryker (1968) and McCall and Simmons (1966) suggested over a decade ago that various identities are organized in hierarchies of salience that influence the liklihood that a given identity will be enacted in a given situation. More recently, Turner (1978) has presented a rather detailed theory similarly concerned with the organization of role identities within the self, but with emphasis less on the episodic alterations of identity portrayal stressed by these previous writers and more on role–person merger. By the latter term Turner refers to the extent that attitudes, developed as the expression of one role, carry over into other situations, coloring the way other roles are played. This tendency, the opposite to role compartmentalization, is seen as resulting from both interindividual tendencies that are reflected in the manner other role partners tend to see the person, and intraindividual tendencies, largely as they lead to the preferences for some identities over others. While the theory needs considerable empirical testing, many of the propositions are consistent with attribution theory. Fortunately the measurement of role merger as well as the relation between cultural stereotypes of roles, individual role images, and relevant aspects of behavior has been facilitated by the development of a measurement procedure by Burke (1980). The development of such techniques, which combine measurement of the semantic differential type with discriminant function analysis, should hasten empirical exploration.

   A final area of sociological research relevant to personality theory concerns the effects of social structures and processes at the macro level of sociological analysis. These, originally studied under the rubric of *culture and personality* include the effects of such macro social structures as societies, types of organizations, social classes, racial and ethnic groups, and processes at this level such as industrialization, urbanization, and social mobility. The work of Rosenberg (1979) on the effects of age, sex, and race on children's self concepts; the work of Kohn, Schooler, and others (Kohn and Schooler, 1978; Pearlin and Kohn, 1966) on the effects of social class and related work environments on psychological functioning; and the work of Inkeles and Smith (1974) on the effects of modernization are illustrative of this area of research. All of these researchers have traced the linkage between macro structures and processes, often mediated by the types of micro processes that we have been examining in more detail here, and a variety of personality variables. As House (1981) in a recent review of this literature suggests, many of these findings have yet to be integrated adequately into the general social psychological literature. Yet the social psychological contribution to personality theory will remain incomplete until this is done.

H.   THE DISSOLUTION OF RELATIONSHIPS AND IDENTITY
     CHANGE

The discussion in this section has drawn upon a theory of relationship development to develop further a theory of identity formation. A basic premise underlying this attempt is the view that relationship formation and identity formation are both the source and the product of each other. The emphasis throughout has been on the development and maintenance of identity elements and the relationship of these elements of self to behavior, although the treatment of the latter part of the theory has been brief, and the emphasis has been on some relevant lines of research and theory from sociology.

The last part of the present discussion of this theory dealing with the implications of relationship dissolution and identity change will also be brief. This brevity is necessitated by the fact that the empirical groundwork has largely yet to be developed, although the growing interest in the dissolution of relationships should provide the basis for additional developments in this direction. It would be convenient if we could sum up this portion of the theory with the assertion that just as identity formation and relationship formation go hand in hand, so relationship dissolution and identity destruction are similarly related. The growing body of research concerning adjustment to divorce and separation (Levinger and Moles, 1979; Weiss, 1975) does suggest that considerable identity disorganization accompanies the dissolution of pair relationships, particularly if they have lasted for several years. Yet identity destruction is far from complete.

It can be hypothesized that the previously discussed processes that contributed to the development of the relationship and the identities embedded therein will in a somewhat reverse fashion undermine both. Thus the process of self-disclosure and the accompanying motivation to support and accept present or nascent elements of self will diminish. At the same time the tendency to attribute negatively evaluated identity elements to the other partner, which accompanies a reduction in outcomes associated with conflict in a declining relationship, will further the process of identity destruction and relationship dissolution.

Persons tend to cope with these changes in part through the formation of new relationships and probably also by shifting their dependency to other already-existing ones. My arguments so far suggest the choice of any new relationship will be influenced by the personality residues from the declining relationship. Yet at the same time it would be rare to find, given the dialectic character of each relationship, that any new relationship would duplicate the old and thus maintain unchanged the earlier identity elements. The kinds of changes and their sources of identity will not only be a product of accommodation and conflict and the vicissitudes of the processes of identity negotiation previously described, but also of behavioral change and changes in interpersonal networks that typically accompany the dissolution of a central relationship such as that of marriage

(Weiss, 1975). These changes, as they interact with the accompanying relationship dissolution, further extent the transformation of identity elements.

V. Summing Up

This chapter began with the suggestion that the preoccupation with the possibility of a convergence between the sociological and psychological traditions in social psychology was part of a paradigmatic shift within the latter in the direction of the former. I hope this chapter has made a case for the advantages to be gained from such a shift and has also underscored the fact that there is some distance yet to be traveled.

While the idea of persons as active agents seems fully accepted by psychologists, a full appreciation of their active role in the joint construction of the meanings of situations, including the identities ascribed to themselves and others, has not yet been fully realized. Also the role of cultural and social structural influences on the construction of meaning has been paid insufficient attention. This can be seen in the three areas of research focused upon in this chapter. There we noted that while psychologists have succeeded in reinventing situated identity theory, certain implications of the sociological origin of the theory are not fully realized. In particular, the existence of shared meanings, including norms, as the basis for self- and other-attribution is less explicit. As a result, the identity implications of various responses in experimental settings as these interact with features of the experimental scenario and relevant norms are apt to be missed, along with ways for controlling these effects.

In the second empirical area, the study of moral behavior, the social construction of meaning is recognized; however, what is underestimated is the human ability to construct meaning to one's advantage. Further, psychologists have failed to view such constructions as causes of action rather than as after-the-fact remedial forms of self-presentation. This causal interpretation has a long history in sociology and is not only consistent with recent developments in cognitive psychology and social learning theory but also suggests further avenues of research on the effects of individual differences, situational variables, and social structural factors on conformity to norms.

The third focus on recent research on relationship formation and identity creation, while briefly reviewing and updating research concerned with self-maintenance processes and the relation between self and behavior, emphasized the dialectical processes of identity creation observed in the context of developing relationships based on attraction. This treatment not only underscored a basic sociological premise concerning the emergent properties of interaction but also directed attention to cultural and social structural sources of identity elements that tend to be ignored by psychologists. While some in psychology may regard the study of these influences of little value, since their content shifts with the vicissitudes of history, I have suggested that social psychology can play a role in explaining this content which is of importance in understanding the behavior of persons in any historic epoch. I hope, in making more explicit the sociological premises consistent with the current drift of research and theory within the psychological tradition in social psychology, that the movement toward a fully interdisciplinary study of social behavior will be accelerated. If there is anything to the notion that one's journey is shortened by knowing where one is going, this should occur.

REFERENCES

Abelson, R. P. Script processing in attitude formation and decision making. In J. S. Carroll and J. W. Payne (Eds.), *Cognition and social behavior*. Hillsdale, New Jersey: Erlbaum, 1976, 33–45.

Alexander, C. N., and Knight, G. Situated identities and social psychological experimentation. *Sociometry*, 1971, **34**, 65–82.

Alexander, C. N., Weil, H. G. Players, persons, and purposes: Situation meaning and the prisoner's dilemma game. *Sociometry*, 1969, **32**, 121–144.

Alexander, C. N., and Wiley, M. G. Situated activity and identity formation. In M. Rosenberg and H. R. Turner (Eds.), *Social psychology: Sociological perspectives*. New York: Basic Books, 1981, 269–289.

Altman, A., and Taylor, D. A. *Social penetration: The development of interpersonal relationships*. New York: Holt, Rinehart and Winston, 1973.

Arkin, R. M. Self presentation. In D. M. Wegner and R. R. Vallacher (Eds.), *The self in social psychology*. New York: Oxford University Press, 1980, 158–182.

Asch, S. E. Forming impressions of personality. *Journal of Abnormal and Social Psychology*, 1946, **41**, 258–290.

Asch, S. E. Studies in independence and conformity: A minority of one against a unanimous majority. *Psychological Monographs*, 1956, **70**, (9, Whole No. 416).

Austin, J. L. *Philosophical papers*. London: Oxford University Press, 1961.

Backman, C. W. Explorations in psycho-ethics: The warranting of judgments. In R. Harre (Ed.), *Life sentences: Aspects of the social role of language*. London: Wiley, 1976, 98–108.

Backman, C. W. Epilogue: A new paradigm. In G. P. Ginsburg (Ed.), *Emerging strategies in social psychological research*. London: Wiley, 1979, 289–303.

Backman, C. W. Attraction in interpersonal relations. In M. Rosenberg and R. H. Turner (Eds.), *Social psychology: Sociological perspectives*. New York: Basic Books, 1981, 235–268.

Backman, C. W. Identity, self presentation, and the resolution of moral dilemmas: Towards a social psychological theory of moral behavior. In B. Schlenker (Ed.), *Self and identity: Presentation of self in social life*. New York: McGraw Hill, in press.

Backman, C. W., and Secord, P. F. Liking, selective interaction, and misperception in congruent interpersonal relations. *Sociometry*, 1962, **25**, 231–235.

Backman, C. W., and Secord, P. F. The compromise process and the affect structure of groups. *Human Relations*, 1964, **17**(1), 19–22.

Ball, R. A. An empirical exploration of neutralization theory. *Criminologica*, 1966, **4**, 22–32.

Ball, R. A. and Lilly, J. R. Juvenile delinquency in a rurban county. *Criminology, 1971*, **9**, 69–85.

Ballif, B. L. The significance of the self-concept in the knowledge society. In M. D. Lynch, A. A. Norem-Hebeisen, and K. Gergen (Eds.), *Self concept: Advances in theory and research.* Cambridge, Massachusetts: Ballinger, 1981, 251–260.

Bandura, A. *Social learning theory.* Englewood Cliffs, New Jersey: Prentice-Hall, 1977.

Bandura, A. The self system in reciprocal determinism. *American Psychologist*, 1978, **33**, 344–358.

Bandura, A. Self-efficacy mechanism in human agency. *American Psychologist*, 1982, **37**, 122–147.

Bandura, A., Underwood, B. and Fromson, M. E. Disinhibition of aggression through diffusion of responsibility and dehumanization. *Journal of Research in Personality*, 1975, **9**, 253–269.

Becker, H. *Outsiders.* New York: Free Press, 1963.

Bem, D. J. Self perception theory. In L. Berkowitz (Ed.), *Advances in experimental social psychology*, (Vol. 6). New York: Academic Press, 1972, 1–62.

Bentler, P. M., and Speckart, G. Attitudes "cause" behaviors: A structural equation analysis. *Journal of Personality and Social Psychology*, 1981, **40**, 226–238.

Berger, P., and Kellner, H. Marriage and the construction of reality: An exercise in the microsociology of knowledge. Diogenes, 1964, **46** (summer), 1–24.

Berger, P., and Luckmann, T. *The social construction of reality.* New York: Doubleday/Anchor, 1967.

Berkowitz, L., and Daniels, L. R. Affecting the salience of the social responsibility norm: Effects of past help on the response to dependency relationships. *Journal of Abnormal and Social Psychology*, 1964, **68**, 275–281.

Berkowitz, L., and Friedman, P. Some social class differences in helping behavior. *Journal of Personality and Social Psychology*, 1967, **5**, 217–235.

Blank, T. S. Two psychologies: Is segregation inevitable or acceptable? *Personality and Social Psychology Bulletin*, 1978, **4**, 553–556.

Bolton, C. D. Mate selection as the development of a relationship. *Journal of Marriage and Family Living*, 1961, **23**, 234–240.

Bradley, G. W. Self-serving biases in the attribution process: A reexamination of the fact or fiction question. *Journal of Personality and Social Psychology*, 1978, **36**, 56–71.

Braiker, H. B., and Kelley, H. H. Conflict in the development of close relationships. In R. L. Burgess and T. L. Hutson (Eds.), *Social exchange in developing relationships*. New York: Academic Press, 1979, 135–168.

Burke, P. The self: Measurement requirements from an interactionist perspective. *Social Psychology Quarterly*, 1980, **43**, 18–29.

Buss, A. H. *Self consciousness and social anxiety.* San Francisco, California: Freeman, 1980.

Cartwright, D. Contemporary social psychology in historical perspective. *Social Psychology Quarterly*, 1979, **42**, 82–93.

Carson, R. C. *Interaction concepts of personality.* Chicago, Illinois: Aldine, 1969.

Cooley, C. H. *Human nature and the social order.* New York: Charles Scribner's Sons, 1902.

Coopersmith, S., and Gilbert, R. Behavioral academic self-esteem. In M. D. Lynch, A. A. Norem-Hebeisen and K. Gergen (Eds.), *Self concept: Advances in theory and research.* Cambridge, Massachusetts: Ballinger, 1981, 237–250.

Cozby, P. C. Self disclosure: A literature review. *Psychological Bulletin*, 1973, **79**, 73–91.

Cressey, D. R. *Other people's money.* Glencoe, Illinois: Free Press, 1953.

Darley, J. M., Klossen, E. C., and Zanna, M. P. Intentions and their contexts in the moral judgments of children and adults. *Child Development*, 1978, **49**, 66–74.

Darley, J. M., and Latané, B. Bystander intervention in emergencies: Diffusion of responsibility. *Journal of Personality and Social Psychology*, 1968, **8**, 377–383.

Darley, J. M., and Latané, B. Norms and normative behavior: Field studies of social interdependence. In J. Macaulay and L. Berkowitz (Eds.), *Altruism and helping behavior: Some social psychological studies of some antecedents and consequences.* New York: Academic Press, 1970, 83–101.

Diener, E. Deindividualism: The absence of self awareness and self regulation. In P. Paulas (Ed.), *The psychology of group influence.* Hillsdale, New Jersey: Lawrence-Erlbaum Associates, 1980, 209–242.

Duval, S., and Wicklund, R. A. *A theory of objective self awareness.* New York: Academic Press, 1972.

Edwards, A. L. *The social desirability variable in personality assessment and research.* New York: Holt, Rinehart and Winston, 1957.

Goffman, E. *The presentation of self in everyday life.* New York: Doubleday/Anchor, 1959.

Greenwald, A. G. The totalitarian ego: Fabrication and revision of personal history. *American Psychologist,* 1980, **35,** 603–618.

Heider, F. *The psychology of interpersonal relations.* New York: Wiley, 1958.

Heiss, J. Social roles. In M. Rosenberg and R. H. Turner (Eds.), *Social psychology: Sociological perspectives.* New York: Basic Books, 1981, 94–129.

Hoffman, M. L. Moral development. In R. H. Mussen (Ed.), *Carmichael's manual of child psychology* (3rd ed.), Vol. 2. New York: Wiley, 1970, 261–360.

Hoffman, M. L. Is altruism part of human nature? *Journal of Personality and Social Psychology,* 1981, **40,** 121–137.

House, J. S. The three faces of social psychology. *Sociometry,* 1977, **40,** 61–77.

House, J. S. Social structure and personality. In M. Rosenberg and R. H. Turner (Eds.), *Social psychology: Sociological perspectives.* New York: Basic Books, 1981, 525–561.

Hughes, E. C. Dilemmas and contradictions of status. *American Journal of Sociology,* 1945, **50,** 353–359.

Inkeles, A. and Smith, D. *Becoming modern: Industrial change in six developing countries.* Cambridge Massachusetts: Harvard University Press, 1974.

James, W. *The principles of psychology,* (Vol. 1). New York: Holt, 1890.

Jellison, J. M. and Green, J. A self presentational approach to the fundamental attribution error: The norm of internality. *Journal of Personality and Social Psychology,* 1981, **40,** 643–649.

Kelley, H. H. *Personal relationships: Their structure and processes.* Hillsdale, New Jersey: Erlbaum, 1979.

Kelley, H. H., and Thibaut, J. W. *Interpersonal relations: A theory of interdependence.* New York: Wiley, 1978.

Kohn, M. L., and Schooler, C. The reciprocal effects of the substantive complexity of work and intellectual flexibility: A longitudinal assessment. *American Journal of Sociology,* 1978, **84,** 24–52.

Kuiper, N. A., and Rogers, T. B. The encoding of personal information: Self-other differences. *Journal of Personality and Social Psychology,* 1979, **37,** 499–514.

Langer, E. J., and Abelson, R. P. The semantics of asking a favor: How to succeed in getting help without dying. *Journal of Personality and Social Psychology,* 1972, **24,** 26–32.

Latané, B., and Darley, J. M. Group inhibition of bystander intervention in emergencies. *Journal of Personality and Social Psychology,* 1968, **10,** 215–221.

Latane, B., and Rodin, J. A lady in distress: Inhibiting effects of friends and strangers in bystander intervention. *Journal of Experimental Social Psychology,* 1969, **5,** 189–202.

Leary, T. *Interpersonal diagnosis of personality.* New York: Ronald, 1957.

L'Ecuyer, R. *Le concept de soi.* Paris Presses Universitaires de France, 1978.

Levinger, G., and Moles, O. C. (Eds.). *Divorce and separation: Context, causes, and consequences.* New York: Basic Books, 1979.

Levinger, G., and Snoek, J. D. *Attraction in relationship: A new look at interpersonal attraction.* Morristown, New Jersey: General Learning Press, 1972.

Lewis, M., and Rosenblum, L. A. (Eds.) *The effects of the infant on its caregiver.* New York: Wiley, 1974.

Lofland, J. *Identities and deviance.* Englewood Cliffs, New Jersey: Prentice-Hall, 1969.

Lynch, M. D., Norem-Hebeisen, A. A., and Gergen, K. (Eds.) *Self concept: Advances in theory and research.* Cambridge, Massachusetts: Ballinger Publishing Company, 1981.

Macauley, J., and Berkowitz, L. *Altruism and helping behavior: Social psychological studies of some antecedents and consequences.* New York: Academic Press, 1970.

Mantell, D. M., and R. Panzarella. Obedience and responsibility. *The British Journal of Social and Clinical Psychology,* 1976, **15,** 239–246.

Markus, H. Self-schemata and processing information about the self. *Journal of Personality and Social Psychology,* 1977, **35,** 63–78.

Marlowe, D., and Gergen, K. J. Personality and social interaction. In G. Lindzey and E. Aronson (Eds.), *Handbook of social psychology,* (Vol. 3). Reading, Massachusetts: Addison-Wesley Press, 1969, 590–665.

McCall, G. J., and Simmons, J. L. *Identities and interactions.* New York: Free Press, 1966.

McCall, G. J., and Simmons, J. L. *Identities and interactions* (2nd ed.). New York: Free Press, 1978.

Mead, G. H. *Mind, self and society.* Chicago: The University of Chicago Press, 1934.

Merton, R. K. The self fulfilling prophecy. *Antioch Review,* 1948, **8,** 193–210.

Milgram, S. Behavioral study of obedience. *Journal of Abnormal and Social Psychology,* 1963, **67,** 371–378.

Milgram, S. *Obedience to authority.* New York: Harper and Row, 1974.

Minor, W. W. The neutralization of criminal offense. *Criminology,* 1980, **18,** 103–120.

Mischel, T. (Ed.) *The self.* Totowa, New Jersey: Rowman and Littlefield, 1977.

Mixon, D. Instead of deception. *Journal for the Theory of Social Behavior,* 1972, **2,** 145–177.

Morton, T. L. Intimacy and reciprocity of exchange: A comparison of spouses and strangers. *Journal of Personality and Social Psychology,* 1978, **36,** 72–81.

Muir, D. E., and Weinstein, E. A. The social debt: An investigation of lower class and middle class norms of social obligation. *American Sociological Review,* 1962, **27,** 532–539.

Murstein, B. A. Stimulus-value-role: A theory of marital choice. *Journal of marriage and the family,* 1970, **32,** 465–481.

Ostrom, T. M. The relationship between the affective, behavioral, and cognitive components of attitudes. *Journal of Experimental Social Psychology,* 1969, **5,** 12–30.

Pearlin, L. I., and Kohn, M. L. Social class, occupation and parental values. *American Sociological Review,* 1966, **31,** 466–479.

Piliavin, I. M., Rodin, M. J., and Piliavin, J. A. Good samaritanism: An underground phenomenon? *Journal of Personality and Social Psychology,* 1969, **13,** 289–299.

Prus, R. C. Resisting designation: An extension of attribution theory into a negotiated context. *Sociological Inquiry,* 1975, **45,** 3–14.

Quinn, C. O., Robinson, I. E., and Balkwell, J. W. A synthesis of two social psychologies. *Symbolic Interaction,* 1980, **3,** 59–88.

Redl, F., and Wineman, D. *Children who hate.* Glencoe, Illinois: The Free Press, 1951.

Regan, D. T. Attributional aspects of interpersonal attraction: In J. H. Harvey, W. J. Ickes, and R. F. Kidd (Eds.), *New Directions in Attribution Research,* (Vol. 2). Hillsdale, New Jersey: Erlbaum, 1978, 207–233.

Reiss, I. L. Toward a sociology of the heterosexual love relationship. *Marriage and Family Living,* 1960, **22,** 139–144.

Reigel, K. F. The dialectics of human development. *American Psychologist*, 1976, **31**, 689–700.

Rogers, T. B., Kuiper, N. A., and Kirker, W. S. Self-reference and the encoding of personal information. *Journal of Personality and Social Psychology*, 1977, **35**, 677–688.

Rosenberg, M. *Conceiving the self*. New York: Basic Books, 1979.

Rosenberg, M. The self-concept: Social product and social force. In M. Rosenberg and R. H. Turner (Eds.), *Social Psychology: Sociological perspectives*. New York: Basic Books, 1981, 593–624.

Rosenberg, M., and Kaplan, H. B. (Eds.) *Social psychology of the self concept*. Arlington Heights, Illinois: Harlan Davidson, 1982.

Rubin, Z. *Liking and loving: An introduction to social psychology*. New York: Holt, Rinehart and Winston, 1973.

Sagatun, S. J., and Knudson, J. H. The interactive effect of attributor role and event on attribution. Paper presented at the annual meeting of the American Sociological Association, September, 1977.

Schank, R. C., and Abelson, R. P. *Scripts, plans, goals, and understanding: An inquiry into human knowledge structures*. Hillsdale, New Jersey: Erlbaum, 1977.

Scheier, M. F., and Carver, C. S. Private and public aspects of self. In L. Wheeler (Ed.), *Review of personality and social psychology* (Vol. 2). Beverly Hills, California: Sage Publications, 1981, 189–216.

Schlenker, B. R. *Impression management: The self-concept, social identity, and interpersonal relations*. Monterey, California: Brooks/Cole, 1980.

Schlenker, B. R. Translating actions into attitudes: An identity-analytic approach to the explanation of attitudes. In L. Berkowitz (Ed.), *Advances in experimental social psychology*, (Vol. 15). New York: Academic Press, 1982, 194–247.

Schwartz, S. H. Words, deeds and perception of consequences and responsibilities in action situations. *Journal of Personality and Social Psychology*, 1968, **10**, 232–242. (a)

Schwartz, S. H. Awareness of consequences and the influence of moral norms on interpersonal behavior. *Sociometry*, 1968, **31**, 355–369. (b)

Schwartz, S. H. Normative explanations of helping behavior: A critique, proposal, and empirical test. *Journal of Experimental Social Psychology*, 1973, **9**, 349–364.

Schwartz, S. H. Normative influences on altruism. In L. Berkowitz (Ed.), *Advances in experimental social psychology*, (Vol. 10). New York: Academic Press, 1977, 222–279.

Scott, M. B., and Lyman, S. M. Accounts. *American Sociological Review*, 1968, **33**, 46–62.

Secord, P. F., and Backman, C. W. Personality theory and the problem of stability and change in individual behavior: An interpersonal approach. *Psychological Review*, 1961, **68**, 21–32.

Secord, P. F. and Backman, C. W. Interpersonal approach to personality. In B. H. Maher (Ed.), *Progress in experimental personality research*. (Vol. 2). New York: Academic Press, 1965, 91–125.

Secord, P. F., and Backman, C. W. Social Psychology (1st Ed.). New York: McGraw-Hill Book Company, 1964.

Secord, P. T., and Backman, C. W. Social Psychology (2nd Ed.). New York: McGraw-Hill Book Company, 1974.

Secord, P. F., Backman, C. W., and Eachus, H. T. Effects of imbalance in the self concept on the perception of persons. *Journal of Abnormal and Social Psychology*, 1964, **68**, 442–446.

Sherif, M. *The psychology of social norms*. New York: Harper, 1936.

Shrauger, J. S. Responses to evaluation as a function of initial self-perceptions. *Psychological Bulletin*, 1975, **82**, 581–596.

Shrauger, J. S., and Schoeneman, T. J. Symbolic interactionist view of self-concept: Through the looking glass darkly. *Psychological Bulletin*, 1979, **86**, 549–573.

Snyder, M. Self monitoring processes. In L. Berkowitz (Ed.), *Advances in experimental social psychology*, (Vol. 12). New York: Academic Press, 1979, 86–128.

Snyder, M., Tanke, E., and Berscheid, E. Social perception and interpersonal behavior: On the self-fulfilling nature of social stereotypes. *Journal of Personality and Social Psychology,* 1977, **35,** 103–122.

Snyder, M., and Uranowitz, S. W. Reconstructing the past: Some cognitive consequences of person perception. *Journal of Personality and Social Psychology,* 1978, **36,** 941–950.

Stafford, R., Backman, E., and Dibona, P. The division of labor among cohabiting and married couples. *Journal of Marriage and the Family,* 1977, **39,** 43–57.

Staub, E. Helping a distressed person: Social, personality, and stimulus determinants. In L. Berkowitz (Ed.), *Advances in experimental social psychology,* (Vol. 7). New York: Academic Press, 1974, 294–341.

Stryker, S. Identity salience and role performance: The relevance of symbolic interaction theory for family research. *Journal of Marriage and the Family,* 1968, **30,** 558–564.

Stryker, S. Developments in two social psychologies: Toward an appreciation of mutual relevance. *Sociometry,* 1977, **40,** 145–160.

Sullivan, H. S. *The interpersonal theory of psychiatry.* New York: Norton, 1953.

Suls, J. M. Social comparison theory and research: An overview from 1954. In J. M. Suls and R. L. Miller (Eds.), *Social comparison processes: theoretical and empirical perspectives.* New York: Wiley, 1977, 1–19.

Suls, J. (Ed.). *Psychological perspectives on the self,* (Vol. 1). Hillsdale, New Jersey: Erlbaum, 1982.

Sutherland, E. H., and Cressey, D. R. *Criminology* (9th ed.). Philadelphia: Lippincott, 1974.

Swann, W. B., and Read, S. J. Self verification processes: How we sustain our self-conceptions. *Journal of Experimental Social Psychology,* 1981, **17,** 351–372.

Sykes, G. M., and Matza, D. Techniques of neutralization: A theory of delinquency. *American Sociological Review,* 1957, **22,** 640–670.

Tedeschi, J. T. (Ed.) *Impression management: Theory and social psychological research.* New York: Academic Press, 1981.

Tesser, A. Self esteem maintenance in family dynamics. *Journal of Personality and Social Psychology,* 1980, **39,** 77–91.

Tesser, A., and Campbell, J. Self definition: The impact of relative performance and similarity of others. *Social Psychology Quarterly,* 1980, **43,** 341–346.

Thibaut, J. W. and Kelley, H. H. The social psychology of groups. New York: John Wiley and Sons, Inc., 1959.

Turner, R. H. The role and the person. *American Journal of Sociology,* 1978, **84,** 1–23.

Verlarde, O. J. Do delinquents really drift? *British Journal of Criminology,* 1978, **18,** 23–29.

Warner, D. B. Determinants of bystander intervention: The effects of verbal cues of victims and others present. Unpublished doctoral dissertation, Reno, Nevada: University of Nevada, 1976.

Wegner, D. M. and Vallacher, R. R. (Eds.), *The self in social psychology.* New York: Oxford University Press, 1980.

Weinstein, E. A. and Deutschberger, P. Some dimensions of altercasting. *Sociometry,* 1963, **26,** 454–466.

Weiss, R. S. *Marital separation.* New York: Basic Books, 1975.

Wicklund, R. A., and Gollwitzer, P. M. *Symbolic self competition.* Hillsdale, New Jersey: Erlbaum, 1982.

Wilson, D. W., and Schafer, R. B. Is social psychology interdisciplinary? *Personality and Social Psychology Bulletin,* 1978, **4,** 548–552.

Zurcher, L. A., Jr. *The mutable self: A self concept for social change.* Beverly Hills, California: Sage Publications, 1977.

INDEX

CONTENTS OF OTHER VOLUMES